THE PIRACY YEARS:
INTERNET FILE SHARING
IN A GLOBAL CONTEXT

THE PIRACY YEARS: INTERNET FILE SHARING IN A GLOBAL CONTEXT

Holger Briel, Michael D. High, and Markus Heidingsfelder

XJTLU IMPRINT

First published 2023 by
XJTLU Imprint,
a collaboration between
Xi'an Jiaotong–Liverpool University
and Liverpool University Press.

British Library Cataloguing-in-Publication data
A British Library CIP record is available

ISBN 978-1-80207-054-5 cased

Typeset by Carnegie Book Production, Lancaster
Printed and bound by CPI Group (UK) Ltd, Croydon CR0 4YY

Contents

Contents

1 Introduction

Holger Briel, Michael D. High, and Markus Heidingsfelder

'Sur Internet, on est tous pirates,
et ça c'est bien'.

Jean-Marc Manach

To speak and write about digital piracy is never easy. It is a minefield of contrasting opinions, activism, corporate and artists' interest, emerging technologies, legal challenges, and punishment, and all this amidst changing social mores. In the northern hemisphere, in particular, much money is spent and legions of lawyers are retained in order to control and punish those thought to be breaking copyright law and to keep such practices illegal. Yet digital rights activists remain very vocal when it comes to defending what they see as piratical lacunae of legitimate and necessary resistance.

This book does not want to add to this bifurcation process; arguments for and against piracy abound and there already exists a large body of diverse research, a fact to which the bibliographies at the end of each chapter bear witness. Rather, the volume at hand wants to examine a number of the technological, philosophical, and social filiations that produced piracy in the first place. Within its pages, different – at times opposing – views on piracy will still become visible, but these appear at the end of an argumentative chain whose foundations are of the essence. Thus, it is not so much the fruit such piracy actually produces, although this can be of interest as well, but rather its social, political, and juridical fundaments. It will become apparent that many of these roots reach back far into history – in terms of technology, to the beginnings of mass media production and management, but in terms of social communal practices, still much further than that.

No matter where one stands on the issues of piracy, it is clear that piracy has grown up and today is nowhere near the monster it was portrayed as in its infancy. On the contrary, it has significantly touched upon and changed the arts, the digital, the social, youth interaction, scholarship, and entertainment consumption. To give an example only for the last point, the common practice of 'bingeing' on whole television series would not have appeared without the aggregating power of The Pirate Bay and its peers. It was only after these had popularised this practice that Netflix and Amazon Studios successfully pirated this phenomenon and thereby mainstreamed it to such an extent that even traditional television networks have begun to release their shows, if not perhaps a whole season's worth at a time, certainly several episodes at once, thereby changing consumption patterns extending all the way back to the 1920s and the beginning of radio serials.

Holger Briel's chapter, 'The Question Concerning Piracy', irrevocably evokes Heidegger and discusses the complexity of the issues involved when attempting to approach the field of digital piracy. He introduces major topics in recent piracy research and some of its key actors. In doing so, he demonstrates that the first step of any discussion of digital piracy needs to thematise piracy's relationship with technological advances and the disruption these caused for traditional business models and governmental regulations. He then goes on to discuss several other core issues related to piracy. These include legal issues created by piracy; the mostly mistaken view that piracy can be equated with and reduced to juvenile delinquency; and the relationship between piracy and the economy, exploring and debunking some of the myths created by entertainment industry representatives regarding the financial havoc piracy is supposedly visiting upon small artists and large corporations alike. Arising as a focal point from his previous topics, he finally discusses the entangled fields of the right to entertainment, information, and education; piracy's philosophical foundations; and, lastly, its political manifestations. Throughout his text, Briel illustrates that all of these issues intersect and need to be contextualised in their treatment. Yet they also have to be treated separately, as local differentiations necessitate different assessments and methodologies. Overall, the chapter sets the stage and provides a frame for the more detailed discussions proposed in the ensuing chapters.

Michael D. High's chapter, 'Creating Piracy: Discourse, Property, and Extra-Legal Territory', takes up this challenge and discusses three important phenomena that cohere in piracy. He contends that it is the imbrication of discourse, property, and extra-legal territory that differentiates piracy from other forms of (il)legitimate appropriation. Important for all three of these areas is the fact that they must be continuously 'projected, protected, and promulgated', otherwise their stable status would be threatened, and, by extension, so would that of society at large. Thus, property rights allow for and limit appropriation, a fundamental activity in which people must engage to survive and create. How these are governed, and any changes to these rules, would decide how cultural production either thrives or continues, or ceases altogether. High then details how these three phenomena intersect in maritime piracy and in intellectual piracy alike. He ends his chapter with a discussion of a form of piracy only very recently created, biopiracy, thereby connecting its original model, maritime piracy, with its most recent manifestation.

One particular additional focus of the book is an analysis of the metonymical usage of the word 'piracy' to describe varying political interventions akin to it. Piracy and politics go hand in hand. At times, politics is simply piracy by different means; at others, piracy is politics by different means; and at still others, both are true simultaneously. It is remarkable that many digital pirates are also heavily invested in changing the world for the better and are activists on a whole slew of issues such as digital rights, hacking, ecology, and education. It should not be surprising therefore that the piracy movement spawned its own political parties. It would seem that in many circles the idea of piracy has become a rallying cry for further engagement, not only in digital matters, but, perhaps resulting from these and reversing history, also in what used to be called the 'real' world. Especially the chapter by Markus Heidingsfelder and the conversation with Gary Hall push this viewpoint further and demand a more holistic view and acting out of piracy.

Furthermore, the book also deliberates ways in which piracy has challenged the economic supremacy of Western countries and their capitalist economies. To do so, three of the chapters analyse piracy movements in two developing economies: China, the country with the largest number of Internet users and also the country often charged with being the 'cradle' and 'centre' of piracy globally; and Nigeria, the most populous country in Africa and home to Nollywood, arguably the most vibrant film industry in the world.

The two pieces on China serve two distinct purposes: the first one tells the story of two women growing up in 1990s China and their unique local situation vis-à-vis the burgeoning proliferation of Western media in the country at the time; the second analyses cultural underpinnings of the Chinese 'sharing' economy and its resulting modifications to identity formation. Entitled 'Growing Up a

Pirate', the chapter contains testimonials by Jiarui Tan and Yifan Li, both of whom display a passion for their preferred medium, music and video gaming respectively. Their narratives give a detailed account of different kinds of structures informing and sharing media discourses at the time, but also speak of their inventiveness in overcoming such strictures. At times tinged with nostalgia, perhaps easily shared by people from different generations alike, they show how much the emerging online community of gamers and music fans has succeeded in creating new collaborations, growing up and enlarging horizons together. In all its difference from Western teenagers' accounts of coming of age, especially when considering economic disparities and disadvantages, there is a surprising and emotional bond which is struck between these accounts. There exists a depth of reflection in these narratives that illustrates the liberating, emancipatory, and lasting power of media piracy and the ways in which it can assist individuals and whole generations in developing into far more rounded personalities and societies, thus bearing strong testimony to the positive power piratical practices can bestow upon their participants

In the second chapter on China, entitled 'Poetic Prosumption and Disruptive Creativity: Social Media Uploaders and Influencers as the New Bandits, Pirates, and Guerrilla Winners', Zhen Troy Chen looks at fandom practices on Bilibili, a video-sharing social media site mediating anime, comics, games, and novels (ACGN). Chen uses an ethnographic approach to problematise the Western conceptualis-ations of creativity by looking at the 'Shanzhai' and cultural adaptation phenomenon of Chinese online vernacular cultures. Informed by de Certeau and Foucault, Chen shows how Chinese urban youth poach and transcode media texts through parody, piracy, and their own agentic 'prosumption' (a neologism signifying the blurring boundaries between producer and consumer). Rather than focusing once again on the top-down linear 'thought management' or the seemingly irresistible 'market domination' China's mediascapes are typically charged with, such poetic and tactical prosumption shapes Chinese youth's negotiated identities and nurtures new socialites in the making.

Rounding out the theme of localised piracy narratives, Nelson Omenugha's 'Piracy in Nollywood: Dimensions, Contexts, Hazards, and Ways Forward' shows that it is not so much the fight against copyright that leads to piratical practices in the global south, but rather economic necessity; also, that if in the West it was mostly ideological and technology-based developments that were conducive to piracy's rise, in economically disadvantaged countries it was these economic and also regulatory restrictions, such as import and dissemination prohibitions for certain content, that gave rise to it in the south. Omenugha works through these arguments, with Nigeria as a pertinent example. He interrogates the complex dimension of piracy in Nollywood, the Nigerian modern film industry, and in particular notes the threats piracy portends to quality digital production, creativity, and the economy. His chapter identifies some of the detailed causes of film piracy, such as weaknesses in extant laws, weak law enforcement regimes, ignorance of copyright laws by the public, film circulation gaps due to huge production costs, and general economic hardship in the country. However, it also examines the suggestions by some commentators that film piracy holds some merits, including its effect on wider circulation (exposure) and stimulation of competitive market price (providing users with marginal utility of money). Given that the creative economy supports a substantial part of the nation's economy, Omenugha recommends that the country's copyright law be amended to reflect the dynamics of today's digital distribution of intellectual works, and that the Nigerian government, copyright authorities, law enforcement agencies, Nollywood, and other key players in its entertainment and media industry closely collaborate and work towards a more efficient and differentiating enforcement of copyright laws as well as the sensitisation of the public to these issues. While his chapter is perhaps the one that most firmly dismisses piracy as a criminal act impinging negatively upon artists in general and film directors in particular, he nevertheless also speaks of the liberating force piracy can develop and credits it with the rise of Nollywood, one of the fastest-growing and most innovative film industries in the world, thereby charting some of the post-colonial and de-colonial lessons that can be learned from piracy.

Besides these localised examples, one also needs to pay heed to the by now historical layers impinging on piratical processes. There are distinct differences within piracy developments and histories which at times are separate. If in the early days of the Internet the piracy movement consisted primarily of digitally gifted amateurs engaging in piracy as an act of sharing files with anti-corporate establishment overtones, 20 years on, many acts of mainstream piracy have taken on distinct organised-crime characteristics, especially when considering Internet Protocol Television's (IPTV) stream infringement and near universal in-film betting advertising of CAM copies of recent theatre releases. This is also the assessment of Ernesto Van der Sar in his 'Sharing is Caring and Piracy is Theft'. Van der Sar, an astute observer and participant in piracy discourses, is the founder (2007) of the *TorrentFreak* website, which arguably is the best-informed website on piracy on the web, with tens of thousands of reports listed in its archives. If Van der Sar's original motivation for launching the website had been to provide a more balanced account of piracy, giving a voice to companies and pirates alike (perhaps weighted a bit towards the piratical side), today he fears that much of the idealistic dynamic in the piracy practices of the 1990s and early 2000s has been lost; instead, much piracy has been co-opted by syndicates of large players, at times close to organised crime, who are interested more in financial than intellectual gain or in making a political point. This is especially true for IPTV, over the last few years the fastest-growing segment of piracy. His worry is that these commercialised services are beginning to drown out other (more reflected and politically motivated) piracy, thereby providing added ammunition to lawyers and industry groups who are summarily charging all piracy with being illegal, illegitimate, and profit-oriented.

At the other end of the spectrum, among the more politically and socially aware segments of piracy, we find people like Gary Hall and Alexandra Elbakyan, the former offering a strong political raison d'être for the continuation of piratical practices and the latter having revolutionised how academic research is conducted globally via her website Sci-Hub. In their writings and actions both sturdily support the application of piracy to the body and tools of criticism of unjust social practices, and take forward a vision of society in which digital practices return to their original idea of developing sharing and caring communities, a way of providing content and interactions for *dividuals* (Deleuze) to grow digitally and beyond. Hall does this via his writing, but also via his involvement in a number of centres and activity hubs; Alexandra Elbakyan via her outstanding work as founder of Sci-hub, the globally most comprehensive academic article aggregator website. Elbakyan's contribution in the form of a short interview and a manifesto highlights once again the metafunction of file sharing in society when it comes to determining how we want to share and build upon knowledge generation. Her spirit certainly infuses much of the writing at hand.

The last chapter of the book, Danai Tselenti's 'Blockchains, Threats, and Parasites', connects cutting-edge developments in digital blockchains with piracy issues and thus propels the latter into the future. Just as is the case for piracy, literature on blockchain technology is multidisciplinary and often approaches blockchain technology via conflicting and polarising terms. Supporters of blockchain technology focus on its positive disruptive potential to revolutionise interactions, foster privacy, and strengthen democracy, even envisaging non-hierarchical socialist forms of governance. Detractors of the technology take a critical view on blockchain technology and tend to emphasise its social and political dangers related to alleged neoliberal strategies in turn leading to greater control and authoritarian outcomes. In an attempt to alleviate such discontinuities, Tselenti studies the blockchain ecosystem in connection to piracy and particularly with regard to the ways it reconfigures and re-evaluates the concept of 'threat' in the general sense of the term. By focusing primarily on the Bitcoin and Ethereum ecosystems, she challenges notions of security and disintermediation by examining how processes of continuous interruptions, modifications, and respective optimisations become operationalised within the blockchain ecosystem. Much of her work is based on Michel Serres's philosophical theorisation of parasitism and Katherine Hayles's concepts of 'cognitive assemblages' and the 'regime of computation'. Via these theories, she arrives at her concept of 'computational parasitism', which 'highlights the numerous parasitic relations that are simultaneously ongoing in, around, and across the blockchain ecosystem and can thus capture the complex and constantly evolving blockchain ecology'.

In conclusion, it is fair to say that piracy is here to stay. Although some of its manifestations may disappear due to technological advances and/or changing consumption patterns, all the chapters in this book, no matter what their focus, conclude that in its many guises piracy is a central and pivotal social practice without which pluralistic societies cannot exist. Variably, they see piracy as a compass; a metonymical and anarchic intervention; a necessary threat and challenge to questionable existing political and commercial activities; an agent of empowerment; an applied critique of particular forms of technologisation; a de-colonising practice; and as an instrument to achieve a post-piratical frame of mind and world. Piracy is not a trivial matter, nor has it ever been. It remains for its practitioners to prove that it neither exhausts itself in (nor is defined by) downloading a few freebies from the web; rather, it extends to actively engaging individuals and creating communities in order to make a positive difference in human and post-human societies at large.

2 The Question Concerning Piracy

Holger Briel

1 Introduction

'Aussie Federal Court orders ISPs to block 101 pirate movie & TV show domains';[1] 'British man gets 22 months in prison over global movie piracy';[2] 'considering the television and film industries alone, there were 79 billion visits to piracy websites between January and September 2021';[3] 'Best Virtual Private Network (VPN) for [*insert your country*]'.[4] Headlines such as these continue to flood inboxes and highlight the fact that what is deemed illegal Internet file sharing, aka piracy, or the enabling thereof via VPNs, has developed, next to discussions of fake news, into an important (perhaps *the* most important) digital battleground. At stake is nothing less than how we want to see our (second) online life governed, which is rapidly becoming our first one. While these headlines highlight the acuteness

Proviso: In the following, the terms 'piracy' and 'file sharing' will be used interchangeably. While the latter is deemed more neutral, the former's etymological, semantic, and metonymic formations make it the preferred term used by many of its participants and detractors alike. It is important to see that it has distinct social and political connotations that need to be thought together with the term when applied. If nothing else, it serves as a good reminder that one person's pirate is always another's freedom fighter.

1   Andy Maxwell, 'Aussie Federal Court Orders ISPs to Block 101 Pirate Movie & TV Show Domains', *TorrentFreak* (22 December 2021), https://torrentfreak.com/aussie-federal-court-orders-isps-to-block-101-pirate-movie-tv-show-domains-211222/.

2   Jonathan Stempel, 'British Man Gets 22 Months in Prison over Global Movie Piracy: U.S. Judge', Reuters News Agency (8 February 2022), www.reuters.com/world/british-man-gets-22-months-prison-over-global-movie-piracy-us-judge-2022-02-07/.

3   Akamai, 'State of the Internet. Most Recent Security Report', SOTI 7, no. 4 (September 2021), ed. Martin McKeay, https://web.archive.org/web/20210923001400/www.akamai.com/our-thinking/the-state-of-the-internet/global-state-of-the-internet-security-ddos-attack-reports.

4   Banner on virtually any pirate website one opens.

of the issues involved, what is not stressed in such generally alarmist missives is that from the beginning of (analogue) media, file sharing of one kind or another has always been at the centre of media distribution and that this has also always included practices which, depending on whom you asked, was deemed legal or illegal, or both.

A short history of such content and the systems charged with protecting it includes the copyright laws set up by book printers and their powerful guild after the invention of the printing press, exchanges of letters and books in the book circles of the eighteenth century, photography, phonographic records, films, radio and television programmes, company and state secrets, patents, and many more. Already in the seventeenth century, piracy was associated with printing, but this time with the publishers and for their pricing policies:

> The bishop of Oxford, for example, defending his nascent Oxford University Press against the London trade, reviled the Stationers en masse as 'land-pirats.' The Stationer John Hancock complained of 'dishonest Booksellers, called Land-Pirats, who make it their practise to steal Impressions of other mens Copies.' And within the Stationers' court itself, references to violators of the register as 'pirates' began to appear in the 1680s.[5]

Precedents for electronic media piracy were, for instance, set by the January 1926 WJAZ Chicago incident, in which the radio station 'pirated' Canadian broadcasting frequencies to add additional hours to its own broadcasting roster. To show its defiance, on 5 February 1926, WJAZ broadcast the operetta *The Pirate*, and distributed photographs of staff dressed as 'wave pirates'.[6] Later on, similar cases can also be found in Europe, with Radio Mercur taking to the airwaves in 1958, literally from a (pirate) ship anchored outside Danish territorial waters, a feat repeated in 1964 by the hugely popular Radio Caroline, originally set up to circumvent the then record companies' almost complete control of music broadcasting and the BBC's radio broadcasting monopoly in the UK. The station, which is still broadcasting today, used several ships, again anchored outside territorial waters, this time the UK's, and garnered a dedicated following. That such radio piracy was not just a youthful act of thumbing one's nose at the radio industry was

5   Adrian Johns, *Piracy: The Intellectual Property Wars from Gutenberg to Gates* (Chicago: University of Chicago Press, 2010), 41.
6   Anon., '"Yo-ho-ho" Sing Pirates Bold', *Radio Digest – Illustrated* (3 April 1926), 5, 8, https://archive.org/details/radiodigest19261618radi/page/n412/mode/1up/.

proven by Abie Nathan, an Israeli peace activist who, in 1973 with the help of John Lennon, bought a ship he named 'Peace Ship'. It would sail outside Israeli waters and became the home of 'The Voice of Peace' pirate radio station that would broadcast music and peace activist messages throughout the region, demonstrating that political activism and piracy could and do go hand in hand. While the station's ship broadcasts ceased in 1993, the station itself is still active today on the Internet.[7]

When compared to such previously established piratical practices, moving to digital content and distribution did not change much, except for one significant difference: scale. If before, record companies had to deal with individual small-scale stations or bootlegged albums sold out of car boots, they were now faced with copies of unauthorised tracks, albums, and films numbering in the millions, potentially subverting or even ending their business models. It was this exponential growth in numbers that would prompt companies rigorously to attempt to find and implement means to stop such practices. However, this would prove to be tricky, if only for the philosophical and technical underpinnings of the very instrument they were trying to rein in, the Internet.

2 A History of the Internet's Piratical Structure

Arguably, there exist three books that shaped the very idea of and practices in early cyberspace: William Gibson's *Neuromancer* (1984), Neal Stephenson's *Snow Crash* (1992), both science fiction novels, and Howard Rheingold's *The Virtual Community* (1993), a quasi-philosophical treatise on the practice of cyberspace life. Not surprisingly, all three address piracy and validate it positively, and even see it as constitutive for the Internet. In this context, it is good to remember that the term 'cyberspace' actually stems from Gibson's novel, set in about 2035, and has as its broken, but likable protagonist 24-year-old Case, for whom cyberspace is a 'pirate's paradise' (p. 78) and also his own paradise, as this is his line of work. In *Snow Crash*, set in 2005, another likable, but damaged protagonist by the name of Hiro Protagonist, 30 years of age, encounters powerful pirates both online and offline. The typical reader of these novels would be a young, male, college-educated media worker or student, engaged in the setting up of the fledgling Internet industry. Such themes were not

7   See https://thevoiceofpeace.co.il/index.php/about/#.

only beginning to crop up in the newly established Sci-Fi genre of Cyberpunk, but also in films. Hugely popular, *Johnny Mnemonic* (dir. Robert Longo, USA, 1995) was based on the William Gibson story by the same name, set in 2021, and starred then young heartthrob Keanu Reeves, action man Dolph Lundgren, and Henry Rollins of Black Flagg fame. The main character, Johnny, yet again a young, damaged, but likable man with a cybernetic brain implant designed to store information, is thrust into a dystopian world in which Asian mega-companies rule the world with an iron fist. Johnny has been forced to carry stolen data in his modified brain – a whopping 320 GB of data in his 180 GB capacity brain, a truly science-fictional amount at the time of writing.

Here, it is significant to stress that due to the dystopic social situations described in these texts, resistance is considered to be a necessity, at least on an individual basis, and also in order to right wrongs and to (re-)enfranchise the disenfranchised. Given the similarity of these plot scenarios, both fictional and not, with today's world, many people might feel that such a necessity exists today in the real world as well.

If the previous texts were fictional, Howard Rheingold's vastly influential 1993 *The Virtual Community* puts emphasis on real-life usage of a then increasingly popular Internet. From today's vantage point it seems strange when he points out that in 1993 the White House set up an email account, thereby legitimising the Internet beyond doubt. What is perhaps more interesting are Rheingold's comments on and description of the fledgling Internet; for one, as a community of similarly minded people committed to social grassroots work and the forging of group-minds which would be able to react to/act out changing practices in an informed and rapid way; for another, the view of an Electronic Frontier and Online Activism, a true virtual community.[8] While he admitted that, '[t]he idea of a community accessible only via my computer screen sounded cold to me at first', he warmed to it quickly, as he realised how comforting virtual comradery and the exchange of ideas and implementation of possible actions could be.[9] After all, the communal idea(l)s of the Whole Earth 'Lectronic Link Bulletin Board (WELL) were not that far

---

8 No surprise then that the arguably most activist of the early communities chose as its name 'Electronic Frontier Foundation'.

9 Howard Rheingold, *The Virtual Community: Homesteading on the Internet* (Cambridge, MA: MIT Press, 1993).

removed from the Whole Earth Catalogue, founded by Stewart Brand, who also became a founding member of the WELL.[10] The connection between the two and the sharing of hippie ideologies was not lost on Steve Jobs who in his 2005 Stanford commencement speech stated that, 'When I was young, there was an amazing publication called *The Whole Earth Catalog*, which was one of the bibles of my generation [...] It was sort of like Google in paperback form, 35 years before Google came along. It was idealistic and overflowing with neat tools and great notions'.[11] Roughly during the same period, Wayne Gregori established the SF Cafe Net/Coffee House BBS (1991) and co-founded the already mentioned WELL, established previously in 1985 as a Bulletin Board Service (BBS), but which only began accepting public traffic in the early 1990s. Both websites hailed from San Francisco and are two of the foundation stones of the Internet, and both engaged in file-sharing practices as the centre of their communities.

File sharing on a much larger scale would begin at the end of the 1990s when Shawn Fanning and Sean Parker launched their

10   See Fred Turner, *From Counterculture to Cyberculture: Stewart Brand, the Whole Earth Network, and the Rise of Digital Utopianism* (Chicago: University of Chicago Press, 2006). Here, another pertinent filiation can be drawn to the successful and highly visible movement Abbie Hoffman created with the publication of his *Steal This Book* in 1971 in New York (Pirate Editions/Grove Press), which had been written while Hoffman was in jail awaiting trial for his part in anti-Vietnam War protests. He gave advice on how to source free food, housing, transportation, and to run a guerrilla movement in order to ensure 'survival in the prison that is Amerika'.

11   www.youtube.com/watch?v=D1R-jKKp3NA&t=12m45s. One might wonder whether Jobs's idealism and Google's oft cited former(!) motto 'Don't be evil' still apply to today's #1 and #4 ranked companies in the world, based on market capitalisation, but both were certainly quick to point out the filiation the Internet inherited and which they still claim for themselves. Peter Lunenfeld, *The Secret War between Downloading and Uploading: Tales of the Computer as Culture Machine* (Cambridge, MA: MIT Press, 2011) portrays the history of the computer and the Internet in a generational mould, beginning with the 'patriarchs' (Vannevar Bush and J.C.R. Licklider) up to the 1960s, continuing on with the 'Plutocrats' (Thomas Watson, Sr and Jr) in the 1960s, then the 'Aquarians' (Douglas Englebart and Alan Kay) in the 1970s, and the 'Hustlers' of the 1980s (Bill Gates and Steve Jobs) and the 'Searchers' of the late 1990s and early 2000s (Larry Page and Sergey Brin), who would revolutionise the Internet with search algorithms. While this is a neat serialisation, the alternative view would ascribe the 1980s to the Aquarians who would continue to exert influence and would eventually bring forth Internet piracy and, as I argue here, the latest stage of Internet development.

free peer-to-peer (P2P) file-sharing service Napster on 1 June 1999, from Northeastern University, Boston, generally considered the first *bourse* or dedicated site for sharing copyrighted entertainment data. It quickly gathered over 26 million users but was forced to close in 2001 due to legal pressure. The issue of (il)legal file sharing has remained alive and well ever since, providing sustenance to an army of lawyers on both sides of the conflict and governments with ammunition to probe their citizens' online (and offline) behaviour. Far from stemming the tide of file sharing, according to one study, during the first nine months of 2021 alone, over 132 billion visits to sharing and streaming websites were recorded,[12] a truly overwhelming number. Partly due to the size of the phenomenon, interest in file sharing on practical and theoretical levels as a social phenomenon has increased concurrently. On 12 February 2022, torrentfreak.com, one of the most comprehensive and open-minded websites writing on file sharing, reported an accumulated 13,604 breaking news stories on file sharing over the last few years on their website alone, together with 179,000 social media followers and 19,900 RSS subscribers.[13] Other topical websites report similar numbers, highlighting the scope of interest and participation in file-sharing processes.

The rapid growth in piracy since the 1980s was accompanied by ever more frantic attempts by entertainment industry bodies to try and frame the issue.[14] Many of these campaigns were heavy-handed and used outdated ideas to counteract piracy and stop particularly young people from engaging in it. A number of these campaigns have led to some very funny and incisive memes circulating on the Internet. Thus, the slogan 'Home Taping Is Killing Music. And it's illegal', a 1980s anti-copyright infringement campaign by the British

---

12 https://torrentfreak.com/pirate-site-traffic-surged-in-2021-research-finds-220127/. Arguably, TorrentFreak is the most important news source for file sharing today and is widely referenced by all news media reporting on piracy. It was established in 2007 in the Netherlands by Ernesto Van der Sar and is led by him and Andy Maxwell. Apart from a very small number of advertisements for VPNs, it is advert-free.

13 https://torrentfreak.com/.

14 See the typically alarmist attempt by the industry-financed yet innocently named Institute for Policy Innovation, in Stephen E. Siwek, 'The True Cost of Motion Picture Piracy to the U.S. Economy', Institute for Policy Innovation, Policy Report (3 October 2007), 186, www.ipi.org/ipi_issues/detail/the-true-cost-of-copyright-industry-piracy-to-the-us-economy.

Phonographic Industry (BPI), was quick to draw fire from home tapers and people friendly to their cause, and quickly a number of ironic repartees followed, such as 'Home sewing is killing fashion – and it's illegal'. Apart from poking fun at the industry, it also made very clear the logical fallacies of such propaganda.

Similarly, Katja Berlin's popular column, Pie Truths, to be found in the pages of Germany's most popular weekly newspaper *Die Zeit*, also shed light on the psyche of Internet users which did not bode well for such campaigns. In one of her columns from 2018, entitled 'Data Security on the Internet', the caption for the left pie asks, 'Do you read the data security conditions [for websites]?' Yes/No. The right caption asks, 'Do you agree to it?' Yes/No, with the overwhelming majority not reading but agreeing to it.[15] While this is satire, judging by most people's practices, one suspects that this is indeed the case, and not only in Germany.

In the following sections, a number of areas pertinent to Internet piracy will be identified to assess and contextualise piratical practices. It will become clear that Internet piracy is not just a small issue that concerns a few reprobate teenagers, but rather that it has serious implications for the way digital life is led and, even more importantly, gives us clues as to what is at stake regarding how we want to live as a society. Piracy will be discussed through analysing seven distinct areas, all of which share a bearing on the issue. These areas are: (i) Piracy and Technology; (ii) Piracy and the Law; (iii) Piracy and Juvenile Delinquency; (iv) Piracy and the Economy; (v) Piracy and the Right to Entertainment, Information, and Education; (vi) Piracy and Philosophy; and (vii) Piracy and Politics. This differentiating approach is necessary as piracy is not just one field that can be easily handled by a singular, disciplinary approach; rather, it is a pan-social phenomenon which necessitates interdisciplinary approaches and solutions. Due to space limitations, it is not possible to present a comprehensive picture of the phenomenon; rather, a discussion of paradigmatic cases is favoured, vignette-style, together with some solutions proffered. There does exist extensive further reading material, though, which has been relegated to the footnotes and the bibliography; it is hoped that in this way readability and the raising of the pertinent points is ensured.

---

15   http://hafneroncrm.blogspot.com/2018/04/facebook-cambridge-dgsvo-uber-den.html.

3 Piracy and Technology

As mentioned above, piracy is an issue that has been in existence ever since humans have engaged in commerce. Product piracy has always existed, as has industrial and governmental espionage, all of which continue still today. Until very recently, media piracy had ultimately been manifested in the realm of materiality, with illegally copied CDs and DVDs appearing in markets all over the world. As Internet bandwidth increased and technology became more advanced, streaming services have taken over and more content has been available online. However, storage and also enabling/connector devices, such as hard disks, servers, or IPTV set-top boxes, still remain as physical realities governed by local laws. As sharing sites learned from earlier mistakes, such as centralised servers hosting files, they professionalised and increasingly made use of mirror sites distributed across the globe. If one site is shut down, another takes over, thereby offering continued service, a method many other websites have learned to make good use of as well, including offering their own VPNs. When compared to pre-Internet times, what is new, of course, is the scale of such piracy, and this was clearly enabled by new technologies. If at first it was written texts that were swapped, as bandwidth increased and storage become cheaper, this soon moved to images, then to music files, and, finally, to video and streaming. Furthermore, with the development of smartphones and the move from first- to second- to third- (etc.) generation mobile devices capable of rapidly receiving data over the air, the Internet and downloading became mobile as well. Since 2020, content is mostly streamed, and downloading has given way to streaming instead. It is fair to say that this development was largely pushed by streaming companies such as Netflix and Spotify.

VPNs are perhaps one of the best examples of the two-edged nature of dealing with piracy. On the one hand, VPNs and, to a lesser extent, the anonymous communication TOR network (often equated with the Darknet), are touted as ways to circumvent authoritarian regimes' attempts to regulate content access. On the other hand, they are often charged with supporting piracy (and sometimes correctly so).

The fight for Internet privacy is a continuing one and its history stretches back to the beginnings of the Internet. Here one can go back to Philip R. Zimmermann's 1991 development of Pretty Good Privacy (PGP), the most widely used email encryption software in the world. Not only did he invent it, he also made its source code freely available and was then promptly sued by the United States Customs Service for allegedly violating the U.S. Arms Export Control Act, as his cryptographic software at the time was considered as a munition. Eventually, the suit was dropped.[16] Here the case clearly involved the view of the US and other governments, still held today, that they should be allowed, if necessary, to have access to an individual's data and emails.

One can perceive the development of VPNs as a filiation of the programming Zimmermann did in the late 1980s and early 1990s. VPNs began with Microsoft in 1996, when point-to-point tunnelling protocols, aka peer-to-peer tunnelling protocols (PPTN) were introduced, which created a secure network between users via encrypting data (creating a 'tunnel') in LAN or WAN connections. This is done by creating a username, password, and server address and involves the three steps of tunnelling, encryption, and authentication. Protocols widely used to do so include Secure Socket Layer (SSL) and Internet Protocol Security (IPSec).

VPNs are nowadays widely recommended by most pirate websites, at times posting warnings on their landing sites and giving suggestions as the which VPNs to use. Long-established and popular German sharing website goldesel.to is a case in point. When in 2019 the Munich District court ruled that German telecoms provider Telekom was required to block access to its site, Goldesel reacted with a statement insisting that its legal status had not been touched by the law as it itself does not host any files and saw the court decision as another attempt by the authorities to do away with the 'free Internet'. It then went on to detail how to circumvent these blocks via DNS jumpers, VPNs, or switching to mirror domains.[17] Apart from these websites themselves, many support groups have sprung up detailing how such circumvention of blockages is easily achieved and giving out legal and other advice regarding file sharing, thereby strengthening the notion of a caring community being at the heart of such file-sharing practices.[18] If indeed file-sharing sites like Goldesel are operating within a legal grey area, the case with file hosters is more clear cut, as they, along with legal material, also do host illegal copies of copyrighted material. Thus, in October 2019, the

---

16 https://philzimmermann.com/EN/background/index.html.
17 See https://tarnkappe.info/artikel/szene/goldesel-to-reagiert-auf-neue-netzsperren-34668.html.
18 E.g., tarnkappe.info, torrentfreak.com, and many others.

then largest German file hoster, share-online.biz, was taken down, as has been happening and is continuing to happen with many other file hosters as well.[19] Needless to say, after a few days, mirror sites sprang up and 'warez" (here meaning (il)legal files to be found on file-sharing websites) were quickly either re-upped or sourced differently. Overall, it is clear that many of the issues springing up around file sharing are technology based and technology enabled, but also that any solution to them must include, but cannot be limited to, technological ones.

4 Piracy and the Law

The first line of the introduction in the 2005 edited volume *Internet Piracy* apodictically states, 'Internet Piracy is a form of theft'.[20] In the first article of the book, written for Music United for Strong Internet Copyright (MUSIC), a coalition of more than 20 trade organisations within the music industry, this claim is strengthened further. It reads: 'The explosion in the illegal copying of music is having a terrible effect on the music industry and everyone who works in it. Downloading copyrighted music off the Internet without permission from the copyright owner is theft, plain and simple'.[21] And, indeed, judging by the thousands of convictions the world over due to copyright breach, the issuance of millions of takedown notices on a daily basis, with torrent website owners having been convicted of a host of illegal activities and at least some of them having been sent to prison, it seems that, legally at least, piracy is a tried and closed case. But even the book cited above, staunchly coming down on the side of copyright protection, at times expresses some lingering doubt about the issue, no matter how faint. Editor and contributor James Torr quotes John Naughton, an *Observer* columnist, who wrote:

> We have to remind legislators that intellectual property rights are a socially-conferred privilege rather than an inalienable right, that copying is not always evil (and in some cases is actually socially beneficial) and that there is a huge difference between wholesale

---

19   Markus Böhm, '"Share-Online.biz" Ermittler schalten größten deutschen Filehoster ab' (17 October 2019), www.spiegel.de/netzwelt/web/share-online-biz-ermittler-schalten-groesstes-deutsches-filesharing-portal-ab-a-1291986.html.

20   James D. Torr (ed.), *Internet Piracy* (Detroit, MI: Greenhaven Press, 2005), 4.

21   Torr, *Internet Piracy*, 8.

"piracy" – the mass-production and sale of illegal copies of protected works – and the filesharing that most Internet users go in for.[22]

It seems therefore that the case for summarily declaring all forms of Internet file sharing as illegal is not quite as airtight as it is made out to be.

Apart from associations, lobby-groups, and companies associated with the entertainment industry, who have a clear and vested financial interest in seeing Internet piracy stopped, there are many within and outside of the legal profession who express serious doubt about it. Already in his 1968 text, *Copyright in Historical Perspective*,[23] Lyman Ray Patterson argued that copyright was a historical formation dependent more on rules than principles. For him, this makes copyright issues inherently problematic, if not illegal, as its genesis took place outside legal principles. In his text, he goes back to the English Star Chamber Decree of 1586, which for 'all times' gave the right to copy to stationer companies, pre-modern printing and publishing houses, thereby leaving the authors and their rights out of the equation. This would change with the Statue of Anne of 1709, in which an author was duly represented. But for Patterson, while this rectified earlier misdeeds, it did not solve the general problem that somebody's copyright was considered a *natural* right. Copyright was seen as helping the monopoly of the book trade and was limited to a time period of 28 years. Today, depending on the country, copyright can stretch up to 70 years past a copyright holder's death. In the United States, the 1998 Copyright Term Extension Act, aka the Mickey Mouse Protection Act, controversially extended even this time period for works of corporate authorship to 120 years after creation, or 95 years after publication, whichever would come first, something Disney had especially lobbied for in order to keep the copyright for Steamboat Willy, Mickey Mouse's predecessor.

While authors and publishers have been looked after generously through such legislation, for Patterson the third stakeholder in the copyright issue is sadly left out: the public. Similarly to other researchers, Patterson argues that the public has a right to ideas and their distribution. And, indeed, one could view copyright as an incitement for the author to publish more. In any case, the Statue of

22 Torr, *Internet Piracy*, 7.
23 L. Ray Patterson, *Copyright in Historical Perspective* (Nashville, TN: Vanderbilt University Press, 1968).

Anne (of Great Britain and Ireland) already views the Copyright Act as 'An Act for the Encouragement of Learning', and the United States Constitution claims that there are good reasons for the public to be made privy to such ideas, when it states in Article I, Section 8, Clause 8 for Congress 'to promote the progress of science and useful arts, by securing for limited times to authors and inventors the exclusive right to their respective writings and discoveries'. For Patterson, the other stakeholders had smugly been overlooked at this pertinent point, making copyright a tool for rules and not for principles when extending copyright beyond a reasonable time period.

For Jessica Litman, a prodigious activist against copyright, this problem with copyright is already enshrined in its linguistic manifestation. She cogently argues that copyright has been a very slippery idea from the beginning and should be treated more as a metaphor than an iron-clad rule and should serve the reader as well as the other stake holders:

> It is becoming increasingly clear that the supposed copyright wars that copyright scholars believed we were fighting – nominally pitting the interests of authors and creators against the interests of readers and other members of the audience – were never really about that at all. Instead the real conflict has been between the publishers, record labels, movie studios, and other intermediaries who rose to market dominance in the 20th century, and the digital services and platforms that have become increasingly powerful copyright players in the 21st. [...] It would make good sense for at least some of us to leave the fight between 20th century publishers and 21st century platforms to the many lawyers that represent both sides, and to focus on some of the issues that aren't as likely to attract their attention.[24]

These issues concern the right of people to education through material, a right which for her supersedes the right to maximise profits for the intermediaries. Interestingly, she compares the 1710 Statute of Anne with the U.S. 1887 Dawes Act,

> which served a crucial function in the American divestment of Indian land. I draw from the stories of the two laws the same moral: Constituting something as a freely alienable property right will almost always lead to results mirroring or exacerbating

---

24   Jessica Litman, 'What We Don't See When We See Copyright as Property', *Cambridge Law Journal* 77, no. 3 (2018).

disparities in wealth and bargaining power. The legal dogma surrounding property rights makes it easy for us not to notice.

Litman then goes on to chart her history of the usage of the copyright laws from a *bargain* between the publisher, the author, and the reader to an *incentive* for the two former parties to the *control* exerted by the same groups over the right of access of the reader and/or the public. The by now generally accepted metaphor of piracy originally described something very different from what Internet 'pirates' are doing. But the choice of words is telling: a large part of the global population is thereby criminalised. Fair use has invariably and increasingly been scaled down in the interest of large companies, as the U.S. Copyright Term Extension Act exemplified. It is only very rarely, for instance in the UK legislature regarding remixing and sampling copyright, discussed below, that actual practices have a bearing on the crafting of laws.

James Boyle[25] and others argue along similar lines but go further still by maintaining that with the abolition of Blackstone's absolute right to property – in his *Commentaries on the Laws of England* (1765–9) – absolute copyright is and should be an impossibility; as some have cogently claimed, even the notion of intellectual property is 'non-sensical and pernicious'.[26]

Another approach to digital material can be the point that anything uploaded onto the Internet is fair game. This point is frequently used when people are warned about their personal data on the Internet and reminded to be vigilant in protecting it. This is part and parcel of the brave new digital Internet world, something that the recent German and EU data laws update (the German Federal Data Protection Law, Bundesdatenschutzgesetz (BDSG 2009) and the EU General Data Protection Regulation (GDPR, 2018)), both of which govern how the personal data of individuals in the EU may be

25 James Boyle, *The Public Domain: Enclosing the Commons of the Mind* (New Haven, CT: Yale University Press, 2008).

26 Samir Chopra, 'End Intellectual Property', *Aeon* (14 November 2018), https://aeon.co/essays/the-idea-of-intellectual-property-is-nonsensical-and-pernicious. For an account of how intellectual property law can stifle creativity, see Siva Vaidhyanathan, *Copyrights and Copywrongs: The Rise of Intellectual Property and How it Threatens Creativity* (New York: New York University Press, 2003). This has already been proven for the unlikely topic of fairy tales, showing how far-reaching such legislation can be. See Helle Porsdam, *Copyright and Other Fairy Tales: Hans Christian Andersen and the Commodification of Creativity* (Cheltenham: Edward Elgar Publishing, 2006).

processed and transferred. Data protection officers warn nonetheless that anything put on the Internet can be accessed by others.[27] If part of the allure and use of the Internet is to make information available, then companies are quick to take advantage of it, and have been doing so over the last 35 years. At the same time, the 'creative commons', the original idea behind the Internet, has been under attack and needs more protection than it has received, as people such as Lawrence Lessig, Christian Fuchs, McKenzie Wark, Gary Hall, and many others do not tire to point out.

A blanket criminalisation of file sharing is therefore problematic, even for those entities who would benefit most from it. Furthermore, there is a distinction to be made between various forms of content, such as text, audio files, and visual material. Since 1908 in the USA, the first-sale doctrine has been in place which creates a basic exception to a copyright holder's distribution right and stipulates that once a work is lawfully sold or given away, the copyright owner's interest in the material object is exhausted. This does not mean that the buyer can make additional copies of the original text, though, as the exception is limited to the original copy obtained. If in 1908 this referred mostly to texts, U.S. Code § 109(a) extended this to 'phonorecords' as well. The same principle also applies to still and moving images. Furthermore, on 3 July 2012, the Court of Justice of the European Union ruled that it was also permissible to resell software licences and any software associated with them. In 2019, the High Court of Paris extended the same rule to video games.[28] Under German law, to make a 'safety' copy

27 See an interview with Falk Lüke from the German Consumer Protection agency, who stated in 2008: 'That is part of the beautiful and partly also not so beautiful world on the Internet. Many people need to be reminded that when they publish something on the Internet, no matter where, that this is the same as publishing it on the front page of a newspaper. At the same time, for the newspaper lying on the breakfast table, nobody wants to see their party pictures from the day before yesterday on the title page' (translation by HB). (The original reads: 'Das ist Teil der schönen und teilweise auch nicht so schönen neuen Welt im Netz. Viele Menschen haben nicht so sehr im Hinterkopf, dass wenn sie etwas im Internet veröffentlichen, egal an welcher Stelle es tatsächlich eigentlich so wäre, als wenn sie es auf die Titelseite ihrer Zeitung drucken würden, aber die Zeitung, die morgens am Frühstückstisch liegt, da würde auch niemand gerne die Partyfotos von vorgestern drin sehen können auf der Titelseite'.) www.deutschlandfunk.de/verbraucherschuetzer-kritisiert-neues-datenschutzgesetz-100.html.
28 See Ian Phau and Johan Liang, 'Downloading Digital Video Games; Predictors, Moderators and Consequences', *Marketing Intelligence & Planning* 7 (2012), 740.

of any digital file owned is also legal, but copyright and fair use issues are distinctly different, depending on what kind of form data takes.

One additional way of using piracy as a way to re-examine existing laws on copyright can also be proposed here. Writing about historical sea-faring piracy, Alexandra Ganser shows that the 'threat of piracy – its instability and unreliability as a legal category […] has always met a need to be negotiated in popular symbolic economies' and should 'therefore be read as fictions of legitimation'. With historian Lauren Benton, she sees pirates as 'oceanic lawyers', well versed in loopholes, ever questioning the 'precarious membrane of the law'. She concludes, 'As cultural texts of "jurisgenesis," pirate accounts are concerned with the creation of a normative universe, "a world of right and wrong, of lawful and unlawful, of valid and void" […] and, in the context of negotiating normativity, with race, class, and gender constructions informing this creation'.[29] One might conclude that if such an enlightened view of piracy as a social generator was applicable to pirates 300 years ago, how much more does it chime a bell with current Internet pirates who were at the forefront of examining and establishing new cyberworlds and challenged and continue to challenge emerging questionable 'jurisgenesis'.[30]

In sum, the legal profession is not quite as unified as it seems when it comes to copyright. There exists a determined movement that is arguing for its abolishment, or at least redefinition, especially when it comes to its application to digital data. Many countries in the world have legislation in place that prohibits the downloading, uploading, or other sharing of copyrighted material; some of them have more lenient laws than others (at present, Switzerland,[31] Poland, and Spain allow downloading but not uploading), and many countries, while having legislation making the sharing of copyrighted material illegal, do not in fact enforce it.[32] As with so many other practices, it is once again a question of who you are and where you are located in the world that makes you either a thief or a file-sharing hero, sometimes even both.

---

29 Alexandra Ganser, *Crisis and Legitimacy in Atlantic American Narratives of Piracy* (Cham: Springer, 2020), 18–19.
30 For a similar, French, view, see Sévane Garibian, 'Hostes humani generis: les pirates vus par le droit', *Critique* 733–4 (2008), 470–9.
31 'Downloading Swiss-Style', *Deutsche Welle* (1 February 2012), www.dw.com/en/swiss-government-confirms-right-to-download/a-15641270.
32 For a recent listing, see 'Are Torrents Illegal? Update by Country 2022', *vpnMentor* www.vpnmentor.com/blog/torrents-illegal-update-country/.

5 Piracy and 'Juvenile Delinquency'

As the chapter in this volume by Michael D. High elaborates, the concept of piracy is a very old one and conflates issues of property, politics, power, and economics.[33] For most members of recent generations, their concept of piracy has been formed by the very international pirate book and film genre. Depending on one's age, the most important examples of the genre would include *The Pirate's Gold* (dir. D.W. Griffith, USA, 1908), *L'Honneur du corsaire* (dir. Victorin-Hippolyte Jasset, France, 1908), *Störtebeker* (dir. Ernst Wendt, Germany, 1919), *Il figlio del corsaro rosso* (dir. Vitale De Stefano, Italy, 1921), *Captain Blood* (dir. David Smith, USA, 1924), *The Black Pirate* (dir. Albert Parker, USA, 1926, with Errol Flynn), *Captain Blood* (dir. Michael Curtiz, USA, 1935, with Errol Flynn and Olivia de Havilland), *The Buccaneer* (dir. Anthony Quinn, USA, 1958, with Yul Brynner), *Treasure Island* (dir. Hsin-yan Chang and Qi Fu, PRC, 1964), the Pirates of the Caribbean franchise, starting with *The Curse of the Black Pearl* (dir. Gore Verbinski, USA, 2003, with Johnny Depp, Geoffrey Rush, Orlando Bloom, and Keira Knightley), and, more recently, *The Pirates: The Last Royal Treasure* (dir. Jeong-hoon Kim, South Korea, 2022). Hundreds of additional examples could be cited, with heroes allowing for easy identification.[34] It is important to realise that in most of these films, pirate life is given the veneer of adventure and also of justice posited against an unjust system, be it in their own countries or in enemy countries they were prompted to attack by their own governments. This is also the reason why over many years pirate outfits have consistently ranked in the top ten of Halloween and Mardi Gras/Carnival costumes.[35]

It was especially the *Pirates of the Caribbean* franchise that was screened during the beginning of file sharing times and that, with its irreverence and humorous take on the powers that be, would become influential for Generations X, Y, and Z, who also happened to be the respective target audiences for file sharing. Thus, these generations saw piracy as a legitimate way to respond to a broken, corrupt system

---

33 See Jonathan Paul Marshall and Francesca da Rimini, 'Paradoxes of Property Piracy and Sharing in Information Capitalism', in Tilman Baumgärtel, *A Reader on International Media Piracy: Pirate Essays* (Amsterdam: University of Amsterdam Press, 2015), 146–66, summarising property arguments.

34 In fictional accounts, one could do worse than looking at Daniel Defoe's *Histoire générale des plus fameux pyrates* (Paris: Phébus, 1990).

35 See https://watchmojo.com/video/id/14592.

and to take advantage of it was seen as a badge of valour.[36] Especially Generation Z, the first digital native generation, grew into this practice and simply consider it something that is available and to which they are entitled. This is the case, irrespective of a number of texts which are trying to highlight the illicitness and outright lawlessness of the pirate life.[37] Pirate glamour, so well peddled by Hollywood studios, by far outweighs any historical analysis of the role they played in world politics, especially so with a younger audience.

In many areas of file sharing or streaming, more organised and revenue-conscious individuals and organisations have become visible over the last few years (see the chapter by Ernesto Van der Sars in this volume). Especially when it comes to younger Internet file sharers, the motivation for using file sharing is arguably of a different kind. For most scene release groups, reputation is key.

36 See Samuel Hyat and Camille Paloque-Bergès (eds), 'Transgressions pirates', *Tracés. Revue de Sciences humaines* 26 (2014), https://journals.openedition.org/traces/5894; 'Pirater', *Tracés. Revue de Sciences humaines* 26 (2014), https://journals.openedition.org/traces/5892 stresses the positive, transgressive quality of piracy. Similarly, Sonny Perseil and Yvon Pesqueux (eds), *L'organisation de la transgression: formaliser l'informel?* (Paris: L'Harmattan, 2014). On digital art as transgression and trespassing in India, see Sarai Media Lab, 'Contested Commons/Trespassing Publics: A Public Record', Conference on Inequalities, Conflicts and Intellectual Property, New Delhi, 6, 7, 8 January 2005, www.sarai.net/events/ip_conf/.

37 See, for instance, the recently published *Piraten: Vom Seeräuber zum Sozialrevolutionär* [Pirates: From Sea Robbers to Social Revolutionaries] (Springe: zu Klampen Verlag, 2022) by Siegfried Kohlhammer, in which the author tries to dispel the social–romantic notion of pirates being the Robin Hoods of the seas. This might be true to a point, but it is not helpful that the author sees all pirates as 'terrorists of the seven seas' [Gewaltdienstleister der Weltmeere], thus grossly oversimplifying and delegitimising the ideological discourse running concurrently with the use of pirates and their services by the then world powers. From this rightist viewpoint, if piracy attracted the dregs of humanity, by analogy, digital piracy would attract people of similar ilk and needs to be rooted out. For a more balanced view, see Alfred S. Bradford, *Flying the Black Flag: A Brief History of Piracy* (Westport, CT: Praeger, 2007) and Daniel Heller-Roazan, *L'Ennemi de tous: le pirate contre les nations* (Paris: Le Seuil, 2010), the latter stressing the stigmatisation pirates experienced when viewed by state actors. Also, Peter Linebaugh and Marcus Rediker, in their *L'hydre aux mille têtes: l'histoire cachée de l'Atlantique révolutionnaire* (Paris: Éditions Amsterdam, 2008), stress the fight of pirates as an 'Atlantic proletariat' against the emerging European states and their state-sponsored terror. For additional arguments on seafaring piracy, see Alfred P. Rubin, *The Law of Piracy* (Newport, RI: Naval War College Press, 1988).

Their goal is not to share files with as many people as possible to create revenue for themselves, but to beat other groups by releasing content first. This kind of brinkmanship is borrowed from the supposedly grown-up world of journalism, where to come out with a news item first is also of great reputational importance. This come-first attitude is also a relic from the beginning of the Internet, when copyrighted media were shared via bulletin boards using very slow dial-up modems, or later using FTP sites and where coming first would indeed garner fame if not fortune. Rankings of scene players or groups are published in real-time tracer rankings, clearly underlining the game character of the exercise.[38] To further illustrate this, here is an excerpt from a 2011 article on the 'scene' by journalist Darren Pauli, who writes,

> The scene lacks a central leadership, yet strict rules apply. The most salient rule is that warez won't remain on a server unless they're the first or the best, but respect must be paid to a group-signed and updated charter that dictates file formats, release terminology and file sizes. Warez that do adhere to the charter, including duplicates and glitched releases, will be deleted, or 'nuked'.[39]

Very clearly, this is a world not governed by financial profit but rather by (juvenile and often male) honour and the 'beating of the system' – points completely neglected by Hollywood.[40] Study after study has shown that besides any honour code there does not exist a stigma which could be attached to file sharing. Arguably, none of the myriad campaigns launched by the entertainment industry across the globe has had any measurable impact on file-sharing practices. A 2019 study on digital piracy conducted amongst students in India, China, and Serbia revealed a complete lack of any idea of wrongdoing on their part when engaging in acts of digital piracy: 'Online piracy lacks negative social stigma. Most of the times, individuals are not conscious that they are involved in infringing rights by purchasing pirated software, books, movies, or music'.[41] On the contrary, those individuals who have newly available pirated material first would be considered popular, even heroes and heroines.

---

38   For instance, at https://predb.org/tracers/TS.
39   www.zdnet.com/article/inside-the-pirates-code-hidden-treasure/.
40   J.D. Lascia, *Darknet: Hollywood's War against the Digital Generation* (Hoboken, NJ: Wiley, 2005).
41   Sanjeev P. Sahni and Indranath Gupta, *Piracy in the Digital Era: Psychosocial, Criminological and Cultural Factors* (Amsterdam: Springer, 2019), 18.

Here a parallel can also be drawn to hacking, which for many years was also the domain of youthful and energetic coders and which was equally regulated by an honour code and less by monetary gains. The creation and retention of an honour code positions file sharing in close proximity to hacking in general, a practice which has overt political and nowadays also strong monetary overtones but used to be as idealistic as the file sharing realm at its idealistic best.[42] In relation to hacking, its ideology has perhaps been expressed best by McKenzie Wark in her *Hacker Manifesto*, when she writes:

> Hackers create the possibility of new things entering the world. Not always great things, or even good things, but new things. In art, in science, in philosophy and culture, in any production of knowledge where data can be gathered, where information can be extracted from it, and where in that information new possibilities for the world produced, there are hackers hacking the new out of the old. While we create these new worlds, we do not possess them. That which we create is mortgaged to others, and to the interests of others, to states and corporations who monopolize the means for making worlds we alone discover. We do not own what we produce – it owns us. Hackers use their knowledge and their wits to maintain their autonomy.[43]

While this appeal of/to autonomy will be discussed further in the Internet and Politics section of this text, another factor for why in the beginning it was youths especially who were involved in file sharing was that entertainment content was and continues to be expensive for those who have little financial means, something that is true for a fairly large number of teenagers in the northern hemisphere and millions of others in the global south. It is therefore an important point to consider, something I do in the next section.

---

42 On Kevin Mitnick and others, see Claire L. Evans, 'Searching for Susy Thunder', *The Verge* (26 January 2022), www.theverge.com/c/22889425/susy-thunder-headley-hackers-phone-phreakers-claire-evans. The film *Takedown* (dir. Joe Chapelle, USA, 2000) also provides an entertaining and insightful Hollywood introduction to the subject.

43 McKenzie Wark, *A Hacker Manifesto* (Cambridge, MA: Harvard University Press, 2004), 4, 5. For a feminist perspective on the politics of hacking, see Jennifer Mae Hamilton, Susan Reid, Pia van Gelder, and Astrida Neimanis (eds), *Feminist, Queer, and Anticolonial Propositions for Hacking the Anthropocene: Archive* (London: Open Humanities Press, 2021).

6 Piracy and the Economy

Common sense would dictate that file sharing is eating into the profits of content-producing companies. And to some degree this is of course true. Any file shared is not bought, and its distributor and creator go (partially) unpaid. On the other hand, a whole economy exists that has always benefited from questioning copyright and providing alternative ways to access such material. This began with second-hand bookshops and the changing of legislation for book selling ('second-use doctrine' as opposed to the 'first-use doctrine' discussed above), and then moved on to bootleg vinyls being sold at festivals, car boot sales, and flea markets, all of which became ever more popular in the 1960s, 1970s, and 1980s and were part of the shadow economy. Whenever a new technology for storing copyrighted data was invented, technology for obtaining such data illegally followed not long afterwards. Predictably, every time this happened, the question of copyright was raised once again, mostly with financial prospects in mind. This was true when paper copying machines (Xeroxes) were invented, but also with cassette tape recorders, VHS recorders, CD writers, DAT recorders, external hard drives, and stream rippers. Besides the legal system, questions of copyright invariably cropped up and were discussed in academia along with these technological developments.[44]

One of the challenges one faces when trying to write about the economic impact of Internet piracy are the financial figures put forward. In a lecture in November 2019 at the Higher School of Economics, Moscow, Joe Karaganis, one of the most authoritative figures in digital piracy research, stated that, 'The war machine to fight piracy continues', and urged his listeners to take a closer look at the ammunition being used in order to fight this war. Many of the figures detailing the alleged damage piracy does to content providers are highly doubtful, as the entities collecting these figures usually have vested interest in them and are often paid by the claimants

---

44   e.g. Gary Hall, *Digitize This Book! The Politics of New Media, or Why We Need Open Access Now* (Minneapolis: University of Minnesota Press, 2008); Gary Hall, *Pirate Philosophy: For a Digital Posthumanities* (Cambridge, MA: MIT Press, 2016); Gerd Leonhard, *End of Control* [blog] (2007), https://gerdcloud.tumblr.com/post/29052773682/the-end-of-control-gerd-leonhard-2007-book; Gerd Leonhard, *Friction is Fiction: The Future of Content, Media & Business* (Morrisville, NC: Lulu.com, 2010); or indeed a recent article leading the German weekly *Die Zeit* on copyright (30 May 2019).

themselves. A case in point is the International Intellectual Property Association (IIPA), created in 1984, and which is made up of the Association of American Publishers (AAP), the Business Software Alliance (BSA), the Entertainment Software Association (ESA), the Independent Film & Television Alliance (IFTA), the Motion Picture Association (MPA), the National Music Publishers' Association (NMPA), and the Recording Industry Association of America (RIAA). All of its members are interested in being able to report high numbers of piracy, as this would allow them to pressure the US government into creating severely punitive laws, thereby strengthening their ability to better sell their products in the US market and globally. This becomes blatantly obvious when considering that the IIPA is the main representative of the US entertainment industry, works closely with the Office of the US Trade Representative (USTR), and assisted the US government with World Trade Organization (WTO), Trade-Related Aspects of Intellectual Property Rights (TRIPS), and North American Free Trade Agreement (NAFTA) negotiations and the 1996 ratification of the World Intellectual Property Organization (WIPO) treaties on copyright performances and phonograms. One of the reasons one can see high piracy rates in the global south is the fact that US companies were successfully creating demand in these countries for content that was mostly unaffordable and unavailable to virtually any and all addressees. Not surprisingly, many people then resorted to easy and cheap piracy to access such content.

But one does not have to go to the global south to find an issue with file sharing. Even within with the economic powerhouses of the northern hemisphere, data suggests that far from stymieing development, piracy has actually had a part in stimulating and growing the creative industries. A 2013 London School of Economics report entitled 'Copyright & Creation: A Case for Promoting Inclusive Online Sharing', by Bart Cammaerts, Robin Mansell, and Bingchun Meng, clearly demonstrated that piracy has been helpful to the creative industries and can arguably be seen as an accelerator for creativity. Key points of the report are:

[1] The creative industries are innovating to adapt to a changing digital culture and evidence does not support claims about overall patterns of revenue reduction due to individual copyright infringement.

[2] The experiences of other countries that have implemented punitive measures against individual online copyright infringers

indicate that the approach does not have the impacts claimed by some in the creative industries.

[3] A review of the UK Digital Economy Act 2010 is needed based on independent analysis of the social, cultural and political impacts of punitive copyright infringement measures against citizens, and the overall experience of the creative industries (Figure 2.1).[45]

Figure 2.1 Trends in revenues of the music industry, 1998–2011 ($US million)

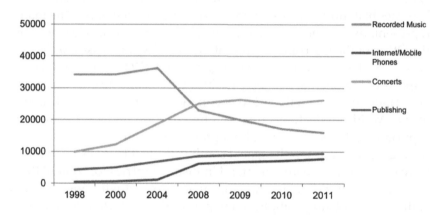

Source: Bart Cammaerts, Robin Mansell, and Bingchun Meng, *Copyright and Creation: A Case for Promoting Inclusive Online Sharing*, LSE Media Policy Brief 9 (2013). https://eprints.lse.ac.uk/54275/.

It is remarkable that just at the time when music file sharing became possible due to the invention of the MP3, increasing computing power and bandwidth, and the invention of Napster, revenues from concerts, publishing, and later streaming would increase. The only declining line on the graph is for recorded music media, which, as Cammaerts et al. cogently claim, was due to changes in the industry; music CDs and vinyl play an ever smaller part in revenues today,

45   Bart Cammaerts, Robin Mansell, and Bingchun Meng, 'Copyright & Creation: A Case for Promoting Inclusive Online Sharing', *LSE Media Policy Brief* 9 (2013), 9. For point 2, see also Trajce Cvetkovski, *Copyright and Popular Media: Liberal Villains and Technological Change* (New York: Palgrave Macmillan, 2013), 5: 'Media piracy is illustrative of a plurality of media consumption within a converging legal, technological, economic and ideological universe'.

which are dominated by streaming services. Piracy therefore did not cause the downfall of this revenue stream but was rather helpful in the creation of an alternative in the first place, in this case very profitable music-streaming services.

A more recent text, 'Empirical Copyright: A Case Study of File Sharing, Sales Revenue, and Music Output', by Glynn S. Lunney, Jr,[46] shows that another mainstay in the arguments by the record industry blaming Napster and other file sharers is also highly dubitable. This argument holds that more revenue means more original works. Lunney demonstrates that the decline in recorded music sales did produce fewer new artists on the Billboard Hot100 chart, but that it also produced more hit songs by each one of the new artists entering the ranking. Ultimately, '[b]ecause the second effect outweighed the first, the rise of file sharing and the contemporaneous decline in record sales was associated with a net increase in the production of new hit songs'.[47] One might furthermore claim that music was also not necessarily being mainstreamed as it had been, with alternative distribution channels being used. One might trace this back to the rave culture of 1990s Britain, which began the renaissance of vinyl records, or, more recently, the creation of soundcloud.com, where new music is streamed without payment, and bandcamp.com, where new music can be listened to with money going directly to the artists played.

Furthermore, a 2015 study supported by the Washington, DC-based Digital Citizens Alliance (DCA) stated that an analysis of 589 pirate websites, including those for counterfeit goods,[48] generated an estimated $US209 million in aggregate advertising revenue, similar to the figures for 2013, and this despite the fact that several large BitTorrent sites had been shut down during that time period – thus demonstrating the resilience of the market.[49] However, a quick check

---

46 Glynn S. Lunney, Jr, 'Empirical Copyright: A Case Study of File Sharing, Sales Revenue, and Music Output', *Supreme Court Economic Review* 24, no. 1 (2016), 261–322.

47 Lunney, 'Empirical Copyright', 261.

48 Tim Phillips, *Knock-Off: The Deadly Trade in Counterfeit Goods* (London: Kogan Page, 2005).

49 See 'Good Money Still Going Bad: Digital Thieves and the Hijacking of the Online Ad Business' (19 May 2015), www.motionpictures.org/research-docs/good-money-still-going-bad-digital-thieves-and-the-hijacking-of-the-online-ad-business/. A 2021 report claimed that advertising on pirate websites garners an estimated $US1.34 billion in annual revenues, again refusing to

in 2022 revealed that none of the six popular torrent sites carries any advertising, except for rare pop-ups on one of them, and that advertising superimposed on CAM videos (i.e., those recorded on cameras during a cinema screening) – something practised recently in particular by XBet – is frowned upon by the downloading community.[50] It is also questionable whether the DCA's statement that over one-third of all files from torrent websites carry viruses is correct, as the claim made remains unsubstantiated and speaks against billions of hits such websites receive annually. Already in 2009, the Rand Corporation had charged that piracy was a threat to (US) National Security, with links alleged (but not substantiated) to terrorism and organised crime.[51] In this regard it is also good to remember that while the name 'Digital Citizen Alliance' tries to suggest it to be an association of concerned (US) citizens, defending citizens' rights, it is actually working with the film industry, lobbies the government on the film industry's behalf,[52] and is a blatant attempt at delegitimising the rights of those citizens who engage in pirate practices.[53] This is despite the fact that seven large BitTorrent sites,

make clear how this estimate is reached. If this proves anything at all, it is the popularity of such websites, as otherwise advertisers wouldn't bother. See 'Breaking (B)ads: How Advertiser-Supported Piracy Helps Fuel a Booming Multi-Billion Dollar Illegal Market', *Digital Citizens Alliance* (August 2021), www.digitalcitizensalliance.org/clientuploads/directory/Reports/Breaking-Bads-Report.pdf.

50   This might differ from country to country. Thus, a 2015 study on Brazilian file-sharing sites does report a large amount of advertising: Paul A. Watters, 'An Analysis of Piracy Website Advertising in Brazil and Its Linkages to Child Exploitation Material', *ECPAT International* (December 2015), https://ecpat.org/wp-content/uploads/2021/05/Piracy-Website-Advertising-in-Brazil_ENG.pdf.

51   Gregory F. Treverton, Carl Matthies, Karla J. Cunningham, Jeremiah Goulka, Greg Ridgeway, and Anny Wong, *Film Piracy, Organized Crime, and Terrorism* (Santa Monica, CA: Rand Corporation, 2009). In a similar vein, see John Arquilla and David Ronfeldt, *Networks and Netwars: The Future of Terror, Crime, and Militancy* (Santa Monica, CA: Rand Corporation, 2001); Moisés Naim, *Illicit: How Smugglers, Traffickers and Copycats are Hijacking the Global Economy* (London: Heinemann, 2005); and Gini Graham Scott, *Internet Book Piracy: The Fight to Protect Authors, Publishers, and Our Culture* (New York: Allworth Press, 2016).

52   'Group Accusing YouTube of Helping Hackers Has Ties to Film Lobby', *vox* (31 July 2015), www.vox.com/2015/7/31/11615256/group-accusing-youtube-of-helping-hackers-has-ties-to-film-lobby.

53   A case in point are the numerous campaigns the DCA and similar associations and lobby groups have been running ever since the inception of piracy.

generating an estimated $US44.3 million in ad revenue, were shut down.[54] That was offset by the growth of smaller and medium-sized sites, as well as video streaming.

It is also true that the Internet industry itself acknowledges the creative potential of pirate practices but does not often do so in public. A rare example is the famous paper by Microsoft's Peter Biddle, Paul England, Marcus Peinado, and Bryan Willman presented at the 2002 Association for Computing Machinery (ACM) Workshop on Digital Rights Management on 18 November 2002, in Washington, DC. Its title was 'The Darknet and the Future of Content Distribution', and it concludes with the following statement:

> There is evidence that the darknet will continue to exist and provide low cost, high-quality service to a large group of consumers. This means that in many markets, the darknet will be a competitor to legal commerce. From the point of view of economic theory, this has profound implications for business strategy: for example, increased security (e.g., stronger DRM systems) may act as a disincentive to legal commerce. Consider an MP3 file sold on a web site: this costs money, but the purchased object is as useful as a version acquired from the darknet. However, a securely DRM-wrapped song is strictly less attractive: although the industry is striving for flexible licensing rules, customers will be restricted in their actions if the system is to provide meaningful security. This means that a vendor will probably make more money by selling unprotected objects than protected objects. In short, if you are competing with the darknet, you must compete on the darknet's own terms: that is convenience and low cost rather than additional security [...] We see the darknet having most direct bearing on mass-market consumer IP-goods. Goods sold to corporations are less threatened because corporations mostly

See Tarleton Gillespie's 'Characterizing Copyright in the Classroom: The Cultural Work of Antipiracy Campaigns', *Communication, Culture & Critique* 2 (2009), 274–318, which chronicles in detail the brainwashing campaign such corporations have carried into schools: 'File trading is painted in moral terms of right and wrong. Moreover, these campaigns perpetuate industry-centric ideas of what copyright is for and how technology is meant to be used. In the process they reaffirm traditional hierarchies of cultural production and reify the long-standing distinction between producer and consumer – far from neutral assertions in the current debates about cultural policy, and that work against the tide of emerging forms of creativity and collaboration'.

54 See 'Good Money Still Going Bad: Digital Thieves and the Hijacking of the Online Ad Business' (19 May 2015), www.motionpictures.org.

try to stay legal, and will police their own intranets for illicit activities. [...] Today's peer-to-peer technologies provide excellent service quality for audio files, but users must be very determined or price-sensitive to download movies from a darknet, when the legal competition is a rental for a few dollars.[55]

Furthermore, two recent studies highlight the fluidity and dynamics of entertainment consumption. The examples also underscore the fact that different agencies come to different, at times diametrically opposed, conclusions. The first study is by Akamai, an Internet security company, entitled 'State of the Internet. Security: Pirates in the Outfield',[56] which concluded that

> between January and September 2021, global piracy demand reached 3.7 billion. Based on the data, we can see that an overwhelming majority of consumers (61.5 percent) are directly accessing pirated materials, while 28.6 percent of them are searching for it. At just over 67 billion total visits, television is the top pirated industry among MUSO's data, as used in the study. This is followed by the publishing and film industries.

According to this study, during the first 9 months of 2021, 132 billion visits to pirate sites were recorded, and that in relation to over 4.66 billion active Internet users in 2020, this represented 56 per cent of the world's population. Looking at these figures, one might agree with Karaganis when he stated that already by 2010, 'Piracy was the media market and not a marginal economy'. These 132 billion visits signal a 16 per cent increase compared to the first nine months of 2020, and more than the number of piracy visits for the whole of 2020. This increase is a recent development, however, and, overall, pirate site visits globally were slightly decreasing for most of the last five years.[57]

---

55 Peter Biddle, Paul England, Marcus Peinado, and Bryan Willman, 'The Darknet and the Future of Content Distribution', 2002 ACM Workshop on Digital Rights Management, Wyndham City Center, Washington, DC, www.semanticscholar.org/paper/The-Darknet-and-the-Future-of-Content-Distribution-Biddle-England/d09ea4f3bb7a0b8ffc596eaa92af8ae367485358.

56 Akamai, 'State of the Internet, Security: Pirates in the Outfield', SOTI 8, no. 1 (January 2022), ed. Martin McKeay, www.akamai.com/resources/state-of-the-internet/soti-security-pirates-in-the-outfield.

57 Ernesto Van der Sar, 'Pirate Site Traffic Surged in 2021, Research Finds', *TorrentFreak* (27 January 2022), https://torrentfreak.com/pirate-site-traffic-surged-in-2021-research-finds-220127/.

The second study, led by Francisco García-Valero for the European Union Intellectual Property Office and entitled 'Online Copyright Infringement in the European Union: Music, Films and TV (2017–2020). Trends and Drivers',[58] comes to a similar conclusion, but draws different lessons from it. If the Akamai study arrived at a 16 per cent year on year increase for piracy from 2020 to 2021, the figures García-Valero and his team present seem to suggests that piracy numbers almost halved between 2017 and 2020, and that this is true across all content categories – but most of all for music, which dropped over 80 per cent, something that might be attributable, at least in part, to the Spotify factor. Here it is good to recollect that both Spotify and the somewhat older iTunes are both built on Napster technology and strategy, having a central server and building a community around its content for sale. Regarding the two studies, important differentiations also come into play, with the most important one being the already familiar one of income and availability. Within the EU, countries with higher incomes, such as Germany and Finland, had less piracy than countries with lower incomes, such as Bulgaria. Furthermore, the legal availability of content also helped to decrease piracy. These European figures can easily be extrapolated across the globe, with the large Internet populations of India, China, Brazil, and Russia dominating piracy website visits, closely following the world leader in piracy website visits, the United States.[59]

Both studies agree that there exists a move away from music downloads and towards pirate streaming sites, with television streaming responsible for the majority of content consumed (over 67 billion television piracy visits, about 50 per cent of all pirate traffic, according to Akamai, and 70 per cent according to the EU study). According to the Akamai numbers, publishing is in second place (30 billion visits – 23 per cent), then films (14.5 billion visits – 11 per cent, EU 20 per cent), then music (10.8 billion visits – 8 per cent, EU 10 per cent) and, in last place, software (9 billion visits – 7 per cent) (with publishing and software piracy not included in the EU study). While

58 Francisco García-Valero, Michal Kazimierczak, Carolina Arias Burgos, and Nathan Wajsman, 'Online Copyright Infringement in the European Union: Music, Films and TV (2017–2020). Trends and Drivers' (2021). DOI: 10.2814/505158.

59 See Vanessa Mendes Moreira De Sa, 'Rethinking "Pirate Audiences": An Investigation of TV Audiences' Informal Online Viewing and Distribution Practices in Brazil', PhD thesis, School of Humanities and Communication Arts, University of Western Sydney, 2013.

there exist differences in numbers, trends clearly seem to be the same across both studies.[60]

But it is significant that the two studies in part also disagree on the direction piracy is taking. There might be several reasons for this. For one, the Akamai study has been commissioned by a company that offers solutions to Internet piracy and might therefore benefit from highlighting and giving maximum numbers for piracy occurring. On the other hand, the official European Union Intellectual Property Office would need to explain why intellectual property (IP) legislation is thought to be working and would benefit from arriving at decreasing numbers. Beyond this obvious difference, the EU study only looked at EU countries, and reached similar results as global studies did when looking at media availability and income distribution. The Akamai study was global and, if piracy happens increasingly in countries of the global south, precisely because of economic factors, then these numbers would make sense as well.[61] An outlier here is the United States, where, according to the Akamai study, 10 per cent of global Internet piracy is taking place; this figure would beg for a closer look in future studies, as neither availability nor economic disadvantages can be said to play a role in this, but perhaps Internet saturation across a large market might.

One other factor may very well have also played a role in the EU study's differing results of declining piracy numbers. The study limited its research data bases to traditional pirate sites, mostly providing torrent downloads; live sports streaming websites were not included, nor were streaming and IPTV service sites. As the last are growing rapidly, this might explain the drop in piracy numbers,

60 As the Akamai study demonstrates, books and journals are rapidly becoming a major new area of file sharing, for instance among academics whose institutions are unable or unwilling to pay the huge sums academic publishers of books and journals are demanding. And even if this money is spent, a recent German study suggests that the increasing concentration of publishing in the hands of a very few players is hampering academic publishing – and thus progress. See Justus Haucap, Nima Moshgbar, and Wolfgang Benedikt Schmal, 'The Impact of the German "DEAL" on Competition in the Academic Publishing Market', *Managerial and Decision Economics* 42, no. 8 (2021), 2027–49; also Adrian Johns, 'Intellectual Property and the Nature of Science', *Cultural Studies* 20, no. 2/3 (2006), 145–64.

61 For a theoretical discussion of how national culture is related to economic piracy, see Bryan W. Husted, 'The Impact of National Culture on Software Piracy', *Journal of Business Ethics* 26 (2000), 197–211.

which actually might not have decreased, but users are just switching to other websites not researched.

Taken together, the reports suggest a mixed picture; no matter whether piracy is increasing or decreasing slightly, the numbers of website visits are in the billions and this is clearly not just a minority or an ephemeral phenomenon. As much as individual artists might be affected negatively by it, most studies suggest that many artists have actually benefited more from the Internet piracy revolution in terms of exposure and access to markets than from any move from CD/DVD to streaming. Profit from these paradigm changes also stretches to and includes record companies and studios, despite their claims to the contrary.[62] One of the most cited reasons why people become involved in illegal downloads is price, be that $US20 or more for an album or $US25 or more for a DVD that costs 50 cents to $US3 in material to produce, or $US150 for an article in an Elsevier, Wiley, or Taylor and Francis academic journal – an article for which the writer had to pay to submit, with peer-reviewers who peer-reviewed it without payment, and a library which had to pay to make it available to its customers. It is hard to see how such prices are defensible as just or appropriate, and the favourite neoliberal argument of market self-regulation does not really fit, as it is an oligarchy of companies which have been in charge of the commercial academic journal market ever since its inception.

Another point to consider is that even when availability and price are less of an issue, piracy still seems to continue, as the American figures suggest, e.g., with individuals complementing their favourite subscription channels with other content available only elsewhere. In 2021, almost 50 different subscription services were available in the United States alone,[63] easily leading to subscription fatigue due to an overabundance of distributed (and chargeable) choices, which might heighten the lure of one piratical source for all even more.[64] Especially

---

62   Cf. the studies cited in Lunney, 'Empirical Copyright'; Cammaerts, Mansell, and Meng, 'Copyright & Creation'; and Joe Karaganis (ed.), *Shadow Libraries: Access to Knowledge in Global Higher Education* (Cambridge, MA: MIT Press, 2018).

63   Derek Baine, 'How Many Streaming Services Can People Consume? OTT Services & vMVPDs Continue To Soar', *Forbes* (22 December 2021), www. forbes.com/sites/derekbaine/2021/12/22/how-many-streaming-services-can-people-consume-ott-services--vmvpds-continue-to-soar/.

64   Tyler Hersko, 'Nearly Half of U.S. Consumers Are Frustrated with a Bloated Streaming Market', *IndieWire* (13 June 2019), www.indiewire.com/2019/06/too-many-streaming-services-television-decentralization-1202149596/.

with large entertainment and technology companies benefiting from this surge of demand, many consumers will refuse to buy into the industry's mainstay tired argument any more, i.e., that it is the small-scale, individual artists who are suffering most from piracy. If this is indeed true for a minority of artists, it was already the case under the analogue regime. This practice continues today as a legal, but perhaps not so legitimate, remuneration model on streaming platforms, as will be discussed further below in relation to the Spotify case.

One further argument in favour of piracy is that due to the progressive technologising of the entertainment/tech industry, it stands to benefit from piracy itself. A case going back to the beginning of content storage devices involving the Sony Corporation sheds some light on this. Sony has been/is on both sides of the fence. This is due to the fact that it is both an electronics company and a creative music/film and distribution company. In 1946, Masaru Ibuka opened an electronics store inside a Tokyo Department Store and was soon joined by Akio Morita, the latter leading Sony for several decades. Its first original product was a transistor radio and the name Sony (combining the Latin word for sound, sonus, with the American familiar form of address to a young boy, 'sonny') was adopted in 1958. CBS Records was purchased in 1988 and Columbia Pictures in 1989, combining media content with its traditional hardware business. In effect, this made it its own enemy.

In 1975, Sony introduced the Betamax video recorder. One year later, it was sued by Universal and Disney, who argued that the Betamax was a copyright infringement device. In 1979, a District Court Judge ruled that the Betamax was covered by fair use, a judgment overturned in 1981. Ultimately, in 1984 the US Supreme Court followed the first judgment and once again allowed its sale. This was not an easy decision, and it was a 5 to 4 split decision. The judgment was based on the decision that (1) Betamax had the potential for non-infringement use; (2) its time-shifting function was considered fair use; and (3) Sony could not be held liable for its customers' misuse of the product.[65]

Betamax tapes, and those of its soon to be victorious VHS competitor, were first only sold as blanks. It was only later that the studios realised the potential of packaged tapes and began

---

65 See Lucas Hilderbrand, *Inherent Vice: Bootleg Histories of Video and Copyright* (Durham, NC: Duke University Press, 2009), 86 ff.

selling them, revolutionising the entertainment market and profitably tapping new markets. But it was the blanks that would allow for illegal copying already back then. However, despite industry rhetoric, the issue of illegal copying was a relatively small one, as copy quality was far below that of any original. Large-scale sequential copying was therefore not a viable option. The anti-copying campaign also simply regurgitated arguments brought against audio cassette tapes and audio cassette recorders in the 1970s. These recorders had been invented in the late 1950s, at first as pure speech recorders.[66] But, as quality improved, by the 1970s they had become a mainstay in adolescents' bedrooms and had led to a 'mixtape' culture, with people mixing tracks recorded either off the radio or from records. When digital audio tape recorders became available in the late 1980s, it was Sony again who was at the forefront of the movement, and once again was sued, now by Songwriter Sammy Cahn and four music publishing companies to stop sales of its digital audio tape recorders. At the time, recording for one's own personal use was not illegal, and this remains the case in most countries today, with the notable exception of the UK. The case was dropped as part of a wider settlement that would lead to the U.S. Audio Home Recording Act of 1992 (AHRA), which amended US copyright law and made it clear that recording copyrighted digital audio for personal use was not a crime.[67] This Act in turn would form the basis for the 1998 U.S. Digital Millennium Copyright Act. By then, though, this was already a lost cause in the case of blank audio cassettes. When the industry went digital in the late 1980s and 1990s, other storage devices such as the computer's internal and external hard discs would take the place of VHS tapes, CDs, and DVDs and, not surprisingly, Sony would again profit massively from tapes and recorder sales. This would not stop the other side of Sony's activities, particularly its film studio and music companies, being at the forefront of suing content and distribution providers for infringement of copyright. A case in point is a 2015 case in Norway:

66 The RAC Tape Cartridge was invented in 1958, the Philips compact cassette in 1963, and the Stereo 8 Cartridge by Lear Jet in 1964.
67 See Joel L. McKuin, 'Home Audio Taping of Copyrighted Works and the Audio Home Recording Act of 1992: A Critical Analysis', *Hastings Communication. & Entertainment Law Journal* 16 (1994), 311–21; Lewis Kurlantzick and Jacqueline Pennino, 'The Audio Home Recording Act and the Formation of Copyright Policy', *Journal of the Copyright Society of the U.S.A.* 45 (1998), 497–501.

Disney, Warner Bros. and Sony are among several movie giants taking legal action to have the world's largest pirate sites blocked in Norway. In a lawsuit targeting 11 local ISPs and eight pirate site operators – including Pirate Bay founder Fredrik Neij – the studios are demanding a nationwide subscriber blockade.[68]

In 2014, Sony was hacked on a grand scale by North Korean hackers, it is alleged, who disliked the resale of the Sony film *The Interview*, a comedy poking fun at the North Korean leader, Kim Jong-un. However,

> [w]hat news reports frequently overlooked in their coverage of the hack of the century was that 'Sony is a company that hackers have loved to hate for 10 years' (Bruce Schneier). In 2005, a decade prior to the hack of the century, it was revealed that, in an ill-informed attempt to force digital-rights management on its customers, Sony BMG introduced a rootkit 'Trojan horse' program that hacked the trusted systems on users' computers, disabled CD ripping, 'phoned home' to Sony every time an affected disc was played, and provided a back door to other malicious software [...]. The company settled subsequent hacking lawsuits without admitting guilt. In 2011 Sony went on the offensive against its PlayStation 3 users who learned to 'jailbreak,' or circumvent, Sony's digital-rights-management software, suing hacker George Hotz and others for criminal federal violations of the CFAA, DMCA, copyright infringement, and trespass. [...] At the same time companies such as Sony manage their own hacking operations as 'skunkworks,' an ongoing cost of maintaining networked enterprises. After the fact Sony employed a classic hacking technique (DDoS) to hack back and sabotage servers providing access to its data [...] Hacking back in such a fashion probably breached legal boundaries.[69]

---

68 Andy Maxwell, 'Movie Studios and Record Labels Target Pirate Bay in New Lawsuit', *TorrentFreak* (1 September 2015), https://torrentfreak.com/movie-studios-and-record-labels-target-pirate-bay-in-new-lawsuit-150901.

69 Patrick Burkart and Tom McCourt, *Why Hackers Win: Power and Disruption in the Network Society* (Oakland: University of California Press, 2019), 49–50. See also Peter Elkin, 'Sony Pictures: Inside the Hack of the Century', *Fortune* (25 June 2015), https://fortune.com/longform/sony-hack-part-1/. For Brian Krebs, such attacks, together with DDoS, are a form of marketing and a 'democratisation of censorship'. Brian Krebs, 'The Democratization of Censorship', *KrebsonSecurity* (25 September 2016), https://krebsonsecurity.com/2016/09/the-democratization-of-censorship/.

Sony is also involved in blocking streaming sites. In April 2019 in Australia, it applied for and was granted a blocking injunction for streaming sites 2conv, Flv2mp3, FLVto, and Convert2mp3. The injunction was based on a 2018 Amendment to Australia's Copyright Act: 'Previously, in order for a platform to be rendered inaccessible by ISPs, it would need to have a "primary purpose of infringing". Last November's [2018] changes lowered the bar so that sites "with the primary effect" of infringing or facilitating infringement can also be blocked'.[70]

This last case of streaming sites being blocked is reminiscent of the Betamax case from the 1970s – catching ephemeral broadcasts/streams – except that Sony has switched sides. If in the 1970s it had been the defendant, it would now become the plaintiff and the defendant simultaneously, in effect suing itself and other entities for comparable infringements it had been charged with at the time. It might be part of neoliberal thought to have your cake and eat it too, and perhaps this is what is being expressed in Sony board meetings. However, either toning down juridical suits or even divesting one or the other area of engagement would have been a more ethical choice.

Other reactions might also have been possible. More recently, the point has been mooted that there indeed exist a number of economic ways to make piracy a springboard to increasing revenues, as a number of initiatives have demonstrated,[71] including use of the Alpha60 system which collects data on select pirate downloading sites.[72] For instance, it revealed that a 2017 episode of *Game of Thrones* garnered over 50 per cent of the official viewing figures from torrent download sites one day after its initial broadcast, with at one point over 800,000 users seeding it. The system also gives download and

70   Andy Maxwell, 'Aussie Music Industry Wins First Ever Stream-Ripping Site Blocks', *TorrentFreak* (16 May 2019), https://torrentfreak.com/aussie-music-industry-wins-first-ever-stream-ripping-site-blocks-190516.

71   Ernesto Van der Sar, '"Piracy Audiences Are Untapped Pools of Wealth"', *TorrentFreak* (21 July 2018), https://torrentfreak.com/piracy-audiences-are-untapped-pools-of-wealth-180721/; Peter T. Leeson, *The Invisible Hook: The Hidden Economics of Pirates* (Princeton, NJ: Princeton University Press, 2009).

72   Abigail De Kosnik and Benjamin De Kosnik, 'The Alpha 60 Project: BitTorrent Cartography for *The OA, Westworld, The Walking Dead, Yuri on Ice, Skam*, and *Game of Thrones*', https://benjamin.dekosnik.com/wp-content/uploads/2017/01/de-kosnik-et-al-hek.pdf.

access data, both of which can help industries better understand their markets.

A cogent case has also been made that it was piracy which helped establish Hollywood products in the global south, in a scope that regular 'legal' material could never have, something that Mattelart and Baumgärtel call, 'globalization from below'.[73] This was, for example, the case with VHS video recorders and tapes of US shows sold on African markets, with these markets also contributing to the exposure of international films, amongst others from Egypt and South East Asia otherwise not available elsewhere, thereby establishing and/or adding to a positive cultural globalisation. Especially in Africa, the video sector developed through pirate networks of the second or shadow economy, as this content was mostly not accessible via official channels, or if it were, it was often censored by governments.[74] These second economies had a strong impact; in South East Asia, it is claimed that the Philippine piracy media economy is larger than the legal sector.[75] Mattelart, together

73 Tristan Mattelart, 'Audiovisual Piracy, Informal Economy, and Cultural Globalization', *International Journal of Communication* 6 (2012), 735–50.

74 See Tristan Mattelart (ed.), *Piratages audiovisuelles: les Voies souterraines de la mondialisation culturelle* (Brussels: De Boeck, 2011). For Nigeria, see Brian Larkin, *Signal and Noise: Media, Infrastructure, and Urban Culture in Nigeria* (Durham, NC: Duke University Press, 2008). The study shows how it was piracy that allowed media content to circulate in Nigeria and was at least in part responsible for the swift rise of Nollywood, as it provided a ready infrastructure for efficient distribution. See Jade L. Miller, *Nollywood Central: The Nigerian Videofilm Industry* (London: BFI, 2016); Jason Crawford, 'Revolution Bootlegged: Pirate Resistance in Nigeria's Broken Infrastructure', in Andrew Opitz, 'Pirates and Piracy', *Darkmatter Journal* 5 (2009), 3–15. A similar case can be made for India and the rise of Bollywood. An interesting case is also Mattelart's study of audiovisual flows which piracy has fuelled and led to 'the rise of new contraflows of non-Western cultural products and then [...] given form to counterhegemonic flows, that is, flows that carry content running counter to the dominant meanings of American programs', thus questioning hegemonic and ideological one-way traffic. See Tristan Mattelart, 'The Changing Geographies of Pirate Transnational Audiovisual Flows', *International Journal of Communication* 10 (2016), 3503.

75 Vivencio O. Ballano, *Sociological Perspectives on Media Piracy in the Philippines and Vietnam* (Singapore: Springer, 2016). Over 49 per cent of the Philippine population admits to using pirate websites: see www.prnewswire.com/news-releases/new-survey-shows-philippines-among-highest-in-online-piracy-in-southeast-asia-301154664.html. See also, Rolando B. Tolentino, 'Piracy and Its Regulation: The Filipino's Historical Response to Globalization', paper presented at the workshop on media piracy and intellectual property in

with D'Almedia[76] point out, though, that piracy is a two-edged sword for these culturally emerging economies of the south: while piracy is combated by Hollywood et al., especially in emerging economies, it paves the way for and heightens recognition of Hollywood wares, to the detriment of local production. For the most part, film distribution would often oscillate between formal and informal channels, giving it extra vibrancy. Here one can also see the dilemma Hollywood faced: while it was happy to have the global south being exposed to its wares, it was less so when it noticed that this happened beyond its monetarising distribution channels, again a case of trying to have your cake and eat it too.[77] As such, piracy is then another highly successful distribution system that develops positive synergies with the 'legal' distribution system, and profits both. It is an additional and necessary informal economy of communication and a shadow economy in its own right.[78]

Last but not least, one might argue that the fact that many media industry companies, from streaming services to journals aggregated and published by the likes of Elsevier and others, do nowadays offer increasing parts of their back catalogue without charge or as open access, something that would arguably not have happened without the strong pressure pirate sites have exerted upon their business plans. It therefore stands to reason that the file-sharing movement as a whole is making an impact on these industries and, with content scarcity a definite thing of the past, is forcing companies to provide more content free of charge. However, this is little comfort for those individuals who are still being persecuted for copyright infringement and handed hefty fines.

Southeast Asia, UP CMC Auditorium, 24 November 2006, http://xn--baumgr-tel-z2a.org/Piracy%20and%20Its%20Regulation2.pdf, and Tilman Baumgärtel, 'The Culture of Piracy in the Philippines', *Pilipinas: A Journal of Philippine Studies* 45 (2005), 29–43.

76   Francisco d'Almeida and Marie-Lise Alleman, *Les industries culturelles des pays du Sud: enjeux du projet de convention internationale sur la diversité culturelle* (Paris: Agence intergouvernementale de la francophonie, 2004). See also P. Sauvé (ed.), 'Trends in Audiovisual Markets: Regional Perspectives from the South' (Paris: UNESCO, 2006), http://unesdoc.unesco.org/images/0014/001461/146192e.pdf.

77   See Toby Miller, Nitin Govil, John McMurria, and Richard Maxwell, *Global Hollywood* (London: BFI, 2001),

78   Ramon Lobato, *Shadow Economies of Cinema Mapping: Informal Film Distribution* (London: Bloomsbury, 2012),

7 Piracy and the Right to Education, Information, and Entertainment

In general, it is in countries' interests to have a well-educated workforce. If one analyses high GDP economies, much of their economic success has been and continues to be their dependence on a thriving, highly diversified, and cutting-edge education sector.[79] The US Constitution makes it clear that information and education are things Congress is charged with providing for citizens, if possible freely or at a reasonable cost.[80] In the United States and in OECD countries, one generally finds free schools and colleges and universities which charge very little or give out generous scholarships. In most other affluent countries, education is overwhelmingly free, which includes countries as diverse as those in the European Union, but also China, India, and many others in the global south.

However, access to such educational content is unevenly distributed and privileges those located in the northern hemisphere. There is an argument to be made regarding the expansion of horizons through file sharing, of being introduced to content otherwise not available, due either to government or commercial restrictions. And, indeed, this is what most users of file-sharing sites also cite when asked why they are downloading files. Other reasons include price and ease of use.[81] Of course, availability of material is deeply connected with power and its ability to decide and implement who gets to see what content and who does not. This can be achieved, often in collusion/collaboration with businesses, via price, but also by artificially closing off access to material, nowadays typically located on the Internet. Recently, Myanmar, Sudan, Russia, and many other countries have demonstrated how to completely switch off the Internet for a whole country or how to severely restrict access to specific educational, journalistic, and scholarly material. A similar case can be made for US sanctions on Iran, which have excluded Iran from being able to

79 See Eva Paus, 'Escaping the Middle-Income Trap: Innovate or Perish', Asian Development Bank Institute, Tokyo, Working Paper 685, 2017, www.adb.org/publications/escaping-middle-income-trap-innovate-or-perish.
80 Article I, Section 8, Clause 8 of the US Constitution states that Congress is asked '[t]o promote the progress of science and useful arts'.
81 'Understanding the Reasons behind Digital Piracy Is the First Step toward Ending It, Researchers Suggest', *Corporate Law Advisory* (18 August 2012), www.lexisnexis.com/communities/corporatecounselnewsletter/b/newsletter/archive/2012/08/18/understanding-the-reasons-behind-digital-piracy-is-the-first-step-toward-ending-it-researchers-suggest.aspx.

access academic websites, a fact which partially explains why Iran is consistently in the top ten for Sci-hub usage.[82]

It is also not just a question of having access, which might be revoked at any time, but also of having things available on a stable basis. For many years, websites such as surrealmoviez.info would offer films that were simply not available through official channels. Such sites were often the only way scholars could access material otherwise unavailable, as other large sharing sites such as The Pirate Bay mostly offer only ranked and more recent material. Such former sites were therefore veritable S2S ('Scholar2Scholar') websites, especially as one would need the recommendation from another (scholar) to be admitted.

Even if educational and entertainment material is available, such content is often severely restricted in its use. A case in point is the recent musical practice of sampling or remixing, often associated with hip-hop music, and involving remixing parts of older songs with new material. Many hip-hop artists have been sued for using snippets of other artists' songs. Arguably, over the last 30 or 40 years, sampling has become an important mainstay of music creation and restrictive laws have had their share of hampering the release of new material. While lawyers will argue over how much remixing is admissible, the more interesting question to ask is why this practice began in the first place and what was the motivation prompting it. Studios and copyright holders will readily claim that all that there is to it is an illegal appropriation of copyrighted material. But the truth is more complicated than that, especially as this practice has also broached out into the moving image field via the so-called scratch method in radical film culture, which borrowed from New York hip-hop artists and their sampling techniques. Pat Sweeney is generally credited with coining the term 'scratch video', in 1984, when a combination of off-air video recording and edit suite improvements led to video material being looped, repeated, and mixed, similarly to hip-hop. Today, scratch has become a mainstay of video production.[83] Ross Rudesch Harley puts it the following way:

82   See https://sci-hub.se/stats.
83   Nick Cope, 'Scratch Video Revisited', in Steve Presence, Mike Wayne, and Jack Newsinger (eds), *Contemporary Radical Film Culture: Networks, Organisations and Activists* (London: Routledge, 2020). In 2010, Kirby Furguson would famously declare, 'Everything is a Remix'. See www.everythingisaremix.info/. Cope draws attention to the fact that the first Fridge nightclub Scratch videos were screened right after the Brixton riots in April 1981 and thus had

Videos circulate and are remixed, mashed up and broadcast over the web at an ever-increasing rate. They are being blown-up, torn apart, ripped, mixed and burned to such an extent that there is no going back to the stability of analog media forms (if ever there were such a state). If images and sounds are coming unstuck, they also open up a new space for the renegotiation of their associated history and critical context. In this sense, the old televisual models have indeed been 'totally busted' by the movement towards user-generated video inaugurated by video art of the 1960s, found footage artists of the 1980s and remixers of the 1990s. This same process has also extended into myriad online experiments that allow users to upload, download, edit and remix a wide variety of audio-visual materials.[84]

It is this participatory practice that works for and against forgetting at the same time that makes such content creation an example of how digital culture has fired up the creative drives of millions of users. As such, this participatory culture would be hard to judge against a very different and proprietary business model of older days, say pre-2000.[85] A related issue associated with piracy is the criminalisation of actions or processes associated with creativity in general. A good example is the fair use legislation which allows, within reason, for copyrighted

a strong political dimension. Scratch videos also often worked with found footage, at times with material whose creator was deliberately not named but within the scene seen as appropriate re-appropriation. See J. Dovey, 'Copyright as Censorship: Notes on "Death Valley Days"', *Screen* 27, no. 2 (1986); also J. Knight (ed.), *Diverse Practices: A Critical Reader on British Video Art* (Luton: University of Luton Press/Arts Council England, 1996), 283–90. Cope also shows how Scratch, as an art movement, influenced the 2014 Fair Dealing Exception for quotations (including aural and visual ones) introduced into UK copyright law, again a clear case in how erstwhile acts deemed piratical were later on established as legal. The 2017 EU Report, 'Exceptions and Limitations to Copyright', would also take a more relaxed view of copyright and allows multiple exceptions. See https://rm.coe.int/iris-plus-2017-1-exceptions-and-limitations-to-copyright/168078348b.

84   Ross Rudesch Harley, 'Cultural Modulation and the Zero Originality Clause of Remix Culture in Australian Contemporary Art', *Fibreculture* 15 (2009), https://fifteen.fibreculturejournal.org/fcj-100-cultural-modulation-and-the-zero-originality-clause-of-remix-culture-in-australian-contemporary-ar/.

85   See Dan Angeloro, 'Thoughtware: Contemporary Online Remix Culture', in Mark Titmarsh (ed.), *SynCity: Remixing Three Generations of Sample Culture* (Sydney: d/Lux/Editions, 2006), 18–25; Eduardo Navas, 'The Bonds of Repetition and Representation', *Remix Theory* (2008), https://remixtheory.net/?p=361.

written material to be quoted and published, thereby propelling science forward. It would be reasonable to say that without this law, science would be made nigh impossible, indelibly hampering human development and progress. This case has already been made in relation to news headlines, which are legally allowed to be included in search engine searches and RSS feeds. Lawrence Lessig's immensely successful creation of the Creative Commons label and practice, offering authors a tiered way of claiming copyright with, typically, no financial remuneration attached, is a good example for how to go about using the commons idea as a way to allow for easy dissemination but to also give credit to the creator(s) of a text.[86] However, the fair use principle in place for texts does by and large not apply to images and videos, making their usage in argument building and creative processes more difficult.

From the aforesaid, it has become clear that the right to educational and entertaining media content has been severely restricted due to ever-extending copyright laws, but that, at the same time, the ever-increasing amount of data available makes it all the harder to police this policy. Whether it should be policed at all is a question posed in the next section.

8 Piracy and Philosophy

There are a number of philosophical underpinnings which inform many of the initiatives of individuals and collectives to offer files for free on the Internet and who fight its continuing commercialisation and 'paywallification'. This thinking goes back to the beginnings of the Internet in 1980s San Francisco, as already explained in the pertinent section above, but also includes additional considerations that speak in favour of such practices. We have noted already Lawrence Lessig and others' Creative Commons initiative, but we should also mention Richard Stallman here, a US free software movement activist and programmer. He holds that software should be free, as indeed information should be also, and wants software to

---

86 Founded in 2001, 'Creative Commons is a nonprofit organization dedicated to building a globally accessible public commons of knowledge and culture. We make it easier for people to share their creative and academic work, as well as to access and build upon the work of others. By helping people and organizations share knowledge and creativity, we aim to build a more equitable, accessible, and innovative world'. https://creativecommons.org.

be unrestricted in usage and modification. To this effect, he launched the GNU Project, a compendium for and reservoir of free software programmes and is the founder of the Free Software Foundation. He also coined the term 'copyleft' and is a vocal critic of the digital rights management legislation that he terms 'digital restrictions management'.[87] Prominent examples of how this can be managed successfully include the Ubuntu open source operating system on Linux, the Firefox web browser, which evolved from Netscape and that had been pitted as a free alternative to Microsoft's Internet Explorer, and VLC, a free and open source cross-platform multimedia player and framework, to name a few.

Recently, prominent philosopher of law Daniel Loick has put the argument of the commons the following way:

> Basically, it is a fact that all goods, whether material or immaterial in nature, are the result of human labour. How this labour is organised and how its results are divided and used, is, in the final analysis, not a question of technological progress, but of social conditions. The argument that goods are limited – becoming ever more important in times of ecological crises – can also be turned around: if land, raw materials, or works of art are limited, what justification does there exist that only some individuals may inhabit, work with or admire them, rather than trying to find a more just system of common, sequenced or compensated usage or sharing?[88]

This kind of sharing – without abusing the right of the author/creator of such content – is also immanent in the hacker ethic, a basic element of Internet etiquette. Himanen has coined the term 'nethic' for such

87   Richard Stallman, 'Opposing Digital Rights Mismanagement (or Digital Restrictions Management, as We Now Call It)', www.gnu.org/philosophy/opposing-drm.en.html.
88   Martin Eimermacher, 'Ist die Idee des Eigentums von gestern? Interview mit dem Rechtsphilosophen Daniel Loick', *Die Zeit* 33 (12 August 2021), 47, translation by HB. The original reads: 'Grundsätzlich ist es so, dass alle Waren, ob materiell oder immateriell, Ergebnis menschlicher Arbeit sind. Wie diese Arbeit organisiert ist und wie deren Früchte verteilt und genutzt werden, ist letztlich keine Frage des technischen Fortschritts, sondern eine der sozialen Verhältnisse. Das Argument mit den begrenzten Gütern – das in Zeiten der ökologischen Krise immer wichtiger wird – kann man auch umdrehen: Wenn es bloß begrenzten Boden, begrenzte Rohstoffe oder Kunstwerke gibt, was rechtfertigt dann, dass nur Einzelne sie bewohnen, bearbeiten oder bewundern dürfen, statt dass wir ein gerechtes System der gemeinsamen Nutzung, der Abwechslung, des Ausgleichs oder des Teilens finden?'

Internet ethics, which would include free access and partially free content.[89] A 2016 briefing by the Harvard-based Berkman Klein Center for Internet Research details how such philosophical ideals can and are being turned into reality, especially when it comes to public access to previously restricted material:

> Political leaders and civic advocates are increasingly recommending that open access be the 'default state' for much of the information held by government agencies. Over the past several years, they have driven the launch of open data initiatives by hundreds of national, state, and local governments. These initiatives are founded on a presumption of openness for government data and have led to the public release of large quantities of data through a variety of channels. At the same time, much of the data that have been released, or are being considered for release, pertain to the behavior and characteristics of individual citizens, highlighting tensions between open data and privacy.[90]

This is certainly a welcome development, but it must be seen in relation to the fact that while the opening up of governmental archives in some countries is progressing well, at the same time, and as the World Trends in Freedom and Expression Reports have emphasised for several years now, blockages and cuts by many other governments have been on the increase globally.[91] Here again, we are left with a mixed picture, one that, on the whole, would still at least condone, if not even endorse, piratical and whistle-blower practices to bring injustices to light.

Already a very basic political philosophy questions the right of those administering copyright. In *The City of God* (IV.4), St Augustine writes: 'Without justice what are kingdoms but great bands of robbers. And what is a band of robbers but such a kingdom in miniature? It is a band of men under the rule of a leader, bound together by a pact of friendship, and their booty is divided among them by an agreed rule. Such a blot on society, if it grows, assumes for itself the proud

89 Pekka Himanen, *The Hacker Ethic and the Spirit of the Information Age* (New York: Random House, 2001), x.
90 Alexandra Wood, David O'Brien, and Urs Gasser, 'Privacy and Open Data Research Briefing', Berkman Klein Center Research Publication No. 2016-16, 28 September 2016, 3, http://ssrn.com/abstract=2842816.
91 UNESCO, 'Journalism is a Public Good: World Trends in Freedom of Expression and Media Development', Global Report 2021/2022, https://unesdoc.unesco.org/ark:/48223/pf0000379826.

name of kingdom'.[92] If people live in an unjust system, then resistance to that system is a duty, a duty which can often be expressed well via piratical practices. In his texts, media researcher, activist, and political scientist Gary Hall shows the manifold ways in which such resistance can work, be it through a website such as aaaargh.fail, giving access to social and media theory texts irrespective of their filiation, or the lobbying he undertook for the UK government in 2019 providing funding for COPIM (Community-led Open Publication Infrastructures for Monographs) and supporting authors to publish open access texts. For Hall, pirate thinking is a way of exposing basic contradictions within the political realm, but also within certain kinds of 'compliant' philosophies themselves.[93] This kind of thinking takes seriously the original meaning of piracy, as the one who 'tests', 'puts to proof', 'probes', or 'contends with', thereby questioning traditional venues of thought and action and attempting new ones.

Hall also experimented with grassroots publishing (culture machine, liquid books, Open Humanities Press, etc.) and continues to connect political activism with Internet practices, in many ways updating and re-grounding the work Rheingold, Lanier, and others undertook at the dawn of the Internet age, thereby not just creating content, but changing Internet infrastructure away from a profit-based to a community-based model, setting agendas and extending boundaries. This is a pan-social activity, with piracy providing a powerful model by questioning ownership of data, the basic unit most Internet users are still trusting. A case in point is the 2019 Pirate Care project:

> Pirate Care is a transnational research project and a network of activists, scholars and practitioners who stand against the criminalization of solidarity & for a common care infrastructure. Pirate Care reflects and brings together those care initiatives which are taking risks by operating in the narrow grey zones left open between different knowledges, institutions and laws, inviting all to participate in an exploration of the mutual implications of care and technology that dare questioning the ideology of private property, work and metrics.[94]

The project stretches to social activities such as caring for migrants and other disenfranchised groups. One might state that as it goes

---

92   Augustine of Hippo, *The City of God*, http://imagining-other.net/pp4augusti-neextracts.htm.

93   See Gary Hall, *Pirate Philosophy*.

94   'The Pirate Care Project', https://pirate.care/pages/concept/.

beyond speech and image acts, as linguistics and visual studies researchers have established, such Pirate Care is comprised of discursive and post-discursive Pirate Acts which have as their goal a change of basic neoliberal social structures into a Foucauldian heterotopia, a place of othering and otherness, linking this effort strongly with Hakim Bey's idea of the Temporary Autonomous Zone (TAZ), with its first chapter explicitly called 'Pirate Utopias', islands which would supply space and material for further pirate actions. This is a zone that is used as a springboard in order to make change permanent, something Bey later on would also bring up.[95]

In his *Pirate Politics* (2014), Patrick Burkart also takes up the challenge of pirate politics in today's world and analyses the Swedish Pirate Party which had emerged as a political force in 2006 when a group of software programmers and file-sharing geeks protested the temporary takedown of The Pirate Bay.[96]

Launched on 21 November 2003, in Sweden, The Pirate Bay continues to be one of the most popular torrent sites on the web. It is visited by millions of people on a daily basis.[97] Besides making downloading copyrighted material easy through its intelligent interface, it spawned a whole fan ecology, including the The Pirate Bureau (Piratbyrån), established to support and disseminate discussions on copyright and to oppose anti-piracy lobby groups, and the Pirate Party (Piratpartiet), a political party that was launched in 2006 in Sweden and for a decade was very successful – at one time being the third largest party in Sweden and spawning pirate parties in other countries as well, leading to the formation of the international Pirate Party movement.[98] With many of its demands (such as strengthened privacy controls and less Internet commercialisation) becoming mainstream issues, several other parties on the left have

---

95 Hakim Bey (Peter Lamborn Wilson), *T.A.Z.: The Temporary Autonomous Zone* (New York: Autonomedia, 1991); Hakim Bey, 'Permanent TAZs', *Dreamtime Village* (1994), http://dreamtimevillage.org/articles/permanent_taz.html.

96 Patrick Burkart, *Pirate Politics: The New Information Policy Contests* (Cambridge, MA: MIT Press, 2014).

97 See Fenwick McKelvey, 'We Like Copies, Just Don't Let the Others Fool You: The Paradox of The Pirate Bay', *Television & New Media* 16, no. 8 (2015), 734–50.

98 See Frederik Miegel and Tobias Olsson, 'From Pirates to Politicians: The Story of the Swedish File Sharers Who Became a Political Party', in *Democracy, Journalism and Technology: New Developments in an Enlarged Europe*, European Media and Communication Doctoral Summer School (Tartu: University of Tartu Press, 2008), 203–15.

successfully absorbed them in their broader manifestos, leaving the pirate parties bereft of large-scale voter support.

Burkart sees piracy as an aspect of cultural production under capitalist conditions. For him, hacking or piratical practices are a repurposing of an unjust social system, and, given that technologies, just as societies, are socially constructed, they help to re-configure society as a whole, i.e., they put the finger on the wound of injustices within and surrounding the entire social system. Hacking is an agnostic move against the system, and its social value lies in the production of knowledge to expose generalised political systems of power and money that have been receiving unquestioned trust from its users until now.[99] Burkart and his co-author McCourt also make a cogent argument that there has been an intensifying development of anti-hacker and anti-piracy legislation, moving from a knee-jerk industry reaction to a full-blown war on both as a matter of, it is claimed, 'national interest'. However, these companies are abusing legislation via policy laundering to firmly protect their interests and at the same time abusing the loopholes provided by the general lack of global legislation.

Pirate parties were successful for some time in Sweden and also in Germany and were associated with free Internet culture, lobbying against European Digital Rights Management legislation. Using second-generation critical theory and new social movement theory, Burkart shows that they were an umbrella cyberlibertarian movement arguing in favour of the public domain and were linked to the Green movement, as they shared an explicit ecological agenda based on the notion of a commons, or public domain. They were also united in a 'cultural environmentalism', which defends free expression and commons culture against both corporate and state attempts at establishing digital sovereignty. In hindsight, while there still exists a smattering of Pirate Party representatives in EU, regional, national, and local governing institutions, the Pirate Party failed to make a lasting impression on the political scene, due to infighting and the (mistaken) perception that they were a one-item party. Much of the critical potential was successfully taken over by the Green parties, who continue to be politically successful in many European Parliaments.[100]

---

99 Burkart and McCourt, *Why Hackers Win*.
100 For a discussion on pirate politics in France, see Razmig Keucheyan, 'Philosophie politique du pirate', *Critique* 733–4 (2008), 458–69.

Pirate practices also played a large part in the Occupy and Arab Spring movements. However, just as with the Pirate Parties in Europe, activists were unable to cash in on their digital prowess and convert it to real power, as they remained tightly ensconced in urban milieux and were unable or unwilling to reach out to the middle and lower classes. Perhaps legitimising political piracy is a contradiction in terms and might not be achievable under such a label. Additionally, one might wonder whether they were caught between either being too digital or not being post-digital enough. To make matters even worse, one can observe that many of the subversive pirate ploys used to 'fight the system' from the left are now being used, equally successfully, by rightist groups in many countries, thereby further questioning the possibility of political action based on a mere technology-centred approach.

Philosopher Tiziana Terranova grounds her hope for change on the 'informational milieu' of cyberspace to describe how the Internet is critically challenging realities in a positive way:

> Information is not simply the content of a message, or the main form assumed by the commodity in late capitalist economies, but also another name for the increasing visibility and importance of such 'massless flows' as they become the environment within which contemporary culture unfolds. In this sense, we can refer to informational cultures as involving the explicit constitution of an informational milieu – a milieu composed of dynamic and shifting relations between such 'massless flows'.[101]

It is exactly these 'massless flows', these *Immatériaux* (immaterials) (as Jean-François Lyotard had called his exceptional and influential 1985 exhibition at the Centre Pompidou in Paris and whose immaterial exponents were closely related to creative processes), that at the same time inform *and* delimit Internet discourses, creating inter-dependent and entangled hypertexts across global servers. While filiations of such texts can and should be topics for research, they have simply become the fabric from which the Internet is woven, and it would do it a disservice to try to disentangle it. A good example is the dedication for the 2015 text *The Pirate Book*, as it makes unmistakeably (and refreshingly honestly) clear how new knowledge is typically created today:

101 Tiziana Terranova, *Network Culture: Politics for the Information Age* (New York: Pluto Press, 2004), 8.

> This book could not have been made without the help of: street
> vendors, photocopiers, bootleg recordings, double cassette decks,
> cracktros, .nfo files, VHS recorders, CD burners, scanners, BBS,
> copy parties, game copiers, Warez, keygens, Napster, eDonkey,
> Soulseek, The Pirate Bay, UbuWeb, Library Genesis, Karagarga,
> Megaupload, FilesTube, and many more.[102]

Today, much of philosophical thought has thus taken up the challenges
of piracy and delineates how such piratical thought and action is a
fitting description of already incumbent positive practices, but also
how it can further describe futures in which especially participation
and personal growth can be achieved via its tenets.[103]

9 Piracy, Politics, and Social Practices

In addition to the argument that piracy is an inherent and constitutive
component of any knowledge creation, there is also an argument to
be made that it is part and parcel of the reigning capitalist system,
as many scholars hold. Already in 2005, Michael Strangelove would
characterise Internet work as legitimate resistance to and part of the
fight against capitalism and explicitly counted Internet piracy among
such actions.[104] It would therefore only seem (digitally) natural that,
given the appearance of new Internet tools, such ways of resistance to
commercial practices would appear concurrently. The most famous of
these phenomena is The Pirate Bay, the most resilient of pirate torrent
websites, as discussed above.

   In his piracy work, Göran Bolin privileges the concept of value,
in a similar way De Kosnik did with the already mentioned Alpha60
project.[105] Rather than detracting value, levels of piracy *indicate* value
to companies that in turn are able to use piracy metrics to gauge and

---

102 Nicolas Maigret and Maria Roszkowska (eds), *The Pirate Book* (Ljubljana:
     Aksioma, 2015), https://archive.org/stream/The_Pirate_Book/The_Pirate_Book.
103 For the necessary differentiation between piracy and piratical paradigm, see
     Matthew K. Dames, 'Distinguishing "Piracy" from the "Piracy Paradigm"',
     Information Today 28, no. 2 (2011), 20–1.
104 Michael Strangelove, *The Empire of Mind: Digital Piracy and the Anti-Capitalist
     Movements* (Toronto: University of Toronto Press, 2005). This thought is also
     displayed in Rodolphe Durand and Jean-Philippe Vergne, *L'organisation pirate:
     essai sur l'évolution du capitalisme* (Lormont: Le Bord de l'eau, 2010).
105 Göran Bolin, *Value and the Media: Cultural Production and Consumption in
     Digital Markets* (Farnham: Ashgate, 2011) and Göran Bolin, *Media Generations:
     Experience, Identity and Mediatised Social Change* (London: Routledge, 2016).

develop their own output. Websites such as The Pirate Bay and other torrent or streaming sites function as huge real-time focus groups and laboratories for these companies. If an audience does not value certain shows and they receive low piracy coefficients, they also lose their value for the producing studio. Media production in digital markets is consequently dependent on such websites. For Bolin, piracy functions as an exchange mechanism situated at the centre of the Internet ecology. If on most commercial and government websites we are losing more and more of our rights due to the uses and regulations declarations we agree to but never read, through piracy, we are able to at least claw back some of the data we expend elsewhere. If we are not free to choose anymore what is to be done with our data, here is a place of resistance. This is a non-trivial contention that covers the whole of the right to entertainment argument to the right for information, and also extends to Nick Couldry's charge of Internet companies engaging in Data colonialism.[106] Furthermore, Bolin differentiates between a run-of-the-mill commodity consumption and a more specific commodity prosumption, with the latter including identity production, social differentiation, and a large non-profit sector. If this is done in good faith, say in unpaid fan-work,[107] then more recently attempts are discernible to commodify this work with large talent agencies and Internet sales companies as their benefactors, especially in Korea, Japan, and China. Piracy, then can be seen as a transgressive act, but one justified via economic-philosophical and creative and aesthetic arguments.

When Mattelart researched 'glocalised' cultural production and distribution, he stressed that people generally engage in what is termed piracy endeavours, which actually are re-mediatising, re-appropriating, and creating new cultural material, akin to the *détournement* process proposed and practised by the Situationists.[108]

---

106 Nick Couldry and Ulises Mejias, *The Costs of Connection: How Data Is Colonizing Human Life and Appropriating It for Capitalism* (Stanford, CA: Stanford University Press, 2019).

107 See Henry Jenkins, *Textual Poachers: Television Fans and Participatory Culture*, 2nd ed. (London: Routledge, 2013 [1992]), who highlights the participatory and re-mediating aspect of such fandom over the free labour one. If this had been the case in the early 1990s, the production aspect not requested of fans, inclusive of time and money spent, has certainly outgrown the more benign earlier aspects.

108 Cf. Nicolas Auray, 'Pirates en réseau: détournement, prédation et exigence de justice', *Esprit* 7 (2009), 168–79, DOI: 10.3917/espri.0907.0168.

His case studies include Francophone Africa and here Senegal especially. Contrary to Western industry voices, he stresses the liberating and creative potential of piratical practices.

Another important area for social engagement, and closely related to the beginning of the Internet, is the idea of sharing as an ethico-emotive principle of Internet engagement. Thus, writes Nicholas A. John in his *The Age of Sharing*:

> This is the age of sharing, then, because 'sharing' stands for both the cutting edge of our digital media-saturated capitalist society and economy, including the way we interact online, and a critical position vis-à-vis this society and economy. Sharing is both supportive and subversive of hegemonic (digital) culture: supportive in that the more you share updates and pictures on social media, for instance, the wealthier those platforms become, and subversive in that the more you share actual stuff with others, the less everyone needs to buy. Moreover, some say that sharing – be that of the distributive or communicative kind – leads to true and deep human connections.[109]

John argues that it is actually sharing that defines and constitutes the spheres of social media and that, rather than taking capitalist practices of exchange for individual monetary gain as a model, it is and indeed should be sharing that defines economic behaviour. That these are not just idle desiderata of a left-leaning philosopher is proven by the telling studies he undertook.

> An analysis of the homepages of forty-four SNSs between the years 2000 and 2010 confirms this, showing the years 2005–7 as the time when 'sharing' became the sine qua non for online partici-pation, pointing to the centrality of powerful media organizations in pushing the word to its current prominence. One exception to this is the field of hacking, where sharing has always been talked of as being a key value and practice. [...] This discussion is supple-mented with an analysis of over 450 posts to file-sharing forum debates about the ethics of a certain form of file sharing known as 'torrenting'. I show how the presence of the metaphor of 'sharing' in the debates shapes some of the positions adopted in it. [...] for at least some of the file sharers engaged in interactions over the best (most ethical, most efficient) way to share files, 'sharing' really is a metaphor they live by.[110]

109 Nicholas A. John, *The Age of Sharing* (Cambridge: Polity Press, 2016), 2.
110 John, *The Age of Sharing*, 16–18.

These studies demonstrate that sharing is the quintessential mode of Internet interaction for many, if not most, of its younger users.

However, even if the idea of sharing is a positive and deeply human one, this sharing economy does not come without its price. This is the concern raised by thinkers such as Yuval Harari. In a recent post for the *Financial Times*, he writes that the new motto for our dataist age is, 'If you experience something – record it. If you record something – upload it. If you upload something – share it'.[111] Apart from benefiting some users, this motto has also become an imperative and, charges Harari, was created by the Internet industry, not for its users' sake but for its own, as with every share and interaction, data is collected about users to know them better and then sell this data to the highest bidder. Harari gives the example of Amazon and its Kindle book reader, which, based on user monitoring, is 'uncannily' able to predict which books we like, better than we ourselves do. This can be extended to proprietary online markets such as Google Play or other app stores, all of which collect user data and thus are able to control our tool intake and shape our virtual interactive toolbox. It is therefore not in the data industry's interests for users to use tools that would obfuscate or completely hide their choices, such as alternative download sites that do not track users or using non-tracking VPNs to do so. Overall, Harari is sceptical that this would make much of a difference, as the overwhelming majority of Internet users do not avail themselves of such devices (yet), but offers the following advice:

> A unified scientific paradigm may easily become an unassailable dogma. If you don't like this, and you want to stay beyond the reach of the algorithms, there is probably just one piece of advice to give you, the oldest in the book: know thyself. In the end, it's a simple empirical question. As long as you have greater insight and self-knowledge than the algorithms, your choices will still be superior and you will keep at least some authority in your hands.[112]

Hence, it is necessary to question critically the virtual superstructure and take a reflected, cautious position in relation to it. One of the most recent battlefields for this are scientific articles and related texts.

111 Yuval Noah Harari, 'Yuval Noah Harari on Big Data, Google and the End of Free Will', *Financial Times* (26 August 2016), www.ft.com/content/50bb4830-6a4c-11e6-ae5b-a7cc5dd5a28c.
112 Harari, 'Yuval Noah Harari on Big Data'.

As suggested by recent research, such as the Akamai study cited above, textual piracy has become the second most popular pirated content, after streaming, easily leaving behind film and music. In a way, this is a return to the earlier days of the Internet, where bandwidth would normally only allow textual exchanges. However, at that time, textual reservoirs were neither very well developed nor very extensive, as it would take a long time to digitise library holdings, agree on formats and produce new e-books and journals. Today, however, this has been largely overcome, but the sharing of texts has been hampered, perhaps not surprisingly, by copyright issues. Already by 2002, Google had initiated a massive digitisation drive, digitising over 25 million books between 2002 and 2014, but due to threatened lawsuits and broken off negotiations with major publishing houses, these books were never shared with the public.[113] Furthermore, owing to the setting up of ever more paywalls to access digital material, sharing libraries sprang up. A good example is Project Gutenberg, whose website hosts over 60,000 books, but is limited to those which were/are either not copyrighted, are in the public domain, or whose copyright has expired.[114] Most pirate websites also have a book section,[115] at times infinitely more comprehensive that what is on offer legally.

By far the most extensive of these shadow libraries are Z-Library and Sci-hub, at last count housing over 8.9 million books and over 80 million articles.[116] The websites are cherished by millions of researchers around the globe, many of whom express their gratitude in the dedications of their scientific works. Sci-Hub was founded in 2011 by then computer student Alexandra Elbakyan, who became frustrated with her inability to access material for her studies. Since then, apart from facilitating the addition of millions of texts to the

113 See James Somers, 'Torching the Modern-Day Library of Alexandria; Somewhere at Google There Is a Database Containing 25 Million Books and Nobody Is Allowed to Read Them', *Atlantic* (17 April 2017), www.theatlantic. com/technology/archive/2017/04/the-tragedy-of-google-books/523320/.

114 See www.gutenberg.org/. At the time of writing, Project Gutenberg contains 60,000 free e-books, which were digitised by thousands of volunteers, making it an excellent showcase for the successful application of a sharing culture and the importance of digital engagement.

115 For a comprehensive discussion of shadow libraries, see Karaganis, *Shadow Libraries*.

116 Z-Library was taken down in 2022. Other important shadow libraries are: www.aaaaarg.org/ and https://library.memoryoftheworld.org/.

website, Elbakyan has become a vocal and prominent propagator of the open access movement and holds that, according to Article 27 of the United Nations Universal Declaration of Human Rights, 'everyone has the right freely to [...] share in scientific advancement and its benefits'.[117] The website, and also Elbakyan herself, have been at the forefront of negative and positive press reports ever since. She has been vilified, but also called 'Science's Pirate Queen' and a modern-day Robin Hood.[118] In 2016, she was voted by *Nature* magazine as one of the ten most influential people in science on the planet.[119] All this came at a hefty price for her, though. Publishing companies such as Elsevier, Wiley, and Springer sued her in several countries' courts and she has a number of judgments against her, amounting to millions of dollars.[120] As a consequence, she is forced to curtail her travels to many countries for fear of possible extradition procedures.

The most recent court case against Sci-Hub (2020) is being battled out in Indian courts where Global publishing giants Elsevier, Wiley, and the American Chemical Society, owners of about 40 per cent of all the scientific journals in the world, are asking the court to block access to Sci-Hub and LibGen in India.[121] On 6 January 2021, the Delhi High Court agreed to wait before passing any possible interim takedown order until additional further statements from scientists, researchers, and students could be heard. The defence charges that the material on Sci-Hub falls under the fair-dealing exception in India's copyright law as it helps to advance science and thus benefits India's citizens, a defence that had previously proven to be successful in the case of the justification for the reproduction

---

117 'Universal Declaration of Human Rights', www.un.org/en/about-us/universal-declaration-of-human-rights.

118 Ian Graber-Stiehl, 'Science's Pirate Queen: Alexandra Elbakyan is Plundering the Academic Publishing Establishment', *The Verge* (8 February 2018), www.theverge.com/2018/2/8/16985666/alexandra-elbakyan-sci-hub-open-access-science-papers-lawsuit.

119 '*Nature*'s 10', *Nature* (19 December 2016), www.nature.com/articles/540507a.

120 Elsevier, Wiley, Springer, and Taylor and Francis own about 70 per cent of all journals. Reed Elsevier's 2021 revenue alone was £7,244m, with an underlying growth of 7 per cent, and an adjusted operating profit of £2,210m, with an underlying growth of 13 per cent, www.uksg.org/newsletter/uksg-enews-509/reed-elseviers-2021-financial-results.

121 See the article by Saad Hasan at www.trtworld.com/magazine/indian-academics-throw-weight-behind-sci-hub-and-libgen-in-landmark-case-51780.

of copyrighted material for use by low-income students by Indian educational institutions.[122] In the present case, prominent anti-copyright campaigners, such as Lawrence Liang and others, assisted in drawing up petitions supporting Sci-Hub's defence.[123]

Censorship and piracy are two sides of the same coin. Writes Frank Caso:

> Censorship suppresses human expression. Throughout recorded history, rulers and religious leaders have abused their powers to forbid speech, writing, and images they considered a threat to their authority or contrary to divine will. Censorship also means manipulating the information people are allowed to receive, including creating official messages that are thrust upon the population. A third form of censorship is secrecy; all governments label some information secret and try to prevent its publication.[124]

It is these kinds of practices against which hackers have been fighting long and hard.

One other important initiative related to and arguably impacting on piracy is the Open Access Movement, which adheres to some of the earlier Internet free sharing culture and aligns with Stallman's GNU project for Open Access software. The Budapest Open Access Initiative of 2002 traces the roots of this movement to the following two fields:

> An old tradition and a new technology have converged to make possible an unprecedented public good. The old tradition is the willingness of scientists and scholars to publish the fruits of their research in scholarly journals without payment, for the sake of inquiry and knowledge. The new technology is the internet. The public good they make possible is the world-wide electronic distribution of the peer-reviewed journal literature and completely free and unrestricted access to it by all scientists, scholars, teachers, students, and other curious minds.[125]

122 Holly Else, 'What Sci-Hub's Latest Court Battle Means for Research', *Nature* (13 December 2021), DOI: 10.1038/d41586-021-03659-0.

123 'Journal paywalls are an example of something that works in the reverse direction, making communication less open and efficient', 'Against Monopoly: Defending the Right to Innovate', www.againstmonopoly.org/.

124 Frank Caso, *Censorship* (New York: Infobase Publishing, 2008), ix.

125 'Budapest Open Access Initiative', www.budapestopenaccessinitiative.org/ read/. See also John Willinsky, *The Access Principle: The Case for Open Access to Research and Scholarship* (Cambridge, MA: MIT Press, 2006).

These views represent a highly noble and desired attitude toward free data exchange, but realities show that Open Access is not (yet) the case for academic publishing in its overwhelming majority. The percentage of scientific articles available via Open Access still remains very low, according to a 2017 study by the Max Planck society at only 13 per cent.[126] However, according to other figures, from 2009, there were about 4,800 active open access journals and, according to the Directory of Open Access Journals, as of February 2022, over 17,506 open access journals were listed.[127] While this constitutes massive progress in regard to making scientific content accessible to the many, one might be allowed a grain of scepticism. It could be argued that the journal industry is only making such content available in a piecemeal fashion and only because they fear the pressure from more and more academics to change their practices. It is thus more a case of open access-washing their paywalled wares than a heartfelt desire to question and change their business models. But, as the case with the music industry has demonstrated, such a change can only be truly achieved via even stronger pressure, in part associated with and coming from pirate sites.

Economists Michele Boldrin and David K. Levine see innovation as a key to reviving the economy. They believe the current patent/copyright system discourages and prevents inventions from entering the marketplace. In their *Against Intellectual Monopoly*, they show that from a public policy view, ideally patent and copyright laws should be abolished altogether. 'There's plenty of protection for inventors and plenty of protection and opportunities to make money for creators. It's not that we see this as some sort of charitable act that people are going to invent and create things without earning money. Evidence shows very strongly there are lots of ways to make money without patents and copyright'.[128]

A strong case of support of such thinking was made in the incisive 2008 *Guerrilla Open Access Manifesto* by Aaron Swartz,[129] when he wrote:

---

126 'Area-Wide Transition to Open Access Is Possible', www.mpg.de/9202262/area-wide-transition-open-access.

127 'Directory of Open Access Journals', https://doaj.org/.

128 Michele Boldrin and David K. Levine, *Against Intellectual Monopoly* (Cambridge: Cambridge University Press, 2008).

129 Swartz was involved in creating the Creative Commons standard and the founding of influential digital and social news site Reddit. In 2010, he was a Fellow at Harvard's Safra Research Lab on Institutional Corruption, directed

Information is power. But like all power, there are those who want to keep it for themselves. The world's entire scientific and cultural heritage, published over centuries in books and journals, is increasingly being digitized and locked up by a handful of private corporations. Want to read the papers featuring the most famous results of the sciences? You'll need to send enormous amounts to publishers like Reed Elsevier.[130]

If one is not privileged either by having the money to access such content or by being associated with a university that has paid for this access via student fees, for Swartz, there remained only one recourse to be taken – to access it illegally: 'But all of this action goes on in the dark, hidden underground. It's called stealing or piracy, as if sharing a wealth of knowledge were the moral equivalent of plundering a ship and murdering its crew. But sharing isn't immoral – it's a moral imperative. Only those blinded by greed would refuse to let a friend make a copy'.[131]

This confluence of activism – online and offline – and support for file sharing can be observed in many more progressive domains of the Internet. If in the early days it had been personified by Howard Rheingold and other San Francisco Internet pioneers, during the 2000s it would be Lawrence Lessig and his work for the Creative Commons, and Jarod Lanier, whose texts *You Are Not a Gadget* (2010) and *Who Owns the Future?* (2013)[132] would speak out against non-paid work for Google and the eradication of the human difference in online networks and databases. Important organisations working towards similar goals were the San Francisco-based Electronic Frontier Foundation (founded in 1990), created to promote Internet civil liberties and defend 'digital privacy, free speech, and innovation',[133] and its German counterpart,

by Lessig, and founded the online group Demand Progress, which lobbied against anti-piracy groups. In 2011, he was arrested at MIT for making available paywalled articles via a hidden server. Having rejected a plea-bargain and awaiting trial, he was found dead in his apartment. He has become an important figurehead of the open access and piracy movements, posthumously being inducted into the Internet Hall of Fame.

130 Aaron Swartz, 'Guerrilla Open Access Manifesto' (2008), https://archive.org/details/GuerillaOpenAccessManifesto. See also the documentary *The Internet's Own Boy: The Story of Aaron Swartz* (dir. Brian Knappenberger, USA, 2014), www.dailymotion.com/video/x21tkoj.
131 Swartz, 'Guerrilla Open Access Manifesto'.
132 Jarod Lanier, *You Are Not a Gadget* (New York: Knopf, 2010); Jarod Lanier, *Who Owns the Future?* (New York: Penguin, 2013).
133 Electronic Frontier Foundation, www.eff.org/.

the Chaos Computer Club (founded in 1984), which fights for a 'new human right to global, unfettered communication'.[134]

Others, including Gavin Mueller, would promote the idea of a 'platform cooperatism' that would allow creative workers to unionise to control the means of digital production and make their digital labour available via a fair exchange.[135] The fact that in late/digital capitalism there does not exist a fair exchange is for many thinkers one of the reasons why piracy is so popular. Writes Yochai Benkler:

> I suggest that the highly distributed capital structure of contemporary communications and computation system is largely responsible for the increased salience of social sharing as a modality of economic production in those environments. By lowering the capital costs required for effective individual action, these technologies have allowed various provisioning problems to be structured in forms amenable to decentralized production based on social relations, rather than through markets or hierarchies.[136]

In his work, Benkler cites both progressing technology and the increase in sharing thus made possible as reasons for massive changes in how data is being created, exchanged, and used.

Reasons for piracy might differ from country to country, but it is fair to say that the number one reason is simple lack of access. This covers a large portion of countries of the global south, but also much of India

134 Chaos Computer Club Constitution, www.ccc.de/de/satzung.
135 Gavin Mueller, *Media Piracy in the Cultural Economy: Intellectual Property and Labor under Neoliberal Restructuring* (London: Routledge, 2019), 121–2. In the same text, Mueller also cites the lack of such worker input and unionisation as one of the reasons why politicisation of the pirate movement offline has, at best, had very mixed results. He writes: 'Pirates created a powerful, technologically enhanced juggernaut against intellectual property, but without a critique of intellectual property as private property, the old relations of production remained intact (122). Similarly, in their 2017 *Radical Markets*, Posner and Weyl also point out the various internal inconsistencies of legacy and digital capitalism and propose critiquing capitalism at its very roots of property, alienated through parameters traditional capitalist economists take for granted but which don't lead to the benefits supposedly characteristic of a capitalist society anymore. One particular way of doing this is the (tacit) support of piracy. Eric A. Posner and E. Glen Weyl, *Radical Markets: Uprooting Capitalism and Democracy for a Just Society* (Princeton, NJ: Princeton University Press, 2017).
136 Yochai Benkler, 'Sharing Nicely: On Shareable Goods and the Emergence of Sharing as a Modality of Economic Production', *Yale Law Journal* 114, no. 2 (2004), 278, www.dropbox.com/s/ig8955sggxjd1h0/Sharing%20Nicely%20Benkler_FINAL_YLJ114-2.pdf.

and the largest cinema (and other media) market on the planet – China. China has the largest absolute numbers of Internet users in the world and thus a large market for entertainment and education content, be that legal or illegal. It is also probably fair to say that in China reasons for piracy include a different cultural mindset – economics – but, most of all, the issues of availability mentioned above.[137] This is due to the Great Chinese Firewall and the strict quota for foreign film releases. In 2021, there existed a quota of 34 'revenue-share' films, where studios receive a cut of the box office. The other way to release a film is through a 'flat fee' (aka a 'buy-out'), in which a Chinese company buys the rights outright. Writes Rebecca Davis:

> Among the 67 foreign films released last year [2021] were 25 revenue-share titles – 21 of them labelled as American – that collectively accounted for 12.5 percent of the annual box office (RMB5.89 billion). That figure is up from 11 percent in 2020, but significantly down from 29 percent in 2019 and way down on years not so long ago when Hollywood vied with Chinese titles for the box office crown.[138]

Add to this strict censorship of music lyrics and books, and it does not take much imagination to understand why many entertainment and educational products are simply not available and are thus procured through back channels. This is very typical for the large student body and early career media and technology workers. And while in 2021 China ranked fourth globally for the first nine months for piracy website visits (Akamai Study), this figure does not even include many of the Chinese websites offering warez specifically for the Chinese internal market. It also does not include the many Fan Groups, making material available online, such as fansub groups that are subbing foreign content and are also still engaged in selling 'retired' hard drives, a practice older readers might still remember from hard drive swapping or 'copy parties' held during the 1990s in the West, during which hard drive content would be swapped.[139] The

137 J.-A. Lee, 'Tripartite Perspective on the Copyright-Sharing Economy in China', *Computer Law & Security Review* 35, no. 4 (2019), 434–52.
138 Rebecca Davis, 'By The Numbers: Foreign Titles Squeezed in China Film Market', *Variety* (12 January 2022), https://variety.com/2022/film/news/foreign-titles-squeezed-in-china-film-market-1235151950/. In this respect, for a more pan-Asian perspective, see also Laikwan Pang, *Cultural Control and Globalization in Asia: Copyright, Piracy and Cinema* (New York: Routledge, 2006).
139 See the section 'Copy Parties' in *The Pirate Book* (2015).

Chinese government has been trying to rein in some of these activities, for instance by rolling out further restrictive laws regarding Western content and heavily censoring popular websites such as Bilibili, but it is hard to gauge whether these measures have had the desired effect.

Especially the digital (online) games market has been growing exponentially in China and much piratical undertakings have been drifting in this direction, with claims made that as many as 90 per cent of video games played in China are illegal copies, in part due to the fact that many foreign game consoles were or are prohibited.[140] In 2018, the Chinese government further tightened the rules on video gaming; no licences for new games were granted for several months and TenCent, one of the biggest players in the Chinese games market, was forced to pull several popular online games from the web.[141] In 2021, the Chinese government restricted the number of hours minors are allowed to play games to three per week and then only on weekends.[142] However, while these measures seem harsh, their circumvention is also flourishing. Soon after the new licence ban on video games came into effect, it was reported that Chinese players now represent the majority of players on the international Steam platform. Furthermore, piracy is of course something that is within the cultural awareness not only of the government, but also of artists, arguably though for different reasons. A case in point was the successful independent, pirate-sympathetic documentary film *Pai Gu* (dir. Liu Gaoming, PRC, 2006), in which is told the story of a junior high school student from the countryside who is selling pirated DVDs in the gleaming metropolis of Shenzhen and in which these foreign films are represented as an exoticised other.

In a 2009 study, Dimitrov had already exposed the difficulties a centralised government has with piracy policies. In his text, *Piracy and the State: The Politics of Intellectual Property Rights in China*, he shows that China has the highest levels of copyright piracy and trademark counterfeiting in the world, even though it also provides the highest

---

140 See Tabea De Wille and Piertommaso Bottura, 'The Rules of Harmony: Video Game Censorship in China', *MultiLingual*, 30, no. 3 (2019), 56–9.

141 Yuji Nakamura and Lulu Yilun Chen, 'China Halts Special Approval Process for New Games', *Bloomberg* (24 October 2018), www.bloomberg.com/news/articles/2018-10-24/china-said-to-halt-special-approval-process-for-new-games.

142 'China Limits Online Videogames to Three Hours a Week for Young People', *Wall Street Journal* (31 August 2021), www.wsj.com/articles/china-sets-new-rules-for-youth-no-more-videogames-during-the-school-week-11630325781.

per capita volume of enforcement. Using China as an example, Dimitrov confirms that states are simultaneously weak and strong vis-à-vis piracy. Thus, 'fully rationalized enforcement of domestic and foreign IPR is emerging unevenly and, somewhat counter-intuitively, chiefly in those IPR subtypes that are least subject to domestic or foreign pressure'.[143] This clearly demonstrates that even highly efficient and centralised systems are unwilling to massively enforce copyright laws, as it would cause economic disadvantages outweighing any gains.

10 Solutions

As we have seen in the previous pages, digital piracy continues to pose challenges for Internet administrators and affects countless individuals and organisations. It does not seem to want to subside, no matter how efficiently and severely content owners fight against it. As new technologies continue to emerge, it engages ever larger and willing audiences. Furthermore, a significant part of global Internet users and, more and more so, academics do not think it actually should be eradicated, as it allows for and encourages an intelligent and creative practice of modes of resistance and of questioning standard governmental and commercial practices. It would also seem doubtful, as Sahni and Gupta suggested, this will bear any fruit in the near future, despite all the good intentions and legal exhortations cautioning self-control as a way to not download illegal content.[144]

What to do with piracy then? The first insight is that it is a complex and layered issue which cannot be successfully addressed or solved via one single approach. Consequently, in the following, I would like to suggest how piracy positively impacts on several areas of our world of practices online and offline and why, therefore, it should continue to be an open question, one that will continue to inform the way in which people interact with objects, be they material or immaterial, and with each other. The four areas to be considered are piracy's impact on politics, revenue sharing, financial incentives, and artistic practices. While these suggestions are not future-proof, they nevertheless open up spaces in which different futures might be tried out.

143 Intellectual Property Rights (IPR). See Martin Dimitrov, *Piracy and the State: The Politics of Intellectual Property Rights in China* (Cambridge: Cambridge University Press, 2009).
144 Sahni and Gupta, *Piracy in the Digital Era*.

Politicisation?

As was mentioned already earlier, Gavin Mueller strongly suggests that to understand piracy as a politically deictic attempt to show what is wrong with capitalism would therefore see it needed until capitalism itself has been overthrown. '[P]roduction demands to be recognised as social. To put it in the language of cultural production, there can be no author. Or, in another implicit recognition that the work of today relies on the work of many others, past and present: everything is a remix'.[145] Piracy does not want to see the exchange of data fettered; rather, it wants to eliminate the 'cybermediaries', something the Internet had promised to do before, but which it failed miserably to do, leading to the rise of platform emperors. 'The abolition of middlemen, gatekeepers, of mediation, in general, that so captures Internet revolutionaries has never been achieved'.[146] Pirates did not destroy intermediaries, but merely developed technologies that would, they hoped, replace obsolete intermediaries such as record labels and industry trade organisations such as the MPA. Instead, new commercial cybermediaries, such as Netflix and Spotify, have usurped this role, and many artists experience greater exploitation and less power than before the disruption of the music industry, and are still impelled to sign unfavourable recording contracts.

For Mueller, piracy unsettled the existing arrangements of cultural production, but

> severed from any comprehensive critique of the dominant ideologies of cultural production, no new politics could fill the void. Pirates created a powerful, technologically enhanced juggernaut against intellectual property, but without a critique of intellectual property *as private property*, the old relations of production remained intact. The P2P era has ended; indeed, it never truly began.[147]

Mueller is spot on when he lists the issues with production in the digital economy and its surrounding, peripheral labour phenomena, be it Uber-drivers or DHL and Amazon delivery personnel. But, short of a revolution, which does not seem to be on the cards, this knowledge is probably not sufficient to instigate massive changes. So

145 Mueller, *Media Piracy*, 118.
146 Mueller, *Media Piracy*, 119.
147 Mueller, *Media Piracy*, 122.

far, attempts to politicise the offline world via/as cyberpolitics have
fallen flat. If there has been any politicisation due to digital media,
this is rather happening in a more rightist and conservative direction,
via fake news, hate speech, and similar negative trends.

Perhaps a less comprehensive yet possibly more yielding approach
to fighting neo-capitalist digital practices via piratical strategies
might be more successful. What I have in mind here is, for instance,
the *Capitalismo Amarillo* (yellow capitalism) project, as suggested by
Jota Izquierdo. Having learned from pirates, these projects utilise
informal economies of the global south that have

> generated a kind of fissure in the formal economy that works as
> a zone of disturbance in which the informal exploit the structure
> of capitalism by shifting the social formations related to the
> formal and state capitalism. The informal economy displaces
> the frames of production away [from] state control and opens
> the possibility of other flaws of social and cultural production.
> Capitalismo Amarillo addresses the shifting, blind spots and
> modes of appropriation of the informal economy as a way to
> explore the effects and transformations of capitalism.[148]

These strategies, clearly based upon and reappropriated from digital
piracy, are then transferred into the offline world. This is possible as
there are still informal economies in place in many of these places,
whereas in countries of the northern hemisphere, these have to be
unearthed, as most of them had been buried by the strength and
length of capitalist practices. The sharing economy is one of these
practices, which, honed by digital piracy, is rapidly becoming such a
(not so) temporary zone.

Cecilia Soares fortifies this view and also draws a comparison
between shadow economies online and offline when she says that,

> as a 'globalized issue', piracy is a good entry to understand better
> a unification of proceedings under capitalism (parallel production
> eventually converges to the 'formal' one, especially on the case of
> replicas, or of smuggling), and also a trend of governmentality
> tools, by the building of desires, the understanding of what is
> luxury, of how to differentiate oneself among the multitude, and
> especially on feelings and relating to material acquisitions.[149]

---

148 See 'Yellow Capitalism', https://capitalismoamarillo.net/acerca-de/.
149 Cecília Soares, 'Discussing Piracy Today: Between the Concept and the
    Socioeconomic System' (2009), https://capitalismoamarillo.files.wordpress.
    com/2009/02/soares-cecilia-discussing-piracy-today.pdf.

In the wake of Soares' argument, it is important to see that piracy here is also a double-edged sword: one the one hand, it shows a path to beat the system; on the other, the ways and means of beating that system, i.e., getting files for free or for the cheapest possible price feeds into traditional capitalist practices, and rather than destabilising the system fortifies it into a new digital practice. Detractors of recent and commercial large-scale piracy, such as Hall and Van der Sar in their contributions to this book, report similar concerns. In the end, it is a question of how people want to live (socially and politically). And the piracy issue is at the heart of things. If companies such as Peter Thiel's Palantir company (the name borrowed from the crystal ball Saruman uses to connect to evil Sauron in *Lord of the Rings*) or Cambridge Analytics are working together with state organs, pirate sites, among other warez providers, offer means of resistance leading to transformation.

Spotification

Spotify's music streaming service launched in October 2008, one year before the judgment in The Pirate Bay trial was pronounced. Since then, together with Netflix, it has become one of the success stories of the streaming industry. In the fourth quarter of 2021, it reported 180 million premium users, more than doubling its 2017 number.[150] And, indeed, many felt that Spotify would be one of the last nails in the coffin of music piracy. One of these is Stephen Witt, who in his informative and witty 2015 book *How Music Was Set Free*, charted the rise of piracy, but then came to the following emotional conclusion, certainly upsetting to some:

> I'd saved every hard drive from every computer I'd ever had. There were nine of them, dating back to 1997 […] I had more than 100,000 mp3s. It had taken me 17 years to amass all these files, but the rise of cloud computing made the whole thing pointless. My hoarding instincts were fading, curating the library was growing more tiresome by the year, and the older drives didn't even work with modern systems. Finally I caved, bought a Spotify subscription, and accepted the reality: what I'd thought of as my personal archive was just an agglomeration of slowly demagnetizing junk. […]

150 Marie Charlotte Götting, 'Number of Spotify Premium Subscribers Worldwide from 1st Quarter 2015 to 2nd Quarter of 2022', www.statista.com/statistics/244995/number-of-paying-spotify-subscribers/.

I watched as he donned a pair of safety goggles, then picked up a large pneumatic nail gun. He took a drive from the bag, placed it on a workbench, and systematically blasted a half dozen nails through its metal housing. Then he picked it up and shook it next to his ear, to listen for the telltale rattle of its shattered magnetic core. One by one he repeated this process, until the bag was empty. When he had finished, he gathered the ruined drives in his arms, then threw them in a nearby dumpster, on top of thousands of others.[151]

Witt's radical and dramatic move away from piracy due to the availability of Spotify is an emotional read for many who have had similar experiences. However, I would argue that most are not willing to follow him in this move, as curated collections are still something to be cherished, at least in many fan circles. It is also the sharing of these large lacunae of knowledge that allows for new inventions.

Diametrically opposed to Witt's rejection of piracy is futurist Gerd Leonhart who already in 2007 had declared the End of Control on the Internet,[152] stating that the Internet could not be reined in with paywalls and other censorial measures. Rather, he sees this end of control as a chance to develop new business models and create new chances for new players, for instance much more frictionless websites, combining free and pay-for content. It would seem that this approach has had some success across diverging media and content already, and, arguably also due to piracy pressure, many content providers have been working on such projects.

Furthermore, recently Spotify has come under a lot of scrutiny.[153] Viewed as a commodified 'taste-maker' and 'ideological construct',[154] it is seen as propagating a similar ideological mode as the record studios of old, which via their Billboard and Payola practices

151 Stephen Richard Witt, *How Music Got Free: A Story of Obsession and Invention* (London: Penguin, 2015), 264–5.

152 Gerd Leonhard, *End of Control* [blog] (2007), https://gerdcloud.tumblr.com/post/29052773682/the-end-of-control-gerd-leonhard-2007-book.

153 Cecilia Ferm Almqvist, Susanna Leijonhufvud, and Niclas Ekberg (eds), *Explorativ bildning i strömmande medier: Spotify som ett case* (Huddinge: Södertörns högskola, 2020); Patrick Burkart (ed.), *Spotification of Popular Culture in the Field of Popular Communication* (London: Routledge, 2021). Regarding what is seen as Spotify's unfair remuneration practices, see L.T. Wright, 'Why Do So Many Musicians Hate Spotify?', *Spinditty* (3 February 2022), https://spinditty.com/industry/why-so-many-artists-hate-spotify.

154 Burkart, *Spotification*.

were able to dictate and then sell taste. Spotify thereby clearly fits Ravi Sundaram's bill, who eloquently warns against the fact that an unfettered neoliberal company such as Spotify would simply recycle old ideological structures and capitalist practices rather than act as a true innovator.[155] This comes on top of the fact that Spotify itself had pirated earlier piratical practices (website structures, chat rooms, individual chat functions, friends lists, etc.) of file sharers in the first place.

Regarding Spotify, Maria Erickson, who worked for the company for some time, would tell us: 'Spotify's business model never benefited all musicians in the same manner but rather appeared – and still appears – highly skewed toward major stars and record labels, establishing a winner-takes-all market familiar from the traditional media industries'.[156] Far from being a simple music streaming service, Spotify has recently been faulted for distributing fake news and allowing COVID-deniers to propagate their views. On 24 January 2022, Neil Young announced that he would take his music off the streaming service because the Joe Rogan podcast, 'The Joe Rogan Experience', was 'spreading false information about vaccines' and, with the entertainer India Arie sharing clips of Rogan using the n-word, other musicians have followed Young's lead.[157] It would therefore seem that Spotify, despite its great success, is not the new gold standard, and is also (morally) unable to fill the pirates' shoes.

Arguably, this claim for piratical ecologies used as cultural intermediaries can also be extended to recent Netflix commissioning practices. Within its network, relevant content from user forums was analysed and so, for instance, access to LGBTQA+ and non-Hollywood material not before included in its search algorithms appeared, so displacing the same old top 20 in its suggestion field with rather more remote material. On the one hand, this is a positive development, as more diverse content could be screened.

155 Ravi Sundaram, 'Recycling Electronic Modernity' [blog] (1998), www.nettime. org/Lists-Archives/nettime-l-9809/msg00040.html.

156 Maria Eriksson, Rasmus Fleischer, Anna Johansson, Pelle Snickars, and Patrick Vonderau, *Spotify Teardown: Inside the Black Box of Streaming Music* (Cambridge, MA: MIT Press, 2019), 4.

157 'Ava DuVernay is the latest artist to follow Neil Young's exit from Spotify because of Joe Rogan', *Los Angeles Times* (30 January 2022), www. latimes.com/entertainment-arts/music/story/2022-01-30/spotify-joe-rogan-covid-neil-young-list-of-artists.

On the other, it saved Netflix revenue-share money, as blockbusters would typically require higher fees to be paid to Hollywood. Such diversification would in turn also feed into its commissioning practices. It was these discursive community-based features, honed by file-sharing sites, that were then used by Netflix when devising its successful global production palette, financing local content for global consumption, but also saving it money.

It would also seem that the erection of more and more paywalls does not seem to work, just a Gerd Leonhard had warned. A case in point was Rupert Murdoch, who in 2009 built a paywall around *The Times* newspaper, not even allowing Google spiders in. In 2012, the newspaper reversed course, because of falling recognition online and offline and as the lack of Internet business hurt the publication more than it helped it.[158] Publishing, and here especially newspapers, has been in a steep decline, except for a few very select publications (e.g., the *New York Times* and, to a lesser degree, the *Wall Street Journal*) that, for very specific reasons, are able to weather the storm. Needless to say, both of these newspapers have embraced online publishing and their continuing success is mostly due to their having done so successfully. This is the case despite the fact that pirated copies of their issues continue to circulate. Another case in point is the music industry. While CD sales are virtually non-existent due to streaming, and despite vast and long-time piracy of music files, consumption has rebounded and streaming is now more profitable than before. The same can be said for streaming sites for films and television, such as Netflix, Hulu, and many others. One might even venture to say that certain films and series are successful precisely because of their rank in top ten pirated film lists. It would therefore seem that the symbiotic relationship between pirates and content providers might benefit both, and that continued piracy scapegoating, as has been the practice by national agencies and industry organisations, has merely become an outdated and knee-jerk reaction.[159]

158 John Biggs, 'Murdoch Finally Invites the Google Spiders to Search London *Times*', *TechCrunch* (27 September 2012), https://techcrunch.com/2012/09/27/murdoch-finally-invites-the-google-spiders-to-search-london-times/.

159 On the flawed process of such scapegoating, see Ernesto Van der Sar, 'Canadian Study: Piracy Boosts CD Sales', *TorrentFreak* (3 November 2007), https://torrentfreak.com/piracy-boosts-cd-sales-071103/.

Alternative Revenue Stream Sourcing for Content Creators

One interesting and very much underdeveloped possibility of managing the fallout of Internet piracy are levies put on recordable media, typically collected by semi-governmental authorities and the distributed among content creators according to formulae dependent on how much output they had. The practice had started already in the early 1960s in Germany when levies on photocopier purchases were introduced.[160] This system is of interest, as it moves toward a certain kind of collectivisation of content creation, thereby at least partially doing away with a more typical property approach. Questions do arise though as to the fairness of the system. A system would have to be found which would remunerate artists equitably. If it is only based on popularity, airtime, and sales, this would unfairly privilege a few artists disproportionally, and thus reintroduce the broken system already in existence today. Other artists, less popular, or perhaps catering to cultural minorities, would not be properly compensated. A system where such considerations are heeded would be preferable; models here could be public broadcasting systems, themselves having recently become controversial due to political outlook discussions. But they clearly have a duty to include minority concerns in their programmes, funded as they are through levies or broadcasting fees and feeding into a larger process of cultural diversification, creation, and conservation, seeking a broad social consensus.

Different countries use different systems to charge such levies, Belgium, for instance, has a system of tiered levies based on the size of the media storage device.[161] However, as technology progresses and consumption patterns change, levies on DVDs or CDs seem to become quickly outdated, and indeed some countries which had them before, such as Australia and Finland, have abolished them. Others, such as the Netherlands, are simply extending the definition of what kinds of devices fall under the levy; thus, computers, mobile phones, and televisions were added to the list. This seems to be the preferred approach. An added benefit to this system is that it necessitates a broad social discussion on what kinds of cultural works should be supported and at which level, and which kinds of processes ought to be used to ensure such support.

160 World Intellectual Property Organization (WIPO), 'International Survey on Private Copying: Law and Practice 2012', www.wipo.int/edocs/pubdocs/en/copyright/1037/wipo_pub_1037_2013.pdf.
161 *Moniteur belge* (23 December 2009), 56–7, www.ejustice.just.fgov.be/mopdf/2009/12/23_1.pdf.

In 2015, the European Parliament approved the so-called non-binding Reda Report, which requested a review of EU-wide levy practices – not surprisingly drafted by an EU Parliament member from a Pirate Party.[162] Unfortunately, seven years on, this review is still on the waiting list. It would seem that lawmakers are slow in acting upon these suggestions, due possibly, one might speculate, to a lack of lobby group pressure.

Financial Incentives?

Financial incentives have been largely gained *from* piracy and not against it. Initiatives to pay users for their content, such as Andrew Yang's Data Divided Project,[163] are, as morally and financially convincing as they might be, so far falling on the deaf ears of Alphabet, Facebook, and others. A number of studies have suggested that ever since the success of Spotify and other streaming portals, largely due to ease of use and moderate pricing, piracy is on the wane in some contexts. A case in point is a 2019 cross-country study conducted amongst young adults in Finland and Austria, analysing Internet consumption.[164] The results clearly show that young adults use legal sources when available, preferring free-of-charge providers, but readily turn to illegal means if this is where they find their sought-after content. However, in Finland, it is considered that using illegal material is acceptable only 'when the material cannot be found from legal sources', whereas Austrians are more likely to use illegal P2P networks regardless of whether the content they seek is available elsewhere. Additionally, for both cohorts, at least with young adults. the concept of 'owning' files is quickly losing popularity.[165]

---

162 Felix Reda, draft report on the current copyright framework for the European Parliament, https://felixreda.eu/copyright-evaluation-report-explained/; European Parliament, Harmonisation of certain aspects of copyright and related rights, www.europarl.europa.eu/sides/getDoc.do?pubRef=-//EP//NON SGML+TA+P8-TA-2015-0273+0+DOC+PDF+V0//EN.

163 'Take Control of Your Data', www.datadividendproject.com/. See also, in a more general vein, 'Should Tech Companies Be Paying Us For Our Data?', *Forbes* (30 October 2020), www.forbes.com/sites/forbestechcouncil/2020/10/30/should-tech-companies-be-paying-us-for-our-data/.

164 Veikko Halttunen, Stephan Schlögl, and Raphael Weidhaas, 'Digital Content Consumption: A Finnish–Austrian Cross-Country Analysis', Mediterranean Conference on Information Systems, Proceedings, 2019, https://aisel.aisnet.org/mcis2019/12.

165 Halttunen et al., 'Digital Content Consumption'.

Another worthwhile approach is taken by anti-piracy company DMCAForce, which is trying to create a win–win situation for both copyright holders and torrent and streaming sites. Instead of copyright holders asking for takedowns or for content to be removed, it is experimenting with an advertising revenue share model. Thereby, copyright holders retain full control, but also allow their content to be available for consumption. Cooperation is seen as key. The company's CEO states that

> Pirates will always find a way to upload and share content somewhere. That's not going to change anytime soon. So instead of fighting it, bringing both sides together may prove to be more fruitful. Users are going to steal and share and need somewhere to upload content. They're just going to do it and there's no way to stop it. So our stance is to protect content, but leverage it as well.[166]

It would seem then that enlightened parts of the entertainment industry are beginning to explore new ways in which to allow certain forms of piracy to exist and also to cooperate with them, thereby subscribing to at least a small part of pirate logic. Whether this is a genuine change of heart or rather something done out of exasperation or calculation, only time will tell.

Artistic Practices?

The relationship between piracy and the arts is an interesting one, as both are inextricably entangled with each other. If one of art's tasks is to challenge and change cultural practices, piracy and hacking seek to do the same, questioning cultural norms that lead to them being labelled illegal in the first place. As the artistic sphere is paradigmatically transforming from an era of aggregation to an era of curation, based upon models of communities being at the centre of pirate ecologies,[167] such curation-based art engagement leads to different creative practices spread out among such communities.

---

166 'Pirate Sites and Copyright Holders Can Both Profit From Advertising', *TorrentFreak* (6 April 2019), https://torrentfreak.com/pirate-sites-and-copy-right-holders-can-both-profit-from-advertising/. A similar willingness to negotiate and cooperate with pirates, this time from the music industry, can be found here: Tim Ingham, 'Major Label Bosses Don't Usually Talk Like This …', *Music Business Worldwide* (27 August 2015), www.musicbusi-nessworldwide.com/major-label-bosses-dont-usually-talk-like-this.

167 See Keiko Bang (Singapore) in her keynote address at the 2019 ACCS conference in Tokyo, 26 May 2019, https://iafor.org/archives/conference-pro-grammes/accs/accs-programme-2019.pdf.

French philosopher Jacques Racine sees the role of art as necessary in order to reinvent the relationship between time and space, something interrupted by capitalist structures. Only in applying art in this way would humans be able to find their way back to collective practices.[168] Especially in the absence of erstwhile gatekeepers and intermediaries, users appreciate such interventions, especially if they themselves can easily chime in and make a difference. Many people would even willingly pay for curation via their attention or pecuniary means, thereby ensuring the working and prospering of such cultural networks, following the model of national public broadcasting systems charging a broadcasting fee. A good compendium of recent practices is the 2021 volume *Aesthetics of the Commons*, where its editors list a number of artistic/piratical practices which unpack the idea of the commons on a piratical, artistic, and political level, and locate it within a '(post)digital field'.[169] These include a feminist web server, an art space in a London park, a pirate library, and a collective art school. As for a common denominator, the editors cite the following:

> [All these projects] have a 'double character'. They are art in the sense that they place themselves in relation to (Western) cultural and art systems, developing discursive and aesthetic positions, but, at the same time, they are 'operational' in that they create recursive environments and freely available resources whose uses exceed these systems. The first aspect raises questions about the kind of aesthetics that are being embodied, the second creates a relation to the larger concept of the 'commons' [...] understood not as a fixed set of principles that need to be adhered to in order to fit a definition, but instead as a 'thinking tool'. [...] They all demonstrate that art can play an important role in imagining and producing a real quite different from what is currently hegemonic; that art has the possibility to not only envision or proclaim ideas in theory, but also to realize them materially.[170]

It is these recursive environments and their material realisation as embodied practices that piracy aims for and where it becomes a natural ally of art.

168 'La proclamation de l'autonomie de l'art et son identification à une forme de l'expérience collective', Jacques Rancière, *Le partage du sensible: esthétique et politique* (Paris: La Fabrique, 2000). See also Pierre Rosanvallon, *La contre-démocratie: la politique à l'âge de la défiance* (Paris: Le Seuil, 2006).
169 Cornelia Sollfrank, Felix Stalder, and Shusha Niederberger (eds), *Aesthetics of the Commons* (Zurich: Diaphanes, 2021), 9.
170 Sollfrank et al., *Aesthetics of the Commons*, 9.

Another example of such a kind of hybrid practice is the work undertaken by the Disnovation Art Collective. They position themselves 'at the intersection of contemporary art, research and hacking', developing 'situations of disruption, speculation, and debate, in order to question dominant techno-positivist ideologies, and to stimulate post-growth narratives'.[171] Among their works and exhibitions count publications on piracy, but especially also art works thematising sustainability and post-nature phenomena drawing a connecting line again between pirate sharing practices and the kind of shared, transborder thinking necessary to address climate change.[172] Apart from being available online, their works have been exhibited in museums and biennales all over the world. One of their recent publications, *A Bestiary of the Anthropocene*, combines found footage from the Internet and, typically of a hybrid nature, images that question any online–offline dichotomies.[173]

These images throw up the question of who is pirating whom: nature, the online world, or vice versa? An art project of similar propensity is Silvio Lorusso and Sebastian Schmieg's 'Five Years of Captured Captures' (2017) at the Photographers' Gallery, London. It consists of thousands and thousands of 'capture' images, which typically have to be solved when requesting access to many Internet sites, prominently including pirate ones, a practice that continually frustrates users but that is used universally to differentiate users from automated search bots. It is a playful yet thought-provoking way to question and challenge digital access and downloading site and practices.[174]

Such artistic interventions share the belief that it is pirate practices that positively shape our thinking about the world of today and of

171 Disnovation Art Collective, https://disnovation.org/about.php.
172 Examples of their work include post-growth biosphere work, solar income and social metabolism installations; life support system, an ecosystem services estimation experiment, 2020; energy slave tokens, human labor to fossil fuel conversion units, 2020; a predictive art bot, which turns the latest media influences into artistic concepts, 2015–17; profiling the profilers, sousveillance of big tech companies using their own tools, applying big data analytics, 2018–20; and a 'Shanzhai archeology', a collection of hybrid phones through technological interbreeding made in China, 2015–18.
173 Nicolas Nova and Disnovation.org (eds), *A Bestiary of the Anthropocene* (Amsterdam: Onomatopee, 2021).
174 https://web.archive.org/web/20220612213818/http://five.yearsofcapturedcapt. ch/imgs/fyocc_lorusso_schmieg_04_1600.jpg.

tomorrow and that work the ever-thinner dividing line between online and offline living practices. They question and attack hereditary policing practices, try to establish themselves in the cyberworld, and imagine ways in which online practices make both online and offline worlds more equal.

11 Conclusion

We started this journey with alarmist news bites detailing how piracy is undermining and threatening 'our way of life'. By digging a bit deeper, it became apparent that the situation is not quite as simple and closed as certain powerful industry and government agencies are trying to make users believe. On the contrary, the oft-quoted, but seldom followed, maxim of 'sharing is caring' was found to be the impetus of many web activists and pirates. Social sharing is more than ever a modality of economic production beyond the established and neoliberalised market economy still held up as the gold standard for people to follow and submit to.

Compared to how things were 20 years ago, the piracy and warez scene is changing. Despite government and industry's concerted and ongoing efforts to close down pirate sites, online sharing is not easily eradicated, and due to its inherent structural and decentralised qualia it is very difficult to suppress data on the Internet as long as there is a dedicated number of users insisting on sharing it. Furthermore, and perhaps in some way similar to the recent decriminalisation of certain recreational drugs due to public pressure and changing social attitudes, there have also been instances where piracy itself has become if not decriminalised then at least not persecuted so much; at times, pirate philosophy was even used to draw up and/or change legislation. Among younger Internet users, piracy is a given resource, easily available and non-stigmatised – the new normal. There even exists a belief in 'access entitlement'.[175] What eventually counts is availability and ease of use, but not whether data mining is legal or not.

More and more, pirate practices concentrate less on the amount that is shared or the speed of the upload, but rather the making available of high quality, critical content and its curation, educating users about the warez they are sharing. As Karaganis argues in *Shadow Libraries*, we have less to worry about piracy than about the

175 Hilderbrand, *Inherent Vice*, 10.

faulty and dangerous process used to fight it, including summative data deletion and takedowns.[176] If there had been 62 takedown notices filed with Google in 2011, in 2018 this figure had increased to over 1 billion.[177] In Karaganis's study of the process, it became clear that at least 4 per cent of takedown notices were wrong outright and up to another 30 per cent at least questionable. Due to the amount of data, takedown processes have become automated, which is contributing to the problem. Karaganis therefore cogently argues that it is not the multiplication of data, inclusive of piracy, that should worry us, but rather the ephemerality of data and the attempt at homogenisation witnessed, for instance, in the syllabuses used in universities globally. Karaganis's latest project, opensyllabus.org, is addressing this issue, with a first step of visualising syllabus practice globally.[178] In a second step these will be analysed and, with data openly available to all, will give academics a chance to revisit their own data sources and those given to students. It is a reflective process that, based on semi-pirated practices (who owns a syllabus: the author, the institution, or the state?), attempts to question institutionalised pedagogical practices that had not been able to be deliberated before the era of big data.

Content can be digitised and distributed at near-zero marginal cost; thus, the new economy has created unparalleled challenges for the protection and enforcement of copyright. But it has also eliminated media scarcity, with most providers offering at least some content without payment. A sustainable copyright-sharing model must carefully align the legal interests of businesses and the legitimate ones of individual users, and making content available at a fair price and as barrier-free as possible is a *sine qua non*, if the industry wants to reclaim Generations X–Z.

The success of streaming services is demonstrating that money can be made from them and the music industry has been growing and making profits over the last few years with the business model changing. But if Witt felt that Spotify would be enough to render piracy obsolete, then this view is wrong on several accounts. For

176 Joe Karaganis (ed.), *Shadow Libraries: Access to Knowledge in Global Higher Education* (Cambridge, MA: MIT Press, 2018).

177 'Top 3 Copyright "Owners" Sent Google a Billion Takedown Requests', *TorrentFreak* (25 December 2018), https://torrentfreak.com/top-3-copyright-owners-sent-google-a-billion-takedown-requests-181225/.

178 'Mapping the College Curriculum across 7,292,573 syllabi', https://opensyllabus.org.

one, availability of content is still very much dependent on the company itself, with little if any outside supervision. And second, the remuneration artists are receiving through the Spotify system is for most a negligible quantity. Third, and this might be the most important point, while Spotify's bounty might address the market needs of the many, it does not alleviate a deeper discourse on owning and content restriction. Just like other platforms, Spotify is a law unto itself and is committed to profit making in the first place.

It is much less the individuals who are re-appropriating and mediatising digital content that give rise to worry; just as throughout history, it is the large players, be they governments, commercial entities, or, as of late, platform cyber-intermediaries, that provide reason to worry. As many of the authors quoted above state, piracy throws up questions of property, the law, and participation. That is also why the legacy term of 'media literacy' is inappropriate, as it merely describes a more or less skilful buying into a rendering system. Rather, notions of digital entanglement – equipping users with the tools and techniques to be as self-determined as possible – have become much more desirable, as such practices afford and require active participation, an active engagement in transformative digital and post-digital processes. In part due to piratical practices, this is beginning to happen, but such practices are on a sliding scale on which the poles are inhabited by opposing views: on the one hand there is the Lev Manovich option, who in a recent Facebook post happily described his willingness to accept any and all cookies from websites visited;[179] on the other, there is the Žižek–Varoufakis option, which rejects the system wholesale, but without giving viable alternatives.[180] I find both options problematic, as the first gives up the idea of, and any positive results reaped from, resistance, and the second does not allow for knowledge gained through the system in which big data can also be turned against itself, for instance via piratical practices. This also includes the

179 'After getting new iPhone 13 Max yesterday and starting to use it, I said YES to every "share data", "allow access to", and all "can we track you" request from EVERY app. Why? I enjoy seeing possible recommendations resulted from all the tracking and I also like the idea of all the servers, AI systems, databases and algorithms having some knowledge of me. It's nice to get all this attention, from humans or machines', www.facebook.com/lev.manovich (14 November 2021).

180 See Yanis Varoufakis and Slavoj Žižek in conversation at the Indigo Festival 2021, *YouTube*, www.youtube.com/watch?v=0ODuleYZwbs.

knowledge that, besides autocratic systems, there have always also been in existence more communitarian, shared, and distributed social practices – practices which were at the heart of the development of modern society, as David Graeber and David Wengrow have recently shown.[181]

Hacking and piracy are also at the heart of many consumer protection agencies. Many users (including pirates) feel that large businesses are reaping an undue amount of data from their customers and are requesting lawmakers to do something about it. This might be a bit ironic, if pirates ask for protection, but the idea is that if such protection were given, at least some piracy would not be necessary any more. Recent approaches to transparency and user protection have shown promise here. Under the EU General Data Protection Regulation (GDPR), organisations are required to uphold privacy rights of anyone in EU territory, and to safeguard any personal data collected or processed. Companies and governments must lay bare what kinds of data they harvest and aggregate from visitors to their websites and visitors are enabled to decide what kind of personal data they are willing to have processed – how and by whom. For many, this is a cumbersome process, but I would argue that it is a healthy choice because it forces participants to come face to face with the at times uncomfortable truth that frictionless surfing is costly: one pays in two currencies, with one's attention and with one's personal data.[182] The friction the law causes is a reminder that seamless and frictionless usage of the Internet does bear a cost. It also schools users in being more aware of what is at stake.

Such a view would also include the tools one uses, for instance search engines. They were the tools that made the Internet possible in the first place and older readers might remember the browser wars of the mid- to late 1990s; already then, these tools had become powerful objects making or breaking the success of a website. Today, this has proven true to a point hardly imaginable 20 years ago, with Google taking in 30 per cent of global advertising revenues through its search engine. At the time of this writing, Google.com is arguably one of the best search engines around, but, and these are rarely advertised, there

---

181 David Graeber and David Wengrow, *The Dawn of Everything* (London: Allen Lane, 2021).

182 For an artistic/activist view on this point, see Clément Renaud (ed.), *Cost of Freedom* (Pourrières: Clément Renaud, 2015) (public domain), http://costof-freedom.cc/.

are alternatives such as DuckDuckGo, which might not be as comprehensive as Google, but which allows its users a much larger say in what data it collects from them. Active participation, be it in political processes or in data streams, always comes at a cost, but so does doing nothing and simply accepting a provider's terms. GDPR also comes at a cost, as content is regulated, and at the time of its devising and inception, many people and organisations protested against it. However, this law does move in the direction of empowering users to manage their data and assigns the state the task to rein in companies and the decision of what is (and the management of) the common good, in a similar way public media have been conceived and regulated since the onset of electronic media over a hundred years ago. Ultimately, these media were regulated by the state and not by companies' untransparent rules of what is allowed on their website and what is not. Of course, any such regulation must be continually legitimising itself via cooperative and member-empowering measures, such as public oversight bodies. Especially since it is mostly (private) technology that is a driving force behind all matters Internet, an oversight framework can and should be provided; to ensure fair participation of all in technology and content is something tech companies might need help from regulatory bodies to achieve. And here piracy is helpful. As we have seen, large academic data wholesalers such as Elsevier and Wiley have recently begun sharing freely on their websites much more content than before. This is a clear result of sharing websites questioning and threatening their business plan (profit maximisation from education) and has led them, at least to a very small extent, to reconsider their practices; the same goes for other content providers such as music companies and film studios.[183]

Resistance to models of power and economic exchange is not a wholesale rejection thereof, but rather an insistence to be offered a

183   This is also proof of Yochai Benkler's extensive work on the wealth networks can produce when based on the commons. See Yochai Benkler, 'Sharing Nicely'; Yochai Benkler, TED talk [video] 2005, http://open.sina.com.cn/course/id_335; Yochai Benkler, *The Wealth of Networks* (New Haven, CT: Yale University Press, 2006); and Matthew Hindman 'What is the Online Public Sphere Good For?', in Joseph Turow and Lokman Tsui (eds), *The Hyperlinked Society: Questioning Connections in the Digital Age* (Ann Arbor: University of Michigan Press, 2008). For an overview of its philosophical underpinnings and emerging practices, see Mathieu O'Neil, Christian Pentzold, and Sophie Toupin (eds), *The Handbook of Peer Production* (Hoboken, NJ: Wiley, 2021) and Sollfrank et al., *Aesthetics of the Commons*.

fair say in what happens with one's participation in and entanglement with Internet technology and beyond. As we are moving into the post-digital era, especially the latter becomes more important. Taking a leaf out of quantum physics, many researchers, such as Karen Barad and Francois Laruelle, embrace quantum philosophy in order to better describe our relationship to technology, arguing that individuality and ownership have become problematic categories.[184] This poses serious questions for governments and companies alike and it would seem that piratical practices can be helpful in thinking these categories through. It is clear that not all piratical practices are positive and that much of recent commercialised piracy is largely committed to illegally generating revenue for shady business practitioners only.[185] However, this does not take away from piracy's original impetus that questioned traditional business practices built on financial gain and the fostering of inequality.

Furthermore, with the rise of the alt right and its usage of erstwhile piratical practices for their own gain, piracy has received yet another twist. Be it Truth Social, Gab, Gettr, Rumble, Parler, Telegram, but also Facebook, Twitter, and others – the issues surrounding piracy and hacking are those that increasingly impact on society. It is too facile only to look at piracy as an economic and legal problem, without seeing its contextualising, glocalising, and decolonialising practices as positive potential.[186] Distinct cultural differences can be observed, especially between the countries of the northern hemisphere and the global south. But even for the former, differentiations need to be put into place. Thus, for instance, in former Warsaw Pact countries, 'forbidden' material such as Samizdat literature was prized and illegally distributed in order to criticise the powers that be. It might follow that especially in countries that were or are prone to authoritarian regimes, piracy is viewed with different eyes than in more 'liberally' oriented regimes. Piracy research can profit from such de-globalisation moves, and especially research into cultural practices

---

184 Karen Barad, *Meeting the Universe Halfway* (Durham, NC: Duke University Press, 2007); François Laruelle, *The Last Humanity* (London: Bloomsbury, 2021).

185 This is by and large, of course, also true for the hacking scene, which is becoming more and more dominated by state-controlled and commercial hackers. See Ben Buchanan, *The Hacker and the State: Cyber Attacks and the New Normal of Geopolitics* (Cambridge, MA: Harvard University Press, 2020).

186 Lars Eckstein and Anja Schwarz (eds), *Postcolonial Piracy: Media Distribution and Cultural Production in the Global South* (London: Bloomsbury, 2014).

of smaller groups in localised areas can be fruitful in bringing out the creative aspect of media reappropriation.[187]

Piracy is, and continues to be, a complex issue which has much to teach us about society at large. Issues that were fought out in real life before now have the chance to be worked through in cyberspace as well, a space that despite its commercialisation and attempts at weaning us away from offline realties also always produces new critical practices. For every metaverse there is a *Dynamicland*, 'a communal computer, designed for agency, not apps, where people can think like whole humans' and attempt to 'incubate a humane dynamic medium whose full power is accessible to all people',[188] thereby producing an alternative to any disembodied capitalist metaverses. Such moves would integrate the virtual into the offline world and not vice versa; data goggles are not required.

This is not an easy solution, and the fights over VPNs and TOR make this clear. If, on the one hand, Western governments praise the use of these programmes and networks as they allow subverting politically authoritarian regimes ('freedom tools'), it is these very tools that these same governments, prompted by media

---

187 Information-sharing has always been viewed as an important cultural element, e.g., in the cultural history of China; see William P. Alford, *To Steal a Book Is an Elegant Offence: Intellectual Property Law in Chinese Civilization* (Stanford, CA: Stanford University Press, 1995). It is therefore no surprise when Yu argues that the Western intellectual property regime, on top of being viewed as a thoroughly foreign concept, has resulted in a massive outflow of traditional knowledge, folklore, genetic material, and native medical knowledge, and has threatened the very existence of indigenous cultures. 'By scrutinizing the structural and ideological assumptions built within the Western intellectual property regime, the policymakers in the two countries would be able to pay special attention to the interests of *nonauthorial* producers. By doing so, the policymakers would also be able to acknowledge the importance of protecting folkloric works, works of cultural heritage, and biological and ecological know-how of traditional peoples'. Peter K. Yu, 'From Pirates to Partners: Protecting Intellectual Property in China in the Twenty-First Century', *American University Law Review* 50, no. 131 (2001), 241–2. See also Jinying Li, 'From "D-Buffs" to the "D-Generation": Piracy, Cinema, and an Alternative Public Sphere in Urban China', *International Journal of Communication* 6 (2012), 542–63, who states: 'By organizing spectatorship and filmmaking through the shadow system of piracy, this alternative public sphere provides an inclusive, heterogeneous, and non-controllable social horizon for organizing collective experience and identities' (542).

188 See https://dynamicland.org/.

and tech companies, condemn when it comes to piracy. It is not just non-democratic countries which subscribe to surveillance practices. As Moinipour and Troullinou argue,

> Even if corporate[/state] surveillance does not operate through overt coercion, it is argued that it yet results in self-regulation and subjugation to neoliberal rationality. Since telecoms and social media companies generally work hand in hand with the state and legal and practical standpoint boundaries overlap on a great scale, how can privacy be safeguarded for citizens?[189]

Piracy has always been at the heart of cultural social practices. It is also closely related to negotiations on how we want to live and how risks are defined and managed. This begins with issues of property and copyright, continues to questions of legality/illegality, and arrives at current practices that allow for a certain margin of reappropriation/theft to be condoned. Certain risks are always present and tolerated, something exemplified by traffic systems, where some use/abuse scenarios are tolerated in order to achieve mobility for societies at large and are considered a greater good. Piracy could be seen as such a risk, and its toleration necessary for the system to continue.[190] The example cited above of advertising revenue shared between pirates and rights holders would point in that direction.

In a next step, rather than viewing piracy as a necessary evil associated with the capitalist system, why not think of the capitalist system as the necessary evil piracy needs to tolerate? It would therefore only be seen as one possible, and in many of its guises, negative offshoot of an anarchical approach to social living, one that can and should be contested. In that way, the focus would be on the piratical practices themselves, which could be critiqued and honed to better serve the common good, something that I think is in line with the many Internet theorists quoted above. While such a view would have its share of utopian thinking, it would nevertheless orient itself on current practices and would incorporate these in visions of the future for a hybrid online/offline life.

Piratical practices can be regarded as legitimate protests against an ever-increasing global commercialisation and are aimed at local and

---

189 S. Moinipour and P. Troullinou, 'Redesigning or Redefining Privacy?', *Westminster Papers in Communication and Culture* 12, no. 3 (2017), 1–4, www.westminsterpapers.org/article/id/251/.

190 Similarly, in Matt Mason, *The Pirate's Dilemma: How Youth Culture is Reinventing Capitalism* (New York: Free Press, 2008).

global exclusionary practices privileging or denying specific media content. Contrary to what parties with vested interests describe as a pandemic or an epidemic, undermining and corrupting businesses and society at large,[191] piracy is an inherent and always already *endemic* part of late digital capitalism and as such offers venues of resistance to authoritarian and illegitimate regimes and monopolising business venues alike. As we are poised to move into a post-human *and* post-digital future along the lines many theorists and practitioners imagine and work towards with their creative commons, temporary autonomous zones, and similar concepts, might it not also be possible to move into a post-piratical future, in which the need for piracy diminishes as it becomes the new normal and people can perform many identities, including the one that used to be called 'pirate'?[192]

Select Bibliography

Akamai, 'State of the Internet: Most Recent Security Report', SOTI 7, no. 4 (September 2021), ed. Martin McKeay. https://web.archive.org/web/20210923001400/www.akamai.com/our-thinking/the-state-of-the-internet/global-state-of-the-internet-security-ddos-attack-reports. Accessed 10 October 2022.
—. 'State of the Internet, Security: Pirates in the Outfield', SOTI 8, no. 1 (January 2022), ed. Martin McKeay. www.akamai.com/resources/state-of-the-internet/soti-security-pirates-in-the-outfield. Accessed 10 October 2022.

191 See Majid Yar, 'The Global "Epidemic" of Movie "Piracy": Crimewave or Social Construction?', *Media, Culture & Society* 27, no. 5 (2005), 677–96.
192 See Tilman Baumgärtel, 'The Triumph of the Pirates – Books, Letters, Movies, and Vegan Candy – Not a Conclusion', *A Reader*, 234–47, in which he expresses his belief that a 'techno-deterministic' view of the Internet would always have pirates come on top. Patrick Burkart's *Why Pirates Win* (Oakland: University of California Press, 2019) makes the same argument, albeit from a socio-ethical perspective; here, one can point to Jonas Andersson, who posits piracy as an established 'backdrop to everyday cultural life' based on 'the perceived "need" for culture and the associated "right" to it'. Jonas Andersson, 'The Quiet Agglomeration of Data: How Piracy is Made Mundane', in Manuel Castells and Gustavo Cardoso (eds), *Piracy Cultures: How a Growing Portion of the Global Population is Building Media Relationships through Alternate Channels of Obtaining Content* (Los Angeles, CA: USC Annenberg Press, 2013). Lastly, consider the account by Mikael Böök, 'Herding the Wind: A Journey to the Strange World of the e-Library in the Autumn of the Year 2020' (2020), www.kaapeli.fi/book/libpub/Z-Library_en.pdf, which clearly exemplifies present laissez-faire cultural practices regarding piracy.

Alford, William P., *To Steal a Book Is an Elegant Offence: Intellectual Property Law in Chinese Civilization* (Stanford, CA: Stanford University Press, 1995).

Angeloro, Dan, 'Thoughtware: Contemporary Online Remix Culture', in Mark Titmarsh (ed.), *SynCity: Remixing Three Generations of Sample Culture* (Sydney: d/Lux/Editions, 2006), 18–25.

Arquilla, John, and David Ronfeldt, *Networks and Netwars: The Future of Terror, Crime, and Militancy* (Santa Monica, CA: Rand Corporation, 2001).

Auray, Nicolas, 'Pirates en réseau: détournement, prédation et exigence de justice', *Esprit* 7 (2009): 168–79. DOI: 10.3917/espri.0907.0168. Accessed 13 March 2022.

Barad, Karen, *Meeting the Universe Halfway* (Durham, NC: Duke University Press, 2007).

Baumgärtel, Tilman (ed.), *A Reader on International Media Piracy: Pirate Essays* (Amsterdam: Amsterdam University Press, 2015).

Benkler, Yochai, 'Sharing Nicely: On Shareable Goods and the Emergence of Sharing as a Modality of Economic Production', *Yale Law Journal* 114, no. 2 (2004): 273–358. www.dropbox.com/s/ig8955sggxjd1h0/Sharing%20 Nicely%20Benkler_FINAL_YLJ114-2.pdf. Accessed 10 October 2022.

—. TED talks [video] 2005. http://open.sina.com.cn/course/id_335. Accessed 13 March 2022.

—. *The Wealth of Networks* (New Haven, CT: Yale University Press, 2006).

Böhm, Markus, '"Share-Online.biz" Ermittler schalten größten deutschen Filehoster ab' (17 October 2019). www.spiegel.de/netzwelt/web/ share-online-biz-ermittler-schalten-groesstes-deutsches-filesharing-portal-ab-a-1291986.html. Accessed 13 March 2022.

Boldrin, Michele, and David K. Levine, *Against Intellectual Monopoly* (Cambridge: Cambridge University Press, 2008).

Bolin, Göran, *Value and the Media: Cultural Production and Consumption in Digital Markets* (Farnham: Ashgate, 2011).

—. *Media Generations: Experience, Identity and Mediatised Social Change* (London: Routledge, 2016).

Böök, Mikael, 'Herding the Wind: A Journey to the Strange World of the e-Library in the Autumn of the Year 2020' (2020). www.kaapeli. fi/book/libpub/Z-Library_en.pdf. Accessed 13 March 2022.

Bradford, Alfred S., *Flying the Black Flag: A Brief History of Piracy* (Westport, CT: Praeger, 2007).

Buchanan, Ben, *The Hacker and the State: Cyber Attacks and the New Normal of Geopolitics* (Cambridge, MA: Harvard University Press, 2020).

Burkart, Patrick, *Pirate Politics: The New Information Policy Contests* (Cambridge, MA: MIT Press, 2014).

Burkart, Patrick, and Tom McCourt, *Why Hackers Win: Power and Disruption in the Network Society* (Oakland: University of California Press, 2019).

Cammaerts, Bart, Robin Mansell, and Bingchun Meng, 'Copyright & Creation: A Case for Promoting Inclusive Online Sharing', *LSE Media Policy Brief* 9 (2013). https://eprints.lse.ac.uk/54275/. Accessed 13 March 2022.

Castells, Manuel, and Gustavo Cardoso (eds), *Piracy Cultures: How a Growing Portion of the Global Population is Building Media Relationships through Alternate Channels of Obtaining Content* (Los Angeles, CA: USC Annenberg Press, 2013).

Cope, Nick, 'Scratch Video Revisited', in Steve Presence, Mike Wayne, and Jack Newsinger (eds), *Contemporary Radical Film Culture: Networks, Organisations and Activists* (London: Routledge, 2020), 175–87.

Couldry, Nick, and Ulises Mejias, *The Costs of Connection: How Data Is Colonizing Human Life and Appropriating It for Capitalism* (Stanford, CA: Stanford University Press, 2019).

Creative Commons License (n.d.). https://creativecommons.org/share-your-work/licensing-types-examples. Accessed 13 March 2022.

Cvetkovski, Trajce, *Copyright and Popular Media: Liberal Villains and Technological Change* (New York: Palgrave Macmillan, 2013).

Dames, Matthew K. 'Distinguishing "Piracy" from the "Piracy Paradigm"', *Information Today* 28, no. 2 (2011): 20–1.

Defoe, Daniel, *Histoire générale des plus fameux pirates* (Paris: Phébus, 1990).

de Wille, Tabea, and Piertommaso Bottura, 'The Rules of Harmony: Video Game Censorship in China', *MultiLingual* 30, no. 3 (2019): 56–9.

Dimitrov, Martin, *Piracy and the State: The Politics of Intellectual Property Rights in China* (Cambridge: Cambridge University Press, 2009).

Durand, Rodolphe, and Jean-Philippe Vergne, *L'organisation pirate: essai sur l'évolution du capitalisme* (Lormont: Le Bord de l'eau, 2010).

—. *The Pirate Organization: Lessons from the Fringes of Capitalism* (Boston: Harvard Business School Press, 2012).

Eckstein, Lars, and Anja Schwarz (eds), *Postcolonial Piracy: Media Distribution and Cultural Production in the Global South* (London: Bloomsbury, 2014).

Eriksson, Maria, Maria Eriksson, Rasmus Fleischer, Anna Johansson, Pelle Snickars, and Patrick Vonderau, *Spotify Teardown: Inside the Black Box of Streaming Music* (Cambridge, MA: MIT Press, 2019).

Furguson, Kirby, 'Everything is a Remix' [video] 2010. www.bilibili.com/video/av33222732?from=search&seid=12788915517576967793. Accessed 13 March 2022.

Ganser, Alexandra, *Crisis and Legitimacy in Atlantic American Narratives of Piracy* (Cham: Springer, 2020).

García-Valero, Francisco, Michal Kazimierczak, Carolina Arias Burgos, and Nathan Wajsman, 'Online Copyright Infringement in the European Union: Music, Films and TV (2017–2020). Trends and Drivers' (2021). DOI: 10.2814/505158. Accessed 13 March 2022.

Garibian, Sévane, 'Hostes humani generis: les pirates vus par le droit', *Critique* 733–4 (2008): 470–9.

Gibson, William, *Neuromancer* (New York: Ace, 2000 [1984]).

Gillespie, Tarleton, 'Characterizing Copyright in the Classroom: The Cultural Work of Antipiracy Campaigns', *Communication, Culture & Critique* 2 (2009): 274–318. DOI: 10.1111/j.1753-9137.2009.01039.x. Accessed 20 October 2022.

'Good Money Still Going Bad: Digital Thieves and the Hijacking of the Online Ad Business' (2015). www.digitalcitizensalliance.org/clientuploads/directory/Reports/goodstillbad.pdf. Accessed 13 March 2022.

Graeber, David, 'La démocratie des interstices', *Revue du MAUSS* 26, no. 2 (2005): 41–89. DOI: 10.3917/rdm.026.0041. Accessed 13 March 2022.

Graeber, David, and David Wengrow, *The Dawn of Everything* (London: Allen Lane, 2021).

Hall, Gary, *Pirate Philosophy: For a Digital Posthumanities* (Cambridge, MA: MIT Press, 2016).

—. 'Postdigital Politics: or, How to Be an Anti-Bourgeois Theorist' (2021). https://hcommons.org/deposits/item/hc:38325/. Accessed 13 March 2022.

Halttunen, Veikko, Stephan Schlögl, and Raphael Weidhaas, 'Digital Content Consumption: A Finnish–Austrian Cross-Country Analysis', Mediterranean Conference on Information Systems, 2019. https://aisel.aisnet.org/mcis2019/12. Accessed 13 March 2022.

Hamilton, Jennifer Mae, Susan Reid, Pia van Gelder, and Astrida Neimanis (eds), *Feminist, Queer, and Anticolonial Propositions for Hacking the Anthropocene: Archive* (London: Open Humanities Press, 2021).

Harley, Ross Rudesch, 'Cultural Modulation and the Zero Originality Clause of Remix Culture in Australian Contemporary Art', *Fibreculture* 15 (2009). https://fifteen.fibreculturejournal.org/fcj-100-cultural-modulation-and-the-zero-originality-clause-of-remix-culture-in-australian-contemporary-ar/. Accessed 13 March 2022.

Hayat, Samuel, and Camille Paloque-Bergès (eds), 'Pirater', *Tracés. Revue de Sciences humaines* 26 (2014). https://journals.openedition.org/traces/5892. Accessed 13 March 2022.

—. (eds), 'Transgressions pirates', *Tracés. Revue de Sciences humaines* 26 (2014). https://journals.openedition.org/traces/5894. Accessed 13 March 2022.

Heller-Roazan, Daniel, *L'Ennemi de tous: le pirate contre les nations* (Paris: Le Seuil, 2010).

Hilderbrand, Lucas, *Inherent Vice: Bootleg Histories of Video and Copyright* (Durham, NC: Duke University Press, 2009).

Ingham, Tim, 'Major Label Bosses Don't Usually Talk Like This ...', *Music Business Worldwide* (27 August 2015). www.musicbusinessworldwide.com/major-label-bosses-dont-usually-talk-like-this. Accessed 13 March 2022.

The Internet's Own Boy: The Story of Aaron Swartz [video] 2014. Brian Knappenberger, dir. www.dailymotion.com/video/x21tkoj. Accessed 13 March 2022.

Jenkins, Henry, *Textual Poachers: Television Fans and Participatory Culture*, 2nd ed. (London: Routledge, 2013 [1992]).

John, Nicholas A., *The Age of Sharing* (Cambridge: Polity Press, 2016).

Johns, A., *Piracy: The Intellectual Property Wars from Gutenberg to Gates* (Chicago: University of Chicago Press, 2010).

Karaganis, Joe, *Media Piracy in Emerging Economies* (New York: Social Science Research Council, 2011). http://piracy.ssrc.org. Accessed 13 March 2022.

—. (ed.), *Shadow Libraries: Access to Knowledge in Global Higher Education* (Cambridge, MA: MIT Press, 2018).

Keucheyan, Razmig, 'Philosophie politique du pirate', *Critique* 733–4 (2008): 458–69. DOI: 10.3917/criti.733.0458. Accessed 13 March 2022.

Kohlhammer, Siegfried, *Piraten: Vom Seeräuber zum Sozialrevolutionär* (Springe: zu Klampen Verlag, 2022).

Lanier, Jarod, *You Are Not a Gadget* (New York: Knopf, 2010).

—. *Who Owns the Future?* (New York: Penguin, 2013).

Larkin, Brian, 'Degraded Images, Distorted Sounds: Nigerian Video and the Infrastructure of Piracy', in Tilman Baumgärtel, *A Reader on International Media Piracy: Pirate Essays* (Amsterdam: Amsterdam University Press, 2015), 183–205.

Laruelle, François, *The Last Humanity* (London: Bloomsbury, 2021).

Lascia, J.D., *Darknet: Hollywood's War against the Digital Generation* (Hoboken, NJ: Wiley, 2005).

Lee, J.-A., 'Tripartite Perspective on the Copyright-Sharing Economy in China', *Computer Law & Security Review* 35, no. 4 (2019): 434–52. DOI: 10.1016/j.clsr.2019.05.001. Accessed 20 October 2022.

Leeson, Peter T., *The Invisible Hook: The Hidden Economics of Pirates* (Princeton, NJ: Princeton University Press, 2009), DOI : 10.1515/9781400829866. Accessed 13 March 2022.

Leonhard, Gerd, *End of Control* [blog] (2007). https://gerdcloud.tumblr.com/post/29052773682/the-end-of-control-gerd-leonhard-2007-book. Accessed 13 March 2022.

Lessig, Lawrence, *Code and Other Laws of Cyberspace* (New York: Basic Books, 1999).

—. *Free Culture: How Big Media Uses Technology and the Law to Lock Down Culture and Control Creativity* (New York: Penguin, 2004). http://free-culture.org/get-it. Accessed 13 March 2022.

—. *Remix: Making Art and Commerce Thrive in the Hybrid Economy* (New York: Penguin, 2008).

Li, Jinying, 'From "D-Buffs" to the "D-Generation": Piracy, Cinema, and an Alternative Public Sphere in Urban China', *International Journal of Communication* 6 (2012): 542–63.

Linebaugh, Peter, and Marcus Rediker, *L'hydre aux mille têtes: l'histoire cachée de l'Atlantique révolutionnaire* (Paris: Éditions Amsterdam, 2008).

Lunney, Glynn S., Jr, 'Empirical Copyright: A Case Study of File Sharing, Sales Revenue, and Music Output', *Supreme Court Economic Review* 24, no. 1 (2016), 261–322. www.journals.uchicago.edu/doi/10.1086/695561. Accessed 13 March 2022.

McKelvey, Fenwick, 'We Like Copies, Just Don't Let the Others Fool You: The Paradox of The Pirate Bay', *Television & New Media* 16, no. 8 (2015): 734–50.

Maigret, Nicolas, and Maria Roszkowska (eds), *The Pirate Book* (Ljubljana: Aksioma, 2015). http://thepiratebook.net. Accessed 13 March 2022.

Marshall, Jonathan Paul, and Francesca da Rimini, 'Paradoxes of Property Piracy and Sharing in Information Capitalism', in Tilman Baumgärtel (ed.), *A Reader on International Media Piracy: Pirate Essays* (Amsterdam: Amsterdam University Press, 2015), 146–66.

Mason, Matt, *The Pirate's Dilemma: How Youth Culture is Reinventing Capitalism* (New York: Free Press, 2008).

Mattelart, Tristan (ed.), *Piratages audiovisuelles: les voies souterraines de la mondialisation culturelle* (Brussels: De Boeck, 2011).

—. 'Audiovisual Piracy, Informal Economy, and Cultural Globalization', *International Journal of Communication* 6 (2012): 735–50. https://ijoc.org/index.php/ijoc/article/download/1164/728. Accessed 13 March 2022.

—. 'Piratages: apports et limites d'une infrastructure d'accès à la culture', *Traces* 26 (2014): 175–82. https://doi.org/10.4000/traces.5953. Accessed 13 March 2022.

—. 'The Changing Geographies of Pirate Transnational Audiovisual Flows', *International Journal of Communication* 10 (2016): 3503–21.

Maxwell, Andy, 'Movie Studios and Record Labels Target Pirate Bay in New Lawsuit' (2015). https://torrentfreak.com/movie-studios-and-record-labels-target-pirate-bay-in-new-lawsuit-150901. Accessed 13 March 2022.

—. 'Aussie Music Industry Wins First Ever Stream-Ripping Site Blocks', *TorrentFreak* (16 May 2019). https://torrentfreak.com/aussie-music-in-dustry-wins-first-ever-stream-ripping-site-blocks-190516. Accessed 13 March 2022.

—. 'Aussie Federal Court Orders ISPs to Block 101 Pirate Movie & TV Show Domains', *TorrentFreak* (22 December 2021). https://torrentfreak.com/aussie-federal-court-orders-isps-to-block-101-pirate-movie-tv-show-domains-211222/. Accessed 13 March 2022.

Miegel, Frederik, and Tobias Olsson, 'From Pirates to Politicians: The Story of the Swedish File Sharers Who Became a Political Party', in *Democracy, Journalism and Technology: New Developments in an Enlarged Europe*, European Media and Communication Doctoral Summer School (Tartu: University of Tartu Press, 2008), 203–15.

Moinipour, S., and P. Troullinou, 'Redesigning or Redefining Privacy?', *Westminster Papers in Communication and Culture* 12, no. 3 (2017): 1–4. www.westminsterpapers.org/article/id/251/. Accessed 13 March 2022.

Mueller, Gavin, *Media Piracy in the Cultural Economy: Intellectual Property and Labor under Neoliberal Restructuring* (London: Routledge, 2019).

Naim, Moisés, *Illicit: How Smugglers, Traffickers and Copycats are Hijacking the Global Economy* (London: Heinemann, 2005).

Navas, Eduardo, 'The Bonds of Repetition and Representation', *Remix Theory* (2008). https://remixtheory.net/?p=361. Accessed 13 March 2022.

Negarestani, Reza, 'Hacker-Engineers and Their Economies: The Political Economy of Decentralised Networks and "Cryptoeconomics"', *New Political Economy* (12 August 2020). www.tandfonline.com/doi/10.1080/13563467.2020.1806223. Accessed 13 March 2022.

Opitz, Andrew (ed.), 'Pirates and Piracy', *Darkmatter Journal* 5 (2009). www.darkmatter101.org/site/2009/12/20/editorial-notes-pirates-and-piracy-material-realities-and-cultural-myths/. Accessed 13 March 2022.

Pang, Laikwan, *Cultural Control and Globalization in Asia: Copyright, Piracy and Cinema* (New York: Routledge, 2006).

Perseil, Sonny, and Yvon Pesqueux (eds), *L'organisation de la transgression: formaliser l'informel?* (Paris: L'Harmattan, 2014).

Phau, Ian, and Johan Liang, 'Downloading Digital Video Games; Predictors, Moderators and Consequences', *Marketing Intelligence & Planning* 7 (2012): 740. doi:10.1108/02634501211273832.

Phillips, Tim, *Knock-Off: The Deadly Trade in Counterfeit Goods* (London: Kogan Page, 2005).

Porsdam, Helle, *Copyright and Other Fairy Tales: Hans Christian Andersen and the Commodification of Creativity* (Cheltenham: Edward Elgar Publishing, 2006).

Posner, Eric A., and E. Glen Weyl, *Radical Markets: Uprooting Capitalism and Democracy for a Just Society* (Princeton, NJ: Princeton University Press, 2017).

Rancière, Jacques, *Le partage du sensible: esthétique et politique* (Paris: La Fabrique, 2000). DOI: 10.3917/lafab.ranci.2000.01. Accessed 13 March 2022.

Renaud, Clément (ed.), *Cost of Freedom* (Pourrières: Clément Renaud, 2015) (public domain). http://costoffreedom.cc/. Accessed 13 March 2022.

Renaud, Clément, Florence Graezer Bideau, and Marc Laperrouza (eds), *Realtime: Making Digital China* (Lausanne: Presses polytechniques et universitaires romandes, 2020).

Rheingold, Howard, *The Virtual Community: Homesteading on the Internet* (Cambridge, MA: MIT Press, 1993). www.rheingold.com/vc/book/intro.html. Accessed 13 March 2022.

Rosanvallon, Pierre, *La contre-démocratie: la politique à l'âge de la défiance* (Paris: Le Seuil, 2006).

Rubin, Alfred P., *The Law of Piracy* (Newport, RI: Naval War College Press, 1988).

Sahni, Sanjeev P., and Indranath Gupta, *Piracy in the Digital Era: Psychosocial, Criminological and Cultural Factors* (Amsterdam: Springer, 2019).

Sarai Media Lab, 'Contested Commons/Trespassing Publics: A Public Record', Conference on Inequalities, Conflicts and Intellectual Property, New Delhi, 6, 7, 8 January 2005. www.sarai.net/events/ip_conf/. Accessed 13 March 2022.

Scott, Gini Graham, *Internet Book Piracy: The Fight to Protect Authors, Publishers, and Our Culture* (New York: Allworth Press, 2016).

Siwek, Stephen E., 'The True Cost of Motion Picture Piracy to the U.S. Economy', Institute for Policy Innovation, Policy Report (3 October 2007), 186. www.ipi.org/ipi_issues/detail/the-true-cost-of-copyright-industry-piracy-to-the-us-economy. Accessed 13 March 2022.

Soares, Cecília, 'Discussing Piracy Today: Between the Concept and the Socioeconomic System' (2009). https://capitalismoamarillo.files. wordpress.com/2009/02/soares-cecilia-discussing-piracy-today.pdf. Accessed 13 March 2022.

Sollfrank, Cornelia, and Felix Stalder, 'Introduction', in Cornelia Sollfrank, Felix Stalder, and Shusha Niederberger (eds), *Aesthetics of the Commons* (Zurich: Diaphanes, 2021), 11–38.

Stempel, Jonathan, 'British Man Gets 22 Months in Prison over Global Movie Piracy: U.S. Judge', Reuters News Agency (8 February 2022). www.reuters.com/world/british-man-gets-22-months-prison-over-global-movie-piracy-us-judge-2022-02-07/. Accessed 13 March 2022.

Stephenson, Neal, *Snow Crash* (New York: Del Rey, 2000 [1992]).

Stevenson, Robert Louis, *Treasure Island* (Calgary, AB: Qualitas Classics, 2010).

Strangelove, Michael, *The Empire of Mind: Digital Piracy and the Anti-Capitalist Movement* (Toronto: University of Toronto Press, 2005).

Swartz, Aaron, 'Guerrilla Open Access Manifesto' (2008). https://archive. org/stream/GuerillaOpenAccessManifesto/Goamjuly2008_djvu.txt. Accessed 13 March 2022.

Terranova, Tiziana, *Network Culture: Politics for the Information Age* (New York: Pluto Press, 2004).

Turner, Fred, *From Counterculture to Cyberculture: Stewart Brand, the Whole Earth Network, and the Rise of Digital Utopianism* (Chicago: University of Chicago Press, 2006).

Vaidhyanathan, Siva, *Copyrights and Copywrongs: The Rise of Intellectual Property and How it Threatens Creativity* (New York: New York University Press, 2003).

Van der Sar, Ernesto, 'Piracy Icon ETTV Officially Shuts Down Due to a Lack of Funds', *TorrentFreak* (6 February 2022). https:// torrentfreak.com/piracy-icon-ettv-officially-shuts-down-due-to-a-lack-of-funds-220206/. Accessed 13 March 2022.

WAREZ 无形帝国. www.cnblogs.com/yaoz/p/11320520.html. Accessed 13 March 2022.

Wark, McKenzie, *A Hacker Manifesto* (Cambridge, MA: Harvard University Press, 2004).

Weyl, Glen, 'The Political Philosophy of RadicalxChange', *RadicalxChange* (19 December 2019). https://blog.radicalxchange.org/blog/posts/2019-12-30-gqx4th/. Accessed 13 March 2022.

Willinsky, John, *The Access Principle: The Case for Open Access to Research and Scholarship* (Cambridge, MA: MIT Press, 2006).

Wilson, Peter Lamborn, *Utopies pirates: corsaires, maures et renegados* (Paris: Éditions Dagorno, 1998).

Witt, Stephen Richard, *How Music Got Free: A Story of Obsession and Invention* (London: Penguin, 2015).

3 Creating Piracy: Discourse, Property, and Extra-Legal Territory

Michael D. High

In a representative passage on the presumed relationship between intellectual property and piracy, the Australian jurist and law professor Stephen Waddams emphatically states that 'the taking of a photograph, the rebroadcasting of television signals, the use of confidential information, or the copying of a design cannot, in fact or in law, be piracy, robbery (on or off the highway), or theft, and if it were any of these things the rhetoric would be unnecessary'.[1] Likewise, the legal scholar Patricia Loughlan proclaims, 'The use of the term "pirate" is clearly metaphorical and not even the most naive of participants in the discourse of intellectual property could or would take it literally'.[2] This position, that the use of the term piracy is rhetorical when applied to the infringement of intellectual property, is widely held by legal studies scholars, rhetoricians, and many others who aim to counter the expansion of intellectual property rights. They hold that the conflation of infringement with the crime of piracy obscures the differences between the two activities and the bodies of law that underlie them, and they maintain that there is no moral equivalent between using another's ideas without permission and attacking a ship at sea. And they are certainly correct, if the focus is only on the separate laws and actions of maritime and intellectual piracy. But what if the use of the term 'piracy' is not rhetorical? Or, more accurately, what if the use of the term piracy is, in fact, always rhetorical and discursive? What if all claims of piracy not only make an argument but attempt to create and defend a property right? What if piracy is not situated in the action of

1   Stephen Waddams, *Dimensions of Private Law: Categories and Concepts in Anglo-American Legal Reason* (Cambridge: Cambridge University Press, 2003), 175.
2   Patricia Louise Loughlan, '"You Wouldn't Steal a Car": Intellectual Property and the Language of Theft', *European Intellectual Property Review* 29, no. 10 (2007), 401. See also Patricia Litman, *Digital Copyright* (Amherst, NY: Prometheus Books, 2006).

taking something (tangible or intangible) but in the act of declaring another person a pirate?

If we dare to be naive and approach both maritime and intellectual piracy as a homologous discursive phenomenon, then we can begin to understand the long history of extending property rights into extra-legal territories through claims of piracy. This chapter looks at the three phenomena that cohere in piracy: discourse, property, and extra-legal territories. While none of these is distinctly piratical, it is their imbrication that differentiates piracy from other forms of illegitimate appropriation. The first aspect, discourse, is the creation of social facts through speech, writing, and other forms of representation. It is the process through which humans make and remake the social world. The second aspect, property rights, are the rights in things (both tangible and intangible) that allow a person not only to use them but exclude others from them. Property rights allow for and limit appropriation, which is a fundamental action in which people must engage to survive and create. The third, extra-legal territory, is any region beyond which the law extends, such as the sea, the sky, and, previously, the intangible. These regions, because their material composition resists occupation, must be continuously projected, protected, and promulgated. After detailing how these three phenomena cohere in maritime piracy, this chapter then examines how they do so in intellectual piracy, and it ends with a consideration of a recently created form of piracy.

1 Discourse

Language does not just define the world; it also creates it. While some things, like atoms, mountains, and animals, would clearly exist without humans, many aspects of reality would not. Diplomas, presidents, and who is and is not a pirate, while clearly having an objective, social reality, could not exist as diplomas, governments, or pirates without language and social agreement. Without us, these would just be objects, blunt physical actualities. It is language that distinguishes them from each other, and it is social agreement that gives them different values, statuses, and uses. In 1955, J.L. Austin proposed that the performative aspects of language, which he called 'speech acts', contested the then prevalent notion that language was primarily concerned with the truth-value of statements.[3] At that time,

3   J.L. Austin, *How to Do Things with Words* (Cambridge, MA: Harvard University Press, 1975).

linguists and philosophers focused on whether a statement correctly described the world. However, according to Austin, the judging of a statement's validity should occur not only on the constative (true/false) axis, but also on the performative (felicitous/infelicitous) axis. Whereas the constative axis focuses on a speech act's truth value, the performative axis focuses on whether a speech act successfully fits the social conventions of its invocation. For a statement to be successful (i.e., felicitous), there 'must exist an accepted conventional procedure having a certain conventional effect, that procedure to include the uttering of certain words by certain persons in certain circumstances'.[4] The performative aspects of speech are *conventional*, as are the roles of the speaker and listener in the acceptance of such speech. If the speech act does not match convention, or it is not made in a socially conventional situation, it is likely to fail (i.e., be infelicitous).

John Searle, developing the work of Austin, has theorised in detail how the performative aspects of language produce the social world. Speech acts, or as he often calls them, 'performative utterances', produce many, if not all, of the important 'facts' of collective life. As Searle states, 'there are portions of the real world, objective facts in the world, that are only facts by human agreement. In a sense, there are things that exist only because we believe them to exist'.[5] These facts exist not only because humans have agreed upon them, but because humans have established institutions, such as language, governments, colleges, etc.,[6] which produce, maintain, and reproduce these facts' existence. Institutional facts even have a particular formula by which they operate: 'X counts as Y in context C', in which one thing counts as, or becomes an institutional fact, in a particular context.[7]

Searle calls speech acts that create institutional facts 'declarations', and they imbue language with a 'somewhat magical capacity' as they create the reality that they assert through the very act of asserting that reality.[8] Like Austin, Searle theorises that a declaration

4   Austin, *How to Do Things with Words*, 14.
5   John R. Searle, *The Construction of the Social Reality* (New York: Free Press, 1995).
6   Searle's conception of institutions is more expansive than the usual use of the term or how it is used in this chapter.
7   Searle, *Construction of the Social Reality*, 40.
8   John R. Searle, *Expressions and Meaning: Studies in the Theory of Speech Acts* (Cambridge: Cambridge University Press, 1979).

must conform to conventions and rules, particularly those of institutions. For example, a judge must declare a defendant guilty at the culmination of a trial for the defendant to become a felon. If the judge declares the defendant guilty at the beginning of the trial, or if someone other than a judge declares the defendant guilty, the declaration will not change the defendant into a felon. But Searle adds that the transformation that accompanies a declarative speech act is not simply the appending of a name or status, but also the creation of a 'function': the imposition of an entire system of obligations, values, and beliefs (or, in Searle's terminology, deontology).[9] In the trial example, the judge's declaration of the defendant's guilt transforms the defendant into a felon and obliges those who maintain the prison system to incarcerate the felon. As well, those in the society who acknowledge the validity of the criminal system will then treat the felon, to a greater or lesser degree, as a criminal: a person to be feared, ostracised, surveilled, etc. Due to the free and open nature of speech, anyone can make declarative speech acts. What determines the success of the declaration is whether others accept it, adopt it, or at least do not impede its status function (i.e., the duties that follow from it).

Searle's conception of speech acts reveals the underlying process of the construction of social reality, but it does not account for how this process is achieved in practice. Fortunately, Pierre Bourdieu has articulated how social actors compete and promote their view of the world through discursive contestations.[10] According to Bourdieu, recognition of groups, and recognition by groups, determine to a large degree how people experience social reality. Groups, collectivities, and institutions can affect the conventions of linguistic performance, while the isolated individual is much more limited in their ability to do so. When individuals speak on behalf of groups though, they draw on what Bourdieu deems symbolic power. The forms such power takes when considered legitimate – honour, title, respect, prestige, and recognition – grant an individual the ability to shape the world: 'The power to impose and to inculcate a vision of divisions, that is, the power to make visible and explicit social divisions that are implicit, is political power par excellence. It is the power to make groups, to manipulate the objective structure of

9   Searle, *Construction of the Social Reality*, 46.
10   Pierre Bourdieu, 'Social Space and Symbolic Power', *Sociological Theory* 7, no. 1 (1989), 14–25.

society'.[11] Symbolic power thus brings into existence groups out of the mass of individuals within a society and empowers those who are recognised by these constituted groups. For example, the concept of race has led to the domination of minority racial groups in Western society, affecting their freedom, enfranchisement, wealth accumulation, education, etc. Yet this racial division has also empowered civil rights activists to speak on behalf of their fellow group members and to argue for equal rights. Similarly, sexual identity not only separates the straight from the gay, enabling homophobic discrimination and violence, but also provides LGBTQA+ people with political categories around which to organise and advocate for civil rights.[12]

In modern societies, symbolic power functions diffusely, and various groups use their various forms of capital to affect perception. Economic capital, social capital (networks of relationships), and cultural capital (education, taste, speech, etc.), become symbolic capital when recognised as legitimate, and such recognition grants their bearers symbolic power.[13] Spokespeople, experts, officials, etc., are both granted power by and empower their groups. Affiliations and memberships contribute to the power to name, categorise, and make successful declarations. These groups, through their repeated utterances, create discourses, which are systems of representation that describe and shape the social world. As there are numerous groups within any society, as well as factions within groups (all with their own interests and relative amounts of capital), there will be conflicts and coalitions between different groups and factions as they produce and reproduce the social world. Thus, the groups in any society engage in a hegemonic struggle over reality through their production, reproduction, and rejection of discourses. The fights in the last few years over the meaning of terms like terrorist, thug, socialist, patriot, and, especially, pirate, testify to the importance of naming, categorising, and dividing individuals in the social, cultural, and political arenas. With their various capitals, groups petition the

11 Bourdieu, 'Social Space and Symbolic Power', 23.
12 Judith Butler has described this political/sexual self-identification as appearing 'under the sign of lesbian'. See Judith Butler, 'Imitation and Gender Insubordination', in Ann Garry and Marilyn Pearsall (eds), *Women, Knowledge, and Reality: Explorations in Feminist Philosophy* (New York: Routledge, 1996), 371.
13 Pierre Bourdieu, *Language and Symbolic Power*, ed. John B. Thompson, trans. Gino Raymond and Matthew Adamson (Cambridge, MA: Harvard University Press, 1991).

state, which is 'the holder of the monopoly not only of legitimate physical violence but also of legitimate symbolic violence'.[14] The state then, as the collective of collectives, ultimately has the most symbolic power, although the state itself is not monolithic and there are often conflicts between and within different agencies and governmental institutions.

In the case of piracy, it is the designating of another as pirate, or of another's action's as piratical, that creates pirates and piracy. A single, isolated designation does not have this power, but the sustained repetition of such designations by those with social capital does. A group that views another's actions as piratical, if they have enough power within their society, can change the perceptions of those actions and, possibly, convince the sovereign (individual or collective) of that society to assign a status function to that particular action. Several academics have noted the discursive construction of piracy. Alexander Dent proposes a loose framework for 'piracy's essence' in which speech plays a key role. Dent holds that piracy has three characteristics: it is a discursive performance, it involves the unauthorised use of goods or ideas, and it is a group affair.[15] Similarly, two historians studying maritime and intellectual piracy have hinted that the study of piracy should focus on speech acts. Philip de Souza, in *Piracy in the Graeco-Roman World*, structures his work around 'the use of the labels pirate and piracy in their historical and cultural contexts [...] to determine why the individuals or groups described as pirates have been labelled in this way'.[16] Likewise, Adrian Johns, in his magisterial work, *Piracy: The Intellectual Property Wars from Gutenberg to Gates*, does not detail acts per se, but rather acts that '*would* be grouped together as piratical'.[17] The only piracies that 'count' in his history are those that 'have been characterised as

---

14 Loïc J.D. Wacquant, 'From Ruling Class to Field of Power: An Interview with Pierre Bourdieu on *La noblesse d'État'*, *Theory, Culture, and Society* 10, no. 3 (1993), 40.

15 Although both Dent and I place importance on speech acts in the construction of piracy, Dent does not see them as being primary, as his focus remains on the supposed piratical action. Alexander Sebastian Dent, 'Introduction: Understanding the War on Piracy, or Why We Need More Anthropology of Pirates', *Anthropological Quarterly* 85, no. 3 (2012), 664.

16 Philip de Souza, *Piracy in the Graeco-Roman World* (Cambridge: Cambridge University Press, 2002), 2.

17 Adrian Johns, *Piracy: The Intellectual Property Wars from Gutenberg to Gates* (Chicago: University of Chicago Press, 2010), 19.

piratical by contemporaries themselves'.[18] The discursive approach to piracy proposed by these scholars and adopted in this book acknowledges that piracy does not reside in the supposed pirate or his (and, less frequently, her) actions, but rather in the designation of particular actions as piratical.

All human institutions work to construct reality. However, it is not sufficient only to focus on the discursive construction of piracy. As Searle describes, 'X counts as Y in context C', and the context of piratical designations involves not just the symbolic power of those declaring and being declared pirates, but also the actions at hand and the location of those actions. Declarations of piracy, both maritime and intellectual, are only felicitous when they claim the right to appropriate in extra-legal territories and claim the right to exclude others. Which is to say, language creates piracy when it lays claim to territory beyond sovereignty's traditional, land-based and physical dominion. This is the context of the declarative act, and it has been a very special context throughout history. As will be detailed in the following sections, the context of piracy is singular, in that it creates a property right in a territory that has been previously beyond the law.

2 Property

Although historians have disagreed as to whether rights are a universal phenomenon or a Western invention, it seems likely that all cultures, whether or not they have a term for the concept, have general ideas about duties and restrictions created through social relationships.[19] Which is to say, in order for humans to have relationships, to work together and to exist harmoniously, they must be able to expect certain kinds of behaviour from those around them; they must have rights. Whether or not these expectations develop into a rights discourse is largely dependent on the social institutions in the society, not the existence of such relationships. However, the universality of rights in general in no way guarantees the universality of particular rights, nor does it lead to the univer-sality of laws, which is to say formal, enforceable rules for ensuring the upholding of particular rights. As Duncan Ivison notes, 'rights

18 Johns, *Piracy*, 7.
19 See Joel Feinberg and Jan Narveson, 'The Nature and Value of Rights', *Journal of Value Inquiry* 4, no. 4 (1970), 243–60 and Margaret Gilbert, *Rights and Demands: A Foundational Inquiry* (Oxford: Oxford University Press, 2018).

presuppose a wider account of the social and political order in which they are to be situated. Rights presuppose community or, better yet, *communities*'.[20] The lack of universality of particular rights and laws and the existence of multiple communities inevitably leads to conflicts over what rights exist, how they are understood, and where they are acknowledged and legally enforced. Conflicts between communities with different conceptions of rights, as well as between communities with different laws, have undoubtedly occurred since the dawn of humanity. Therefore, just as rights have probably been a constant in human relationships, conflicts over rights have probably accompanied them. While disagreements can often be settled if parties have an interest in working together, if parties to a dispute about rights do not both see a benefit in compromising and there are no intervening social or legal structures, conflict is likely. When such conflicts happen, contestants often engage in discursive battles to legitimate their claim to the contested right and to delegitimise that of their opponent.

For piracy, the right at issue is that of property, and although there is no historical record detailing the origins of private property rights, there are explanations for how they arose. One earlier explanation attempts to understand their formation from a state of nature, in which, it is assumed, human beings owned everything in common.[21] Hugo Grotius, a seventeenth-century Dutch jurist who also wrote significantly about international law and piracy, posited that 'God gave to mankind in general, dominion overall the creatures of the earth, from the first creation of the world'.[22] According to Grotius, this state did not last and humans at one point made an agreement authorising the institution of private property, not unlike the social

20 Duncan Ivison, *Rights* (London: Routledge, 2014), 21.
21 This strain of reasoning differs, admittedly, from that of the Roman statesmen Cicero, who writes in *De Officiis*, 'There is, however, no such thing as private ownership established by nature, but property becomes private either through long occupancy (as in the case of those who long ago settled in unoccupied territory) or through conquest (as in the case of those who took it in war) or by due process of law, bargain, or purchase, or by allotment'. However, the natural law tradition, which dominated legal thought through the early modern period, attempted to locate the origins of law and morality in divine revelation, even if such things were never actually revealed. Marcus Tullius Cicero, *De Officiis*, trans. Walter Miller (Cambridge, MA: Harvard University Press, 1913), sect. 1.22.
22 Hugo Grotius, *On the Law of War and Peace*, trans. A.C. Campbell (Kitchener, ON: Batoche Books, 2001 [1814]), 72.

contract of later political theory.[23] This mythical agreement justified the exclusivity of ownership by one person despite the supposed biblical proclamation of communal property. Relatedly, Samuel Pufendorf, also a seventeenth-century jurist, claimed that in the state of nature no one owned anything, then humans agreed to communal ownership, only to later agree to private ownership, although he does not describe why this was the course of events.[24] It is worth noting though that both jurists attempted to justify the property system of their society, even though their Christian beliefs posited a different, divinely ordained order.

John Locke, whose views on property have been very influential in the United States, likewise believed in a communal state of nature. He, however, justified property in his *Two Treatises of Government* through the natural right of labour: 'Though the earth, and all inferior creatures, be common to all men, yet every man has a property in his own person: this no body has any right to but himself. The labour of his body, and the work of his hands, we may say, are properly his'.[25] Although the work of his hands may extend beyond the property of his body, Locke does not find a contradiction here, as 'he who appropriates land to himself by his labour, does not lessen, but increase the common stock of mankind'.[26] He does, however, add a proviso: 'for this labour being the unquestionable property of the labourer, no man but he can have a right to what that is once joined to, at least where there is enough, and as good, left in common for others'.[27] Locke's proviso hints at and attempts to account for the ethical issue at the heart of private property, which is that private property systems often result in an unequal distribution of wealth.

These theories, which are based on an unhistorical and unlikely state of nature, all posit an initial appropriation of property and then try to justify that appropriation. Modern philosophers have dubbed this initial act of appropriation *first acquisition*, as it marks the first possession in the chain of ownership that will eventually become a property system. Considering that humans evolved over hundreds of thousands of years, rather than existing wholly evolved

23 Grotius, *On the Law of War and Peace*, 75.
24 Samuel Pufendorf, *Of the Law of Nature and Nations: Eight Books*, ed. Jean Barbeyrac, trans. Basil Kennett (London, 1729), 362.
25 John Locke, *Two Treatises of Government*, Book II (London, 1689), sect. 5.27.
26 Locke, *Two Treatises of Government*, II, sect. 5.37.
27 Locke, *Two Treatises of Government*, II. sect. 5.27.

in a communal state of nature, the idea of an initial acquisition as an intentional action is problematic, but the moral conundrums produced by such a hypothetical act are very clear. First acquisition is morally unjustified because those who first appropriate land will be in a better economic position than those who later follow them, as there will ultimately come a time when there is not enough land or resources for everyone to appropriate. First acquisition is an appropriation that forecloses further appropriation, as there are natural physical limitations on the amount of land or objects available on earth. Temporal limitations ensure that latecomers (those born after initial occupiers) will be at an inherent disadvantage, excluded from the initial grab.[28] As such, the distribution of private property creates a serious ethical dilemma. To deny this injustice and obscure the initial seizure, Grotius hypothesised a pact, Pufendorf adopted it, and Locke qualified his labour-dessert theory with a provision for the lack of abundance. However, as several commentators have noticed, Locke devised his theory of labour to justify the expropriation of land in the new world, and his theory would not have actually applied to England, his own country, because at that time all of the land in the country was already claimed.[29] It is clear that these philosophical justifications for private property, regardless of their plausibility, fail to account for initial acquisition limiting the ability of late comers to equally acquire. As such, later philosophers have insisted that there is an aporia at the heart of private property, one for which there 'is no Holy Grail',[30] no philosophical justification or moral defence.[31]

More recently, legal studies scholars have proposed a theory for how property rights develop that is based on rational transactions between actors. Harold Demsetz, in an article entitled 'Toward a Theory of Property Rights', details the development of private hunting rights amongst the indigenous peoples of Quebec during the eighteenth century. As demand for furs increased with Europeans colonising the surrounding areas, a private system developed to accommodate the increasing demand, thus replacing a previously common hunting

---

28   See John T. Sanders, 'Justice and the Initial Acquisition of Property', *Harvard Journal of Law & Public Policy* 10 (1987), 377.
29   See Peter Garnsey, *Thinking about Property: From Antiquity to the Age of Revolution* (Cambridge: Cambridge University Press, 2007), 144.
30   Garnsey, *Thinking about Property*, 175.
31   Sanders, 'Justice and the Initial Acquisition of Property', 369.

system. From this history, Demsetz then claims that property rights arise as a response to externalities, as an attempt to internalise them and prevent the inefficient sharing of common resources. With the increased demand for furs spurring increased hunting, the move to private hunting grounds by native peoples ensured that the animals would not be overhunted, thereby internalising the externality caused by increased demand. According to this narrative, while communal ownership of a resource can function well when people are known to each other and have developed an equilibrium in relation to their shared resource, when people do not know each other or when a new technology or situation changes the nature of demand and production, the use of the resource will become inefficient and probably result in a tragedy of the commons. Or, as Demsetz puts it in relation to land, 'Negotiating costs will be large because it is difficult for many persons to reach a mutually satisfactory agreement, especially when each hold-out has the right to work the land as fast as he pleases'.[32] Whereas, Demsetz claims, a private owner will take into account future uses and economise fully without having to negotiate with others, communal owners must agree to abridge their use of the property, must actually do so, and must police those who do not, all of which increase costs. As such, private property is more efficient at managing costs and maximising benefits than communal or state property regimes.

Although this efficiency theory has been largely accepted in legal studies, it does not explain all the mechanisms for the creation of private property. Terry L. Anderson and Peter J. Hill have expanded Demsetz's theory to include not just a response to externalities but also the production of property rights to capture previously unnoticed rents. They note that the successful entrepreneur is 'the person who is alert to Ricardian rents that are not seen by others and are available from better defined and enforced property rights. Just as the entrepreneur sees and produces products that generate net consumer and producer surplus, he can also see and establish property rights that eliminate open access dissipation of these rents'.[33] Although this expansion of Demsetz's theory is still concerned with economic efficiency, and assumes all economic efficiency produces

---

32 Harold Demsetz, ''Toward a Theory of Property Rights', *American Economic Review* 57, no. 2 (1967), 354.

33 Terry L. Anderson and Peter J. Hill, 'Cowboys and Contracts', *Journal of Legal Studies* 31, no. S2 (2002), S489–S514.

consumer benefit, it nonetheless acknowledges that property rights do not result solely from managing externalities but also from the capture of rights due to entrepreneurial initiative. Stuart Banner, noticing that the transition between property regimes often produces large management costs, argues that 'societies reallocate property rights when some exogenous political realignment enables a powerful group to grab a larger share of the pie'.[34] Which is to say, those powerful enough to benefit from a transition bear the brunt of the initial costs and therefore make valuations that benefit themselves: 'A powerful oligarchy can thus overcome the problem of administrative cost simply by not being particularly rigorous in the valuation and assignment of the property rights of the majority'.[35] Thus, the transition between property regimes is enacted in a way that minimises costs, and benefits those managing the transition, otherwise no such transition would occur. Whether one looks at the transition to private property during the great enclosure of Europe or following European colonisation of the Americas, the transition is political, initiated by the ruling members of society for their own benefit.

Similarly, Saul Levmore writes that the efficiency theory of property is one story, but not the only one, for understanding how such rights develop.[36] There is another story that is much more suspicious: 'private property and closed access may in fact have emerged not because they were efficient, or not yet efficient, but instead because some of those who stood to gain from closed access could not buy out the losers but nevertheless succeeded in encouraging the government to close access on their behalf'.[37] This special interest story is arguably more convincing than Demsetz's theory, because it is likely that special interest groups lobbying for privatisation will offer to share gains with those in power, thereby making privatisation appear more attractive to them. These different responses to Demsetz's theory demonstrate that the creation of property rights, which may produce efficiency and social utility later, create injustices in the transition that are unlikely to be addressed. Like the theory of initial acquisition, the efficiency theory

---

34   Stuart Banner, 'Transitions between Property Regimes', *Journal of Legal Studies* 31, no. S2 (2002), S360.
35   Banner, 'Transitions between Property Regimes', S369.
36   Saul Levmore, 'Two Stories about the Evolution of Property Rights', *Journal of Legal Studies* 31, no. S2 (2002), S421–S451.
37   Levmore, 'Two Stories about the Evolution of Property Rights', S429.

for the development of private property fails to fully address the moral issues created by the denying of access to those who cannot capture the initially created rights.

Regardless of how it is believed to develop, private property always leads to inequities, because private property is fundamentally concerned with the right to exclude. According to Oliver Wendell Holmes, Jr, one of the most revered and influential Supreme Court Justices in US history, 'The notion of property [...] consists in the right to exclude others from interference with the more or less free doing with it as one wills'.[38] Similarly, legal scholars have repeatedly insisted on the centrality of exclusion to private property. Morris R. Cohen bluntly states that 'the essence of private property is always the right to exclude others',[39] and Thomas W. Merrill argues that the right to exclude is not just one of the essential aspects of property: 'it is the *sine qua non*. Give someone the right to exclude others from a valued resource, i.e., a resource that is scarce relative to the human demand for it, and you give them property. Deny someone the exclusion right and they do not have property'.[40] The right to exclude is what gives property its value, yet it is also what makes it unjust.

The fundamental moral problem with property rights is that they restrict the appropriation of others for one's own benefit (i.e., exclude).[41] This is a fundamental and intractable problem, because appropriation is necessary for human life. Unable to sustain ourselves, humans must take from nature and other humans: they must appropriate. As appropriation is essential to human survival and flourishing, control over appropriation is a fundamental form of power. It is, and this is not hyperbole, the control over life and death. Not surprisingly, many philosophers have railed against the inequalities created by private property. Jean Jacques Rousseau deemed property the source of all 'crimes, wars, murders [...] miseries and horrors'.[42] Pierre-Joseph

---

38 *White-Smith Music Publishing Co.* v. *Apollo Co.*, 209 U.S. 1, 28 S. Ct. 319, 52 L. Ed. 655 (1908).

39 Morris R. Cohen, 'Property and Sovereignty', *Cornell Law Quarterly* 13 (1927), 12.

40 T.W Merrill, 'Property and the Right to Exclude', *Nebraska Law Review* 77 (1998), 730–55.

41 Some writers on property rights see the right to exclude as being *the* fundamental right of property.

42 Jean Jacques Rousseau, *A Discourse on a Subject Proposed by the Academy of Dijon: What is the Origin of Inequality Among Men, and Is It Authorised by Natural Law?* trans. G.D.H. Cole (London, 1754).

Proudhon famously declared 'property is robbery'.[43] And Karl Marx and Fredrich Engels argued for its abolishment in the *Communist Manifesto*.[44]

Although scholars have long engaged in debate over the right to exclude, there have been few attempts by anyone to theorise appropriation in and of itself, perhaps because it is so fundamental to existence. The little scholarly work on appropriation that exists focuses on cultural appropriation, which is the taking of ideas and forms from a culture other than one's own. In their situating of cultural appropriation, Bruce H. Ziff and Pratima V. Rao observe that the meaning of appropriation is 'open-ended', that it 'concerns relationships among people', that it occurs through a wide range of modes, and that it is pervasive.[45] It is open-ended because what defines culture is dependent on legal status, society, and perspective. It is relational in that it involves relationships between stakeholders, particularly between individuals in Western conceptions of cultural appropriation. It occurs through a range of modes, in that what counts as appropriation, particularly in reference to culture, involves many kinds of taking (from wholesale theft of cultural relics to the borrowing of generic forms). And it is pervasive because all artists take from others to create. All these aspects of cultural appropriation can be applied to appropriation in general, and they demonstrate that appropriation is, very simply, inescapable.

Thus, to exclude people from some property naturally creates a conflict when there are people who lack property, and very quickly after a private property regime is established (if not before) inequities will develop. There will thus always be a discord between legal rights about property and the moral right to property. Which is to say, there is an underlying tension between the legal rights of private property holders, which grant the right to exclude others, and the moral right everyone has to sustain and develop their own life. This is an important distinction, because as the rights theorist Hillel Steiner relates, theories of moral rights 'have constitutional

---

43 P.-J. Proudhon, *What is Property? An Inquiry into the Principle of Right and of Government*, trans. Benjamin R. Tucker (New York: Dover, 1970).

44 Karl Marx and Friedrich Engels, *Manifesto of the Communist Party*, in *Marx and Engels: Selected Works*, vol. 1, trans. Samuel Moore (Moscow: Progress Publishers, 1969), 98–137.

45 Bruce H. Ziff and Pratima V. Rao, *Borrowed Power: Essays on Cultural Appropriation* (New Brunswick, NJ: Rutgers University Press, 1997), 3.

reference',[46] which is to say, moral rights are the ground upon which legal rights are justified. If legal rights do not uphold moral rights, they risk being viewed as unjust, because 'moral rights are, so to speak, the instantiating progeny of justice'.[47] Modern nation states have attempted to rectify the inequities of private property through many different forms of social welfare; however, increases in wealth and income inequality globally over the past 30 years demonstrate that these attempts have been stymied by vested interests.

The tension between the moral right to appropriate and the legally enshrined right to exclude creates a mirroring between theft and property, whereby both can be viewed as moral and immoral. This is why the tale of Robin Hood continues to fascinate, why the gangster's meteoric rise and eventual decline continues to make great cinema, and why the pirate is often viewed variously as a villain and a hero. Shannon Lee Dawdy and Joe Bonni see this moral ambiguity as being a key feature of pirates, as well as of pirates' appeal.[48] They link the recent resurgence in piracy, and the widespread cultural celebration of piracy, to the excesses of neoliberal capitalism, and situate the bivalent reception of piracy in their definition of it: piracy is *'a form of morally ambiguous property seizure committed by an organized group* which can include thievery, hijacking, smuggling, counterfeiting, or kidnapping'.[49] This view of piracy, as an ambivalent reaction to the excesses of capitalism, helps to explain why piracy and the interest in it grow and wane at different times and why pirates have often been championed in popular culture. However, this view continues to see piracy as primarily an action rather than as a result of a discursive act which claims a right. As well, it fails to note that all theft can be viewed as morally ambiguous, depending on one's position.

More importantly, any theory of piracy is incomplete without considering sovereignty. This may seem counterintuitive, as piracy is concerned with private property, but the ownership of private property is, in many aspects, a form of sovereignty. The seminal English jurist William Blackstone, in what is probably the most widely quoted statement on property, conflates the rights of the

---

46 Hillel Steiner, 'Moral Rights', in David Copp (ed.), *The Oxford Handbook of Ethical Theory* (Oxford: Oxford University Press, 2006), 460.

47 Steiner, 'Moral Rights', 460.

48 Shannon Lee Dawdy and Joe Bonni, 'Towards a General Theory of Piracy', *Anthropological Quarterly* 85, no. 3 (2012), 673–700.

49 Dawdy and Bonni, 'Towards a General Theory of Piracy', 695.

property owner with that of the sovereign: 'There is nothing which so generally strikes the imagination, and engages the affections of mankind, as the right of property; or that sole and despotic dominion which one man claims and exercises over the external things of the world, in total exclusion of the right of any other individual in the universe'.[50] Here, Blackstone makes explicit the emotive link between sovereignty and property, the common feeling that property grants sovereignty to the property owner. As many have pointed out, though, property rights do not grant 'sole and despotic dominion'.[51] Property rights are a subordinate form of sovereignty; the property owner must bend to the will of the sovereign. Due to this, property can be expropriated by the state, and there are limits on how exclusionary different forms of property can be. Yet this does not fundamentally negate the fact that property is still a form of sovereignty. As Cohen makes very clear in his mediation on the relationship between the two,

> The money needed for purchasing things must for the vast majority be acquired by hard labour and disagreeable service to those to whom the law has accorded dominion over the things necessary for subsistence [...] we must not overlook the actual fact that dominion over things is also imperium over our fellow human beings.
>
> The extent of the power over the life of others which the legal order confers on those called owners is not fully appreciated by those who think of the law as merely protecting men in their possession. Property law does more. It determines what men shall acquire.[52]

Here, Cohen collapses the distinction between dominion and imperium that existed in Roman law, and which informs modern legal thinking. He articulates very clearly how the modern rent seeker holds similar power to the feudal lord, able to control the lives of those who must use his property. The next section will discuss how sovereign power creates and, reflexively, needs the pirate to justify extensions of domain beyond established territory.

50 William Blackstone, *Commentaries on the Laws of England*, vol. 2 (Oxford: Clarendon Press, 1765), chap. 1, para. 2.
51 Cohen, 'Property and Sovereignty' and Keith Aoki, '(Intellectual) Property and Sovereignty: Notes Toward a Cultural Geography of Authorship', *Stanford Law Review* 48 (1996), 1293–355.
52 Cohen, 'Property and Sovereignty', 12.

3 Extra-Legal Territory

In the beginning of his study of ancient piracy, de Souza notes that ancient Greeks often used the same words to describe banditry and piracy. This prompts him to ask what, fundamentally, separates the two activities? He answers, 'piracy involves the use of *ships*, which require greater initial commitment of resources and offer a greater range of freedom of opportunity to the would-be plunderers than can be obtained from wholly land-based activities'.[53] Yet to view the use of ships as the differentiating feature of piracy puts the cart before the horse. It is not the use of ships but rather the territory in which piracy takes place that separates it from other forms of theft. Theft, banditry, robbery, etc., take place on land, and as such they are more embedded in society (physically and normatively) than piracy, which takes place on the sea, in the air, and probably someday in space. To understand the similarities between maritime and intellectual piracy, as well why the term piracy has been used to describe so many different forms of appropriation, it is essential to see it as concerned with the expansion of sovereignty into extra-legal territories.

The English word *pirate* comes from the Latin *pirata*, which is itself derived from the Ancient Greek word *peirates* (πειρατής). *Peirates* is related to *peira* (πειράω), 'to make an attempt, endeavour, try', and *peiratn* (πειρατῶν), 'pierce, run through'.[54] Yet, as de Souza and other historians of ancient piracy have detailed, *peirates* is not the only ancient Greek word used to describe pirates, nor was it commonly used in the ancient epics.[55] While the two related words *peira* and *peiratn* appear in epics from the Mycenaean Age (1100–600 BCE), *peirates* first appears in inscriptions in the third century BCE,[56] and only becomes common once the Roman Republic exerts influence in the Mediterranean, thereafter occurring frequently in Polybius' *The Histories* (c.170 BCE), Strabo's *Geography* (c.18 CE), and Plutarch's *Lucullus* (c.75 CE).[57] Before *peirates* became common, Homer and other

---

53 de Souza, *Piracy in the Graeco-Roman World*, 11.
54 Henry George Liddell and Robert Scott, *An Intermediate Greek–English Lexicon* (Oxford: Clarendon Press, 1889).
55 de Souza, *Piracy in the Graeco-Roman World*, 9–11.
56 Henry A. Ormerod, *Piracy in the Ancient World* (Baltimore, MD: Johns Hopkins University Press, 1996), 59n2.
57 The classical Greeks (500–300 BCE) did have a word that only meant pirate, καταποντιστής (literally, 'one who throws into the sea') (Liddell and Scott), which appears in Isocrates writing in the late fifth century BCE. The word

ancient Greeks authors used *leistes* (Ληστής), literally 'robber', to describe both banditry *and* piracy. In Latin, the Romans used *pirata* like the Greeks used *peirates*, inconsistently and often interchangeably with the term *praedo*, which literally meant 'one that makes booty, a plunderer, robber' and could be applied to both bandits and pirates.[58] The semantic conflation of piracy and banditry signals a similarity between the spaces in which these kinds of activities occurred for the people who described them. The Greeks of this time, having neither dominion over the sea nor the area outside of their city states, often conflated pirates and bandits. Although the Romans were much better able to extend and control their territory, and though they used both the Greek and Latin terms that solely described theft at sea more frequently, the continued use of the more encompassing terms *liestes* and *praedones* reveals that they viewed much of the territory beyond their cities and roads similarly to the way they viewed the seas: beyond their control.

As the Romans attempted to expand their empire and gain dominion over more territory, they naturally encountered and created more bandits. According to Brent D. Shaw, in the Roman Empire the space of the bandit was the gap between the 'Roman Society' and the 'Roman State': the disjunction between the two 'resulted most often from geopolitical factors that inhibited the state from effectively extending its networks of communication and control over whole regions'.[59] Bandits arose not from actions or individual choices, but rather from competing systems of relation and definition: the 'ebb and flow of state-defined power in the ancient Mediterranean which automatically created, in the very process of definition, groups of men called bandits'.[60] As Rome solidified control and developed its territories, more aspects of local societies came under its purview

must not have been common, as it does not appear often in other texts. When it does appear, in Isocrates and Demosthenes (384–322 BCE), it appears next to *leistes* or *peltastai* (πελταστής) (mercenaries; literally, 'one who carries a light shield') (Liddell and Scott). The word only becomes common much later, around the end of the Roman Republic in the writing of Pausanias, Lucian, Claudius Aelianus, and Cassius Dio. All statements of word usage refer to the statistics compiled by the *Perseus Digital Library*'s searchable texts and index.

58   Charlton Thomas Lewis, William Freund, and Charles Short, *A Latin Dictionary: Founded on Andrews' Edition of Freund's Latin Dictionary* (Oxford: Clarendon Press, 1879).
59   Brent D. Shaw, 'Bandits in the Roman Empire', *Past & Present* 105 (1984), 42.
60   Shaw, 'Bandits in the Roman Empire', 35.

and supervision, reducing the space of disjunction. As this happened, Roman law ceased to treat the bandit as a non-person and instead, once he became some form of Roman subject, treated him as a criminal.[61]

As Shaw depicts, and as many other commentators have noted of piracy, it is conflicting regimes and claims that create special criminal categories. Rudolph Durand and Jean-Philippe Vergne claim that 'as a state seeks to expand its reach, the number of individuals it considers to be pirates tends to increase [...] [and piracy] appears precisely at the point where territorial space and the normative network emanating from a sovereign authority meet'.[62] Piracy is thus, like banditry, intimately bound up with legal and physical dominion over a territory. However, banditry has largely disappeared from modern legal and cultural discourse. Today, when state sovereignty is the global, normative form of sovereignty, and almost all land on the planet is part of a sovereign state, or claimed by one, banditry is no longer relevant.

Notably, piracy has not disappeared, and it is unlikely it will ever be subsumed under another legal category. The physical difference of the sea undermines humans' ability to dominate it. There are no people whose domain is the sea; it cannot be held. It has no fixity and, in a certain sense, no history, as it cannot be settled, colonised, or controlled without unceasing effort. A person cannot even float on the sea in the same spot without being buffeted back and forth by the current. The sea is thus a threat to those in power on land, as it is never in place, it is never ordered and proper, and it is never secure. The sea's physical composition precludes any kind of stability to its surface or interior.[63] Any attempt at control of the sea will always be contingent on land-based stability, extending from the shore or up from the ocean floor.

Thus, the sea has a fundamentally different *nomos*, or order, than the land.[64] The instability and mutability of the sea accounts for the lack of any universally binding maritime or international law. As the

61 Shaw, 'Bandits in the Roman Empire', 6–8.
62 Rodolphe Durand and Jean-Philippe Vergne, *The Pirate Organization: Lessons from the Fringes of Capitalism* (Boston: Harvard Business School Press, 2012), 39.
63 Leif Dahlberg, 'Pirates, Partisans, and Politico-Juridical Space', *Law and Literature* 23, no. 2 (2011), 262–81.
64 See Carl Schmitt, *The Nomos of the Earth in the International Law of the Jus Publicum Europaeum*, trans. G.L. Ulmen (New York: Telos Press, 2003).

German Jurist Carl Schmitt writes, 'In every case, land-appropriation, both internally and externally, is the primary legal title that underlies all subsequent law [...] Land appropriation thus is the archetype of a constitutive legal process externally (vis-à-vis other peoples) and internally (for the ordering of land and property within a country)'.[65] All law and sovereignty comes, inevitably, from the forceful acquisition and occupation of land.[66] It is dominion over an area that establishes the rule of law, and creates the basis for production (which is impossible without appropriation of resources). As dominion over land is the basis of sovereignty, and hence law, any attempt to rule the sea will be a wishful projection onto a physical order that cannot maintain it. While it is possible to mark places within the ocean through the geographic coordinate system of longitude and latitude, that system exists in reference to the stability of land, particularly to the longitude of Greenwich, in England, and therefore the history of land-based British colonial power. Those coordinated places within the sea are not of the sea, but rather laid on it. The opposition between land and sea, the essential incongruence of the *nomos* of the earth and the *nomos* of the water, creates the distinct space of maritime piracy, as opposed to that of banditry, although both partake of the same action (i.e., appropriation).

The fact that the pirates operate outside of land and hence sovereign territory is partially why the pirate has received such a special status in legal and political discourse. Daniel Heller-Roazen, writing of piracy's 'paradigm', stresses that it is the pirate's actions 'outside regions of ordinary jurisdiction' that disrupt the normal distinctions between criminal and political.[67] Because the pirate operates outside normal legal spaces, he appears as a different kind of antagonist, one who is dealt with by the justice system *and* by the military. This, according to Heller-Roazen, helps to explain why the pirate has historically been perceived as a universal enemy of humankind, as the *hostis humani generis*, and was therefore able to be seized and executed by anyone. This epithet is generally credited to the Roman statesmen

65 Schmitt, The Nomos of the Earth, 46.
66 As the seminal theorist of space, Henry Lefebvre, articulates, 'Sovereignty implies "space", and what is more it implies a space against which violence, whether latent or overt, is directed – a space established and constituted by violence'. Henri Lefebvre, *The Production of Space*, trans. Donald Nicholson-Smith (Oxford: Blackwell, 1991), 280.
67 Daniel Heller-Roazen, *The Enemy of All: Piracy and the Law of Nations* (New York: Zone Books, 2009), 11.

and orator Cicero,[68] who writes in *De Officiis*, 'for a pirate [*pirata*] is not included in the number of lawful enemies, but is the common foe of all the world; and with him there ought not to be any pledged word nor any oath mutually binding'.[69] However, Cicero does not write *hostis humani generis*, but actually *communis hostis omnium*: common enemy of all. *Hostis humani generis* is actually a later emendation by the fourteenth-century Italian Jurist Bartolus de Saxoferrato, which adds a provocative nuance to its meaning. Dan Edelstein, tracing the history of the phrase, reveals that it originally referenced the Devil and not the pirate. Appearing in Christian texts as early as the fourth century CE, the use of *hostis humani generis* for the Devil links the pirate with 'a menace to each and every soul', a menace for which 'the imperative for extermination [is] all the greater'.[70] As the original Christian figure both outside and inside the cosmological order, the Devil occupies a special position as the figure which, through his evilness, helps to define God's goodness. Relatedly, Robert Elliot Mills has detailed how the pirate has functioned rhetorically as a negative identification for the sovereign, as the constitutive other of the modern order: 'sovereignty is predicated upon the simultaneous existence of its opposite, the anti-sovereign: the pirate'.[71] The pirate has thus been crucial in Western legal discourses, functioning as the opposite of the sovereign. Not surprisingly, many of the important early modern legal scholars, like Grotius, Pufendorf, and de Saxoferrato, wrote extensively on property, sovereignty, and piracy, demonstrating the critical relationship between these three phenomena: the pirate stands against the sovereign and his little reflection, the property owner, defining, constituting, and justifying their power.

Yet, as is nicely illustrated by St Augustine's parable of the pirate and the emperor, the difference between the pirate and the sovereign is, at least initially, normative:

> Indeed, that was an apt and true reply which was given to Alexander the Great by a pirate who had been seized. For when

---

68 Alfred P. Rubin, *The Law of Piracy* (Newport, RI: Naval War College Press, 1988), 10.

69 Cicero, *De Officiis*, sect. 3.107.

70 Dan Edelstein, *The Terror of Natural Right: Republicanism, The Cult of Nature, and The French Revolution* (Chicago: University of Chicago Press, 2009), 31.

71 Robert Elliot Mills, 'The Pirate and the Sovereign: Negative Identification and the Constitutive Rhetoric of the Nation-State', *Rhetoric & Public Affairs* 17, no. 1 (2014), 108.

that king had asked the man what he meant by keeping hostile possession of the sea, he answered with bold pride, 'What thou meanest by seizing the whole earth; but because I do it with a petty ship, I am called a robber, whilst thou who dost it with a great fleet art styled emperor'.[72]

This normative difference is something that other writers have also noted. As Heller-Roazen details, ancient Greek laws of reprisal and asylum from reprisal were not meant to end the practice of capturing ships and goods, but rather to formalise it.[73] Thus, in the ancient world, what separated piracy from legitimate capture was social and legal authority, not territory, action, or justice.[74] Similarly, the signing of the Treaty of Westphalia in 1648 formalised and codified state sovereignty at exactly the same moment that European powers were colonising the Americas.[75] The codification of state sovereignty actually helped legally to enable colonialism because an essential aspect of modern state sovereignty is 'reciprocal recognition' by other states: a state or any entity that is not recognised by other states is not entitled to be respected and treated as an autonomous power.[76] As such, the development of state sovereignty not only created the nation state, it also created its opposite: the territory that could be raided with impunity. Correspondingly, claims of piracy during the colonial period proliferated, and the pirate became an important figure in literature and popular songs. Today, piracy continues to occur in

72 Augustine of Hippo, *The City of God*, ed. Philip Schaff (Edinburgh: T&T Clarke, 1888).
73 Heller-Roazen, *Enemy of All*, 41–56.
74 As Heller-Roazen relates, this is not a modern projection onto the past: 'More than once, ancient authors present the rise of commonwealths as marking not the end of acts of depredation but their formal and lasting establishment'. Heller-Roazen, *Enemy of All*, 42.
75 In its modern conception, state sovereignty coalesces with the rise of the nation state and the collapse of the Holy Roman Empire's political authority in the sixteenth and seventeenth centuries. European monarchs, and their lawyers, philosophers, and statesmen, developed the idea of state sovereignty to escape the power of the pope and the church, which exerted its authority without regard to territory. In this conception, a sovereign is an absolute authority within a bounded territory and a sovereign state has a permanent population. A government is independent from outside influence and is recognised by other sovereign states. See Robert Jackson, *Sovereignty* (Cambridge: Polity Press, 2007).
76 Immanuel Maurice Wallerstein, *World-Systems Analysis: An Introduction* (Durham, NC: Duke University Press, 2004), 44.

places where sovereignty is contested or difficult to maintain,[77] such as in parts of Indonesia and the Philippines, were archipelagos make holding and policing territory difficult, and in the waters of failed states, like Somalia. As these different examples illustrate, territory, sovereignty, and piracy are fundamentally intertwined.

4 Intellectual Piracy

As detailed in the beginning of this chapter, many scholars have insisted that maritime and intellectual piracy are different because they described infractions of different kinds of laws. Western legal codes treat private property and intellectual property separately, and the use of the term 'intellectual property' is itself a relatively recent invention. In the nineteenth century, the different forms of intellectual property were viewed and described as statutory monopolies: monopolies that were dangerous but nonetheless necessary for the public interest.[78] Another reason scholars and jurists have argued that private property and intellectual property are dissimilar is intellectual property has mechanisms to alleviate the inequities produced by initial acquisition. Limits on patents and copyrights, exemptions for fair use, and licensing schemes can reduce the control granted and provide for the public interest. These mechanisms, which allow for a public domain of ideas from which people can appropriate, mitigate the temporal and sufficiency problems inherent in tangible property. However, over the last century there has occurred a 'propertisation' of intellectual property, in which its role as a public utility has receded and its conceptualisation and treatment as a property right have increased.[79] This propertisation has worked to return intellectual property to its original, unmitigated form of control, which was inherent in 'literary property' when it was first created in Britain in the sixteenth century.[80]

The current intellectual property system was not born of the desire to control the exchange of books, but rather to limit ideas. In 1557, Mary Tudor granted a royal charter to the Worshipful

77 Bjørn Møller, *Piracy, Maritime Terrorism and Naval Strategy*, DIIS Report (Danish Institute for International Studies, 2009), 13.

78 William W. Fisher, 'The Growth of Intellectual Property: A History of the Ownership of Ideas in the United States', *Eigentum im internationalen Vergleich* (1999), 20.

79 Fisher, 'The Growth of Intellectual Property', 20.

80 Johns, *Piracy*, 38.

Company of Stationers and Newspaper Makers of London, a livery company or guild of booksellers, bookbinders, and printers. The company created by the charter, the Stationers' Company, thereafter had the de jure monopoly on publishing, although they already controlled the trade to a large extent.[81] The charter granted them two important rights: first, it granted the Stationers' Company the exclusive right to establish alienable, perpetual copyrights in books that they registered in their register book, and second, the right to search any property they suspected of printing books illegally and, finding such books, to seize and destroy them and the presses that printed them.[82] The second right was the reason for the first. Mary Tudor granted the charter to the Stationers so that they would censor seditious, treasonable, and heretical material, particularly that of Protestants. The Stationers became, thus, the agents of the government, with their monopoly as reward for their role as royal censor.[83] The Stationers' monopoly was extended and amended over the next 150 years through a series of decrees and licensing acts, many of which were more concerned with newspapers than with book publishing. After the Glorious Revolution of 1688, England's Parliament enacted (partial) religious tolerance and government censorship of the book trade was no longer necessary.

During the intervening years, the Stationers' monopoly on printing angered many as rising literacy rates created a lucrative market for literature. In 1694, the Licensing Act of 1662 lapsed and the Stationers' Company petitioned for a renewal, which Parliament ignored and continued to ignore thereafter. When Parliament finally acted in 1709, it crafted the Statute of Anne, which was significantly different than the previous law. The new statute aimed to destroy the Stationers' monopoly and ensure that authors had some control over the publication of their works. Although the booksellers still maintained control of the book trade through the purchase of rights from authors, the rights were now vested in the authors, not the publisher, and the copyright term was now limited to an initial 14

---

81 Cyprian Blagden, *The Stationers' Company: A History, 1403–1959* (Stanford, CA: Stanford University Press, 1977).

82 The Stationers' Company Charter (1557), www.stationers.org/news/features/the-stationers-company-charter (9 June 2021).

83 Craig Joyce and L. Ray Patterson, 'Copyright in 1791: An Essay concerning the Founders' View of the Copyright Power Granted to Congress in Article I, Section 8, Clause 8 of the US Constitution', *Emory Law Journal* 52, no. 909 (2003), 910–52.

years with the allowance of a renewal for another 14 years by the author. As the title of the new statute demonstrates ('An Act for the Encouragement of Learning, by Vesting the Copies of Printed Books in the Authors or Purchasers of such Copies, during the Times therein mentioned'),[84] Parliament acknowledged that learning and creation necessitated a common stock of ideas and texts from which to take. They legally enshrined the creation of new ideas through the appropriation of old.[85] This act changed copyright from a perpetual, absolute right to a limited, utilitarian, and collective one, thereby creating the public domain.[86] By granting authors a limited monopoly over their works, it ensured the incentive to create, and by limiting the term of copyright the statute ensured the public a continually expanding collective resource from which to appropriate. Thus, it made literary property more just.

The Statute of Anne would later influence the American founding fathers and the copyright clause of the US Constitution: 'To promote the Progress of Science and useful Arts, by securing for limited Times to Authors and Inventors the exclusive Right to their respective Writings and Discoveries'.[87] Unfortunately, US copyright law has slowly abandoned its utilitarian and collective aspects. At the beginning of the last century, due to the increasing complexity of the law, Congress primarily ceded the legislation of copyright law to industry representatives. These representatives, naturally, crafted laws that protected their interests and limited the laws' ability to adapt to changing practices and technologies.[88] Most importantly, by ceding legislation to industry represent-atives, Congress abdicated its responsibility to ensure the public benefit of copyright that was enshrined in the Constitution.[89] Over the last hundred years in the United States, Congress has signifi-cantly extended copyright limitations, penalties, and the nature of infringement. From an original 14 years plus a 14-year renewal, the current term is the life of the author plus 70 years. If the work is made for hire (i.e., contracted by a company), the term is 95 years from publication or 120 years from creation, whichever is shorter.

---

84 Copyright Act 1710.
85 Justin Hughes, 'The Philosophy of Intellectual Property', *Georgetown Law Journal* 77 (1988), 287–366.
86 Joyce and Patterson, 'Copyright in 1791', 914.
87 United States Constitution, Article I, Section 8, Clause 8.
88 Litman, *Digital Copyright*.
89 Fisher, 'The Growth of Intellectual Property', 20.

Assuming a life of 80 years and publication at age 30, copyright terms have thus increased 8.57 times, and 4.28 times if renewed. Copyright now surpasses the author's period of creative production (i.e., their life) by as long as they might have lived, decoupling copyright protection from any incentive to create. Damages have increased from 107:1 to 4,285:1 for regular infringement and 21,428:1 for wilful infringement. A criminal offence for commercial infringement, originally added in 1897, now extends to non-commercial infringement, and that criminal offence has since changed from a misdemeanour to a felony.[90] By continually extending copyright terms, and even retroactively extending some terms, many key cultural works have been prevented from entering the public domain, and if things continue it is possible that many corporations will be able to lobby to keep their works, and many others, from entering it.[91]

Patent law was likewise intended to ensure incentives for creation and to allow for a robust public domain. Patents protect the implementation of specific ideas, even if those ideas have been independently produced by others.[92] Because patents provide for the control of technologies and medicines that are necessary for personal survival and societal and economic development, their period of protection is much briefer than that of copyright. The current patent terms in the United States are 20 years for industrial patents and 15 years for design patents. Even with such short terms though, the patent system still enables forms of control and inefficiencies that harm the public interest. As several critics have noted, the control over scientific knowledge through patents, especially as patent law has expanded to cover genetic material, restricts the ability to research.[93] The refusal of patent holders to license patents to others can and has stifled technological development.[94] Most importantly, patents in medicine can

90   I. Trotter Hardy, 'Criminal Copyright Infringement', *William & Mary Bill of Rights Journal* 11, no. 1 (2002), 305–41.
91   Specialised copyright licences, like the Creative Commons License, allow for non-standard copyrights, but they do not actually replace the original copyright, which is granted instantly at the time of creation – they only modify it.
92   Michele Boldrin and David K. Levine, *Against Intellectual Monopoly* (Cambridge: Cambridge University Press, 2008), 8.
93   Peter Drahos and John Braithwaite, *Information Feudalism: Who Owns the Knowledge Economy* (New York: Routledge, 2017).
94   Drahos and Braithwaite, *Information Feudalism*, 76.

allow for rent-seeking behaviour that increases their price astronom-ically and can, in general, prevent medicines from reaching people who need them.

Although this chapter focuses primarily on the Anglophone law, this is not just an American, English, and Australian issue. The United States not only exports its intellectual property, but also its intellectual property law, through treaties, trade agreements, and economic pressure. Over the last 100 years, the United States has become the most aggressive proponent of international IP treaties, often mandating other nations change their national laws to receive trade benefits, thereby undermining (or at least impinging) foreign sovereignty to fit US interests.[95] The fair use of limited parts of texts for education, criticism, or parody mitigates the closure of the public domain to some extent, but fair use and fair dealing, its less flexible Commonwealth counterpart, are common law provisions, which can only be used as a defence after a copyright infringement suit has been brought. Onerous and expensive litigation can easily have a chilling effect on those who would appropriate fairly or on emerging competitors by patent holders.[96]

Rather than see this as a recent change to intellectual property, it is better to understand it as its underlying goal. Unlike physical property, intellectual property is a non-rivalrous good: it cannot be used up. As such, the entire intellectual property system exists to create scarcity in ideas. By granting intellectual property owners the power to restrict how others use ideas, states create the scarcity necessary for profit. Without this scarcity, intellectual property loses its value.[97] This is not to say that there are no other ways to incentivise production of ideas, but rather that current intellectual property regimes only recognise the value created by those very same regimes. As Mark Rose relates, the production of authorship in the creation of copyright entailed 'the abstraction of the concept of literary property from the physical book and then the presentation of this new, immaterial property as no less fixed and certain than

---

95 Shujen Wang, *Framing Piracy: Globalization and Film Distribution in Greater China* (Lanham, MD: Rowman & Littlefield, 2003).

96 The Lumen Database, a project at the Berkman Klein Center for Internet & Society at Harvard University (in partnership with the Electronic Frontier Foundation), documents cease and desist orders of online content at https://lumendatabase.org.

97 Christopher May, *The Global Political Economy of Intellectual Property Rights: The New Enclosures* (New York: Routledge, 2015), 45.

any other kind of property'.[98] Yet intellectual property is not fixed and certain, like physical property.[99] A person can build walls around the edge of their property, but not around their ideas, just as a nation can build walls around its territory to mark and defend it, but it cannot build walls around the sea. The constant vigilance of copyright holders, the need to unceasingly police their intellectual property, is the correlative of a navy's ceaseless patrols on the sea. In fact, the only way to control the adoption and proliferation of an idea is not to share or benefit from it. Preventing the appropriation of intellectual property, like maintaining sovereignty over the sea and air, is an impossibility, and the staggering and ever increasing rhetorical, legal, and technological means employed to protect IP testify not to its security but to its vulnerability.

The long history of intellectual property may have obscured its origins as a radical extension of the law and as a control regime, but as texts have become digital, once again claims of piracy have become the main means to constrain the spread of information and to claim ever new territories. The legal scholar Timothy Wu convincingly argues that discussions of copyright often miss the importance of copyright's 'communications policy': 'copyright's poorly understood role in regulating competition among rival disseminators'.[100] Throughout its history, copyright has functioned as a mechanism for limiting or encouraging competition that arises from the development of new dissemination technologies. Depending on how the law is interpreted or enforced, copyright can enable incumbent industries to stifle competition from emerging competitors or enable market entrants to compete with incumbents and innovate in ways that the incumbents either cannot or do not. In these struggles, the incumbents naturally call their new competitors 'pirates', as the newcomers profit from the dissemination of incumbents' content, and emerging competitors

---

98 Mark Rose, *Authors and Owners: The Invention of Copyright* (Cambridge, MA: Harvard University Press, 1993), 7.

99 Rose also states, 'After all, authors do not really create in any literal sense, but rather produce texts through complex processes of adaptation and trans-formation. Literary property is not fixed and certain like a piece of land. Indeed, not even the notion of landed property [...] is ever simple or certain. All forms of property are socially constructed and, like copyright, bear in their lineaments the traces of the struggles in which they were fabricated'. Rose, *Authors and Owners*, 8.

100 Timothy Wu, 'Copyright's Communications Policy', *Michigan Law Review* 103 (2004), 279.

complain about being stifled by incumbent industries. Again and again, the development of a new technology shows this pattern, whether it be the complaints of musicians against piano roll manufacturers, complaints of the Motion Picture Association against Sony and other video tape manufacturers, or the more recent lawsuits of the recording industry against Napster. This is particularly important, as the pace of technological change has quickened, and because a historical view of the development of incumbent disseminators shows that previous pirates often become incumbents who themselves later make claims of piracy.[101] What copyright's communication policy demonstrates, although only if looked at historically, is that piracy is relative: that claims of piracy are based on one's position in the market, not on the morality or justice of the claim. Or, as Peter Decherney insists, it is important when thinking about new media to ask, 'Which forms of piracy today will be tomorrow's norms? Which of today's pirates will be tomorrow's media moguls?'[102]

Digital technology has made communication policy more important and piracy more prominent because it has separated information from its analogue container. Digital technology breaks the bond between the ideational and the material, freeing content from its physical cage and making it infinitely reproducible. Of course, to distribute digital content a material substrate is still required, with computers and servers containing and reproducing the information that moves between them in the wires and on the electromagnetic waves that form a network. However, once it is freed from its analogue container, information becomes more like ideas themselves: available to all.

The sea and the immaterial realm of ideas are examples of what Gilles Deleuze and Félix Guattari term smooth spaces.[103] Smooth spaces are amorphous, non-formal, and heterogeneous. One does not occupy a smooth space but rather moves through it, as nomads move through the desert without settling it. By their nature, these spaces resist occupation, and as such deterritorialise other spaces. Deleuze and Guattari contrast smooth spaces with striated ones, which are the

---

101 Wu, 'Copyright's Communications Policy', 278–84.

102 Peter Decherney, 'Copyright Dupes: Piracy and New Media in *Edison* v. *Lubin* (1903)', *Film History: An International Journal* 19, no. 2 (2007), 123.

103 Gilles Deleuze and Pierre Félix Guattari, *A Thousand Plateaus: Capitalism and Schizophrenia*, vol. 2 (Minneapolis: University of Minnesota Press, 1987), 474–500.

sedentary spaces of the state and of military manoeuvres: organised, formal, and homogeneous, with clear horizontal and vertical lines, epitomised by longitude and latitude, and capable of long order vision, constant orientation, and movement between points along lines. Not surprisingly, Deleuze and Guattari find the sea to be 'a smooth space par excellence', just as the 'city is the striated space par excellence'.[104] For them, however, the two spaces are not mutually exclusive: 'the two spaces in fact exist only in mixture: smooth space is constantly being translated, transversed into striated space; striated space is constantly being reversed, returned to a smooth space'.[105] The striated constantly traverses the smooth and smoothness results from maximum striation. Territorialisation and deterritorialisation are in constant tension, always working upon each other.

Although Deleuze and Guattari do not mention the pirate, the pirate is very similar to the nomads they focus on, moving from place to place but not settling, resisting the order and restrictions of the nomos of the earth. It is therefore possible to understand maritime piracy as appropriation in smooth spaces, while theft, expropriation, land reform, and enclosure correlate to appropriation in the striated spaces of the state. This spatial dialectic explains why early banditry and piracy were semantically identical: both took place in smooth spaces, but once land became a straited space of the state banditry faded away. Intellectual piracy similarly takes place in the once smooth space of extra-legal territories that sovereigns, governments, and property holders have brought under their control.

5 The Creation of Biopiracy

In the early 1990s, The Rural Advancement Foundation International (RAFI), a Canadian non-governmental organisation focused on development, agriculture, and technology, created a new form of piracy. In 1993, they released a communiqué entitled 'Bio-Piracy: The Story of Natural Coloured Cottons of the Americas',[106] in which

104 Deleuze and Guattari, *A Thousand Plateaus*, 479, 481.
105 Deleuze and Guattari, *A Thousand Plateaus*, 474.
106 Rural Advancement Foundation International, 'Bio-Piracy: The Story of Natural Coloured Cottons of the Americas' (November 1993). Whether this is the first use of the term is unclear. Considering that the word appears only in the title of the document and in the hyphenated form that would later be abandoned, it is most likely the initial published usage. For a discussion of the history of the term and the difficulty determining its exact origin, see Paul

the term 'bio-piracy' referred to the burgeoning practice of Western individuals and corporations monopolising the knowledge and genetic resources of indigenous peoples through intellectual property. RAFI continued to use the term in its communiqués and papers, and shortly thereafter the Research Director of RAFI published a piece in *Biotechnology and Development Monitor* entitled '1993: A Landmark Year for Biodiversity or Biopiracy?'[107] The next year, RAFI produced a study for the United Nations Development Program entitled *Conserving Indigenous Knowledge: Integrating Two Systems of Innovation*, which used the term repeatedly.[108] The *Financial Times* and *Pharma Marketletter* both reported on the study, using the term 'biopiracy' in the titles of their articles.[109] At roughly the same time, James O. Odek published an article in the *Journal of Intellectual Property Law* entitled 'Bio-Piracy: Creating Proprietary Rights in Plant Genetic Resources'.[110] Then, in 1997, the Indian scholar and activist Vandana Shiva published *Biopiracy: The Plunder of Nature and Knowledge*, which popularised the term even further.[111]

Shiva's work most clearly articulates biopiracy. For her, it is not the theft of property, but rather the establishment and use of private property to exploit indigenous peoples. In *Biopiracy*, she argues that transnational corporations and Western governments were attempting, and largely succeeding, in repeating the plunder of the non-European world that occurred during the colonial period: 'Five hundred years

Oldham, 'Biopiracy and the Bioeconomy', in Peter Glasner, Paul Atkinson, and Helen Greenslade (eds), *New Genetics, New Social Formations* (New York: Routledge, 2006), 114–37.

107 Hope Shand, '1993: A Landmark Year for Biodiversity or Biopiracy?', *Biotechnology and Development Monitor* 17 (1993), 24. The *Biotechnology and Development Monitor* was a quarterly magazine published by the University of Amsterdam and the Netherland's Ministry of Foreign Affairs.

108 Rural Advancement Foundation International, *Conserving Indigenous Knowledge: Integrating Two Systems of Innovation* (New York: Rural Advancement Foundation International, 1994).

109 Frances Williams, '"Bio-Piracy" Costs Third World $5.4bn a Year', *Financial Times* (28 October 1994), 7 and 'The Costs of "Bio-Piracy" to the Third World', *Pharma Marketletter* (19 December 1994). Note that both uses of the term in the titles are in quotation marks, signalling the novelty and tentativeness of it.

110 James O. Odek, 'Bio-Piracy: Creating Proprietary Rights in Plant Genetic Resources', *Journal of Intellectual Property Law* 2, no. 1 (1994), 141–81.

111 Vandana Shiva, *Biopiracy: The Plunder of Nature and Knowledge* (Boston: South End Press, 1997).

after Columbus, a more secular version of the same project of colonisation continues through patents and intellectual property rights'.[112] The West uses international agreements like the General Agreement on Tariffs and Trade, private and maximalist notions of property rights, and circumscribed and inaccurate conceptions of creativity to plunder the knowledge of non-Western people and prohibit the collective use of nature. These mechanisms represent the continuation of the colonialist practices begun by Christopher Columbus and Sir Walter Raleigh, though they are now marshalled by the United States Trade Representative and Monsanto. This new enclosure movement, which attempts to render the knowledge of indigenous people as nature, and therefore open for pirating, will undoubtedly result in a similar oppression and dispossession as the earlier colonial encounter. To RAFI, Shiva, and others, the capture of the right to use traditional knowledge and to prevent the use of that knowledge is piracy, even though there were no rights protecting collective knowledge when they first popularised the term.

The idea summed up in the term 'biopiracy' was not novel when RAFI began popularising it. In 1988, Jack R. Kloppenburg, Jr published an anthology about the subject: *Seeds and Sovereignty: Debate Over the Use and Control of Plant Genetic Resources*. A year later, Calestous Juma published *The Gene Hunters: Biotechnology and the Scramble for Seeds*, and RAFI's own Cary Fowler and Pat Mooney published *The Threatened Gene: Food, Politics, and the Loss of Genetic Diversity* in 1990.[113] Although none of these works featured the term, the idea was present in all of them, waiting for lexicalisation. Despite that fact that other phrases such as 'biotheft', 'bioplunder', and 'biorobbery' were possible neologisms, they did not ultimately become popular.[114] RAFI and others ultimately seized on 'biopiracy' as it was the term that best

112 Shiva, *Biopiracy*, 1.
113 Jack R. Kloppenburg, Jr, *Seeds and Sovereignty: Debate Over the Use and Control of Plant Genetic Resources* (Durham, NC: Duke University Press, 1988); Calestous Juma, *The Gene Hunters: Biotechnology and the Scramble for Seeds* (Princeton, NJ: Princeton University Press, 1989); and Cary Fowler and Pat Mooney, *The Threatened Gene: Food, Politics, and the Loss of Genetic Diversity* (Cambridge: Lutterworth Press, 1990).
114 RAFI even produced a paper with the title, 'COPs... and Robbers', referring to the exploitation of the members to the Convention on Biological Diversity, who were designated as the Conference of the Parties [i.e., COPs]. Rural Advancement Foundation International, 'COPs... and Robbers. Transfer-Sourcing Indigenous Knowledge: Pirating Medicinal Plants', Occasional Paper Series, 1, no. 4 (Ottawa: RAFI, 1994).

fit the structure of the phenomenon, allowing these activists to claim a right that did not previously exist.

RAFI and the activists who popularised 'biopiracy' have been very successful in their discursive campaign. By 1997, Alexander Cockburn, writing in *The Nation*, noted, 'Biopiracy, a term barely in use five years ago, has become a central theme in the politics of First and Third World debates over biodiversity'.[115] The term is now widely recognised outside academia and political movements, as it is now used by media outlets to report on the exploitation of biological and genetic material in the developing world.[116] The United Nations has even added an amendment, named the Nagoya Protocol, to the Convention on Biological Diversity mandating the sharing of benefits with the countries from which traditional knowledge comes. The success has not been total, however. The economy of the United States has benefited greatly from American corporations' bioprospecting. Therefore, the United States has never ratified the Convention on Biological Diversity, which limits its applicability to American companies. In this struggle to create and legitimise a new form of piracy, the symbolic power of the US government and its legal authority and influence outweigh that of all other contestants.

6 Conclusion

To summarise, declarative speech acts not only perform actions but also create institutional facts. These institutional facts become social reality if they fit the conventions of the society in which they are uttered and if those uttering them have the correct, conventional social roles. Groups with more symbolic power, with more recognition by members of a society, are better able to shape conventions and therefore better able to establish social reality through discourse. Although appropriation is an essential human activity, property systems

---

115 Alexander Cockburn, 'Bill Burroughs and the Biopirates', *Nation* 265, no. 1 (1997), 8.

116 See, for instance, Anthony Barnett, 'Biopiracy in Africa', *Guardian* (22 September 2006), www.theguardian.com/world/2006/sep/22/outlook.develop ment; Rajeshree Sisodia, 'Biopiracy in India: The Case of the Aubergine', *Al Jazeera* (31 October 2011), www.aljazeera.com/opinions/2011/10/31/biopiracy-in-india-the-case-of-the-aubergine; and Janna Rose, 'Biopiracy: When Indigenous Knowledge is Patented for Profit', *The Conversation* (7 March 2016), https://theconversation.com/biopiracy-when-indigenous-knowledge-is-patented-for-profit-55589.

initiated by those in power or with the collaboration of those in power institutionalise and make real the right to exclude, creating legitimate and illegitimate appropriation and the corresponding criminal categories of theft, banditry, piracy, etc. Yet because appropriation is essential, property is always morally ambiguous, and those who are excluded from initial appropriation are likely to reject such a system in whole or in part and to discursively contest it. Piracy is distinctly different from other forms of illegitimate appropriation, necessitating different laws and enforcement mechanisms. What separates maritime and intellectual piracy from other forms of illegitimate appropriation are the formerly extra-legal territories in which they take place: on the sea and in the intangible realm of ideas, smooth spaces that resist occupation and domination.

If maritime and intellectual piracy are considered not as distinct actions or legal categories but rather as the result of attempts to create a property right in an extra-legal territory, they reveal a long history of homologies, shared discursive strategies, and shared motivations on the part of sovereigns, governments, and property owners. This discursive approach to piracy demonstrates that piracy is created not by a theft but rather by a group of people claiming the right to appropriate (and the right to exclude others from appropriating) in a previously ungoverned territory, whether that territory is a physical or intangible region previously beyond the scope of law. This approach not only accounts for why the term piracy has been used to describe things as separate as maritime predation and the copying of digital files but also explains why new piracies will continue to arise. As long as legal regimes rise and fall, power extends to new territories, and people attempt to enclose and protect new forms of property, new pirates will be created.

Select Bibliography

Anderson, Terry L., and Peter J. Hill, 'Cowboys and Contracts', *Journal of Legal Studies* 31, no. S2 (2002): S489–S514.

Aoki, Keith, '(Intellectual) Property and Sovereignty: Notes Toward a Cultural Geography of Authorship', *Stanford Law Review* 48 (1996): 1293–355.

Augustine of Hippo, *The City of God*, ed. Philip Schaff (Edinburgh: T&T Clarke, 1888).

Austin, J.L., *How to Do Things with Words* (Cambridge, MA: Harvard University Press, 1975).

Banner, Stuart, 'Transitions between Property Regimes', *Journal of Legal Studies* 31, no. S2 (2002), S359–S371.

Barnett, Anthony, 'Biopiracy in Africa', *Guardian* (22 September 2006) www.theguardian.com/world/2006/sep/22/outlook.development. Accessed 20 October 2022.

Blackstone, William, *Commentaries on the Laws of England*, vol. 2 (Oxford: Clarendon Press, 1765).

Blagden, Cyprian, *The Stationers' Company: A History, 1403–1959* (Stanford, CA: Stanford University Press, 1977).

Boldrin, Michele, and David K. Levine, *Against Intellectual Monopoly* (Cambridge: Cambridge University Press, 2008).

Bourdieu, Pierre, 'Social Space and Symbolic Power', *Sociological Theory* 7, no. 1 (1989): 14–25.

—. *Language and Symbolic Power*, ed. John B. Thompson, trans. Gino Raymond and Matthew Adamson (Cambridge, MA: Harvard University Press, 1991).

Butler, Judith, 'Imitation and Gender Insubordination', in Ann Garry and Marilyn Pearsall (eds), *Women, Knowledge, and Reality: Explorations in Feminist Philosophy* (New York: Routledge, 1996), 371–87.

Cicero, Marcus Tullius, *De Officiis*, trans. Walter Miller (Cambridge, MA: Harvard University Press, 1913).

Cockburn, Alexander, 'Bill Burroughs and the Biopirates', *Nation* 265, no. 1 (1997): 8.

Cohen, Morris R., 'Property and Sovereignty', *Cornell Law Quarterly* 13 (1927): 8–30.

'The Costs of "Bio-Piracy" to the Third World', *Pharma Marketletter* (19 December 1994).

Dahlberg, Leif, 'Pirates, Partisans, and Politico-Juridical Space', *Law and Literature* 23, no. 2 (2011): 262–81.

Dawdy, Shannon Lee, and Joe Bonni, 'Towards a General Theory of Piracy', *Anthropological Quarterly* 85, no. 3 (2012): 673–700.

Decherney, Peter, 'Copyright Dupes: Piracy and New Media in Edison v. Lubin (1903)', *Film History: An International Journal* 19, no. 2 (2007): 109–24.

Deleuze, Gilles, and Pierre Félix Guattari, *A Thousand Plateaus: Capitalism and Schizophrenia*, vol. 2 (Minneapolis: University of Minnesota Press, 1987).

Demsetz, Harold, 'Toward a Theory of Property Rights', *American Economic Review* 57, no. 2 (1967): 347–59.

Dent, Alexander Sebastian, 'Introduction: Understanding the War on Piracy, or Why We Need More Anthropology of Pirates', *Anthropological Quarterly* 85, no. 3 (2012): 659–72.

de Souza, Philip, *Piracy in the Graeco-Roman World* (Cambridge: Cambridge University Press, 2002).

Drahos, Peter, and John Braithwaite, *Information Feudalism: Who Owns the Knowledge Economy* (New York: Routledge, 2017).

Durand, Rodolphe, and Jean-Philippe Vergne, *The Pirate Organization: Lessons from the Fringes of Capitalism* (Boston: Harvard Business School Press, 2012).

Edelstein, Dan, *The Terror of Natural Right: Republicanism, The Cult of Nature, and The French Revolution* (Chicago: University of Chicago Press, 2009).

Feinberg, Joel, and Jan Narveson, 'The Nature and Value of Rights', *Journal of Value Inquiry* 4, no. 4 (1970): 243–60.

Fisher, William W., 'The Growth of Intellectual Property: A History of the Ownership of Ideas in the United States', *Eigentum im internationalen Vergleich* (1999), 1–20.

Fowler, Cary, and Pat Mooney, *The Threatened Gene: Food, Politics, and the Loss of Genetic Diversity* (Cambridge: Lutterworth Press, 1990).

Garnsey, Peter, *Thinking about Property: From Antiquity to the Age of Revolution* (Cambridge: Cambridge University Press, 2007).

Gilbert, Margaret, *Rights and Demands: A Foundational Inquiry* (Oxford: Oxford University Press, 2018).

Grotius, Hugo, *On the Law of War and Peace*, trans. A.C. Campbell (Kitchener: Batoche Books, 2001 [1814]).

Hardy, I. Trotter, 'Criminal Copyright Infringement', *William & Mary Bill of Rights Journal* 11, no. 1 (2002): 305–41.

Heller-Roazen, Daniel, *The Enemy of All: Piracy and the Law of Nations* (New York: Zone Books, 2009).

Hughes, Justin, 'The Philosophy of Intellectual Property', *Georgetown Law Journal* 77 (1988): 287–366.

Ivison, Duncan, *Rights* (London: Routledge, 2014).

Jackson, Robert, *Sovereignty* (Cambridge: Polity Press, 2007).

Joyce, Craig, and L. Ray Patterson, 'Copyright in 1791: An Essay Concerning the Founders' View of the Copyright Power Granted to Congress in Article I, Section 8, Clause 8 of the US Constitution', *Emory Law Journal* 52, no. 909 (2003): 910–52.

Juma, Calestous, *The Gene Hunters: Biotechnology and the Scramble for Seeds* (Princeton, NJ: Princeton University Press, 1989).

Kloppenburg, Jack R., Jr, *Seeds and Sovereignty: Debate Over the Use and Control of Plant Genetic Resources* (Durham, NC: Duke University Press, 1988).

Lefebvre, Henri, *The Production of Space*, trans. Donald Nicholson-Smith (Oxford: Blackwell, 1991).

Levmore, Saul, 'Two Stories about the Evolution of Property Rights', *Journal of Legal Studies* 31, no. S2 (2002): 421–51.

Lewis, Charlton Thomas, William Freund, and Charles Short, *A Latin Dictionary: Founded on Andrews' Edition of Freund's Latin Dictionary* (Oxford: Clarendon Press, 1879).

Liddell, Henry George, and Robert Scott, *An Intermediate Greek–English Lexicon* (Oxford: Clarendon Press, 1889).

Litman, Patricia, *Digital Copyright* (Amherst, NY: Prometheus Books, 2006).

Locke, John, *Two Treatises of Government* (London, 1689).

Loughlan, Patricia Louise, '"You Wouldn't Steal a Car": Intellectual Property and the Language of Theft', *European Intellectual Property Review* 29, no. 10 (2007): 401–5.

Marx, Karl, and Friedrich Engels, *Manifesto of the Communist Party*, in *Marx and Engels: Selected Works*, vol. 1, trans. Samuel Moore (Moscow: Progress Publishers, 1969), 98–137.

May, Christopher, *The Global Political Economy of Intellectual Property Rights: The New Enclosures* (New York: Routledge, 2015).

Merrill, T.W., 'Property and the Right to Exclude', *Nebraska Law Review* 77 (1998): 730–55.

Mills, Robert Elliot, 'The Pirate and the Sovereign: Negative Identification and the Constitutive Rhetoric of the Nation-State', *Rhetoric & Public Affairs* 17, no. 1 (2014): 105–35.

Møller, Bjørn, *Piracy, Maritime Terrorism and Naval Strategy*, DIIS Report (Danish Institute for International Studies, 2009). www.econstor.eu/bitstream/10419/59849/1/591900467.pdf. Accessed 20 October 2022.

Odek, James O., 'Bio-Piracy: Creating Proprietary Rights in Plant Genetic Resources', *Journal of Intellectual Property Law* 2, no. 1 (1994): 141–81.

Oldham, Paul, 'Biopiracy and the Bioeconomy', in *New Genetics, New Social Formations*, ed. Peter Glasner, Paul Atkinson, and Helen Greenslade (New York: Routledge, 2006), 114–37.

Ormerod, Henry A., *Piracy in the Ancient World* (Baltimore, MD: Johns Hopkins University Press, 1996).

Proudhon, P.-J., *What is Property? An Inquiry into the Principle of Right and of Government*, trans. Benj. R. Tucker (New York: Dover, 1970).

Pufendorf, Samuel, *Of the Law of Nature and Nations: Eight Books*, ed. Jean Barbeyrac, trans. Basil Kennett (London, 1729).

Rose, Janna, 'Biopiracy: When Indigenous Knowledge is Patented for Profit', *The Conversation* (7 March 2016). https://theconversation.com/biopiracy-when-indigenous-knowledge-is-patented-for-profit-55589. Accessed 10 October 2022.

Rose, Mark, *Authors and Owners: The Invention of Copyright* (Cambridge, MA: Harvard University Press, 1993).

Rousseau, Jean Jacques, *A Discourse on a Subject Proposed by the Academy of Dijon: What Is the Origin of Inequality among Men, and Is It Authorised by Natural Law?* (Discourse on Inequality), trans. G.D.H. Cole (London, 1754). https://aub.edu.lb/fas/cvsp/Documents/DiscourseonInequality.pdf879500092.pdf. Accessed 20 October 2022.

Rubin, Alfred P., *The Law of Piracy* (Newport, RI: Naval War College Press, 1988).

Rural Advancement Foundation International, 'Bio-Piracy: The Story of Natural Coloured Cottons of the Americas' (Ottawa: RAFI, 1993). www.etcgroup.org/sites/www.etcgroup.org/files/publication/496/01/raficom34cotton.pdf. Accessed 20 October 2022.

—. *Conserving Indigenous Knowledge: Integrating Two Systems of Innovation* (New York: Rural Advancement Foundation International, 1994).

—. 'COPs… and Robbers. Transfer-Sourcing Indigenous Knowledge: Pirating Medicinal Plants', Occasional Paper Series, 1, no. 4 (Ottawa: RAFI, 1994). www.etcgroup.org/sites/www.etcgroup.org/files/publication/483/01/occ_vol1no4_1994_copsrobbers.pdf. Accessed 20 October 2022.

Sanders, John T., 'Justice and the Initial Acquisition of Property', *Harvard Journal of Law & Public Policy* 10 (1987): 367–99.

Schmitt, Carl, *The Nomos of the Earth in the International Law of the* Jus Publicum Europaeum, trans. G.L. Ulmen (New York: Telos Press, 2003).

Searle, John R., *Expressions and Meaning: Studies in the Theory of Speech Acts* (Cambridge: Cambridge University Press, 1979).

—. *The Construction of the Social Reality* (New York: Free Press, 1995).

Shand, Hope, '1993: A Landmark Year for Biodiversity or Biopiracy?', *Biotechnology and Development Monitor* 17 (1993): 17–24.

Shaw, Brent D., 'Bandits in the Roman Empire', *Past & Present* 105 (1984): 3–52.

Shiva, Vandana, *Biopiracy: The Plunder of Nature and Knowledge* (Boston: South End Press, 1997).

Sisodia, Rajeshree, 'Biopiracy in India: The Case of the Aubergine', *Al Jazeera* (31 October 2011). www.aljazeera.com/opinions/2011/10/31/biopiracy-in-india-the-case-of-the-aubergine. Accessed 20 October 2022.

The Stationers' Company Charter (1557). www.stationers.org/news/features/the-stationers-company-charter (9 June 2021). Accessed 20 October 2022.

Steiner, Hillel, 'Moral Rights', in *The Oxford Handbook of Ethical Theory*, ed. David Copp (Oxford: Oxford University Press, 2006), 459–79.

Wacquant, Loïc J.D., 'From Ruling Class to Field of Power: An Interview with Pierre Bourdieu on *La noblesse d'État*', *Theory, Culture, and Society* 10, no. 3 (1993): 19–44.

Waddams, Stephen, *Dimensions of Private Law: Categories and Concepts in Anglo-American Legal Reason* (Cambridge: Cambridge University Press, 2003).

Wallerstein, Immanuel Maurice, *World-Systems Analysis: An Introduction* (Durham, NC: Duke University Press, 2004).

Wang, S., *Framing Piracy: Globalization and Film Distribution in Greater China* (Lanham, MD: Rowman & Littlefield, 2003).

White-Smith Music Publishing Co. v. *Apollo Co.*, 209 U.S. 1, 28 S. Ct. 319, 52 L. Ed. 655 (1908).

Williams, Frances, '"Bio-Piracy" Costs Third World $5.4bn a Year', *Financial Times* (28 October 1994): 7.

Wu, Timothy, 'Copyright's Communications Policy', *Michigan Law Review* 103 (2004): 278–366.

Ziff, Bruce H., and Pratima V. Rao, *Borrowed Power: Essays on Cultural Appropriation* (New Brunswick, NJ: Rutgers University Press, 1997).

4 Pirates of Society

Markus Heidingsfelder

> Property was thus appall'd
> That piracy was not the same
>
> (loosely based on Shakespeare, 'The
> Phoenix and the Turtle')

1 Introduction

The theoretical figure of the observer used in this text is neither a substance nor a person, but the theorist who, first, makes the statements concerning the phenomenon of piracy in the following, and second, assigns all these statements to three system references: the economy, the law, and piracy itself.[1]

This theoretical figure is invoked because it allows and forces the social construction of piracy to be contingent on the one hand, and to refer to a specific address of construction on the other. If one engages in it, one gives up the assumption of an observation-free point of view. The projection of the world turns out to be site-dependent, it does not result from itself anymore. The same is true for the social systems that are constructed in this text: the law, the economy, and piracy are also figures of theory. Just like the observer, the figure of the system allows constructions of reality to be reconstructed, in this case the realities of the above systems, because they are not only observed by the theorist as systems, these systems also observe themselves. The guiding question of research then is: how and in what form do the economy and the law observe piracy? In other words, how and in what form does piracy occur in these systems? How does piracy observe the law and the economy? And how does this system observe itself?

---

1   For reasons of space, I exclude the detailed discussion of politics in this essay, as it mainly concerns the spatial areas of application, i.e., the territorial scope of legal regulations. Only the last section will deal more extensively with the political function of piracy, as a large fraction of pirate theorists argue primarily in political terms.

Granting piracy its own system status is likely to meet with scepticism from scientific observers, just as was the construction of terror and the Internet, i.e., the World Wide Web, as independent social systems, initiated by Peter Fuchs,[2] and of pop, as initiated by Fuchs and myself.[3] None of them was licensed by Niklas Luhmann, and for many systems theorists this accolade seems to make all the difference. Therefore, it should be emphasised once again that the observer is not concerned with proving the existence of these systems, but with assuming it.[4] This minimal ontology serves as a heuristic principle for a description of the object – here: piracy – which can then be further used within science. It should be noted, however, that Luhmann himself brought into play the possibility of extending the usual canon to include a class of more chaotic systems operating on the follow-up costs of functional differentiation.[5] His example of such a secondary functional system was social work, which we will deal with later in connection with pirate reflection.[6]

The theory of the observer chosen here accepts the deconstruction proviso but forgoes the deconstruction of its own distinctions in

2   P. Fuchs, *Das System 'Terror': Versuch über eine kommunikative Eskalation der Moderne* (Bielefeld: Transcript, 2004); P. Fuchs, 'Das WorldWideWeb – ohne Technik' (manuscript 2009).

3   P. Fuchs and M. Heidingsfelder, 'MUSIC NO MUSIC MUSIC: Zur Unhörbarkeit von Pop', *Soziale Systeme* 10, no. 2 (2004), 292–324; M. Heidingsfelder, *System Pop* (Berlin: Kadmos, 2012); M. Heidingsfelder, 'Untangling Pop: A Systems Theoretical Approach', *Systems Research and Behavioral Science* 39, no. 4 (2022), 786–806.

4   In the words of Luhmann, 'The following considerations assume that there are systems. Thus they do not begin with epistemological doubt'. N. Luhmann, *Social Systems* (Stanford, CA: Stanford University Press, 1995), 12.

5   Roth and Schütz have cast their dissenting vote against the proposal, as they advocate for setting limits on the rampant proliferation of newly discovered social systems. While their position is understandable, their endeavor is ultimately futile and serves only to encourage researchers to breach the so-called 'ten system commandments'. Moreover, the ontological orientation of their effort presents certain problematic aspects. Rather than inquire into 'how many of these systems actually exist', a theory of observation would suggest addressing the more pertinent query of what number of systems is reasonable to postulate or, as Spencer-Brown would have it, to call into existence. See S. Roth and A. Schütz, 'Ten Systems: Toward a Canon of Function Systems', *Cybernetics and Systems Analysis* 22, no. 4 (2015), 11–31.

6   N. Luhmann, *Theory of Society*, vol. 2 (Stanford, CA: Stanford University Press, 2013), 26.

favour of possible gains in knowledge. These, of course, are just as deconstructible as others, all of which must rely on their own blindness if they are to be able to observe anything at all.[7] By renouncing the 'deconstructivist affect' (Luhmann) towards ontological metaphysics – as in principle towards all passions in connection with theory – first an unexcited position can be taken. This is already advantageous because the self-descriptions of the pirates – as we will see – are quite 'affected' and in many texts stylised into the pretentious. This, however, applies to all self-descriptions, as the qualities of external observation that neutralise the internal perspective are missing here. No pirate questions the existence of piracy; instead, it is assumed to be indispensable (Gary Hall even calls it 'necessary' in the interview with Holger Briel in this volume). One could also say, the system is taken in by itself and 'embellishes' its own operations. Therefore – despite all the scientific veneer that the reflective instances of the pirates strive for – the 'over-tension' (Luhmann) typical of self-observation processes sets in here as well, leading to an increase of certainty that cannot be justified scientifically. Second, the distinction allows us to go beyond the text-and-interpretation level deconstruction is concerned with. It starts more generally with the operations by which an observer produces and reproduces itself. In the case of social systems, these operations are communications. They take place on the basis of a specific difference which is related to a certain functional context, 'because it differentiated with it and seems to be necessary for it'.[8]

As a systems theorist, the observer has exactly two ways to construct the fact of piracy. The first possibility is: piracy is part of a system (the economy, the law, politics, etc.). The second possibility is to conceive of piracy as a state of affairs in the environment of these systems – and perhaps even to conceive of it as a system itself. In the latter case, one would have to identify the specific communicative operation through which piracy is reproduced. In any case, if it

---

7   In a formulation of Peter Fuchs, blindness is the technique that makes sight possible. P. Fuchs, *Das Weltbildhaus und die Siebensachen der Moderne: Sozialphilosophische Vorlesungen* (Konstanz: UVK Verlag, 2001), 30. One could rightly call this the *conditio humana*, our conditional structure, because all human beings are 'blind seers'. A complete and valid view of the world is not possible.

8   N. Luhmann, *Die Wirtschaft der Gesellschaft* (Frankfurt am Main: Suhrkamp, 1988), 209. All translations in the text are the author's own unless otherwise indicated.

is considered part of a system's environment, the system views it differently than a problem that it must solve internally. A super-observer (Über-observer) is not admitted. What piracy is for society as a whole cannot be determined, as there is no observation of the phenomenon that is binding for all of its systems.

This is the limitation of the present observation: it does not go beyond the indication of system references. In this limitation lies its seriousness.[9] The disadvantage of this self-chosen limitation or self-commitment is at the same time its advantage: there are almost infinitely many possibilities of observer constitution for a description of the phenomenon of piracy. If the theorist succeeds in turning such possible determinations into determinations that could then interest other observers, this observation has proven to be worthwhile.

A mechanism that enables systems to bypass their 'closedness' without compromising it is the operative coupling. We can distinguish two variants.[10] I have already alluded to the first. It consists quite fundamentally in the production of operations of the system by operations of this system and is called *autopoiesis*.[11] As mentioned above, in the case of social systems we are dealing with communications. The other is based on the always presupposed simultaneity of system and environment. It allows a momentary coupling of operations of the system with those that the system actually attributes to the environment. We are dealing with two forms of time here. That of autopoiesis is typically observed as the reproduction of events of the same form 'in' one time. That of operative coupling can be illustrated by a simple example. When a doctor confirms an illness in writing and gives the document to the patient for his employer. Then the health care system no longer functions only in the scope

9   M. Lehmann, 'Enthemmter Dissens. Kommunikation in Netzwerken', in L. Koch and T. König (eds), *Zwischen Feindsetzung und Selbstviktimisierung: Gefühlspolitik und Ästhetik populistischer Kommunikation* (Frankfurt am Main: Campus, 2020), 203.

10 On this point and the argument that follows, see N. Luhmann, *Das Recht der Gesellschaft* (Frankfurt am Main: Suhrkamp, 1993), 440–1.

11 H. Maturana and F. Varela, *Autopoiesis and Cognition: The Realization of the Living*, with a preface by Stafford Beer (Dordrecht: Reidel, 1972). Originally aiming at the reproductive circles that make life possible, Luhmann transferred the term from biology to the theory of social systems. One could certainly speak here of a certain interdisciplinary tradition of sociology to which he is connecting, for the concept of differentiation also originates – as is often forgotten – in the research context of biology.

of healthy/sick. Another example is when payments serve to fulfil a legal obligation. The conditioning of this particular coupling of the law with the economy is, as we shall see, provided by the institutions of property and contract – property in the system of economy, contract in the system of law. These couplings, however, remain tied to the recursive networks of the various systems, are identified by them, and therefore have quite different antecedents and quite different futures, depending on which system performs the operation as a unity. Where the money comes from, and what the recipient continues to do with it does not concern the legal side of a transaction. Such events establish and dissolve relations between systems in the form of continuous integration and disintegration; barely coupled, the coupling is immediately released 'for self-determined follow-up operations'.[12]

***

The various dimensions of piracy and the overlapping areas of society can best be illustrated by means of a randomly selected typical case. Imagine you are a moderately successful media theorist sitting in front of your computer. Imagine further that you feel the need to unwind and relax after correcting the 22nd assignment and decide to download an illegal torrent of the latest Marvel film. You already have the appropriate software needed to read the information from the torrent file and start the download.

If your partner were to come along and ask, 'Honey, what are you doing? I thought you were grading papers', and you reply, 'I am being a pirate again and making rich booty!', the intimate system would come into play. And if your partner asked you, 'Just because you can get the movie you want without paying for it, should you?', the communication would cross the line to morality, a form that subverts the distinctions of individual social areas or systems. In other words, it can – theoretically – be applied to *any* situation (but, unlike piracy, many topics cannot be morally coded without further ado).

What else happens at the moment of downloading you are only indirectly responsible for. With torrents the file is not only downloaded, you also upload data from your computer at the same

12 Luhmann, *Theory of Society*, 197ff.

time[13] – which means that you are committing a criminal offence. The obvious question that also moves pirate reflection, namely why caring by sharing is punishable, will be explored later. At this point, it should only be pointed out that sharing content is subject to certain legal conditions.

Your action is not yet relevant to any functional system. But it could become so. That depends on where you are – more precisely: on which state or territory you are trying to satisfy your need for distraction. It is here that the political system must be taken into account, as the situation on the Internet reflects to a certain extent the political situation in any given country. In other words, copyright laws are national in scope; how they are defined and protected varies considerably across the countries of this world.[14] 'What applies to internet users in Germany does not necessarily also apply to Brazilians who access the internet from Rio de Janeiro. The internet is global, but decentralized and legally fragmented. Different rules apply depending on where you are when you access the internet'.[15] The legal situation in Germany, for example, has led to fewer open WLAN networks being offered than in other countries: 'Under the so-called "Stoererhaftung", operators of such networks could be legally prosecuted if, for example, unlicensed copies of films or music were downloaded from their WLAN network'.[16] Besides, torrent networks are relatively well monitored in Germany, so a smart pirate is unlikely to risk a download there.

For the sake of example, let us imagine that you are a dumb pirate. Or, even better, that you are a smart but somewhat absent-minded pirate, which, as an academic, is your right by profession: you return to Germany after a long stay in a small South East Asian country and have forgotten that the program you downloaded there automatically pumps bits and bytes of files from your hard drive to the Internet as soon as your computer is connected to it. Whether you become 'system

---

13 The fact that the servers and their providers are relieved and everyone is helped could well be subsumed under the umbrella term 'pirate care', a concept of pirate reflection that I will discuss in section 5.

14 C. Fink, K.E. Maskus, and Y. Qian, 'The Economic Effects of Counterfeiting and Piracy: A Review and Implications for Developing Countries', Policy Research Working Paper 7586, Washington, DC, World Bank Group (2016), 2.

15 J. Niesyto and K.D. Dapp (eds), 'Who Governs the Internet?', updated ed., Friedrich-Ebert-Stiftung Political Academy, Bonn, 2020, 7.

16 C. Piallat (ed.), *Der Wert der Digitalisierung: Gemeinwohl in der digitalen Welt* (Bielefeld: Transcript, 2021), 408.

relevant' or not is not a foregone conclusion. If you are lucky, nothing will happen – punishable does not mean that you will necessarily be punished, only that you have broken the law. In our example, you come to the attention of an organisation that hunts down the IP addresses of file sharers, and a law firm whose business model is to warn off Internet pirates does just that. Now you are at least potentially relevant.

As mentioned above, any operative coupling remains tied to the recursive networks of the systems involved. Why you want to see the film, how you liked it, or that you forgot about the software, all this has nothing to do with the legal or economic side of your action. Only the recursivity of the operation context of the individual systems identifies the operation as a system element. In the case of the economy, the operation is payment – as long as there is no payment, one is left out, so to speak. In the case of the legal system, the operation is a legally binding decision, i.e., the official determination of what is legal and what is illegal. (One can, if one is uncertain here and wants to keep options open, solve the problem of specification tautologically by saying: the operation of the economic system is an economic communication, the operation of the legal system is a legal communication, and the operation of piracy is a 'piratical' one. For the respective system, there is no problem here, as long as it knows what it has already done so far or will continue to do in order to qualify its own operations as respectively legal or economic or 'piratical'.)[17]

One could consider signing the offer of the law firm to settle the legal violation out of court – against the one-time payment of 1,500 euro – as an operative coupling. After all, the figure of *negotiorum gestio* underlying the warning possibility – which serves to balance both interests and provides certain types of legal action intended to enforce the claim – is a legal one. However, the reference to a legal concept (the already established right of 'gestio') is an operation that does not alter the law, even if it ends in dispute, and the dispute is still legally irrelevant if it is submitted to dispute mediation. Mediation and arbitration, however, are not 'alternatives to law', but strategies to avoid law because it may strike harder or be more unreliable (such as Soviet law; arbitrage is also particularly popular in China).[18] The law only intervenes when there is a corresponding

17   Luhmann, *Das Recht der Gesellschaft*, 57.
18   Klaus Ziegert's question is whether the Asia-wide tradition of the need for harmony or Soviet tradition is responsible for this preference as far as civil disputes are concerned. Email to the author, 15 April 2022.

formal request, e.g., at the trickster lawyer's office or at the public prosecutor's office via the taking of evidence by the police (with the latter not being an operation of the law, but of the political system, i.e., the state). I therefore tend to observe such a declaration as a social communication that, in case of violation, refers to an operation of the legal system, namely the possibility of legal action and subsequent enforcement (or sanctioning) of the (omitted) cease-and-desist.

This peculiarity of the legal system can be well explained by the distinction between centre and periphery: the injunction takes place in the periphery of the system, which acts as a kind of large buffer zone protecting the courts from overload. It extends, among other things, from the gatekeeper lawyer, who has to fend off troublemakers, to the conflict mediation agencies, which sift out potential hard cases to the legislature. (Whereby the systems theorist sees laws as political programmes that receive the benefit of doubt, whether they are right or wrong, until a court so decides. But, in practice, in the preparation of the law, everything is largely settled beforehand in order to pave the way for the law to be lawful. It still remains peripheral, fodder for the courts, and certainty of expectation for the people.) Only when the court is involved do legal operations proceed in a centred manner, with the court – any court – at the centre. The hierarchical chain of instances – from the small district court to the regional court to the Supreme Court, etc. – only makes the legal examination of the legal decision more thorough (more reasoned) or longer.[19]

As we have seen, politics is already involved, even without police – because if you were still in the small East Asian country not particularly interested in monitoring torrent networks, none of this would – presumably – have happened. So, without the German state, which (just like the East Asian one) ensures the stabilisation of boundaries between politics and the other functional systems and provides for legal 'safeguards' institutionalised in politics itself, you would have had to do without official recognition as a net pirate. But you would have also been spared the futile attempt to negotiate down the demanded warning fee, the gnashing of teeth when signing the cease-and-desist declaration, in which you guarantee to refrain from such an act in the future (against the threat of a penalty), and the flattering realisation that you are supporting the industry of trickster lawyers parasitising on piracy with your 1,500 euro. In other words,

19 Many thanks to Klaus Ziegert for important hints at the analogous – not hierarchical – character of legal practice.

you would have been spared the opportunity to sarcastically chalk up this experience to 'research costs' and possibly refer to it in an academic paper.[20]

***

As the example has made evident, the systems theorist's essential differentiation is that of the division between 'inside' and 'outside'; that is, distinguishing what is deemed as part of the system and what is not. The borders of the systems show up as changes in the continuability conditions of economic, legal, intimate, piracy, etc., communication. It is not a matter of, for example, the economy's own reproduction being enveloped by a kind of membrane (as the many spherical representations of systems suggest) so that it can take place protected from disruptive influences in all tranquillity.

That the observation of closed systems plays in the registers of spatiality seems indispensable at least in didactic contexts. The circle is an obvious choice since it has always been the image of perfect unity. With this 'illustration', the distinction of inside/outside becomes plausible.[21] If one wants to prevent this, one can follow Peter Fuch's variation of Spencer-Brown's central instruction: 'Don't draw a system!' or: 'Don't draw a circle!'[22] Because metaphors like closedness, connection, closure, opening, etc. not only lead into paradoxes if one hypostasises them, they also do not do justice to the 'spaceless' character of communication, even if it belongs to a certain 'sphere' or 'field' (to name the two best-known competitors of the system concept in sociology). It is only a question of when the respective reproductive circuit is 'clicked on', as it were. The systems

20 As did T. Baumgärtel, whose experience served as an example for me here. See T. Baumgärtel, 'Lob der Piraterie', *Zeitschrift für Medienwissenschaft*, vol. 13, *Überwachung und Kontrolle 7*, no. 2 (2015), 133–7.
21 Many terms have to fall back on spatial and natural background meanings in order to become comprehensible. The application of Luhmann's centre/periphery difference to modern – not space-dependent – communication conditions is another example. As Koselleck points out, revolution, too, had its initial spatial meaning in the circling of the stars before the term was applied to social and political processes. R. Koselleck, *Begriffsgeschichten: Studien zur Semantik und Pragmatik der sozialen Sprache* (Frankfurt am Main: Suhrkamp, 2010), 161–2.
22 P. Fuchs, 'Die Verschränkung der Systeme' (manuscript 2022), 2. See also G. Spencer-Brown, *Laws of Form* (New York: Julian Press, 1972), 3.

theorist's question can be reformulated accordingly: does piracy satisfy the continuability conditions of this or that unit? 'Belongs to/ does not belong to' is translated to 'satisfies the conditions/does not satisfy them'. In this way, one avoids invoking spatial notions, as if economy or the law or piracy were a vessel.

The problems of an unambiguous assignment are already apparent in our example. Where does a film-enthusiastic media theorist and teacher belong who professes to file sharing because – apart from occasional selfish desires to pass the time – the licence-free copying of film classics and specialist literature offers countries of the so-called 'global south' educational opportunities that they would otherwise not be able to take advantage of (and thus eliminates the economic and cultural asymmetry between the First and Third Worlds to some extent)? What becomes visible is a plurality of system references that do not see the same thing. They all see piracy but identify its reality differently. It is not that someone downloads an illegal torrent of a film that then constitutes the reference to the entity I have conceived as the observer of the system, but that companies that make their money by hunting down file sharers, an industry of trickster lawyers, and possibly also one's own partner refer to it – including the pirate himself, who tries to justify the downloading of the film as part of a 'globalisation from below' or perhaps even refers to a doctrine of the beauty of the commons (and thus aesthetically charges the, so to speak, shameful act of theft).[23] They all refer to this event in different ways. The reference becomes an element of the system that appears at the moment (has its *kairos*, as it were)

---

23 Some reasons are better suited for motif narratives, others less so. That in turn depends on where and when we cite them. M. Heidingsfelder, *Trump – beobachtet: Eine Struktursuche* (Berlin: Springer, 2020), 293. The justification 'I steal films because I am too cheap to pay money for them' is unlikely to find a following, especially in the scientific community, certainly in the context of pirate reflection. Large sections of the public characterise the phenomenon only against the background of foul and fair motives – self-interest, profit maximisation, etc.; they thus reformulate only the perspectives of economy or law, sometimes those of politics. But even a uniform set of pirate motives can only be constructed with difficulty; the individual pirates are looking for very different things. It might therefore be more fruitful to ignore communicated interests and motives, which always have to do with 'applaudability', and look more closely at the situation that determines the action instead – with Goffman, at the moment and its man (or woman or transgender person). E. Goffman, *Interaction Ritual: Essays on Face-to-Face Behavior* (New York: Pantheon, 1967), 3.

and falls apart again the next moment to look for new events; for example, when the law firm is confronted with the pirate's refusal to sign the cease-and-desist declaration, with which the out-of-court ('out-of-law') settlement sought has failed, so that the possibility of legal action becomes an actuality and the sanctioning of the 'omitted omission' is enforced. In the intimate system, the pirate's refusal to sign the declaration could lead to a dispute with the life partner who points out the consequences of such a refusal: that he could end up in prison in the worst case, that a corresponding entry in the police record could have a negative impact on his/her career and thus affect their future plans, etc., etc. If we remove all these system references that synchronise in society, nothing remains but a diffuse everyday life within which we all encounter the phenomenon of piracy. Which is why it makes sense, in the case of research, to choose certain system references, and at the same time ensure the interchangeability of the system references with each other. The system theorist interested in the truth of piracy has no choice but to choose. Those who do not wish to do so must then at least opt for another theory.

This brings us to the consequence of this design: there is no such thing as the file-sharing media theorist from my example. There is also no piracy. There are only certain events that are coded and attributed accordingly. The attempt to grasp downloading a file as 'globalisation from below' points back to the observer, just like the one to point out the destructive consequences of such action for society. For the observer, there is no: 'piracy is what it is' – the possibility of a statement of being that takes him out of the equation, as if all one had to do was look at piracy like one would look at a product whose package lists all the ingredients. An 'objective' outside world given independently of the observer makes sense only for observers who want to deny themselves.[24] Failure to account for this fact is not without risks, it can result in essentialism, sometimes even fundamentalism. The more differences the observer enters into such an imaginary document, the richer the world within which he places piracy. An either–or observer can then ask the question: is the richness of the world or are the richness of distinctions the starting point? The systems theorist points out that his drawing of boundaries

---

24 In Heinz von Foerster's words: 'If the properties of the observer [...] are eliminated, there is nothing left: no description, no observation'. H. von Foerster, 'Ethics and Second Order Cybernetics', *Understanding Understanding: Essays on Cybernetics and Cognition* (New York: Springer, 2003), 289.

comes up against what might be called a natural limit: *the world is a world of and for observers.*

Before we go any further, it is important to draw attention to a kind of second level of observation – not in the sense of second order observation, which is employed in this text, observing primary observations and thus setting them contingent, but in the sense of an additional power located at the first level of observation, which brings evaluations into play. A 'pure' level of observation does not exist (and any theory that aims to eliminate all evaluations runs the risk of being highly informed by them). As a rule, every observation is already accompanied by an evaluation, at the most basic level: piracy is good and serves society, or piracy is bad and harms it, etc.

In what is the theoretical observer embedded? Meaning, life form, practice, habitus – for this embedding preceding the consciousness of the theorist there are many terms, which I unify with Dirk Baecker as the social, historical, and cultural situation. Only this horizon of meaning equips me with the information that piracy is productive, i.e., destructive, i.e., both. The theorist does not owe this horizon of meaning to himself. But this embedding does not change his freedom of choice. First comes the observer who discovers the society that sets the observer and enables him to choose. Of course, only such that are socially available; decisions, which in turn change the society and thus the conditions continuously.

2 The Form of Piracy

Up to this point, the term piracy was used without further clarification. Creating an only apparent precision that lacks foundation, the reader was forced to make assumptions and inferences about what might be meant. If, in a first step, one wants to speak coherently and without contradictions about piracy, one must therefore be able to determine precisely what is peculiar to it, otherwise it cannot be dealt with thoroughly.[25] In systems theory, this is done by means of the

25 I am paraphrasing Kant, *Prolegomena zu einer jeden künftigen Metaphysik* (Hamburg: Felix Meiner, 1976), 13, who does not speak of concepts here, but of the limits of the individual scientific disciplines. Wittgenstein countered Kant's injunction with the idea of cluster definition. The punch line of this counter is that he uses exactly the same image with which Kant makes fun of the conceptual confusion of contemporary philosophy: that of the family. L. Wittgenstein, *Philosophical Investigations*, German text, with an English translation by G.E.M. Anscombe, P.M.S. Hacker, and Joachim Schulte (Chichester:

figure of form, i.e., by focusing on the distinction that is central to the observation and identification of the phenomenon.[26] The assumption is that this distinction generates piracy facts and piracy objects in the first place. The theorist does therefore not ask what piracy is, but how it becomes what it then is (as what it is observed to be). On closer examination, the supposed rigidities prove to be contingent, merely set, the result of an arbitrarily made distinction. They are not a property of a piracy object. It is the observation that stages

Wiley-Blackwell, 2009), 67 ff. The mixture described by Kant, in which the concepts, 'as if they belonged to one family like siblings, run through each other without distinction' (Kant, *Prolegomena*, 13) is itself transformed into a concept denoting the properties of words that respond, as it were, brittlely to a categorical sorting. I cannot discuss Wittgenstein's plea for a redefinition of categorial determinations here – which, by the way, is a much-discussed one on which thousands of experts have expressed themselves in a far more competent manner anyway – only briefly address it. What Wittgenstein tries to do is not to dissolve categories. If the theorist forms a category like piracy, then he must determine it in such a way that similar things are excluded. Otherwise, classically, he would not arrive at a concept. Wittgenstein's approach is about subverting the strictness of categorial thinking and allowing for similarities, pointing at the 'unnatural' ideal of exactitude demanded by science. It aims at the absorption of situational differences and anomalies that characterise a word, denaturalises it, as only such an axiomatised, idealised term opens up the possibility of gaining a position from which a phenomenon like piracy can be analysed without having to resort to specific, pre-existing descriptions. But whoever turns a word into a concept (a precise word) and calls the siblings romping around to order, as it were, does it within the language game of science. The word 'piracy' is not destroyed by this, it retains a lasting influence on the experiences that it makes possible. N. Luhmann, *Die Wissenschaft der Gesellschaft* (Frankfurt am Main: Suhrkamp, 1990), 4. In this sense, Wittgenstein's plea is merely a further development or an 'exposure' (in the sense of François Jullien) of Kant's inquisitorial attempt at conceptual consistency, not a refutation. The follow-up question could be whether certain words fundamentally prove resistant to the terminological claim and cannot be resolved into conceptuality. For Blumenberg, this characteristic applies to those metaphors that he calls 'absolute', designating the special case of metaphors that have made themselves independent of the facts they illustrate. See H. Blumenberg, *Paradigmen zu einer Metaphorologie* (Bonn: Bouvier, 1960). I will leave open the question of how far this might also apply to the metaphor of piracy. My attempt in the following is instead to propose a tailoring and limitation of this metaphor that makes it manageable. On the question of the metaphorical qualities of 'system', see P. Fuchs, *Die Metapher des Systems: Studien zu der allgemein leitenden Frage, wie sich der Tänzer vom Tanz unterscheiden lasse* (Weilerswist: Velbrück Wissenschaft, 2001).

26 Spencer-Brown, *Laws of Form*.

the projection of piracy as a thing and determines which forms at different times constitute what it is.

Without wanting to complicate matters unnecessarily, however, it should be noted that this also applies to the observation of piracy presented here: it is the theorist who chooses this concept of piracy as a starting point. It does not function as a sign for a state of affairs in the external world. Thus, the contingency of distinguishing comes to the fore again, as well as the question of the consequences of such self-limitation. The form determined in the following is nothing but a thoroughly contingent operation: the practice of an observer who makes this distinction because he believes that pirates make it, and who hopes that in doing so he will hit their centre. In this way, I become the observer of what is not only piracy for me, but also the piracy of my distinction.

This constructivist approach has much in common with labelling theory, which Howard S. Becker introduced in connection with the phenomenon of deviance.[27] For him, it is not so much the personal and social characteristics of outsiders that make them outsiders, but the – communicative – process by which they come to be thought of as outsiders. Something similar could be said for the pirates, who only become pirates through a process of attribution. For: 'Just because one has committed an infraction of a rule does not mean that others will respond'.[28] In short: without connection, no norm-breaking – no outsider. I start from a similar consideration in this text when I try to determine the distinction that is constitutive for the attribution of piracy.[29]

---

27 H.S. Becker, *Outsiders: Studies in the Sociology of Deviance* (Glencoe, IL: Free Press of Glencoe, 1963).
28 Becker, *Outsiders*, 2.
29 I conceive the declarative speech acts discussed by High in this volume as a specific form of observation. The figure of the observer goes beyond linguistic actions, i.e., speech acts, in that the concept of the speech act itself is seen as a specific distinction of an observer, which positions other linguistic activities such as the description of facts or the making of allegations on the other side (namely, a scientific observer belonging to a particular programme). The biggest difference might be that the concept of communication used in this text does not denote an action, i.e., something that an agent carries out, even if communication cannot be observed otherwise (i.e., at the moment of a linguistic or non-linguistic utterance). Instead, communication is understood as a continuous self-activity that neither begins nor ends with an utterance, which is why it cannot be observed directly. See N. Luhmann, *Soziale Systeme: Grundriß einer allgemeinen Theorie* (Frankfurt

The observation of piracy, like every observation, distinguishes two sides. The unmarked other side is always carried along. For classical piracy, the central distinction can be defined as the distinction between robbery on the high seas (as a lawless area or an area not subject to state authority) and robbery on land (as an area where laws exist and are enforced, i.e., one that is subject to state authority).[30] A look at the origin of the word reveals a remarkable fact that pirate theorists have unsurprisingly exploited for their own purposes: it is a Latin loanword to the Ancient Greek word *peirates* (πειρατής), which is derived via *peira* (πειράω) ('venture, enterprise, raid') from *peiran* (πειρᾶν) ('to try, undertake, scout'). The word therefore denotes the risk of an enterprise, not necessarily a robbery, and not necessarily one at sea. For the 'sheer' buccaneers or sea robbers, there was a more precise, narrower expression at hand: *katapontistés* (καταποντιστής). However, this designation – and thus the distinction between the mere, blunt buccaneer and his experimental conspecifics – was not able to assert itself. We therefore encounter a certain indeterminacy and ambivalence of expression right at the beginning of its history, which has remained until today.

As legal scholar Patricia Loughlan correctly proclaims, 'The use of the term "pirate" is clearly metaphorical and not even the most naive of participants in the discourse of intellectual property could or would take it literally'.[31] But perhaps it is what Gordon Pask calls a 'defensible metaphor' (and Michael D. High's work on piracy can be seen as engaged in this task). The history of this metaphor begins around the sixteenth century with the invention of the 'paper engines' which made it possible to carry out a whole new form of property crime. For the reprinters, each freshly published book, sometimes even proofs of books that had not yet been published, is a function for a number of different, unlicensed copies. Even then,

---

am Main: Suhrkamp, 1984), 226. As we will see in section 5, the peculiarity is that piracy translates the external description – the exclusion observed by High – into its own conditions in order to be able to observe itself. Drawing from High's depiction of piracy as a rhetorical tool, one could argue that the pirates neutralise those who wield this weapon against them, in order to claim it as their own – akin to the saying, 'turning swords into plowshares'. See M. High, 'Piratical Designations: Power and Possibility in Representations of Piracy', PhD thesis, Stony Brook University, 2014.

30 See U.S. Supreme Court, *United States v. Furlong*, 18 U.S. 184 (1820). Cf. also High, 'Piratical Designations', 16–17.

31 Patricia Louise Loughlan, '"You Wouldn't Steal a Car": Intellectual Property and the Language of Theft', Sydney Law School Research Paper 08/35 (2008), 3.

this activity was viewed critically by the book industry, because by reprinting them cheaper in their own workshops, the demand for the more elaborate and expensive original editions decreased. One of the first authenticated mentions of this new form of piracy is found in 'A Journey to Hell', a poem by Ned Ward:

> *Piracy, Piracy,* they cry'd aloud,
> What made you print my Copy, Sir, says one.[32]

Already in this poem the dispute between the ungrateful bibliopoles, who sell second-hand or rare books, and the servile typographs, who threaten this branch of income, the law is called to the rescue – it ends in court. Awareness of the possible economic consequences of piracy is already present, as the economy is built on the regulation of scarce goods. Initially, it presents itself as a threat to the monopoly business of the bibliopolies. However, as the poem progresses, the focus shifts towards the malevolent material disseminated by pirate printers, losing sight of the economic and legal ramifications of piracy. The fact that legal copyright law today speaks of piracy owes much to this historical coincidence, namely that someone used the term for the unlicensed reproduction of creative works (first only of literature, which is why it was initially called 'literary piracy'). As Yifan Li points out in her contribution to this volume, piracy in Chinese literally means 'to steal a plate (盗 版)', with the word 'plate (版)' referring to the same context of origin. The first originator of calling the fact of unlicensed copying piracy can no longer be identified, but no one can deny that this 'conflation of unjustly printing another person's copy with the crime of piracy', to quote Michael D. High, was itself a creative act. As it was used again and again, the term subsequently established itself – from an evolutionary point of view, it proved to be fit, in other words: it found favourable environmental conditions for its own reproduction, for 'being called so', and a licence was not necessary either.

For Tom Rothmann, former co-chief executive of Fox Filmed Entertainment and current chairman and CEO of Sony Pictures Motion Picture Group, 'allowing this romantic word – piracy – to take hold' was a mistake (he blames himself, 'our' mistake): 'It's really robbery – it's theft, and that theft is being combined with consumer

---

32   Edward Ward, A *Journey to Hell: or, A Visit Paid to the Devil. A Poem* (London: British Library, 2010 [1700]).

fraud'.[33] Leaving aside the question of how the rights holders, who were already unable to stop piracy, envisage such a stop to a certain word use, robbery and theft are by no means the same offence. A look at the legal understanding of 'real' piracy as opposed to 'so-called piracy' (Gary Hall), which the US Supreme Court defines as robbery at sea, might be helpful here. Robbery requires the use of violence or the threat of violence, and precisely this moment is absent from unlicensed copying. What applies to 'space pirate' Mark Watney, aka Captain Blondebeard, who, as it were, seizes a boat without permission that is drifting masterless on the surface of Mars,[34] also applies to the pirates observed in this text, who seize the files floating on the Internet without permission: they steal, they do not rob. In other words, if the act is theft, not robbery, then the assignment to the category of piracy makes little sense, at least in legal terms. The question of what law applies on Mars is another matter, and a far more delicate one than the question of what law applies on the high seas of the Internet.[35] However, an increase in power struggles can be observed, with 'some states [...] trying to stake out their "territory" on the Internet', which is why Kettemann and Paul consider it important to involve the United Nations and implement a global 'Internet update'.[36]

Whenever piracy does not denote an act of criminal violence by ship or boat-borne attackers, but is used as a metaphor, it usually refers to the unauthorised use, copying, modification, or distribution of creative works – books, films, records – in other words: to an offence the law carries under the corporate title of copyright infringement. Designations intended to make this circumstance clearer delimit this type of piracy accordingly as literary piracy, broadcast piracy, digital piracy, online piracy, or video piracy. This understanding of piracy could be a good starting point for an analysis, even if some details – such as what exactly is meant by 'unauthorised', 'use', 'creative', 'works', 'copying', 'modification', etc. – would still need to be clarified. Not least for the historical reasons mentioned above, because this is the context from which the term piracy originally stems: no thing is

---

33 R. Wyatt, 'Lines Drawn on Antipiracy Bills', *Tuscaloosa News* (13 December 2011).
34 *The Martian* (dir. Ridley Scott, USA, 2015).
35 B. Adams, 'Martian Law: Is Mark Watney Really a Space Pirate?', *Overthinking It* (27 October 2015).
36 M.C. Kettemann and A. Paul, 'Ein Update für das Internet: Reform der globalen digitalen Zusammenarbeit', Global Governance Spotlight 4 (2020). Trans. M.H.

stolen, nothing is taken away, as it were – at the latest since we left the printing age behind us: not even a 'plate' – but a thing is multiplied. In this sense, piracy refers to a theft that consists in adding, but the economy and the law regard this multiplication as a theft. If you want to multiply, you need a licence which makes the copying just. The form of piracy would then be: *copyright infringement/copyright compliance*.

Unfortunately, however, this first provision was subsequently extended. Today, piracy also refers to the business of counterfeit goods that are manufactured with the aim of being confusingly similar to an original product. Article 61 of the Agreement on Trade-Related Aspects of Intellectual Property Rights (TRIPS) makes no distinction between 'wilful trademark counterfeiting or copyright piracy'.[37] Designations that are intended to represent this fact more clearly restrict this type of piracy to product piracy, product counterfeiting, or trademark piracy. To the conflation of infringement with the crime of piracy (robbery at sea), we must therefore add the conflation of piracy (unauthorised use of creative works) with the crime of counterfeiting (unauthorised use of trademarks). The confusion is understandable, because creative works can also be reduced to a commodity, i.e., to a monetary expression. Conversely, a commodity can also be translated into a creative work, but it is much harder and therefore takes place much less frequently (as in the case of Duchamp's *Fountain*, a standard urinal from a sanitary shop turned a work of art). Those creative works can then, however, in turn be effortlessly transformed into what the Abbé Morellet calls 'real money' (*monnaie réelle*) – namely, a commodity, usually with a considerable increase in value.[38] But, for scientific purposes, such an imprecise concept, in which – with Kant – the two different forms of piracy, 'as if they belonged to one family, like brothers and sisters, run through each other without distinction', is rather unsuitable.

Even a text that claims to compare the three offences of counterfeiting, piracy, and plagiarism unceremoniously lumps them together: 'Counterfeit products, illegal manufacture of objects and goods, piracy in other words'.[39] And those scholarly observers who, in a first step,

37 C.M. Correa and Xuan Li, *Intellectual Property Enforcement: International Perspectives* (Cheltenham: Edward Elgar, 2009), 208.
38 See Luhmann, *Die Wirtschaft der Gesellschaft*, 238–9.
39 A.V. Toma, 'Counterfeit, Piracy, Plagiarism: Comparison between These Crimes That Threaten National Security', *National Strategies Observer* 1 (2015).

seem to succeed in making a clear distinction between counterfeiting and piracy, proceed to classify them both as IPR infringements. A Nike logo then finds itself in the same weight class as a book by, say, Niklas Luhmann: 'counterfeiting, which is the illegal use of trademarks to sell unauthorised goods, and piracy, which is the duplication and sale of copyrighted goods without the copyright holder's permission'.[40] In both cases, therefore, the aim would be to lead to payment. Only the means are different, but the goal is the same: some counterfeit to sell, others duplicate to sell. This distinction, however, may not accurately represent the actuality of piracy.[41] Not every IPR infringement necessarily leads to a payment or is supposed to enable a payment. Even if the majority of the infringements – the classic 'intellectual property industries' – are quite profitable: high-end fashion (Gucci), low-end fashion (Nike), research-based pharmaceuticals, food products, plant varieties, software all promise high returns. But are pirates interested in profit, i.e., financial pay-offs? Or should we consider the possibility of turning a duplication into real money as a possible next step, which then defines the specificity of the respective pirate activity? Only the connection to the duplication would then determine what form of theft we are dealing with. Similar to the artist who produces a work that can then be sold, but who at the moment of creation does not move the sums in his head that can be earned with it – or more precisely: whose respective choice of form is not motivated by the profit that can be made through it.[42] It is the means to the end that makes the difference here, not the actual act. This is not unproblematic, because at the moment of the act it may not even be certain whether the stolen piece of music is intended to be shared, to be sold, or to serve one's own fame (in case of plagiarised research, one's own reputation). The legal idea behind this is to be able to grasp the purpose as the *present* state of a purpose-oriented perpetrator, whereby purpose can present itself as selectable, i.e., contingent, which in turn makes the attribution

---

40 Fink et al., 'Economic Effects', 2.

41 To be on the safe side: in the sense of how piracy manages the difference between piracy and the environment in relation to itself, not ontologically. It is a matter of bringing one's own observation scheme into congruence with what the system does. See Luhmann, *Soziale Systeme*, 245.

42 If this is the case, which as we know often happens in the field of art or entertainment, one could speak of corruption, because the criteria for making art are then taken from the economy. It is often branded as 'commerciality'. If the criteria are taken from politics, we talk of propaganda.

of guilt possible. In our case, however, it is not about motives and inscrutable inner states, but simply about the factual connection.

Before we go any further, a closer look at what a counterfeiter does might be helpful. The unauthorised imitation of an original product occurs equally in the field of art as in the field of industrial goods. Both forms can be consolidated under the umbrella term of plagiarism, which stems from the Latin word *plagiarius*, meaning someone who claimed another's work as their own. I consider this form of kidnapping in the field of art the counterfeiting (imitation) of famous artistic programmes (i.e., styles), and plagiarism in the field of industry as counterfeiting (imitating) brands or specific products. The difference between mere imitation and plagiarism refers to what is imitated. Thus, artists who imitate nature are usually not called plagiarists but realists, and the philosophical term for this kind of imitation is called mimesis. Artists who are able to imitate the mannerisms of other people's behaviour are called actors, which is where the Greek term *mimesis* initially comes from, with *mimos* meaning both imitator and actor.[43]

Industrial counterfeiters attempt to imitate the features, material, or appearance of a legally protected product, artistic counterfeiters attempt to imitate the features, material, or appearance of works of art. Both are concerned with financial gain, i.e., coupling with the economic system. This preference can be seen most clearly in

43 Particularly interesting are artists who kidnap their own style and repeat the significant features of their paintings. This practice of 'stealing from oneself' is one of the most controversial forms of plagiarism. This is connected to the definition above of what constitutes plagiarism, which is generally always the case when someone else's ideas are passed off as one's own. In this respect, the reuse of one's own work cannot, strictly speaking, constitute plagiarism. While D. Goldblatt, 'Self-Plagiarism', *Journal of Aesthetics and Art Criticism* 43, no. 1 (1984), 71–7, finds this form of self-recycling problematic, A. Bejan, 'Plagiarism Is Not a Victimless Crime', *ASEE Prism* 28, no. 7 (2019), 52, considers self-copying one of the privileges of creativity (in our terminology: the re-entry of non-creativity or boredom into creativity). In academia, self-plagiarism can be considered an attempt to deceive if the reference to the original work is missing. In a legal sense, there are no repercussions for copying. The sanctions, if any, only apply within the respective systems, in this case, art and science. Regardless, the market consistently favors the work of artists who produce similar pieces, creating a personal brand and reputation for themselves. The fundamental difference is merely quantitative, with a copied brand being readily accessible, whereas the work of an artist who copies their own style is limited in availability.

connection with those counterfeiters who forego the diversions via the counterfeit product and instead prefer to counterfeit banknotes straight away. Plagiarism in the field of education and science makes it a little more difficult for us to classify. Here too the duplication serves the goal of 'paying off', although not in financial form but in the form of certificates (students) or reputation (many politicians like to adorn themselves with a doctorate). Clever students have long since switched to ghost-writing – because since most ghost-writing pieces are neither imitations nor copies, it is no longer easy to prove the fraud, and certainly not with the usual plagiarism software. It should be clear that this use of academic mercenaries presupposes the ability to pay and thus possibly consolidates socio-structural differences ('classes'). AI-powered ghostwriting is the newest trend and accessible to all, potentially reducing such disparities.

An artistic counterfeiter who recently caused a stir due to his high technical skills in the field of imitation is German painter Wolfgang Beltracchi, whose forgeries of works by painters like Heinrich Campendonk surpassed the genuine canvases in some cases, and not only by his own admission. His skill is evident from the fact that Beltracchi managed to fool recognised experts who authenticated works among the imitations of existing Campendonk paintings. As the Beltracchis proudly report in their book *Selbstporträt* (Self-portrait), journalists from the *Frankfurter Allgemeine Zeitung* newspaper praised his Campendonk imitation 'Red Picture with Horses' as the 'highlight of the auction', and the *Sueddeutsche Zeitung* even went so far as to speak of a 'key work of modernism'.[44] In the end, only a chemical analysis could bring certainty (the colour component titanium dioxide that was discovered in one of his Campendonk copies was not available during the painter's lifetime). Since then, Beltracchi has benefited from the reputation of the successful daredevil – an art 'pirate' who is sometimes called the forger of the century, sometimes the Paganini of painting.[45] Duplication was out of the question for Beltracchi: replicating a painting that already existed would not have led to the desired payment: 'The forger seeks no credit, the plagiarist seeks it all'.[46] So the only way was to imitate an already existing style.

---

44 H. Beltracchi and W. Beltracchi, *Selbstporträt* (Reinbek bei Hamburg: Rowohlt, 2014) (e-book).

45 M. Iseli, 'Wolfgang Beltracchi: Der Stachel im Kunstmarkt', *Handelszeitung* (6 August 2018).

46 Goldblatt, 'Self-Plagiarism', 1.

And if you wished to copy the style of a certain painter like Heinrich Campendonk, then it can't hurt to take a close look at his paintings: the geometric language of forms used there, the colours, the subjects (e.g., horses). Beltracchi painted Campendonks that could have existed. He achieved the goal, according to his self-assessment, through a mixture of dedication, research, and superstition or shamanistic practice: 'To create a painting in the artistic handwriting of a painter, one must absorb the artist within oneself. That can take months. I did a lot of research, looking at places where they lived, houses where they painted. I read their letters and diaries. And even tried to eat what the artists ate back then [...] At some point I went to my studio and painted'.[47]

Although art counterfeiting is typically intended to deceive by producing fake works that appear authentic, not all counterfeiters are motivated by profit. For example, comedian Stevie Riks is satisfied with persuading his audience that they are listening to a bona fide recording of John Lennon. The sole objective is the attainment of a convincing illusion: 'So insane this exists!' (Jeff Lavezoli).[48] Not unlike those illusory muralists who use perspective to make viewers believe in the continuation of a building where it has actually stopped, he makes the listener believe in the continued mutual admiration and friendship of John Lennon and Paul McCartney. And with this he is as successful as the German painter, as the comments on the Internet show: 'I love the vids of John and friends singing Paul's songs. Heart warming' (Ed Westfall). Even in terms of a certain quality if it weren't for the equally deliberate moment of uneditability, which is also in the service of suggesting authenticity: 'Would be a sublime listen, but Yoko's voice is a black hole of melody' (Jeff Lavezoli). In the recording, the combination of similarity (Riks's voice sounds similar to John's, the droning whine sounds like Yoko Ono's droning whine, and the overall character of the recording is reminiscent of the 'unproduced' low-fi recordings Lennon produced during his bed-in with Ono, representatively: 'Give Peace A Chance') and repeatability (Riks repeats the songs from McCartney's album) that define any imitation, are successfully strung together. Riks succeeds with an *imitatio inventio* that supplements the existing John Lennon and Paul McCartney recordings, as it were, with another, secondary one to the

47   M. Kix, 'Der Glaube an Kunst ist wie in die Kirche gehen', *Die Zeit* (8 March 2017).

48   www.stevieriks.net.

most beautiful completeness. It seems adequate to call him a pirate in the first sense, i.e., someone who dares to undertake an enterprise that consists in deceiving Beatles fans and Beatles connoisseurs who 'should've known better'. The motive is not to make money, but to prove that it can be done. The fact that it is also about highlighting one's own skills and increasing fame is not disputed. In this, too, Riks resembles the spirit of the pirates to whom this text is dedicated.

The difference should have become clear by now: the pirate does not imitate, she is initially nothing more than a copyist who is not willing to pay anything for the copying – and she copies or 'acquires' copies (often, but not always) of creative works in order to share them with others (often, not always: without asking for anything in return), but usually aware of the unlawfulness of this act, whose unlawfulness she questions or considers unlawful. The pirate considers every piece of art, science, or entertainment as a means to produce multiple unauthorised copies – 'reprints'. She accepts that she is violating trademark rights in order to be able to share them. Piracy, according to this provision, would take place outside of the systems mentioned – and only when the pirate is caught in the act does a possible linkage in the form of an operative coupling with the legal system occur, possibly also a linkage with the economy, should there be a penalty payment as a result.

It is thus not the reproducibility itself that is considered the crime here, or with Walter Benjamin, the loss of aura that goes hand in hand with it (and harbours the danger of political appropriation). Benjamin was not interested in the legal or economic questions raised by the possibilities of technical reproducibility, which society answered with the idea of intellectual property and the ban on unauthorised reproduction, but in the aesthetic and political consequences.[49] For him, the technical reproduction itself was, as it were, unauthorised. However, he could have easily steered his reflections in a direction that the pirate theorists of today would probably approve of and understand reproducing as an act that opposes the order of domination rather than reproducing it; for example by describing the one who ignores the prohibitions on reproduction enacted by the rulers to maximise profit as an 'angel

49 W. Benjamin, 'Das Kunstwerk im Zeitalter seiner technischen Reproduzierbarkeit', in *Abhandlungen: Gesammelte Schriften Band*, vols 1–2, ed. R. Tiedemann and H. Schweppenhäuser (Frankfurt am Main: Suhrkamp, 1991), 1st version: 431–70, 3rd version: 471–508.

of reproduction'. It is this myth of the pirate as a fair 'outlaw', a resistance fighter who takes from the rich (corporations) and gives to the poor (users) that still enjoys great popularity today, from which Internet pirates also benefit, only that they no longer carry out their 'raids' on the high seas, but in cyberspace. The story of the pirate figure then reads similarly to that of Robin Hood, who in the oldest written sources from the middle of the fifteenth century is first portrayed as a dangerous highwayman, and in the course of the sixteenth and seventeenth centuries finally becomes a champion of social justice. Instead of robbing greedy clergymen and nobles, the pirates take from greedy corporations, 'the weary giants of flesh and steel' (John Perry Barlow) and the ungrateful Lars Ulrichs of this world to promote 'democracy, human freedom, sharing, caring, cooperation'.[50] That is why a Chief Executive like Rothmann fears the 'romantic' sound that the word piracy has. Favour is on the side of the pirates, who – unlike common thieves and robbers – are recognised rather than ostracised. The increasing social acceptance and understanding of piracy in the positive, metaphorical sense (as early on suggested by Benedict Anderson) is reflected not least in the success of the so-called pirate parties, which want to abandon the extra-parliamentary existence of the pirates in favour of a parliamentary one. Their themes are indeed 'piratist': promoting the strengthening of civil rights, more direct democracy and co-determination, the reform of copyright and patent law, free exchange of knowledge (open access), better data protection, respect for privacy guaranteed by fundamental rights, more transparency and freedom of information, free education, etc. After the founding of the *Piratpartiet* in Sweden on 1 January 2006, other pirate parties emerged throughout Europe, and later worldwide.[51] The German *Piratenpartei* (Pirate Party) can boast a mandate in the European Parliament. It is represented in local parliaments with around 300 mandates. At times it has also been in

---

50 John Perry Barlow, 'A Declaration of the Independence of Cyberspace' (8 February 1996), www.eff.org/cyberspace-independence; Gary Hall, 'Postdigital Politics: or, How to Be an Anti-Bourgeois Theorist' (2021), 47, https://hcommons.org/deposits/item/hc:38325/.

51 It should be noted, however, that the formation of a Pirate Party in Russia was denied because the judiciary considered such a designation to be against the law.

the German state parliaments of North Rhine–Westphalia, Berlin, Schleswig-Holstein, and Saarland.[52]

As we have seen, even a rather staid, fictional NASA employee like Mark Watney takes great pride in calling himself a pirate.[53] Seaborne piracy against transport vessels, on the other hand, is denied any claim to romance today, and films that tell of it take the side of the victims, the people responsible for transporting the 'real money'.[54] Speaking of which, Hollywood lends itself perfectly to making the form of piracy more vivid. For instance, with the help of the first episode of the film series *Pirates of the Caribbean: The Curse of the Black Pearl* (USA, 2003). It distinguishes between a 'good', ethical, albeit eccentric, pirate – Jack Sparrow – and the evil pirates led by Sparrow's mutinous former first mate, Hector Barbossa. Sparrow corresponds to the cultural content-sharing pirates to whom this text is dedicated – although they are pirates, they are good men (and women and transgender persons). Barbossa, on the other hand, would belong to the species of counterfeiters who bluntly want to make money with fake products (and risk the health of people with their defective goods and fake spare parts, regardless).[55] To sharpen the distinction,

---

52 The fact that the Pirate Party in Germany has also received a warning letter for illegal music uploads is not surprising – in spite of the fact that it was initiated by the German rapper Bushido, of all people. The judicial back and forth over the question of whether Bushido himself was guilty of copyright infringement by using an average of ten-second samples from songs by the French band *Dark S* as a sample loop clearly reflects the transitional stage in which society currently finds itself. More on this in section 4.

53 'So here's the cool part. I'm about to leave for the Schiaparelli Crater where I'm going to commandeer the Ares IV lander. Nobody explicitly gave me permission to do this, and they can't until on board the Ares IV. So I'm going to be taking a craft over in international waters without permission, which by definition [...] makes me a pirate. Mark Watney: Space Pirate'. *The Martian* (dir. Ridley Scott, USA, 2015).

54 One thinks, for example, of *Captain Phillips* (dir. Paul Greengrass, USA, 2013).

55 The two types correspond roughly to High's typology of the 'actively piratical villain' (Barbossa) and the 'reluctantly piratical hero' (Sparrow). From High's point of view, on the other hand, Sparrow does not represent a pirate at all, but follows the Hollywood rule that film pirates 'rarely, and in many cases never, commit piracy'. High, 'Piratical Designations', 92. Where High observes a separation of the pirate film from the act of piracy (by omitting the depiction of robbery at sea and the punishment of the perpetrators), I see Sparrow as the embodiment of the 'good' copyright pirate who does not use violence – but who is also not fit to be a clear hero, precisely because he is, despite everything, still a pirate. And maybe because, as High points out, he is also

one could again refer to the original meaning of pirate, which accentuates the risk of an undertaking instead of success or the prospect of 'fat prey'. The pirates that interest me in the following are these *peirates* – the scouts, venturers, enterprisers, raiders who dare to do something – the Shawn Fannings, as it were: 'Initially, Napster was not intended to be a revenue-generating business. Like many great inventors before, Shawn Fanning created the program to see if it could be done, not because of money'.[56]

Metallica's and Dr Dre's lawyer, Howard King, confirms Napster's altruistic approach: 'They could raise hundreds of millions of dollars if they decided to offer shares in the company'.[57] Oddly enough, this was not what they were after, which qualifies Napster as pirates. Andy Greenwald, the online editor of *Spin* magazine at the time, also sees motives that have little to do with the prospect of hundreds of millions of dollars: 'The most positive thing it that it shows absolute passion in music'.[58] Paraphrasing a *Los Angeles Times* editorial on Napster, one could say, Piracy is, in its purest form, 'hard-core Sixties: free love, free music'.[59] On the other side would be the counterfeiters and product pirates. They correspond to the *katapontistes*, their daring motivated solely by the prospect of profit. Maigret and Roszkowska do justice to this definition of piratical practice by understanding piracy as the act of 'sharing, distributing and experiencing cultural contents outside the boundaries of local economies, politics, or laws'.[60] Although some caution is needed in the following not to fall for the romantic self-descriptions of the pirates, I would like to use their proposal below as working hypotheses for a new determination. The form of piracy – in the sense of George Spencer-Brown – would therefore be:

sharing contents outside the boundaries of the law/selling contents outside the boundaries of the law

coded for gay subcultural appeal and therefore exhibits traits of the third type: the 'gender shifting temporary pirate'. As the latest Hollywood pirate film *Our Flag Means Death* indicates, in which the masculine, archaic, and violent ('real') pirates meet the 'gentlemen pirate', Stede Bonnet, this type currently appears to be particularly promising in terms of future market success.

56   J. Tyson, 'How the Old Napster Worked', *HowStuffWorks* (2016).
57   Nick Paton Walsh, 'Mom, I blew up the music industry', *Observer* (21 May 2000), www.theguardian.com/theobserver/2000/may/21/features.review27.
58   Walsh, 'Mom, I blew up the music industry'.
59   Walsh, 'Mom, I blew up the music industry'.
60   Nicolas Maigret and Maria Roszkowska (eds), *The Pirate Book* (Ljubljana: Aksioma 2015). https://archive.org/stream/The_Pirate_Book/The_Pirate_Book.

The emphasis on the legal system stems from the fact that (a) every sale inherently occurs within the realm of the economic system, and (b) this system assumes legal dominion with ownership. The economy only knows either owners or non-owners with regard to a property-capable good, whereas the piracy that this text seeks to define wants to realise the third possibility: every property of a pirate should also be the property of another, for example effectively realised through the torrent dualism of downloading/uploading. The only condition is: in order to be able to participate in file sharing, one must become a pirate oneself, i.e., commit a breach of law. Practically, if you want to download, you must upload, i.e., share. The condition of sharing is sharing. It takes place outside the economy precisely because the pirates do not accept the property coding of the economy with relation to creative works (in Maigret and Roszkowska's terminology, of contents). While in the economy every property of one is the non-property of another, and all non-owners accept this exclusion as a condition for inclusion in the economy, the pirates realise the utopia of a property that does not exclude. They question the concept of property altogether and thus precisely the basic condition of differential distribution that, according to Marx, leads to class formation.

This could be the reason why – as we have seen – some observers prefer to obscure the differences between the two activities by claiming that there is an equivalence between the duplication and sharing of cultural content and the illegal production of objects and goods. Although these are two different types of unsanctioned appropriation, both are grouped under the corporate title of piracy.[61] The counterfeiters and product pirates steal, but they do not challenge the concept of ownership because they validate it by reselling, they are indeed 'just thiefs'; the cultural pirates steal to include those who are excluded from ownership, their offence is far more fundamental because it challenges the legitimacy of the concept. And it is more dangerous because they are – as those who preach participation – on the morally superior, good, 'altruistic' side, standing by the less powerful. The other side denies them this moral superiority.

61   In the words of Michael D. High, 'criminals and anarcho-libertarians are accused of the same offence'. What, according to High, leads to conflicting interpretations in Hollywood's pirate representations is apparently still not perceived as a contradiction for a large part of legal and financial research. See High, 'Piratical Designations'.

According to them, since both pirates and counterfeiters are breaking
the law, sharing cultural content is no better than selling counterfeit
goods. What becomes visible is precisely the attempt to control piracy
through discourse which leads High to treat maritime and intellectual
piracy as manifestations of the same thing.[62] While it is true that they
are both excluded, it is not, in my view, a reason to satisfy this attempt
in terms of scientific control, which requires an axiomatised, idealised
concept that eliminates situational differences and anomalies that
characterise the word. But in principle we are in agreement: the term
ensures exclusion, and by distinguishing counterfeiting as piracy,
the pirates are denied precisely that moral superiority on the basis
of current law that Hollywood fiction ascribes to them, and which
the pirate theorists also claim for themselves in the sense of 'sharing
is caring': that of the thief interested in the common good who
steals in order to ensure a higher level of justice or 'human freedom'
(Gary Hall). The reason for this conflation could be found in their
fundamental negation of property. While the economy provides
sufficient motives for the form of inclusion through exclusion, such
as 'property obliges' (namely socially, as a kind of compensation for
exclusion) or monetisation (money as a possibility to 'share' property,
i.e., to pass it on via exchange), and distribution differences between
rich and poor are made vivid and attackable by means of the concept
of class,[63] piracy returns to a morally generalised reciprocity that
makes balanced sharing a social duty. However, this is only possible
as long as unequal property relations continue. The pirates are
therefore working on their own abolition. The conditions for their
existence are the economic and legal relations they parasitise.[64]

62 For High, five conditions apply to all forms of piracy: maritime, intellectual,
    and digital: (1) an act of appropriation, (2) the use of a technology, (3) a
    spatial relation (physical, metaphorical, or perceived) between the parties
    involved, (4) a speech act designating an action as piracy, and (5) a discursive
    exclusion motivating and manifesting in such a designation. See High,
    'Piratical Designations', 16–17.
63 Luhmann, *Die Wirtschaft der Gesellschaft*, 190.
64 I come back to the term 'parasite' in section 5, which I do not use in a negative,
    pejorative sense. At this point it should only be mentioned that the legal
    guarantee for the high-risk operations of the economic system also are the
    result of a parasitic development which takes place via structural coupling.

3 Piracy and Economy

The question of piracy affects the two systems of economy and law in different ways. In the economic system, it must be determinable who is capable of disposition, i.e., capable of doing business with respect to certain goods (by which I include money and services) and who is not. In the legal system, 'right' and 'wrong' (legal and illegal) must be distinguishable, with the two being mutually exclusive. The everyday context in which these system references unfold in a 'piratical' way and form surprising structures that cannot be controlled economically and legally by traditional means is the digital infrastructure of the Internet.[65]

Economy depends on the satisfaction of organic and cultural needs – for example the need to want to own the entire Metallica catalogue, even if you don't have the money for it or aren't willing to spend the money you have – which become effective as motives. A need is a motive to prefer having the entire Metallica catalogue rather than not having it. When this cultural need takes the form of a 'command', it can, if it is not satisfied, lead to an action. It is then no longer merely experienced. Well-known 'commanding needs' are hunger and thirst – organic needs that demand immediate action. While the satisfaction of such needs can initially only be increased within narrowly defined thresholds, these thresholds can be crossed with the help of property and money: in factual terms in the direction of a practically unlimited variety of needs (one wants to have not only all Metallica songs, but also all of Slayer and Entombed and Napalm Death, and beyond that a Gucci bag and a Basquiat painting, etc.), and in temporal terms as securing the satisfaction of distant future needs.

Property is probably the most important prerequisite of the economy, of which 'intellectual property' is a subcategory. It is a form of observation of objects on the basis of a specific distinction,

65 The world wide web is decidedly not the focus of attention here. Due to its relative centrality, it is not suitable for piracy. The P2P distributed transfer infrastructure eliminates the need for a central index server, as these utilities search each other out online. We will see that this idea of escaping the control given by centrality is one of the most important intellectual motifs of piracy reflection. Today, Blockchain is probably the most promising possibility of such a distributed network whose content is both undeletable and uncensorable. See also the article by Danai Tselenti in this book, which points to the ambivalent role of a digital piracy technology that could help end digital piracy.

namely the distinction of different owners: 'For certain communication successes, it depends on the consent of the owner *and no one
else*'.[66] Since it is of such outstanding importance for our topic – albeit
in the special form of intellectual property – it is worth taking a look
at the peculiarity of this scheme. One could begin, for example, with
the question of what belongs to each of us, as it were, by nature:
what property we are automatically entitled to. The first thing
that comes to mind is what we enter this world with – our body.
But from a systems theory perspective property is an institution
that has emerged historically. In other words: before this concept
existed, there was no 'body property'. Its purpose is to cope with the
phenomenon of scarcity of goods, in the case of piracy: the scarcity
of cultural contents. As scarcity is only possible when goods and
persons can be moved against each other, property is thus constituted
as a schematism of having and not having.[67] Everything that someone
has, wants to have, or should have has social relevance because it
is at the expense of others, from camels to women to Marvel films
to the form of ownership that securitises shares in a company, i.e.,
sharing that ensures continued scarcity. Depending on the respective
system, property acts differently. In the economic system, property
is the primary coding alongside the secondary coding of economic
action through money (payment/non-payment), which has become
widely accepted in developed societies, for which property serves
as a precondition.[68] The realisation of this 'second coding' requires
universalism, that is, it must be applicable to everything that is
economically relevant – and 'intellectual property', such as in the
form of a composition, holds immense economic potential. This
quantifiability in monetary terms, the convertibility of everything
into monetary values, has occupied and worried many theorists,
as it allows all economic interests to be converted into 'cash' and
to distinguish what is thus formulated in money from other things
(formulated in love, formulated in power, formulated in faith or in
beauty). This is where functional differentiation begins. Thanks to
this expansion, more and more possibilities can be transformed into
needs, which are then conditioned accordingly: 'Do I really need the
entire Metallica catalogue? Shouldn't I spend the money on more

66 Luhmann, *Das Recht der Gesellschaft*, 454. Italics in original.
67 N. Luhmann, *Systemtheorie der Gesellschaft*, ed. J.F.K. Schmidt and A. Kieserling
    (Frankfurt am Main: Suhrkamp, 2018), 586–7.
68 Luhmann, *Die Wirtschaft der Gesellschaft*, 196.

meaningful needs?' Piracy, as we know, allows the satisfaction of this need without the diversions of a monetary payment.

The connection between having and not having may not strike us as particularly remarkable. We are familiar with it, have become accustomed to it. But what may not seem particularly remarkable to us is, on closer inspection, quite so. For the view of property duplicates the relation to the thing in question: from your body to the book you got as a birthday present to the software you invented. Pulled apart into a positive and negative version, the thing now exists twice, so to speak – in the same world. Property is the institution-alisation of this binary schematism, and not the simple (entitled or unentitled) possession of something. (Legally, another difference is relevant, namely that of possession and ownership, because someone can also possess something, i.e., 'have it in his power' – in his grip – that does not belong to him.)

As long as everything is in abundance, the scheme is not needed. As soon as something is scarce, it becomes acute; in late archaic societies, for example, the means of production. Especially land is also a means of production, because it allows food to be produced, for the production of which, in turn, one needs water, which can also be scarce. The law has its hands full here, as we will see, because it is also concerned with this political function of property, e.g., with the fact that land ownership serves to supply the population with essential goods. If a citizen of the USA wants to release a piece of land for the purposes of fracking, the situation differs from state to state. In some states it is forbidden, because the injection of chemicals into the ground puts drinking water at risk, and drinking water – see above – is needed for food production, etc. It is this political function of piracy to which many of the piracy theorists refer who call for basic digital provision, or, like Hall, invoke the idea of the commons. However, the institutionalisation of this difference becomes meaningful only when the change from having to not having is possible: when I can get a music file I do not own. Or when I cannot. It may sadden my friend Jungmo if I tear Gramsci's original prison notebooks into a thousand pieces in front of him, but how I use my property is my business. Bob Dylan allegedly used the 'Silver Elvis' that Andy Warhol gave him as a dart board.[69] Of course, the painter could do nothing about it: he did not own it any more. Sting's assumption that Universal, the new

69 At least Warhol reports the rumours in one of his books. See A. Warhol and
    P. Hackett, *POPism: The Warhol Sixties* (Orlando, FL: Harvest, 1980), 108

holder of his entire song catalogue, will give his work 'a home where it is valued and respected'[70] is as touching as it is naive, because what Universal does with the songs is their business (!) alone. This is what ownership is all about. For Sting's sake, let us assume that this 'respect' exists. The $US300 million Universal paid could be an indication; that it will last is by no means a foregone conclusion. And Sting could not even complain about it: sold is sold. Universal's new Sting property is nothing more than a temporary fixation awaiting its dissolution.

The constellation only becomes problematic with regard to change/non-change. Should my friend Jungmo stand idly by if I destroy the original Gramsci notebooks, although he is interested in their preservation? Pirates do not want to stand idly by. They do not want to give up money to access a scarce digital good, and they will not be okay with someone destroying important cultural content, pointing out that the only justification I have for owning the Gramsci notebooks is that I am not selling them (despite my friend offering me a lot of money for them).

The systematic attempts to explain the emergence and justification of the social institution of property, known under the name of occupation theories or property theories, amount to paradoxical constitutions of exclusion. That I have something (my body, the Gramsci notebooks, a demo of 'I Disappear') that someone else does not is somewhat understandable. That I am owner of a meadow (on which possibly a spring originates) is already more difficult, as we have seen, and the same applies to a factory. That I am owner of the sentences strung together in this text, about which my name at the beginning of this text informs, I consider no more than the convention of an attribution.[71]

---

70   A. Steigrad, 'Sting Sells Music Catalog to Universal Music Group for $250 million', *New York Post* (10 February 2022).

71   The relevant texts on this are persistently attributed to Foucault and Luhmann. With Foucault, we can direct the gaze obsessed with authorship to the functional conditions of those language games that he calls 'discourses', while Luhmann directs it to the functional conditions of systems. This text is committed to this basic idea: analysing piracy beyond authors and textual boundaries – despite the constant references to them – in order to draw attention to the functional conditions that make it possible in the first place. See M. Foucault, 'What is an Author?', in S.B. Smith (ed.), *Modernity and its Discontents: Making and Unmaking the Bourgeois from Machiavelli to Bellow* (New Haven, CT: Yale University Press, 2018), 299–314. Luhmann has sometimes

Is there a duty connected with property? Towards society? As we have seen, one of the motives that contribute to the acceptance of different distributional claims is the idea that property is an obligation. However, this obligation is only legally secured in rare cases, and only when it comes to the political functions of property discussed above. Does the pirate fulfil his duty towards society by disregarding exclusion via property? And how can social actors assert their claim to access, and which claims are considered legitimate? In pre-modern times, this question was answered by a 'moral economy', in that cosmological designs also clarified who was entitled to what and to how much.[72] By the eighteenth century at the latest, this natural law conception of economy was no longer compatible with the more complex reality. Instead, the bifurcation of having and not having was translated into the very schematism we are concerned with here – first that of property, then that of money.

The transfer of property occurs through exchange (or, more precisely, through the change of one exchange partner from owner to non-owner and of the other from non-owner to owner) legally whenever the owner agrees, and money can increase the likelihood of agreement decisively (but so can power, love, faith, and beauty).[73] Economy, therefore, cannot be thought of as limited to owners, since exchange would then be impossible: 'The property code consequently says that, with respect to all property capable of ownership, everyone is owner or non-owner, and that third possibilities are excluded'.[74] This also means that all but the owner must accept not having access to a resource. It is precisely this circumstance with which pirates and piracy theorists disagree – and this is not surprising or unusual; what is truly remarkable is the general societal consensus regarding the recognition and acceptance of property. Luhmann therefore speaks of an extreme evolutionary improbability. On the other hand, the

explicitly distanced himself from the assumption that it is he who writes his books; see, for example, N. Luhmann, *Archimedes und wir*, ed. D. Baecker and G. Stanitzek (Berlin: Merve, 1987), 142–3. More on the questionability of this attribution in the excursus on the lie of origin in section 4.

72 Luhmann, *Die Wirtschaft der Gesellschaft*, 185.

73 For reasons of space, I cannot go into the function of the so-called symbolically generalised communication media here, which belong to the essential structures of functional systems. But the example makes the basic assumption clear: that they serve to make improbable communication offers more probable.

74 Luhmann, *Die Wirtschaft der Gesellschaft*, 189.

necessity to accept property in order to participate in the economic system in turn motivates the non-owners to accept the property of others. Napster, who did not own the Metallica catalogue, not even a single one of their songs, could have simply accepted this fact, but then they would not have been able to make the band's catalogue available for free download, nor any other songs (except for those Fanning had recorded with his own non-existent band, perhaps). Lars Ulrich, on the other hand, could have simply accepted that on Napster, in their function as a pioneering peer-to-peer file-sharing service, the band's catalogue was made available to interested listeners for free download, instead of suing them.

This accepting is normal – because if we were to react to everything that happens around us, the potential for action would explode. But accepting certain actions also varies, of course. In the past, one accepted it if a colleague lit a cigarette; today, one does not do it without further ado (if one is outdoors, the probability increases). In the past, you accepted it when your boss made wild compliments (or grabbed your buttocks); today, you don't accept it easily anymore. But if he takes off his glasses to clean them, you don't mind. In the past, music owners got furious about piracy websites sharing their songs. For Ulrich, a music platform like Napster violated the conditions of normality. The reason why he has stopped suing piracy websites is probably not only to be found in the fact that the next Napster, the music exchange Gnutella, is completely decentralised, so that it is no longer possible to track down users, or because it is free software, so that no one can be sued, but because sharing files has become normal. It is what Luhmann calls a 'world event', just as unworthy of further mention as a person who cleans his glasses.

If we want to apply these considerations to the question of piracy, then we must first assume that a certain situation is experienced under the condition of scarcity. If I own something that is scarce – say, a demo of 'I Disappear' – then I will not simply accept it when someone – say, music lover Shawn 'The Napster' Fanning – takes it from me. Even the remark that he is sorry (that he doesn't earn any money from it because it is just about sharing music with Metallica fans and that he – unfortunately – already made this contingent access and has uploaded the piece, which is why I should calm down with the experience that this is so) will probably not be able to change my mind.

Luhmann's inquiry regarding the fundamental restructuring of the social order through property was: how is it conceivable that those who are excluded from access to scarce goods accept this exclusion? Why does someone accept the exchange transaction coming about or not coming about as merely an experienced event, as something that can just happen to you, as something that is just the way it is, that is expected as part of social reality – in other words, that it is normal, a 'world event', in the sense above? 'Why, in other words, is a disposition of scarce and, for many people, desirable goods accepted on the condition that two and only two participants agree?'[75] No one, after all, is forced to do so by political power. No one assumes that this distributional order is just. We already know the answer: a generally accepted means of exchange makes it possible – money. The money code presupposes the difference of having/not having and in turn duplicates this difference with the help of money symbols. This is precisely why one person is allowed to place his labour at the disposal of a certain entrepreneur, even though the need is much more urgent elsewhere. This is why others usually look on impassively at this two-party disposition. Money effectively neutralises any third-party interest.

As we have seen, codes are simple duplication rules. They provide a negative correlate for everything that occurs in their scope (which they themselves define) as information (which they themselves constitute). In science: true/untrue; in an intimate relationship: loved/not loved; in the economy: having/not having property; in education: passing/not passing tests; in politics: exercising official power/being subject to it, etc. Everything that is grasped with the form of the code appears as contingent: also possible otherwise. This duplication is not necessary, it is – with Luhmann: 'superfluous'.[76] I can look at my Gramsci notebooks or listen to my demo. Whatever the books or the demo may be worth, that doesn't change them. With Led Zeppelin: the song remains the same. The notebooks, too. Just like the Basquiat that was once hanging in Lars Ulrich's living room.[77] The reason

75 Luhmann, *Systemtheorie der Gesellschaft*, 511. Translation M.H.
76 Luhmann, *Systemtheorie der Gesellschaft*, 512.
77 According to his own statement, Ulrich is not just an 'owner'. Rather, he sees himself as a 'caretaker'. He had 'taken care' of the 1982 Basquiat painting for a long time, but now, said Ulrich in 2008, 'it is time to put it back into circulation, and let someone else enjoy it as much as I have over the last decade'. Associated Press, 'Lars Ulrich to Sell Basquiat Painting', *Hollywood Reporter* (10 October 2008). Whatever he himself may say about his purchase and resale of the painting, the circulation he is talking about is not a general societal one, but that of the art market, that is, a part of the economic system. If he

why we accept it when someone like Ulrich has a beautiful Basquiat painting – even though our need is much more urgent – is simply that he paid a lot of money for it. If we paid a lot of money for it, we could also buy such a Basquiat and hang it as a trophy above our sofa – we could even, like Ulrich, place two small African wooden sculptures in front of it to clarify that it was painted by a black man.

But how exactly does the neutralisation of third-party interests work? With the help of the idea of equivalence. The $US50,000 that Fanning could have offered Ulrich for the demo in an alternative history corresponds – so the idea goes – to the value of it. It is this equivalence that neutralises possible objections from others who watch Ulrich and Fanning haggle. They accept the disposition over the scarce and, for many people, desirable good. As long as Fanning pays, everyone else excluded from the exchange is reassured. Of course, only as long as he doesn't share the demo with the whole world 'for free' on Napster. The idea is that what he has, no one else has. For by doing so he puts everyone else in a position also to access other, as yet unspecified things, such as the original Gramsci notebooks, a Basquiat, a jewelled egg. Which is why Luhmann converts Karl Marx's well-known aphorism into 'money is the opium of the people'.[78] And money is apparently also the opium for Lars Ulrich – in contrast to Shawn Fanning, who didn't want to believe that at all: 'I thought perhaps this was industry propaganda and some lawyer capitalising on the controversy – not explaining things to Metallica fully. I got very defensive as I like the music and the band members'.[79] If Ulrich had received a large sum of money for the demo, who knows, maybe he would not have objected to giving it away, i.e., exchanging it.

wanted someone to take care of it or 'enjoy' it, he could have simply given it away. Nevertheless, his formulation is revealing. It points to the same need to rhetorically enhance one's own financial orientation that is also encountered in his comments on the Napster case. We can see it as a variant of the above discussed idea that property obliges. It allows Ulrich to appear as someone who is fulfilling his duty to society. The follow-up question could be what problem this resort to the mode of hypocrisy solves. My guess is that it is supposed to mark him out as someone who has mastered the technique of moral communication that is so important for the upper circles of politics and the economy – as symbolic capital in Pierre Bourdieu's sense, which is invested in solving the problem of inclusion.

78   Luhmann, *Systemtheorie der Gesellschaft*, 512.
79   Walsh, 'Mom, I blew up the music industry'.

Certainly, Ulrich himself said, it's not about money, but control.[80] Even if that may have been the case, such statements must of course be judged with scepticism because they are addressed to the public (which, of course, also applies to Fanning's statements). As Musil has his protagonist, Count Leinsdorf, say so beautifully: When one makes a public statement, he flows in a different circuit.[81] If control is supposed to mean that Metallica decide whether and when their songs are available for free download on Napster, the band could have settled with them out of court. If control means that Metallica decide not only when to make these songs available, but also how much money they want to receive for them in return, a lawsuit makes more sense. The aforementioned statement of their lawyer points in this direction: Napster 'could raise hundreds of millions of dollars if they decided to offer shares in the company'.[82] The company was thus not only punished for offering music for nothing, but also for not agreeing to a change of strategy. The misunderstanding here was apparently that Metallica were only seen as artists and the coupling with the economic system, which is of crucial importance for pop music, was not sufficiently taken into account.[83] But this confusion was a mutual one. For the owners Metallica also justified their claim to payment with a reference to their status as artists: 'It is [...] sickening to know that our art is being traded like a commodity rather than the art that it is'.[84] Ulrich's argument makes little sense, because the band's songs were precisely not traded as commodities or material goods on Napster, as is usually the case.[85] Rather, fans skipped the moment of value creation that demeans any art and appreciated the results of the band's activity by directing the commodity straight toward consumption without any intermediate step. Just as in their 'early

---

80   Walsh, 'Mom, I blew up the music industry'.
81   Robert Musil, *Der Mann ohne Eigenschaften* (Munich: Carl Hanser Verlag, 2013), 99; also nn. 23 and 73.
82   Howard King, in Walsh, 'Mom, I blew up the music industry'.
83   About the trajectories of this coupling, see Heidingsfelder, *System Pop*, 470 ff.
84   R. Reed, 'Revisiting the Lessons of Metallica's Napster Lawsuit in the Era of Coronavirus', *Spin* (13 April 2020).
85   Whether Metallica's music is art in the strict sense of the word I would dispute, because the band's music – like all pop music – is determined by its function, the blocking of reflection, and thus opposed to art (see Heidingsfelder, *System Pop*, 111–12, 255, 341–2). For strategic reasons, however, I use the term 'art' in this text in an extended sense, in the same way in which the English-speaking world refers to musicians like Ulrich and Justin Bieber as 'artists'.

days', when – according to a fan – 'they just wanted to get their music out there'.[86] To reflect the facts correctly, Ulrich's sentence should have read: *It is sickening to know that our music is traded as art.*

Paradoxically, access creates what it is supposed to eliminate.[87] In this, scarcity is self-referential: it motivates reserving access and thereby increases scarcity, which in turn leads to increased motivation to access. The paradox can be resolved by looking at the specific actors: in our example, scarcity becomes less for my friend Jungmo, who buys my Gramsci notebooks, but greater for everyone else. In the case of piracy, this medium does not come into play, which is why we had established that it does not occur within the economic system. Thanks to the Internet and the pirates, the non-organic needs for cultural contents can be satisfied even without money, which normally determines whether one can have something or not. Many market participants have chosen this 'cheap' (in fact, free) form of music supply as the main one. The offer that makes file sharing attractive is that it combines the almost endless individual need satisfaction with the idea of the common good, an equal distribution of cultural or 'content property'. The price one pays for the unauthorised copying and exploitation of copyrighted works is the currency of possible civil law consequences – it becomes more likely if you live in one of the First World countries. The other disadvantage has to do with the fact that you often come across low-quality copies or 'defective goods' – an argument that the World Bank research strangely does not use in the case of artworks, presumably because the psychological costs (annoyance, displeasure) are of little consequence – and the search for high-quality ones takes time or remains unsuccessful. Which is why most users follow a double strategy: sometimes pay, mostly not.

Of course, a property-based economy is not necessarily a money economy; it can be, and historically has been for a long time, based on the exchange of property of things. Fanning could also have offered Ulrich two African sculptures in exchange for the possibility of sharing 'I Disappear'. But the socially unifying, bonding nature of such an exchange is rather repugnant to many contemporaries today. Most prefer a socially emptied form of exchange – that of money symbols.

86   Reed, 'Revisiting the Lessons of Metallica's Napster Lawsuit'.
87   Luhmann, *Die Wirtschaft der Gesellschaft*, 179.

***

Economy is only ever at issue when the binary code payment/ non-payment is in use. It is oriented exclusively to this distinction. The preference value is the payment or the optimisation of the ability to pay. The form of piracy investigated here – the sharing of cultural contents – does not lead to profit, nor is it in most cases being done for the sake of profit. File sharers don't exchange files for files either. Because this 'share economy' (in contrast to the shares economy) is completely independent of the social status of the participants and the concrete consideration, it is first of all free of external influences, and second, because nothing is paid for the files, these operations can be completely decoupled from the economic system. In the share economy, nobody is excluded from accessing the resource 'Metallica catalogue' – the only restriction is that Internet access is required, and a certain 'speed' (data transmission rate) must also be guaranteed.

The communal aspect emphasised by piracy theorists becomes evident in this context. It is this moment of self-exclusion that makes a rights holder like Ulrich so uncomfortable – in his words: the loss of 'control'. From his perspective, access should only take place if a payment is made. That is why piracy is seen as a problem. Not because the supposed artistic character of song artefacts is despised here, or because it could cause damage to health – one of the most important arguments against piracy's big ugly sister, counterfeiting. If prosecution is successful, however, it can be turned into profits that at least compensate to some extent for the alleged losses and thus make the expected communication about scarcity in the form of payments or payment expectations possible after all – almost as if the economy itself wanted to take revenge for being left out or operationally excluded from piracy. Since there is a whole industry that parasitises on this compensation practice, we can assume that these profits are not infinitesimally small, even though they are unlikely to be of an economically relevant magnitude. But why – or more precisely how – can piracy be then held responsible for the economic effects of infringements? The assumption represents a bet on the future: that piracy takes place at the expense of profits that would surely have materialised without it.

However, while it is a fact that thousands of people who made thousands of copies of copyrighted songs via Napster, for example, gave neither the music industry nor the artists any money for these copies, this does not mean that all downloaded data, without exception, would have been purchased by the users in question at full price instead. Metallica lawyer Howard King even blamed Napster for the insolvency of small record shops: 'There are colleges across the States – where the Napster is particularly popular – whose record stores are going out of business'.[88] But the extent to which the exchange of unlicensed content has influenced and continues to influence the development of revenues and sales in the recorded music market is more than questionable. The numerous studies come to completely different conclusions. Many consider file sharing to be the cause of the drop in sales, while others see no connection here.[89] An official study published in 2010 by the U.S. Government Accountability Office has sharply criticised the assumption that all downloaded data would have been purchased at full price by the users concerned. It is no longer allowed to be applied in official papers and statements in the United States due to a lack of evidence and dubious study conduct.[90]

The situation is different in the case of counterfeiting. The aim here is to make profits on a large scale, which is why it also attracts the greatest interest on the part of the rights holders. In other words, unlike piracy, counterfeiting takes place in the economic system. It is understandable that the copied companies do not consider this desirable; however, in order to give their claim more 'social weight' they do not cite the losses incurred by the industry due to counterfeiting and piracy, but refer to other damages caused by them. In doing so, both types are considered equally 'bad': 'Policy makers around the world recognize the potentially harmful consequences of trademark counterfeiting and copyright piracy'.[91] A closer look reveals that the

88   Walsh, 'Mom, I blew up the music industry'.
89   Rufus Pollock has compared the various studies and considers a share of between 0 per cent and 30 per cent to be realistic. For 2009, the German Music Industry Association (Bundesverband Musikindustrie) assumed that only about 10 per cent to 20 per cent of the downloaded songs would have generated sales and estimated the resulting damage at about 400 million to almost 1 billion euro. See S. Zach, *Labelgründung 2.0: Der Weg zum eigenen Label in Zeiten von Web 2.0* (manuscript 2008), 53 ff.
90   U.S. Government Accountability Office, 'Intellectual Property: Observations on Efforts to Quantify the Economic Effects of Counterfeit and Pirated Goods', Reports and Testimonies GAO-10-423 (12 April 2010), www.gao.gov/products/gao-10-423.
91   Fink et al., 'Economic Effects', 2.

two offences entail fundamentally different consequences, which is hardly surprising considering their different functions.

According to the US Congress report mentioned above, '[n]egative effects on U.S. industry may include lost sales, lost brand value, and reduced incentives to innovate'.[92] This assessment, which in addition to the loss of expected financial gains primarily denotes a loss of confidence and a loss of motivation that could then in turn have financial implications, is apparently highly connectable. Fink et al. second that infringements of intellectual property rights 'undermine trust in rules-based systems that are at the core of modern market-based economies'.[93] The specific concern in the case of counterfeit products – apart from an inadmissible confusion of consumers and mere ineffectiveness (the product 'does not work') – are national security or civilian safety implications, for instance adverse health consequences: the fake products may be 'dangerous, as with adulterated medicines and foodstuffs or noncertified engine replacement parts'.[94] The third argument then brings the two offences together again and concerns the supposed inhibition of creative motivation, i.e., socio-psychological effects: 'extensive counterfeiting can significantly deter the emergence of new products and firms, and piracy can block the development of creative industries, especially in poor countries where entry conditions are already weak'.[95] Piracy and counterfeiting appear equally as dangerous destabilisers of the social order, acting on three levels: first, on a society-wide level, as the loss of trust negatively affects 'modern market-based economics'; second, the counterfeit products could pose a threat to life and limb; and third, they weaken the inventive spirit and motivational drive of the creative industries. The last aspect resonates with a premise in Paul Starr's reasoning for copyright in his book *The Creation of Media*. As per Starr, the absence of the legal safeguards of patent and copyright would render an open society dysfunctional, as 'this right of appropriation [...] has helped to enlarge the public sphere

92   U.S. Government Accountability Office, 'Intellectual Property'.
93   Fink et al., 'Economic Effects', 2. The similarities between the authors' choice of words and the wording of the Congress report are sometimes striking. Are advocates of IPR (Intellectual Property Rights) guilty of copyright infringement here? In my view, this circumstance points to a fundamental paradox related to this historical construct, of which the authors seem to be unaware. They simply take it for granted. I will come back to this.
94   Fink et al., 'Economic Effects', 2.
95   Fink et al., 'Economic Effects', 2.

by creating incentives to produce and disseminate knowledge and new technology.[96] Apart from the debate over the legitimacy of the perceived disadvantage of 'closed' societies, including the classification of China as such, there is doubt regarding the fairness of access available to investors and authors from the global south to participate in this realm of innovation and emerging knowledge from the outset, and thus, whether they can fully benefit from it. Starr also acknowledges that copyright monopolies, depending on their breadth and comprehensiveness, can impede further innovation.[97] This is where the argument of the pirates becomes relevant, highlighting the conflict between private interests and the broader interests they purport to promote. Additionally, Starr identifies the drawbacks of a purely market-based regime for education and research, which will be discussed further in section 5.

Fink et al. acknowledge that the traditional intellectual property sectors have less influence on the manufacturing systems of impoverished nations. Local businesses may concentrate more on mimicking and duplicating products, and consumers may be more accepting of counterfeit items, meaning that stricter enforcement of intellectual property rights would primarily benefit multinational companies and foreign content providers. However, the authors claim that 'even poorer countries have significant interests in stronger enforcement for at least two reasons. One is that their citizens disproportionately suffer from adulterated counterfeit medicines and ineffective or dangerous foods and beverages'.[98] One could argue that the harm to someone who purchases a counterfeit Gucci bag is rather small, even in the unlikely event that the purchaser assumes the bag is genuine. (It is more likely that the person is well aware of the fact that they are buying a counterfeit product, because otherwise it would not be available at such a low price, and therefore also of its defects.) But even counterfeiting Gucci bags, according to Fink et al., can have harmful effects on a developing country, as 'weak trademark enforcement can sharply diminish prospects for effective brand development, firm entry, and national marketing success among potentially innovative companies

---

96 P. Starr, *The Creation of the Media: Political Origins of Modern Communications* (New York: Basic Books, 2004), 10.

97 Starr, *Creation of the Media*, 11.

98 Fink et al., 'Economic Effects', 32. Of course, one would have to ask all of the governments of these 'poor countries' individually whether this claim of interest in stronger copyright enforcement is true – or whether a norm is being passed off as fact here.

in poor countries'.[99] Others argue that local counterfeiting often targets domestic enterprises at least as much as foreign brands.[100] Similarly, extensive unauthorised copying of music, designs, and other creative activities allegedly limits the ability of artists to build local markets, ultimately affecting their ability to 'sell worldwide' (in other words, become a global player in the same way as those whose copyright is protected). The researchers recommend a strategy that relies on public investment in law enforcement and creative infrastructures on the one hand and focuses ever-scarce law enforcement resources on reducing fraudulent counterfeiting on the other hand. Additionally, educational campaigns are to be conducted to raise consumer awareness of how unauthorised copying negatively impacts local artists.

The ineffectiveness of these approaches has long been recognised. For Burleson, the failure of massive marketing campaigns aimed at educating the public about the correct moral implications of copyright infringement is unsurprising, not only because it is questionable whether either the government or private interests can forcibly alter existing morals or social norms that have already taken root in society – but simply because a strategy that relies on winning people's hearts and minds by calling them thieves is not very promising.[101]

Professionally conducted counterfeiting and piracy are also considered as a political means for the purpose of the destabilisation of national economies. This is the US accusation against China: 'According to the Commission on the Theft of American Intellectual Property, intellectual property theft costs the U.S. economy hundreds of billions of dollars annually, and China is "the world's principal IP infringer"'.[102]

We encounter a tactic of fear generation that has also been employed before the music industry's conversion to digital commerce: If 'the economic growth engine of the culture industry' starts to sputter, German licence owners argued in an open letter to then-Chancellor Merkel in 2008, 'we cannot guarantee anything'. (That the petitioners invoke the Frankfurt School-created theoretical figure of the culture industry as a positive force is a wonderful footnote to the history of

99   Fink et al., 'Economic Effects', 32.
100 A.C. Mertha, *The Politics of Piracy: Intellectual Property in Contemporary China* (Ithaca, NY: Cornell University Press, 2005).
101 K. Burleson, 'Learning from Copyright's Failure to Build Its Future', *Indiana Law Journal* 89, no. 3 (2014), 1313 ff.
102 M. Farivar, 'US Intensifies Crackdown on China Intellectual Property Theft', *Voice of America* (15 May 2020).

piracy.) One of the suggestions was to take the anti-piracy policies of the UK and France as a model; in both countries, there had been discussion of simply cutting the Internet connections of users who are repeatedly caught file sharing. It seems that the infinities of causalities make a 'stop rule' (Peter Fuchs) like the pirate necessary: not the technical course of events, not overpriced, bad products let the revenues shrink – the malicious pirate is to blame for the misery. In the case of the music industry, a wrong pricing policy and the too late adaptation of offers to the wishes of the consumers could also have played a role in the decline in sales. It can also be attributed to the decoupling of individual tracks made possible by digital distribution, which inevitably had a negative impact on album sales. Even the US Congress was sceptical in the face of the music industry's accusations against pirates (here, file sharers) and speculation about lost profits; more than that, the above-mentioned report from 2010 emphasised 'that piracy may also benefit the entertainment industries and third parties'.[103]

Many researchers subscribe to this view.[104] They look at the gains that the economy owes to the piracy factor as an impetus for important structural changes, as a 'constructive destructor'. Here, for once, it would indeed be appropriate to speak of positive socio-economic consequences, because the beneficiaries are not individual companies, but entire regions and business sectors. From this perspective, piracy appears as a motor and driving force of the economy. For Baumgärtel, only the threat of piracy has led the media industry to switch to distribution methods that correspond to the technical possibilities and audience desires in the age of the Internet: 'Without piracy, there would be no streaming, no Spotify, no Netflix, and no media libraries – all forms of distribution that correspond to the technical shape of the Internet, and which were initially operated illegally before the industry could bring itself to make its own legal

---

103 U.S. Government Accountability Office, 'Intellectual Property'; Ernesto Van der Sar, 'U.S. Government Recognizes Benefits of Piracy', *Torrentfreak* (13 April 2010), https://torrentfreak.com/es/u-s-government-recognizes-benefits-of-piracy-100413/.

104 It is worth noting that some of these researchers are also advocates of piracy. While this does not necessarily invalidate their research findings, it may shed light on certain exaggerations in their arguments. However, the same exaggerations are found in what I call World Bank research, which I count among the reflective instances of the economy, so the two balance each other out, so to speak.

offerings'.[105] Li argues similarly with regard to China.[106] Following up on Johnson et al.,[107] she suggests not to interpret the phenomenon politically or legally, but to consider it an industry and acknowledge piracy as a sector of the informal economy, of which especially 'video spoofing' and 'fansubbing' appear as important practices of the pre-Internet.[108] Rather than seeing weak trademark enforcement as a threat to effective brand development, corporate market entry, and national marketing success, Li emphasises the social energies that encouraged the formation of these online practices, which eventually became assimilated within a nascent Chinese video industry. In that respect, her argument is 'that the vernacular cultural forms and practices associated with these phenomena were central, and indeed essential, to the formation of an online video industry in China'.[109]

Similar considerations arise with regard to the phenomenon known as 'Shanzhai'. Literally meaning 'mountain fortress' or 'mountain village', it was initially used to describe a bandit stronghold outside government control. Today, it refers to Chinese businesses based on fake and pirated products. Instead of condemning Shanzhai as the embodiment of China's 'knock-off' industries, scholars argue that it might be more appropriately viewed as an instance of its emerging creative economy and an example of rapid prototyping.[110] 'Many businesses with humble Shan Zhai origins are becoming formidable market disruptors, and in many cases, market leaders [...] The Shan Zhai phenomenon is not about low-cost fake products anymore; it is about how one type of Chinese company achieves success without following conventional wisdom and develops competitive advantage through innovation'.[111] The self-proclaimed 'Shanzhai archeologists',

---

105 Baumgärtel, 'Lob der Piraterie'.
106 N. Li, 'Rethinking the Chinese Internet: Social History, Cultural Forms, and Industrial Formation', *Television & New Media* 18, no. 5 (2017), 393–409.
107 M. Johnson, K.B. Wagner, K.T. Yu, and L. Vulpiani, *China's iGeneration: Cinema and Moving Image Culture for the Twenty-First Century* (New York: Bloomsbury Academic, 2014).
108 See also Shujen Wang, *Framing Piracy: Globalization and Film Distribution in Greater China* (Lanham, MD: Rowman & Littlefield, 2003), who examines film piracy in China as an example of laissez-faire capitalism.
109 Li, 'Rethinking the Chinese Internet', 393.
110 Michael Keane and Elaine Jing Zhao, 'Renegades on the Frontier of Innovation: The Shanzhai Grassroots Communities of Shenzhen in China's Creative Economy', *Eurasian Geography and Economics* 53, no. 2 (2012), 216.
111 E. Tse, K. Ma, and Y. Huang, *Shan Zhai: A Chinese Phenomenon* (Beijing: Booz & Company, 2009), 1.

who promote the scientific study of Shanzhai companies through the recovery and analysis of their products, point out the bleakness and unimaginativeness of the design of most Western manufacturers.[112]

Another counter-example of the productive energies and positive socio-economic effects of piracy can be found in the so-called Dakou discs: 'These CDs and cassette tapes arrived in China as waste to be recycled; they were cut on their edges to prevent them from being resold'.[113] The word 'Dakou', which literally translates as 'strike cut', refers to precisely this defect that was meant to devalue the goods and thus prevent resale. Because Chinese custom officials turned a blind eye and sold them on, they became available for listeners to buy from semi-legal markets for – not unimportant in order to be able to judge the Dakou practice as piracy – ridiculous amounts. The defect thus quickly became its own brand. Dakou albums and cassettes allowed 'a new generation of young Chinese [...] to listen to foreign music – pop, rock or even classical music – to form new bands, or to write as music critics'.[114] The phenomenon has been described and analysed in an impressive number of articles as a crucial source of inspiration for Chinese musicians, writers, or music lovers, and the importance of Dakou for the emergence of a new Chinese rock music scene in the 1990s.[115] Contrary to Starr's argument of the judicial protection of copyright, it was actually the deliberate neglect that led to the creation of production incentives and even served as a component of state-building.

As mentioned in the beginning, there are considerable national differences in terms of legal restrictions on counterfeiting and piracy. While in the West no direct economic gains through piracy could be

---

112 Clément Renaud, 'An Archeology of Shanzhai Phones', in Clément Renaud, Florence Graezer Bideau, and Marc Laperrouza (eds), *Realtime: Making Digital China* (Lausanne: Presses polytechniques et universitaires romandes, 2020), 86–109. For more on the phenomenon and the 'Shanzhai archeologists', see section 5. See also Zhen Troy Chen's article in this book.

113 N. Amar, 'The Lives of Dakou in China: From Waste to Nostalgia', *Études chinoises* 38, no. 2 (2018), 35.

114 Amar, 'Lives of Dakou', 35.

115 Jeroen de Kloet, 'Dakou Culture', in E.L. Davis (ed.), *Encyclopedia of Contemporary Chinese Culture* (London: Routledge, 2005), 183; J. Yan, *Génération dakou: écouter, recycler, expérimenter* (Paris: Van Dieren Éditeur, 2012), 29 ff. The text by Jiarui Tan in this volume adds a first-hand account to the relevant Dakou analyses by Western researchers. It also confirms the assumption that Dakou was not about achieving high profits, but rather a kind of sharing: 'They didn't sell a lot of stuff, and things they did sell usually looked more like they originated from personal collections'.

claimed, the positive side-effects have been observed in the increased reach and perception of pirated contents. According to this logic, today's highly acclaimed US series like *The Wire* or *The Sopranos* owe their global acceptance not least to an international army of fans who discussed and analysed every episode on their blogs and social networks. HBO programming president, Michael Lombardo, called piracy 'a compliment of sorts' that accompanies 'a wildly successful show (e.g., *Game of Thrones*, M.H.) on a subscription network'.[116] Unlike Metallica, Billy Corgan of the Smashing Pumpkins welcomed the practice of file sharing, which guaranteed precisely this wide dissemination of one's art.[117] From this perspective, piracy, while not the driver of success, contributes to it – as a moment of 'symbiotic' partnership.[118]

4 Piracy and Law

Next to the economy, the law represents the most important system reference of piracy, which in turn is related to the observation form of property. This is due to the fact that property is, so to speak, no longer property, i.e., can no longer be observed and distinguished as somebody owning something, if its forcible removal is not prevented and, if necessary, sanctioned.[119] The law monitors the control or power of disposal over property by means of the system's own mutually exclusive distinction between illegal and legal. This exclusivity is also present with regard to ownership. If a song, say, 'I Disappear', belongs to Hetfield/Ulrich, it cannot also belong to Hanneman/King.

116 G. Gilman, '"Game of Thrones" Tops "Breaking Bad" as 2013's Most-Pirated TV Show', *The Wrap* (26 December 2013).
117 Walsh, 'Mom, I blew up the music industry'.
118 By the way, I too belong to this group of beneficiaries. The film about Rem Koolhaas produced by Min Tesch and me, *A Kind of Architect*, ended up on YouTube shortly after its DVD release, and a photo of the elderly George Spencer-Brown taken by my friend Mirko Ludewig when we visited this remarkable man in his home in Horningsham was also copied and shared without following the Commons guidelines we had made conditional. I see it like Lombardo – it is a compliment.
119 Luhmann, *Das Recht der Gesellschaft*, 454. The interesting case of expropriation, i.e., lawful removal in the public interest, which has become topical again as a result of the Ukraine war and Russia's threat to expropriate Western corporations, cannot be dealt with here. What is interesting about it in any case is the fact that compensation must nevertheless be paid for this removal, even though it is lawful.

If the owners of 'I Disappear' don't approve of it being used for a commercial or election campaign or being sampled or shared, then none of this can happen because only the owner gets to decide on that use. Unless, of course, he gets to deal with a pirate.

Property represents a 'hinge' that couples the two systems of law and economy, even if this observation scheme produces quite different forms in both, so that this hinge presents itself entirely distinct depending on the system from which one looks at it. Only because the observation scheme of property in law and in the economy allows different forms is it capable of structurally coupling both areas. In its operations, the economy ignores the question of what restrictions the legal system attaches to the concept of property; it simply uses the scheme because it depends on it. In other words, there would be no economy without property. The economy is indifferent to the restrictions that the law associates with the concept of property, and the law, in turn, is only concerned with the legality of the constitution of property. It throws sand into the gears of the economy; just as, conversely, the economy makes it more difficult for the law to make consistent case decisions (more emphatically, to establish 'justice').[120] Harder, but not impossible. The search for profitable capital investments in the economy continues but must take into account the conditions dictated by law. This strange combination of mutual obstruction and ignorance is already evident in classical natural law theory, which assumes that property stands in the way of any just legal order (a fact to which pirate theorists repeatedly point) but at the same time recognises the economic advantages that are gained by it.[121] The adaptation of unjust property demands to this natural law was not without problems, not least because it also had the task of fulfilling the promise of humanity itself.[122] How to justify an unjust right that constitutes a paradoxical relation of exclusion – as the act of first seizure is actually an act of injustice, which is then used to establish a right?[123] Every attempt to justify property can only be understood as the unfolding of a paradox and considered

120 Luhmann, *Das Recht der Gesellschaft*, 455.
121 Luhmann, *Das Recht der Gesellschaft*, 455.
122 N. Luhmann, *Die Moral der Gesellschaft* (Frankfurt am Main: Suhrkamp, 2008), 25.
123 N. Luhmann, 'Der Ursprung des Eigentums und seine Legitimation – ein historischer Bericht', in W. Krawietz, A.A. Martino, K.I. Winston (eds), *Technischer Imperativ und Legitimationskrise des Rechts* (Berlin: Duncker & Humblot, 1991), 43–57.

in terms of its respective historical–social plausibility. Property thus denotes nothing more than a form of observation of the access of socially constructed actors to objects of any kind. While some natural law theorists see the right to property as something that needs to be discovered, others claim that the discovery can only consist in nature's renunciation of any claims to property. This is how – in contrast to John Locke – Thomas Jefferson and Stewart Brand see it, the latter obviously being very familiar with the needs of organised data: 'information wants to be free'.[124] If information wants to be free, it will 'find a way' to escape this attempt at control. Of course, information itself does not want anything, and the Internet does not have any interests either, only to be discovered in its depths.[125] The critique of property, as we find it in many texts by pirate theorists, overlooks the fact that this formalism is precisely society's reaction to the disintegration of all material justifications as we find them in natural law. Replacing such a formalism with a new 'contentism' is unfortunately not an option.

As noted above, the most important historical development for transactions is the invention of money. The coding of the economy reflects this circumstance in that money is the secondary coding and property is the primary coding of the system. But only the recursive interconnection of money transactions, which take the place of thing transactions, makes the differentiation of the economy as an independent system possible. Whereas before all transactions had simply presupposed property, it is now property valued in money that becomes the presupposition. Since then, the money factor dominates the property factor, which ultimately means that all property is observed from the point of view of transformation into cash – as a temporary illiquidity.[126]

Especially for the high-risk money operations of the economic system, certainty of expectation with regard to legal decisions is important. However, a differentiated monetary economy places high demands on the law – as Luhmann so aptly puts it, 'priceless'

---

124 See R.P. Wagner, 'Information Wants To Be Free: Intellectual Property and the Mythologies of Control', *Columbia Law Review* 103, no. 4 (2003), 995–1034.
125 Therefore, even M.C. Kettemann's honourable attempt to discover a kind of natural normativity there, which could then be used to justify a corresponding legal practice, cannot help this practice any further. See M. Heidingsfelder, 'Guest Editorial: Shifting Spheres', *Kybernetes* 40, no. 4 (2020), 880.
126 Luhmann, *Das Recht der Gesellschaft*, 456.

demands.[127] And this is precisely the point: the law cannot fulfil the function of the economy, i.e., it must not be purchasable – a commodity or service. Then the terms of money-mediated transactions would have to be traded and paid for in turn, and a downward spiral would result. The solution for this is the forms of property and contract that allow a structural (not operative) coupling between the fields of law and economy. The observation scheme of exchange allows for the coupling of the economy with the law, and the observation scheme of contract allows for the coupling of the law with the economy.[128] It determines the terms for giving up ownership, for instance for sharing your demo of 'I Disappear' on Napster. The first requirement is that you are able ('free') to negotiate these terms. It was exactly this possibility that Napster denied to the song owners Metallica, i.e., Lars Ulrich, and Universal Music granted to Sting.[129]

***

The form of ownership that is most important in the context of this chapter is that of intellectual property – an 'esoteric legal subject' (Liang), whose increased relevance has much to do with the rise of pirate practice. Liang observes a remarkable transformation that has taken place in a relatively short time: 'the aggressive expansion of property claims into every domain of knowledge and cultural practice'.[130] What once applied to the appropriation of material wealth or trespassing onto private property is now massively extended to all objects that – in Liang's words – 'embody thought, knowledge or feeling'.[131] Yet this expansion of intellectual property is taking

127 Luhmann, *Die Wirtschaft der Gesellschaft*, 453.
128 Luhmann, *Das Recht der Gesellschaft*, 456.
129 Steigrad, 'Sting Sells Music Catalog'.
130 Lawrence Liang, 'Copies without Originals: The Work of Love in the Age of Mechanical Reproduction', Marg Foundation (29 November 2022), 50; Lawrence Liang, 'Beyond Representation: The Figure of the Pirate', in Lars Eckstein and Anja Schwarz (eds), *Postcolonial Piracy: Media Distribution and Cultural Production in the Global South* (London: Bloomsbury, 2014), 69–70.
131 Liang, 'Beyond Representation', 50. Niklas Luhmann's work – including the famous 'Zettelkasten' – was itself the subject of a dispute between his children over ownership and copyright that dragged on for several years. Luhmann had transferred all copyrights to his daughter in an advance bequest in 1995, as it was his wish that his intellectual legacy remain in one hand, and the judiciary ruled in his favour. On this one-hand solution,

place in very different ways in different regions of world society. In the United States, Liang observes a shrinkage of the public domain and of the commons and the linking of file-sharing and peer-to-peer activities with the global war on terror, while as previously outlined, in many parts of Asia, the proliferation of cheap technologies of media reproduction creates a parallel economy that threatens the monopoly of old media.[132]

Intellectual property brings two evolutionary achievements together. First, the possibility of considering property as invested capital, and second, the possibility of extending property to the realm of the 'mind', whose owners are henceforth interested in the transactional exploitation of works or inventions that are the result of creativity: art works, designs, symbols, names, images, and computer codes like the one developed by Shawn Fanning. On the other side we find creations that are not the result of creative work: boring, simple-minded, uninspired. The often expressed misunderstanding that intellectual copyright also protects 'mind property' – ideas – has to do with this questionable designation. But copyright shelters only fixed creative expressions, not the ideas or facts upon which the expressions are based. For example, copyright may protect a film like *Jaws*, but it cannot protect the idea of a great white shark preying upon a small resort town and the voyage of three men trying to kill it. At least this restriction makes sense when comparing the different reproduction conditions: an idea does not develop into a novel or a film like an egg develops into a mouse. The egg contains a set of instructions in its genes, the idea does not. In fact, the reason for this restriction is hardly to be found in the biological knowledge of the legislators, who merely want to ensure that creative work continues to be diligently carried out: 'Allowing authors to monopolize their ideas would thwart the underlying purpose of copyright law, which is to encourage people to create new work'.[133]

The dubiousness of the construct of intellectual copyright, which is based on the idea of individual authorship, cannot be given much space in this text. Not for methodological reasons alone, since the

however improbable, a German sociologist and a British rockstar seem to agree.

132 Philippe Cullet, *Intellectual Property Protection and Sustainable Development* (London: Butterworth, 2005).

133 Rich Stim, 'Copyright Basics FAQ', Stanford Libraries, https://fairuse.stanford.edu/overview/faqs/copyright-basics/.

aim is to reconstruct (and thus construct) the piracy observations of the law, the economy, and piracy itself. In the form of a brief digression, however, it should be pointed out that its plausibility owes much to the circumstances of our perception. Hardly anything is phenomenally as evident 'as the sense of owner-ship, the constantly revitalising "feeling" of authorship'.[134] Everyone who sees, hears, or feels experiences themselves as the centre of the world, because what we perceive is built around this centre. Communication reinforces this 'deception'. It can be compared to the process of formatting: as a much more comprehensive and fundamental form of socialisation than we normally assume. We are not only given certain themes and schemes, we are also equipped with a certain basal way of using meaning, for which the difference between self-reference (who said something) and 'reference' (what was said) is central. The very process of socialisation creates the idea of an inside/outside, it creates sensory perception just like consciousness and the self.[135] But if this is so, then there is no reason for us to use a possessive pronoun here. 'My' consciousness is not my consciousness.[136]

In fact, no communication is private and thus cannot belong to one person – otherwise, it would not function as communication at all. Which is why communicated and socially circulating individuality is always general individuality. The idea of originality itself is a result of social, that is, general processes. In simpler terms, there is no alternative to copying. Peter Fuchs has therefore referred to the notion of an originator as a 'lie of origin' (or *proton pseudos*, in Aristotelian terms).[137] This false premise assumes that a communication belongs

134 P. Fuchs, *Am Fuß des Leuchtturms* (Weilerswist: Velbrück, 2019), 13.
135 Fuchs, *Am Fuß des Leuchtturms*, 13.
136 Derrida approaches the question of paradoxical origin with the help of the soufflage metaphor. What inspires the poet is this 'positive incursion of speech'. We do not know where it comes from, who speaks it; it is another voice that reads out ideas to us, as it were. See J. Derrida, 'Die soufflierte Rede', in *Die Schrift und die Differenz* (Frankfurt am Main: Suhrkamp, 1997), 269. If this soufflage is to have consequences, it must be offered to perception. It succeeds through a kind of proxy Luhmann signs with the metaphor of 'flagging out' (which makes sense in the pirate context). With the help of this simplification, communication is marked as an action and attributed to the persons who talk, speak, compose, paint, sing... And because every utterance appears as a selection from a horizon of other possibilities, the thought suggests itself that there is someone selecting: an author, an authority telling the story of *Ulysses* or Jesus Christ or *Robinson Crusoe* or the Avengers.
137 Fuchs *Am Fuß des Leuchtturms*, 209, with reference to Žižek 1996.

to an author, to an 'I' that resides in consciousness and transforms a thought into an expression, from which further false statements are derived. The humanist tradition of the 18th and 19th centuries subscribed to this idea, emphasising self-expression and freedom through individuality, and current copyright law still upholds this perspective, while ignoring the alternative tradition that emphasises copying and imitation. This text takes a pragmatic approach, assuming that there are psychic systems whose perception is organised in a way that appears to revolve around a kind of central registry. It is this 'appearance' (this phenomenon) that makes notions of intellectual property seem plausible.

The third complication is psychological and has to do with the way our brain works. Don't the thoughts in our heads often produce ideas all by themselves? In that case, one would almost have to speak of plagiarism: the thoughts that make themselves, without waiting for an originator, are passed off as something that one has created. Robert Musil speaks of something 'impersonal' that happens here: 'namely, the affinity and togetherness of the things themselves that meet in a head'.[138] Niklas Luhmann has compared his work to that of a computer, 'which can also be creative in the sense that it produces new results by combining input data that were not foreseeable in this way'.[139]

From this point of view, the impostor syndrome that is currently widely discussed in the Western media appears less as a disease than as a kind of allergic reaction to the constant insinuation of authorship and individual responsibility – to the demand to wear a mask that identifies us as selectors, as 'author-heroes'.

***

Media theory assumes several stages in the history of communication owing to breaks, most of which refer to the upheavals brought about by new technical media.[140] All these upheavals restructure thought and bring forth new social formations. There can be few better proofs for this thesis of the power of a new technology than the way

138 Musil, *Der Mann ohne Eigenschaften*, 112.
139 Luhmann, *Archimedes*, 144.
140 Albion, Johns, Baecker, Luhmann, or Behringer.

the Internet imposed its rules on the world and within a decade completely reformatted the way we consume music and films.

Especially in connection with the question of novelty, which is a decisive market requirement today, decisive shifts can be observed. For an enormously long period of time, society saw it the same way as nature: new mutations are more likely to be harmful to survival than adaptive.[141] One considered innovations to be inadvisable, and even more so, highly dangerous. Only since modernity, the 'modern age', has the demand for novelty replaced the demand for preservation. What must now be preserved is the new, and the innovative work that is judged to be new is protected: it may not be copied – the next work has to be new itself, another one-off.[142] This devaluation of the once positively connoted concept of copying at the beginning of the modern era, notes Luhmann, is initially surprising – after all, thanks to the printing press, 'copying is going on anyway and in an emphatically welcomed way'.[143]

A look at these upheavals also informs us about the contingency of a construction called 'authorship'. The first communicative revolution concerns the invention of the means of recording called writing, which Plato viewed so critically. The question of who owned a story such as the *Odyssey* or that of Jesus Christ or *The Empty Cup* did not even arise for contemporaries. Lord makes the distinction between non-literate authors of the Homeric epics and the scribes who later wrote them down.[144] The actual story of the *Odyssey*, for instance, had no definitive text, but consisted of innumerable variants, which were then improvised by the teller (Lord: singer) in the act of telling the tale. This makes the question of the author who owns the rights

---

141 Which of course poses the question of why the diversity of organisms that surround us are all wonderfully adapted: non-adaptation leads to adaptation? J.M. Smith and E. Szathmáry's *The Origins of Life: From the Birth of Life to the Origin of Language* (Oxford: Oxford University Press, 1999) is an attempt to answer this question. Part of this answer concerns natural features that are able to reduce the harmful effects of mutations, which in turn leads to the question of how these adaptive functions came about. According to Smith and Szathmáry, not by natural selection, which can of course only adapt something that varies.

142 See M. Heidingsfelder, 'Retrology: Addicted to the Future', *Society & Culture in South Asia* 2, no. 2 (2016), 12–13.

143 N. Luhmann, *Die Kunst der Gesellschaft* (Frankfurt am Main: Suhrkamp, 1995), 434.

144 Albert B. Lord, *The Singer of Tales* (Cambridge, MA: Harvard University Press, 1960).

to this story obsolete: the story of the *Odyssey* belonged to the one who 'sang' it. We can speak of a kind of temporary possession, as fleeting as the pressure and density fluctuations in the medium of air: hardly coupled into forms, they disintegrate again. The question of textual fidelity, i.e., the exact reproduction of a given text, did not arise for the singers of old because this original text did not exist. On the contrary, the moment of recreation was central to this oral tradition, in which improvisation and composition merged and became one process. An oral poet did not reproduce, he composed. And because this composition could not be recorded, only remembered, variation was guaranteed: the next, different, deviating composition. The concept of *poiesis*, which we have already encountered in connection with the 'self-making' of systems, points the way. It denotes a creative process which persists in the word 'reproduction', and this is exactly how sociology interprets it, as a re-creation. In everyday language it usually denotes a process in which something is duplicated, as well as the copy produced as a result of the process; and this replica is understood as inferior to the 'original' (a circumstance to which Benjamin may have made a not inconsiderable contribution). Even the question of whether the version of the *Odyssey* that has been handed down – the variant that presumably represents the transcription of a single telling of the story – belongs to one author, Homer, is likely to be misleading, because whether this literally legendary author ever existed, even if he was the last redactor and compiler, is still open to this day – a multiple authorship is more likely. The same applies to many other mythical authors of prehistoric times.

With the next media revolution, which owed itself to the printing of books, the question of authorship or the original arose in a different form. Textual uniformity, an essential ingredient for the acceptance of the Bible as a single, authoritative book, was not the forte of manuscript culture. To say that prior to printing the Bible existed in scribal multiformity is to make the point that no manuscript was exactly like any other. It was only with print technology that a standardised Bible and the dissemination of a virtually limitless number of fully identical copies became an attainable objective. The Greek text of the New Testament is entirely the creation of the medium of modernity: the product of an ongoing process of selection from a number of manuscripts and from a vast and growing pool of textual variants. It is an eclectic or composite text that has never existed before, most certainly not during the ancient and medieval centuries of oral, chirographic, performative communication.[145] Given the existence of 'tens of thousands of medieval manuscripts', what is the rationale, Kelber quotes Dagenais, for marginalising, discarding, and categorising them into lists of variants, instead of appreciating them as 'living witnesses to the dynamic, chaotic, error-fraught world of medieval literary life'? 'What is the intellectual value (and cultural significance) of taking a text that was written and read in a variety of forms in numerous medieval manuscripts and transforming it into a single printed book?'[146] The question could be wrongly posed – it was probably not the intellectual value that was in the foreground. But rather the possibility of handling this chaotic work for market purposes.

The idea of intellectual property emerged in the transit from the stratified to the functional form of differentiation (in semantically commensal form: the modern era). It began as a privilege, i.e., an exceptional law granted only to a single person or a group of persons. The ecclesiastical and secular rulers issued these privileges, and, just like today, these regulations were only used in the respective sovereign territory. Already in the next larger town, or at least on the national border, a printing privilege – or one to sell timber – was no longer worth much. When the bourgeoisie grew stronger, so did cross-border trade. A market for modern literature was established, which authors were only too happy to serve. Now the problem was no longer that of a physical reprint but of intellectual theft. People accused each other of stealing each other's ideas. Two worlds collided. The medieval culture of copying and commenting was still alive; but at the same time, notions of originality, authorship, and intellectual property had gained space – the idea of authorship of an idea.

It took time for the new understanding to take hold. In the transitional period, the oral, moment-oriented performance practices mixed with the new, literal orientations. When Bach and Handel composed, it was not – or only rudimentarily – about the creation of an immortal work that lives on after the death of the creator and thus needs to be protected. Instead, the music of the time was replaced by the new music of the next generation. This understanding found its direct expression in the musical assembly technique of montage called 'pastiche' (*pasticcio*), which

145 W.H. Kelber, *Imprints, Voiceprints, and Footprints of Memory: Collected Essays of Werner H. Kelber* (Atlanta, GA: Society of Biblical Literature, 2013), 449–54.
146 J. Dagenais, *The Ethics of Reading in Manuscript Culture: Glossing the Libro* de buen amor (Princeton, NJ: Princeton University Press, 1994), xvi.

was practised until the eighteenth century as a kind of analogue sampling procedure. It envisaged compiling operas or church music works from already existing music by different composers or from different works by one composer. Of interest here was not so much the question of whether this montage satisfied legal claims to authorship, but to what extent it succeeded as a work of art. The form of the *opera seria*, which separates the acting and contemplative parts (to which recitative and aria correspond musically), proved to be advantageous; the arias, which are not very concrete textually, could be easily transferred from one opera to another. The consideration of the different performance conditions (for example, concerning the abilities of the singers), which are hardly taken into account today, played as much a role as the information value: then *pasticci* turned into a kind of greatest hits compilation, which offered the audience a cross-section of the latest works of the most famous masters. Even Vivaldi was to make use of the form in his opera *Tamerlano/Bajazet*, for which he recomposed some pieces and took the rest of the music partly from his own works and partly from those of other composers. John Cage was to help the form, which had become aesthetically questionable in the nineteenth century (expressed in pejorative terms such as 'flick opera'), to new relevance in the twentieth century with his *Europeras*, which – as appropriations of several European opera pieces, especially arias – can confidently be called pirate works, even if they do not violate any copyrights. Cage took advantage of a copyright peculiarity, namely the fact that the associated monopoly expires after a maximum of 80 years. This possibility is not available to those who want to interpret a work by Cage today. They have to pay obscenely high royalties to John Cage's estate – whether it's for his flick operas or the legendary 4'33". Even silence can be copy-protected, it seems.[147]

With regard to the gradually installed temporary copyrights that started from the Statute of Anne (of Great Britain and Ireland) and were gradually adopted by other countries, one can observe the interesting fact that copyrights themselves were copied. One can therefore speak of a paradox: pirates prohibiting piracy. From Anderson's point of view, this applies quite fundamentally to those

147 At least when one relates this silence to Cage's name – an experience that Mike Batt had to make, who foolishly passed him off as a co-composer for his piece 'One Minute Silence'.

imagined communities we call nations: they, too, are the result of piracy.[148] Nations not only pirate one another's histories, but also legal guidelines that prohibit copying (today especially European ones, which is why observers speak of a 'Brussels effect').[149] And the Third World countries, as we have seen, are encouraged to copy the copyright laws of First World countries – in short, to act as pirates too in order to be able to fight piracy. A decade ago, almost anything could be freely downloaded in China, from music and books to movies and software. The increasing awareness of intellectual property rights in the country is probably related to the fact that China now tops the rest of the world in terms of patent applications.[150] In November 2017, China's State Council on Intellectual Property Rights concluded that 'penalties for IPR infringements will be increased and the cost of safeguarding such rights will be lowered. Quick and low-cost ways of safeguarding IPR must be expanded'. Consequently, there has been a rise in the number of legal cases. That times have changed was shown not least during the Olympic Winter Games 2022, where official mascot Bing Dwen Dwen became a hot commodity due to its scarcity – 'a fact Chinese state media celebrated, as it meant that copyright protection laws were upheld, with hardly any fakes on the market – something admittedly unlikely to have happened a decade ago'.[151] Additionally, as Michael D. High rightly notes in one of his comments on this text, the increasing protection of foreign copyrights in China is also being used as a means to restrict access to foreign content for ideological purposes.[152] However, that 'plagiarism is still rampant in China' is not due to disregard of the law.[153] Rather, it is ignored. Awareness of the laws protecting intellectual property is obviously still lacking, which may have something to do with decades of practice.[154]

148 B. Anderson, *Imagined Communities: Reflections on the Origin and Spread of Nationalism*, rev. ed. (London: Verso, 2006), 80 ff.

149 C. Piallat, *Der Wert der Digitalisierung*, 233.

150 Qian Chen, 'Plagiarism is Rampant in China, and Its Media Companies Are Raking in Billions', CNBC (23 January 2018).

151 M. Malzer, 'Reflections on the Winter Olympics in Beijing' (manuscript 2022).

152 At this point I would like to express my gratitude for his excellent review of this text. Any remaining deficiencies are entirely my own fault.

153 Chen, 'Plagiarism is Rampant in China'.

154 'It's China. No one's gonna sue you', one of my colleagues at UIC shrugged when I expressed my scepticism regarding the practice of downloading books from Sci-Hub and making them available to my students.

The conflict between a convention of transmission that has become historical and a new one that is just becoming established is something we encounter again today, albeit in the opposite variant: the ideas of originality, authorship, and intellectual property collide with ideas that encounter a new kind of culture of copying (and commenting) under conditions of digital modernity. The fundamental crisis into which the Internet plunged the music industry in particular at the end of the twentieth century seems to be a direct result of the functioning of digital reproduction and distribution technology, of programs such as the μTorrent software on our media theorist's computer. 'Since file sharing emerged in the late 1990s, copyright infringement has been widespread and virtually impervious to legal sanctions. Despite the best efforts of industry representatives and the lawmakers acting at their behest, attempts to scare and shame copyright infringers into compliance with the law have fallen flat'.[155] Piracy is so widespread precisely because the Internet so effectively lowers the cost of reproduction and makes it easy and inexpensive for users to duplicate numerous copies and transmit them instantly to numerous recipients worldwide. The same circumstance also explains the origin of the belief called 'Internet Myth No. 9' by Kettemann and Dreyer: that content on the Internet is free or not protected by copyright.[156] Even the insight into the fact that one is committing a breach of law here does not change the practice – the Internet seems to virtually demand this violation. However, the effortlessness of copying given by digital technology does not yet correspond to any legal regulation that declares copying to be legitimate. What can be said, however, is that being a pirate in Captain Blackbeard's time required far more initiative than it does today.

***

The world is turning, and the laws are turning – with a time lag – along with it. For when the norms of behaviour laid down by law, as the set of general rules of conduct guaranteed by the community, are no longer accepted as binding and are consequently

---

155 Burleson, 'Learning from Copyright's Failure', 1299.
156 M.C. Kettemann and S. Dreyer (eds), *Busted! The Truth about the 50 Most Common Internet Myths* (Hamburg: Verlag Hans-Bredow-Institut, 2019).

continually ignored, as is the case with users' dealings with digital data, new norms of behaviour emerge. Then unwritten law becomes written law. The legalisation of cannabis is a good example. Just like cannabis, P2P is here to stay, regardless of legality disputes. Since the introduction of Napster, many other similar utilities and websites have appeared. And most of them do not limit file sharing to just MP3s as Napster did. Some, like Gnutella, allow virtually anything to be shared. But for all the scope of these changes, the consequences in the fields of law and economics are only rudimentary. The social structural changes that have led to individual copyright infringement becoming a world event have not led *pari passu* to changes in the understanding of law.

What is the justification of the copyright currently in force, the right to protect content property? The justification is just the fact that it is not changed, despite legal possibilities to change it. From the point of view of the pirate, this 'ought' defined by lawyers ('Thou shalt pay for content') is a historically contingent artifact. It has outlived its usefulness, because the situation created by the fourth media revolution is different from the situation after the introduction of printing, when copyright law was first introduced. Which is why our factual behaviour with respect to copyright infringements and the reality of the legal system currently diverge further than usual. This clash of different expectations and attitudes is typical of the transit spaces in which social upheavals brought about by media take place. It also explains the fact that a certain arbitrary component can be observed. The law wanders between different assessments and uses vague formulations (such as the one that speaks of the 'commercial scale of copyright infringement'). Items like the Audio Home Recording Act of 1992 added to the confusion.[157]

157 The legislation allows consumers to make digital recordings for their personal use but mandates manufacturers of devices such as the DAT machine and the mini-disc recorder to pay a royalty to the copyright owners. The argument of Napster's lawyers that the company cannot do anything illegal if it helps to facilitate copyright infringements on a larger scale, since individual users are protected by this law, did not change the judges' minds. This reveals another remarkable peculiarity of the legal system that should not be underestimated. Because which interests the law considers worthy of protection and how it decides any conflicts can only be found out by observing its practice – which, from the perspective of realist legal theory, can only mean ignoring interests and instead trying to predict judge behaviour. See Heidingsfelder, *Trump*, 215–16.

The current legal norms of copying provide no information whatsoever about what the morality of contemporary society is, but only about how legislators and courts imagine this morality to be. What for the law is an offence that must be legally sanctioned is for most users a world event. From Burleson's point of view, public morality and the law have therefore ceased to coincide, which is why 'the law must be re-examined and the discrepancy must be addressed. Copyright law must be modernized, returned to a legitimate legal foundation, and reconciled with public intuitions about what is morally right'.[158] The Börsenverein des Deutschen Buchhandels (German Publishers and Booksellers Association) summarised these intuitions more than ten years ago under the title 'Illegal? Doesn't Matter!'[159]

Fortunately, piracy is a social fact, and the law is concerned with the regulation of social relations, not with environmental problems or biological and chemical facts (which has turned out to be a disadvantage in connection with global warming or environmental pollution). The typology of legal problem perception is thus attuned to piracy. There is also a certain social consensus (what Luhmann calls 'a kind of mobile substitute natural law') with regard to the phenomenon. Politicians have long realised that enforcing all copyright claims would cause far too much turmoil. The unrest triggered by ACTA (the Anti-Counterfeiting Trade Agreement) – a planned multilateral trade agreement that would have existed as international law and which, among other things, would have set international standards in the fight against product piracy and copyright infringements – may serve as an example here: 'Hundreds of thousands of young Europeans took to the streets to protest Article 17 of the EU Copyright Directive or ACTA because they saw their online freedom threatened'.[160] The EU Parliament was forced to reject ACTA by a considerable majority in July 2012.

158 Burleson, 'Learning from Copyright's Failure', 1319.
159 According to a non-representative survey conducted by the Börsenverein in 2010 among young people aged 12 to 19, 62.8 per cent have already passed on files to others. Some 86.8 per cent of respondents were aware that this may be illegal, but only 55.3 per cent felt that file sharing was wrong. It can be assumed that these figures have now shifted significantly in the direction of file sharing acceptance. BDB (Börsenverein des Deutschen Buchhandels), *Illegal aber egal? Ein Forschungsüberblick zum Unrechtsbewusstsein von Jugendlichen*, Börsenblatt (14 April 2010).
160 Niesyto and Dapp, 'Who Governs the Internet?', 38.

The limits of the law's adaptability are related to the specificity of this historical machine. Just like all the other systems, it binds time through its communicative operations – in its case, legal decisions. But it is the only social system that can really do so! This means that even in the future, these decisions remain law, and thus remain a connecting factor for further legal decisions. In this way, expectations relating to legal decisions can be kept highly stable and the law provides this security of expectation (legal certainty) for all other social systems. As mentioned above, this is especially important for the operations of the economic system. In other words, copyright law will not simply vanish into thin air, but continues to be the starting point, as every legal innovation has to ensure its connectivity in the system.[161]

So far, property claims are only reduced when it comes to 'natural persons', i.e., users like you and me. The legal point of attack is regularly not the downloads of the copyrighted works, but the uploads (the redistribution) made automatically by the file-sharing programs. Pure downloading continues to be prosecuted neither under civil law nor under criminal law. This is due in particular to the fact that the amount in dispute and the unlawfulness of the download are weighted comparatively low in comparison to the upload, and it is therefore only financially worthwhile for rights holders to prosecute uploads. At the level of the German district courts, the fees incurred for a first-time infringement of the property rights of others have settled at around 150 euro – a tenth of the sum our media theorist from the example had to pay. While those who offer files for sale are treated differently from those who access them, there have been only a few convictions of providers of music in file-sharing networks in Germany (or, more precisely, at least no other cases have become known).[162]

---

161 Burleson views the law's ability to change with similar scepticism, albeit for different reasons. Given the enormous lobbying power of those invested in the current legal scheme, he thinks even the attempt at reform futile: 'existing copyright cannot be reformed in a constructive way, only supplemented'. Burleson, 'Learning from Copyright's Failure', 1320.

162 One way of elegantly turning the pirate's non-payment into a payment I encounter time and again on my private music website, where I loop pieces of music without the permission of the rights holders and then have friends improvise over them. The solution: instead of prosecuting me, i.e., sending me a copyright warning, a Content ID claim is made on my video, advertising

5 Piracy as System

A system is the reproduction of a specific difference. It processes itself through time by producing a certain type of form again and again. Piracy reproduces the difference of *sharing contents outside/selling contents outside*, with sharing as its preference value, while counterfeiting and product piracy prefer the other value. All forms of piracy are united by the fact that their operations take place *outside* of the law. The thesis is that only the form of piracy examined in this text generates its own inside. It is thus about a context of communication, not just about mere rebellion, individual violations, occasional raids. Any communication of piracy is only an event 'in' the system if it is ordered along this difference. Of course, in what we experience every day as piracy, infinitely more is talked and written than can be captured by the content-empty code of sharing/selling. A comparative case would be the organisation where I work. There is incessant talk, about the president, the dean, the programme director, the TAs, the students, the exams, but the organisational operation is only staged by the fact that something can be observed as a decision, that is, as a communicative event by which this reproduces itself (for instance, by hiring/firing someone, etc.).

There are two basic ways of defining piracy as a social system. One way is the identification of operative elements in whose perpetual reproduction the system produces itself – as an entity that, through this very concatenation, separates itself from an environment in which differently specified communications occur: economic, legal, political, or scientific. We have determined the operation as content sharing that connects to content sharing and so forth. As not every shared content contributes to the continuation of piracy as a system, one could also consider using a placeholder like 'pirate communication' here, which can be specified by later research. Another way is the combination of code (content sharing as a preference value) and programme. I am not talking about Emule, LimeWire, Soulseek, verycd here, but about the programming of piracy itself, that is, the possibility of using the code. Here, the focus is on the question of what the sharing should lead to, and also what 'real' sharing looks like. This is again basically done in two ways that correspond to the division of programmes into theories

is placed, and the advertising revenue is paid to the copyright owner. An elegant solution that helps everyone – except maybe the pirate agenda.

and methods in science.[163] On the one hand, environmental orientations are articulated, and, on the other, self-reference – certain reform programmes (represented by Tim Wu's approach at net neutrality, for instance) rather represent the complexity of the environment, the ideas of pirate care take an intermediary position, and other more radical ideas (represented, for instance, by computer programmer and Internet hacktivist Aaron Swartz) stand for the 'hardness' of the autopoiesis of piracy. Either way, it is only at the level of programming that environmental influences can be taken into account, societal needs can be brought to bear, and extra-piratical needs can be met, as it were.

The question of which type of system we are dealing with in the case of piracy is more difficult to answer. I have already pointed out that the system type of a secondary functional system is a way of extending Luhmann's recognised primary systems of society. The idea is that these systems 'step in' when the primary systems fail to fulfil their function. Such systems do not fit into the known schemes and realise a more sophisticated possibility of differentiation. Luhmann explicitly related this proposal to the system of social work.[164] These systems owe their existence to the fact that every difference creates orders, which in turn give rise to possibilities of deviation, which can then be exploited for the creation of new orders; and every order, of course also that of functional differentiation, enforces exclusions. Areas of deviation emerge, 'domains of deviance' (Peter Fuchs), which are either used to build up their own complexity or not. Michel Serres speaks of parasites in this context, and the pirates can also be understood as parasites in this sense – as 'pirasites'.[165] They are discoverers and exploiters of the opportunities provided by the prevailing legal and economic order. Before there was copyright law, intellectual property theft was simply not possible. The pirasite feeds on the crumbs that fall from the table of this new order; it builds conformities in the non-conformity.

It is the primacy of a certain form of differentiation (here: the functional one) that illustrates the breaking points where such

163 Luhmann, *Die Wirtschaft der Gesellschaft*, 250.
164 Luhmann, *Theory of Society*, 2.26.
165 M. Serres, *The Parasite* (Baltimore, MD: Johns Hopkins University Press, 1982). See also the chapter by Tselenti in this volume, to which I referred earlier; apparently she and I parasitise on the same theoretical figure to describe piracy. By the way, the legal safeguards provided by the law are also the result of a parasitic development via structural coupling, and not the outcome of communication between the two systems.

parasites can feed, set up bifurcations, tread new historical paths. A never-ending story, because the pirate, too, in turn produces an area of exclusion, in which parasites then settle again – for instance, the trickster lawyers mentioned in our example.[166] Thereby, what the parasite does is by no means dysfunctional, rather it transforms the flipsides of the dysfunctionalities produced by the current order into functionalities and thus makes them operatively manageable. This also applies to the pirates: they parasitise on what the autopoiesis of the economy and the law as their flipsides exclude. In other words, piracy is functional. With their activities, the pirasites not only draw attention to certain consequential problems of functional differentiation, but also present an alternative self-description of modern society that is not provided for within the functional schemata of the economy and the law.

But does it make sense to consider this parasite as a secondary functional system? Then one would have to be able to specify not only the operation that closes the system, but also name the medium, the code, and other structures typical of functional systems.[167] It may be more fruitful to understand piracy as a special form of social movement that uses negation to question certain structures of expectation, namely economic and legal ones.[168] As such, it is able to recruit actions. And as soon as actions are assigned to piracy, one is no longer dealing with the communicative attribution process observed

---

166 A similar 'flipside exploitation' can be observed with regard to social media, which have only been able to move into this position thanks to the Internet. The idea here is that the mass media system, because it operates in the medium of public opinion, creates a counterside of non-public opinion, a world of non-publics who escape the operations of the system. This forum-free, idiosyncratic world has so far fallen outside the self-descriptions of modern society. Thanks to the Internet, the communication of private states of consciousness of arbitrary private individuals could be brought into the form of its own medium – into the form of private generality, into the form of an electronic *locus communis*, as it were. They parasitise on that which the autopoiesis of mass media excludes as its flipside of non-publicity, and: 'It would put into operation another self-description variant of modern society, thus assuming the function of including that which is excluded by mass media'. Fuchs, 'Das WorldWideWeb – ohne Technik'.

167 See N. Luhmann, *Theory of Society*, vol. 1 (Stanford, CA: Stanford University Press, 2013), 214 ff.

168 Luhmann, *Soziale Systeme*, 545. It is precisely their proximity to law that is often overlooked, as social movements provide a procedure that selects and addresses contradictions in society as a whole – exactly what the law does.

by High, but with this external observation reinforcing the pirates' identification and self-reference. In the terminology of systems theory, we speak of a re-entry[169] – and what re-enters in the case of piracy is the description of piracy into what is described as piracy.

The fact that the theft they commit goes by the 'romantic name' of piracy, as criticised by Rothmann, is definitely to their advantage. Just like the possibility of being able to hijack a meaningful symbol like the 'Jolly Roger' (the pirate flag, sometimes also called 'Black Jack', showing a skull with two bones crossed), so that the pirates themselves wilfully contribute to the conflation which links their activity of non-violent service theft to violent robbery on the high seas. Not only *The Pirate Book* by Maigret and Roszkowska makes extensive use of the flag's symbolic power; even football clubs do not miss the opportunity to charge their own existence with the meaning components the motif indicates.[170]

Equally helpful are events like the court case brought by Metallica against Napster. They make it possible for piracy to describe itself as a movement in the first place, and to promote identification processes in order to sail under the pirate flag from then on: 'On April 13, 2000, Metallica became a very visible villain for a hoard of infuriated fans. By attempting to block over 300,000 users who swapped their songs on Napster, they marked a symbol of celebrity greed and melted morality – multi-platinum metal stars too distracted by dollar signs to realise the little-guy side casualties of their quest for legal vengeance'.[171] The Napster defeat could be included in the history of the movement. In this way, previous occurrences contribute to establishing a peculiar, if indeterminate, type of system or context of reproduction. It allows the pirates to refer to a self that others also refer to, which in the case of Metallica vs. Napster draws on a long semantic tradition: here the fans, the lovers, the 'little guys' who love music, there the rich owners, the music landlords who

---

169 Luhmann, *Soziale Systeme*, 547.
170 See Maigret and Roszkowska, *The Pirate Book*. In the case of the football club FC St Pauli, the Black Jack logo helps the Hamburg club position itself as 'community-based' on the opposite side to the 'money-based' clubs of the Bundesliga. Not unlike the pirates, those responsible at FC St Pauli also emphasise their social commitment: 'We will always take a stand against racism and homophobia, always look out after the weak and the poor'. U. Hesse, 'St Pauli: The Club That Stands for All the Right Things … except Winning', *Guardian* (2 September 2015).
171 Reed, 'Revisiting the Lessons of Metallica's Napster Lawsuit'.

control its distribution. Animator Bob Cesca created a video clip that portrayed the band as 'demented buddy cops who patrol college campuses to squash downloading among students'.[172] Although the Recording Industry Association of America (RIAA) had previously sued the P2P music exchange, this legal attack was, as it were, the norm for the fans; it was only when the band itself stood up for its economic interests – with Ulrich serving as their mouthpiece – and took the trouble to do so with the help of a consulting firm to track down 335,435 users – that the event could be used to specify its own context of action. All of this set in motion a reproduction of piracy-related communications and actions that allow speaking of a social system that distinguishes associated and non-associated activities. In the case of piracy, the reproduction of communication – the connection of content sharing that connects to content sharing, from the perspective of law: copyright infringement; from the perspective of economy: illegal transaction – refers to a 'no': a no to copyright, to intellectual property rights, even to property itself.

Self-observation reinforces the selectivity of the pirates, who can now respond to themselves, grow, and organise. One could, paraphrasing Rammstedt, speak of a 'teleologization of the violation'.[173] The goals set out by the pirates – open software, open educational resources, net neutrality, pirate care, etc. – guarantee the movement's ability to discriminate (or distinguish) which organised crime, for example, does not have (even if organised crime sometimes actually provides similar services to the population and, for example, in some districts of Third World countries, is able to compensate for the deficits of corrupt governments, which is why the inhabitants of these districts actively support their criminal quasi-mayors and react with protest in the event of police raids). The goals serve the pirates at the same time as an 'alibi' (Luhmann) for having to continue, and as a symbol of their own self-reproduction.[174]

Unlike other social movements, no radicalisation can be observed among the pirates, and this is probably because they have achieved their goals in part, i.e., they have fulfilled their function of keeping the economy and the law in motion. Their 'corrective' interventions have led to remarkable rearrangements in both economical and judicial terms: 'Free-MP3-as-promotion is normal in 2020, given our

172 Reed, 'Revisiting the Lessons of Metallica's Napster Lawsuit'.
173 O. Rammstedt, *Soziale Bewegung* (Frankfurt am Main: Suhrkamp, 1978), 146.
174 Luhmann, *Soziale Systeme*, 547.

current streaming landscape, but that's a side effect of an infection Napster spread'.[175] The need to cling too conservatively to the state-of-affairs and thereby miss out on necessary developments was particularly evident in the case of the music industry, which wanted to retain the old analogue distribution methods when Napster was already demonstrating new possibilities. As early as 1995, Nicholas Negroponte wondered about the record companies' obsession with 'plastic discs' to predict an imminent change: 'The systematic transport of recorded music on plastic discs will [...] be replaced in the near future by the immediate and inexpensive transfer of electronic data'.[176] This changeover was much longer in coming than he anticipated, which has to do with the fact that the decisions of record companies – like those of any other form of organisation – must be hedged against uncertainty. They therefore resisted these innovations as long as they could. The Internet piracy made possible by Napster was one of the reasons why they finally agreed to a change of structures. In this sense, Napster was able to overcome the limits of formal organisation and at the same time put the still analogue music bureaucracy in its place. This was accompanied by a certain expectation of emancipation that is still cultivated today.

In the field of science, these fundamental changes are still pending. Here, too, the pirates are creating facts, e.g., in the form of the Sci-Hub project, the first pirate website in the world to provide mass and public access to tens of millions of research papers.[177] Their 'no' reacts to the extension of copyright and with it the exclusive marketing model to digital networks in the 1990s. This business model made possible by copyright consists of the access-controlled online database, which conveys full control over scientific information. Thus a digital dilemma is realised: digitalisation allows maximum access and at the same time maximum control.[178] An ever decreasing number of scientific publishers demanded ever higher prices for ever increasingly large database packages, forcing libraries to cancel orders for other journals and monographs. The result is a growing digital divide between those who can benefit from a campus or national licence, those

175 Reed, 'Revisiting the Lessons of Metallica's Napster Lawsuit'.
176 N. Negroponte, *Being Digital* (New York: Random House, 1996), 10.
177 See Holger Briel's interviews in Chapter 5.
178 A. Peukert and A. Sonnenberg, 'Das Urheberrecht und der Wandel des wissenschaftlichen Kommunikationssystems', in P. Weingart and N. Taubert (eds), *Wissenschaftliches Publizieren. Zwischen Digitalisierung, Leistungsmessung, Ökonomisierung und medialer Beobachtung* (Berlin: de Gruyter, 2019), 231.

outside of academic organisations, and, more generally, those in the global south. However, the publishers' behaviour only follows the logic of the database model made possible by copyright: the more content is available, the more researchers need access, and the higher prices can be charged to provide even more content, etc. While some propose to change substantive science copyright law and others advocate (in various guises) making publicly funded research results available according to Open Access principles, the pirates of Sci-Hub provide access to hundreds of thousands research papers every day, effectively bypassing any paywalls and restrictions, actively challenging – and thus changing – the current status quo. Their argument is that the artificial restriction of the widest possible distribution of research papers, as well as of other scientific or educational sources by copyright laws, 'effectively slow(s) down the development of science in human society'.[179] Here too, piracy becomes functional. Just like the regularly repeating crises – Corona, climate, Ukraine war – piracy has its function for the 'periodic de-dogmatization and re-adaptation' of society.[180] One could therefore say that piracy steps in where the economy fails to fulfil its function of linking a future-stable provision for satisfaction with ever-present distributions. So is piracy 'necessary', as Gary Hall believes, as it fills 'the gaps in care left by the state and market'?[181] The concept of pirate care proves plausible above all where the pirates compensate for the deficits that affect copyright confirmation, which is dependent on the dictates of the market. For even those who consider the pirates to be nothing but thieves, and who value paying for content always and forever, will in many cases have to realise that where there is a will, there's not always a way, because some books, for example, are no longer being distributed (pirates speak of 'orphaned' works), so the only way to access them is that of the pirate. Even in the case of negligent rights holders who do not attach great importance to the enforcement of copyright claims, the pirate steps in. Then granting access – the piratist social worker's concern – to this work seems justified, even imperative. 'Technically, such practices can be considered piracy, while in reality they embody elements of a commons, as

179 Sci-Hub, https://sci-hub.yncjkj.com/.
180 N. Luhmann, 'Status quo als Argument', in A. Kieserling (ed.), *Universität als Milieu: Kleine Schriften* (Bielefeld: Haux, 1992), 27.
181 Hall, 'Postdigital Politics', 1.

they create and preserve "shared resources" available for reuse'.[182] Thus, in a wondrous reversal, the pirates now take the place of the bibliopoles who had been on the opposite side of the pirates in Ned Ward's poem.

One of their more moderate and concrete proposals concerns the issue of large and ever-growing volumes of data transport. There are two basic ways here. Either one permanently increases the capacity of the networks and transports all data equally, i.e., with the same quality (best-effort principle), then these networks remain 'neutral'. This is the option that pirate theorists, net activists, and 'left' politicians (especially in the United States) are voting for. It has become known as net neutrality and was introduced into the academic discourse in 2003 by Tim Wu.[183] The irony is that net neutrality is an extension of the longstanding concept of a common carrier, which belongs to admiralty law or maritime law – quite appropriate in the context of a piracy issue. One of main things ISPs would do in the United States is throttling torrenting speed, sometimes even reporting users to the FBI. Net neutrality wants to remove these restrictions. But, for many pirate theorists, this reformist approach does not go far enough; even more, it realises a contradiction: 'Net neutrality is a confining framework in itself. It is like trying to argue for freedom in a cage – typical of US reformism'.[184]

The other option is to transport different data at different speeds and with different quality. The yardsticks for this quality are mainly data rate (often referred to as bandwidth in everyday use), delay, jitter, and packet loss. This is the option that most telecommunications networks find reasonable, who want to transmit data on their networks with different quality guarantees. The argument they are making is, again – just like in Tim Wu's case, who talks of 'broadband discrimination' – a socially acceptable one: that this form of network management is a more efficient way to prevent data congestion and, in the event of congestion, to ensure that important data continues to be transmitted with guaranteed transmission quality.

This rationale makes sense, as it gives some legitimacy to the cause of 'net partisanship'. That this rationale also satisfies the rationality

182 Cornelia Sollfrank, Felix Stalder, and Shusha Niederberger (eds), *Aesthetics of the Commons* (Zurich: Diaphanes, 2021), 16.
183 T. Wu, 'Network Neutrality, Broadband Discrimination', *Journal on Telecom and High Tech Law* 2 (2003), 141–79.
184 E-mail conversation with G. Zhang, 23 March 2022.

of the economy can be doubted. What is legitimate for society as a whole cannot fulfil the requirements for economic legitimacy that are evident in the possibility of charging for this special data quality. The business community is motivated by the idea of payment, not by the idea of welfare or 'equality': 'At the very least, research results to date indicate that network neutrality tends to slow down investment in high-speed Internet access'.[185] The pirates, on the other hand, are motivated by the idea of participation and 'content care'. These two preference values can hardly be brought down to a common denominator – let alone a 'commons denominator'. In fact, however, not even the mass media, which are entrusted with the 'supply of information' to the public, comply with the demand for information neutrality. Instead, they hide highly relevant information from the public (for example, regarding the necessary measures in the case of a Corona infection) behind paywalls, charging their readers a fee in exchange for the information that would allow them to fulfil their role of active citizen. The democracies of this world thus afford exactly what, according to Jürgen Habermas, they cannot or should not be able to afford: they leave the media to themselves.[186] Only that this is precisely not a 'market failure', as Habermas assumes, but, on the contrary: a market success.[187]

It therefore seems appropriate to pay tribute to piracy, as many of the piracy theorists demand, because it draws society's attention to deficits, especially in the area of the economy. While file sharing does not take place on an exchange basis and thus operates outside the economic system, it did point the industry to earning opportunities in cyberspace. That economic practice has been massively irritated by this form of theft is evident. The economy reacted with self-resonance and translated these irritations into its own operativity. The fact that file sharing has acted as a motor to keep precisely this area in motion, and here especially that of the music industry, is somewhat ironical, if not paradoxical. (Luhmann therefore understands social movements as immune systems of society, which, precisely because they change things, protect society from solidification in old, no longer adequate behaviour patterns, and thus ensure its continuation.)[188] Whether

185 Fink et al., 'Economic Effects', 2.
186 See Heidingsfelder, 'Shifting Spheres', 871.
187 J. Habermas, 'Keine Demokratie kann sich das leisten', *Süddeutsche Zeitung* (19 May 2010).
188 Luhmann, *Soziale Systeme*, 507.

piracy merely accelerated developments that would have occurred later anyway is another question. But it is also an unhistorical one: piracy did occur, and it did change the course of events.

This success could well pose a problem for piracy at some point because its existence as a system depends on maintaining difference. This difference can be lost for exactly two reasons: on the one hand because of failure, but on the other hand also in the case of success. Therefore, some of the current demands made by piracy theorists could be deliberately unrealistic in nature because their non-fulfilment ensures the continued existence of piracy as a context of reproduction. (I will come back to this in the last section.) On the other hand, there is still a lot for the pirates to do, because the business community has translated the irritations into their own operationality and in this way created new zones of exclusion. Legal file-sharing services like Spotify, for example, 'pay artists using a widely criticized 'pro-rata' model, resulting in the top performers taking home the most money'.[189] As an anonymous pirate (whom I know personally) likes to put it: 'Spotify is more like the shitty contemporary version of convenience store culture that entices you at first but then you realise it does not even provide what you want anyway once you venture beyond the confines of pop music'.

What is certain is that piracy has produced effects and thus contributed to the survival of the very system it attacks, i.e., the reproduction of a social unit consisting of payments. The 'side paths' it used became in part normal paths. This circumstance has not escaped the attention of the pirates' reflective authorities.

**

Theories help with the 'difficult business of self-reflection' (Kai-Uwe Hellmann) and thus strengthen the selectivity of the system.[190] Here, another peculiarity of piracy becomes apparent: there is no theory deficit here (a criticism that Luhmann repeatedly raises with regard to social movements).[191] The naivety and carefree slogans typical for social movements are much less common here, as pirate theorists

189 Reed, 'Revisiting the Lessons of Metallica's Napster Lawsuit'.
190 Kai-Uwe Hellmann (ed.), *Protest: Systemtheorie und soziale Bewegungen* (Frankfurt am Main: Suhrkamp, 1996).
191 See, as a representative example, N. Luhmann, *Ökologische Kommunikation:*

are largely in control of the distinctions underlying their own observations. With representatives like Gary Hall and others, they can claim a kind of reflective authority. They try to make clear why one is on one side of the form, on the side of the 'no'.

However, as already mentioned at the beginning, piracy reflection is not identical with its context of affiliation, science. While science has neither a positive nor a negative attitude towards piracy, and can also imagine a society without it, no reflection instance is unbiased towards its own system. One only needs to imagine theology denying religion. Thus, as should become clear, a relationship of loyalty and affirmation to piracy can be observed among pirate theorists.[192] This relationship is the precondition of all pirate reflection.

The term piracy in particular offers the movement a variety of possibilities for strengthening its meaning – for example with regard to the etymology of the term, which helped us determine its form: 'The word piracy derives from a distant Indo-European root meaning a trial or attempt, or (presumably by extension) an experience or experiment. It is an irony of history that in the distant past it meant something so close to the creativity to which it is now reckoned antithetical'.[193] Thus, self-identification as brutal criminals (seagoing warlords) is replaced by that as explorers and artists; instead of continuing to be conceived as opponents, the antithesis of civilisation, the constructive, creative potential of piracy is asserted and thus freed from the stigma of nefarious theft and greedy self-enrichment. Maigret and Roszkowska take this hint seriously by demonstrating the creative potential *of* piracy aesthetics in a book *about* piracy.[194]

The ground for this claim to pirate creativity has been initiated by the Birmingham School, namely John Fiske[195] following Stuart

Kann die moderne Gesellschaft sich auf ökologische Gefährdungen einstellen? (Wiesbaden: VS Verlag für Sozialwissenschaften, 2008), 232.

192 Luhmann, *Theory of Society*, vol. 1.

193 Adrian Johns, *Piracy: The Intellectual Property Wars from Gutenberg to Gates* (Chicago: University of Chicago Press, 2010), 35.

194 Of course, it is available for free download, https://archive.org/stream/The_Pirate_Book/The_Pirate_Book. Pirate theorists, for all their Marxist and structuralist influences, try very hard to live up to Kant's categorical imperative when it comes to questions of open access, etc.

195 See representative J. Fiske, 'The Cultural Economy of Fandom', in L.L. Lewis (ed.), *The Adoring Audience: Fan Culture and Popular Media* (London: Routledge, 1992), 30–49.

Hall,[196] and Henry Jenkins[197] following Fiske, who emphasised the active aspect of media reception, granting fans, bloggers, and other 'prosumers' a crucial role in the reception, recoding, and reinterpretation of media. For Jenkins, fans who created their own works from media content were 'textual poachers' who ushered in a new era of participatory culture. Instead of condemning these forms of appropriation, as befits a law-abiding citizen, he praised them as one of the most important elements of media literacy in the twenty-first century, explicitly referring to the concept of 'culture jamming' (the subversive reworking of existing media messages) developed by Mark Dery in his momentous essay of the same name.[198] The importance of this approach for theory formation is reflected in the texts of this volume, for example in Zhen Troy Chen's attempt to describe the media ways of the urban Chinese youth with the help of Jenkins's concepts, or in Jiaru Tian's autobiographical account, which makes use of Lev Manovich's related remix considerations.[199]

Evidence of this creative potential can be found in pirate historiography that points to the beauty and uniqueness of counterfeiting: it is not the fake products that are 'defective' but the protected ones.[200] One could understand Renaud's already mentioned 'Shanzhai archeology' as an attempt to prove the aura of copies: objects that are

196 S. Hall, 'Encoding, Decoding', in S. During (ed.), *The Cultural Studies Reader* (London: Routledge, 1999), 507–17.

197 Jenkins, *Textual Poachers*.

198 M. Dery, 'Culture Jamming: Hacking, Slashing, and Sniping in the Empire of Signs' [blog] (1993), www.markdery.com/books/culture-jamming-hacking-slashing-and-sniping-in-the-empire-of-signs-2/. The extent to which this observation represents an inadmissible exaggeration or transcendence of piracy that cannot keep up with its reality would have to be examined specifically. A YouTuber and singer like Jincheng Zhang (金成張), who claimed a lot of music from the YouTube audio library as his own to sell them as his original compositions, represents the antithesis of the creative, innovative pirate for many observers – a media illiterate. While I find many of his pieces extremely amusing, even instructive – especially in terms of observing pop music; his hilarious song titles, which, combining a random word and 'I Love You' at the end, can be read as clues to the function of pop – I would consider Zhang a plagiarist who accidentally creates works that go beyond mere imitation. My assumption is that his failure to achieve success made him a darling of the academic discourse on piracy.

199 See L. Manovich, 'What Comes after Remix', *Remix Theory* 10 (2007).

200 Renaud, 'Archeology of Shanzhai Phones'. By doing so, Renaud refers to a form of piracy that I have positioned on the other side. Again: it is a contingent operation – the piracy of my distinction.

cheaply made, poorly counterfeit, 'or just plain crappy' (Renaud), are appreciated in terms of their aesthetic innovation and presented to the astonished eyes of Europeans as part of an exhibition project: 'The collection has been exhibited numerous times in Europe, where most models were unknown because of border regulations forbidding their circulation'.[201] The smartphones valued by Shanzhai archaeologists demonstrate that copyright primarily protects unoriginal and uninspired design of Western manufacturers: their right to copy. What consumers are protected from is the flexibility and ingenuity of the pirates. The poor performance is found on the side of the rights holders, who prefer not to take creative risks (see above). Here, the understanding of piracy as an experiment comes into its own. It is the 'practice of trial-and-error, with small incremental iterations of products' that leads to quite unique, unusual solutions, which – although geared to quick profit and short-livedness – have 'in some cases led to innovations with long-lasting consequences'.[202] The 'crap archeologists' do not miss the opportunity to point out the mendacity and double standards of the Western piracy discourse towards Asia and China in particular. Their Chinese kiosk of counterfeiters explicitly serves the purpose of recalling the 'long lineage of piracy and the looting of Chinese knowledge to the benefit of arty European salons'.[203] In thus writing an alternative history of the losers, they take up one of the central philosophical considerations of the historical materialist Benjamin, 'to give nothing that has ever occurred away for history'.[204] Piracy appears as deconstruction, a critique of the rule of copyright or intellectual property, and piracy historiography strives to 'wrest tradition [...] from conformism'[205] and to 'call into question every victory that has ever fallen to the rulers'.[206] The Shanzhai archeologists 'wake the dead (and piece together) what has been shattered'.[207] What Benjamin still considered hopeless, because the storm of progress was driving the angel of history inexorably into the future, today makes the abatement of this storm possible – a reflection on 'the pile of rubble', the plastic waste that was transformed into sustainable cultural products – thanks to the 'confidence, the courage,

201 Renaud, 'Archeology of Shanzhai Phones', 91.
202 Renaud, 'Archeology of Shanzhai Phones', 93.
203 Renaud, 'Archeology of Shanzhai Phones', 99.
204 Benjamin, 'Das Kunstwerk', 694.
205 Benjamin, 'Das Kunstwerk', 695.
206 Benjamin, 'Das Kunstwerk', 694.
207 Benjamin, 'Das Kunstwerk', Engel.

the humour, the cunning' of the pirates.[208] But the political factor, which has only played a minor role in this text, should not be underestimated in this context. Without the Chinese Communist Party's decision to invest heavily in the IT sector and allow direct, tax-free foreign investment in the Shenzhen Economic Zone (SEZ), piracy could have not 'created the possibility of affordable phone computers and mobile phones worldwide'[209] and thus – paradoxically – enabling autocracy to be 'instrumental in democratizing access to mobile phones globally over the past decade'.[210] For this reason, even the use of 'crappy' products can be understood as a nationalist commitment, as the following advertising slogan makes clear: 'Buy *Shanzhai* to show your love for your country'.[211] The same moment can also be observed in connection with the Dakou discs discussed above: the enjoyment of foreign music contributed to strengthening national consciousness; today, the Dakou era is an important part of Chinese history.

Such justifications are often accompanied by references to a cultural

208 They also contribute to this on the level of textual research, for example with the reference to the industrial espionage of a Jesuit priest: 'Father d'Entrecolles arrived in China as a missionary in 1698, where he was praised for his deep knowledge of the Chinese language and sent to Jingdezhen – the capital of the famous art of Chinese porcelain – to appreciate the highest levels of refinery in the Empire. In a letter dated September 1712, the missionary related to his French correspondents that he had finally managed to witness first-hand how the precious pottery was cast, revealing in detail his host's secrets that would, a few decades later, give birth to the European porcelain industry'. Renaud, 'Archeology of Shanzhai Phones', 99. Schmidt points in a humorous travel book to other Chinese inventions 'clearly stolen from the West', 'such as – and this is only a small selection – noodles, folding umbrellas, kites, the compass, silk, paper money, steel, and toilet paper'. He marvels, 'But today, when the Chinese copy a few Gucci bags, Ritter Sport chocolate bars or Rolex watches, the whole world talks about intellectual theft, instead of just being happy that China isn't suing the rest of the world for trillions just for re-cooking steel'. C.Y. Schmidt, *Allein unter 1,3 Milliarden: Eine chinesische Reise von Shanghai bis Kathmandu* (Dresden: Kahl, 2008).
209 Renaud, 'Archeology of Shanzhai Phones', 93.
210 Renaud, 'Archeology of Shanzhai Phones', 103.
211 Fan Yang, *Faked in China: Nation Branding, Counterfeit Culture, and Globalization* (Bloomington: Indiana University Press, 2016). In the case of Russia, one could even speak of self-defence. The country has altered its law on piracy to help circumvent massive tech and software bans that have been placed on it since it invaded Ukraine. J. Jimenez, 'Russia Considers Legalizing Software Piracy to Combat Tech Bans', *PC Gamer* (10 March 2022).

emergency. Piracy appears as the solution to a North–South problem: 'Given that most of the fansubbed programs were not officially imported by the Chinese state, fansubbing constituted a specific form of digital piracy organized around P2P networks'.[212] Baumgärtel even stylises piracy as part of a process he calls 'globalisation from below', a globalisation not of corporations but of enthusiasts. His example is the Philippines, which – like so many other countries of the global south – was denied access to most of the world's cinema for more than a century. Not only were film classics neither released in theatres there nor available on DVD, but a significant portion of the world's knowledge available in the form of literature was also unavailable. Which is why he and his colleagues were 'seized with enthusiasm when pirate DVDs and file-sharing services allowed access to large parts of the world's cinema from the end of the 1990s. For those teaching, it was simply a way of eliminating, at least in this area, the economic as well as cultural asymmetry between the First and Third Worlds'.[213] In addition, there was access to the relevant, but for many schools in the global south too-expensive, specialised literature. Which is why Philippine dictator Marcos introduced state-licensed piracy in the 1970s by means of the so-called 'Asian Edition', allowing the reprinting of key US textbooks without paying royalties to publishers, a practice that was ended only after his overthrow. Baumgärtel's conclusion: 'Piracy can therefore be a source of education and an invitation to free speech; an act of resistance and a condition for new forms of creativity. The beginning of a conversation about intellectual property under the changed conditions created by the Internet. Piracy is about access to knowledge and information and the foundations of cultural production and authorship'.[214]

This is where the proximity of the pirate activists with forms of political opposition becomes apparent. Similar to the protest movement of socialism, piracy is also about the problem of scarcity, i.e., the unequal distribution of goods and services: 'How can we act differently with a view to transforming society through the creation of more commons-oriented ways of being and doing?'[215] In other words, pirate theory starts from paradox, not from tautology.[216] It

212 Li, 'Rethinking the Chinese Internet', 10.
213 Baumgärtel, 'Lob der Piraterie'.
214 Baumgärtel, 'Lob der Piraterie'.
215 Hall, 'Postdigital Politics', 2.
216 N. Luhmann, 'Tautologie und Paradoxie in den Selbstbeschreibungen der

considers society something it is not. The community in which the pirate goals are realised is prevented by certain forces (also called the 'power bloc' in other contexts), among which are the theorists themselves:

> Consequently, while most critical theorists position themselves as being politically on the left – some even writing books and articles about the importance of equality, solidarity and the radical redistribution of wealth and power – many end up operating as rampantly competitive, proprietorial individuals nonetheless. Driven by a goal-fixated instrumentalism, what's important to them are the number of books published, grants captured, keynote lectures given, followers acquired, or likes and retweets gained.[217]

The assumption is that structural-logical development will realise, via revolution or evolution, this community – what is presently and provisionally 'not yet'. That which is not yet, however, has to be realised.

The semantic tradition, in which many pirate theorists find themselves, assumes that by nature – in the early history of mankind – there was no private property, and that this invention is the main cause of wars and other violent conflicts. In doing so, they can refer to a multitude of collectivist property theories, from Plato's *Politeia* to Thomas More's *Utopia* and other venerable compilations of private thoughts which are no longer protected by copyright. No one, says Plato, should own anything as his property, unless it is necessary. The result would be a wonderful, relaxed life among confederates, instead of among hostilely eyeing people who spend their whole life chasing others' goods. The important word here is 'not necessary'. For who determines which property is necessary and which is not necessary? For Plato, it is Plato, i.e., the philosopher-king, who determines what is necessary and what is not necessary. Gold and silver do not fall

modernen Gesellschaft', *Systemtheorie der Gesellschaft*, 79–106.
217 Hall, 'Postdigital Politics', 3. A remarkably self-critical comment by Gary Hall which nevertheless fails to grasp the fundamental problem that leads the author who pleads for the renunciation of distinction gains associated with publications to publish this very demand under his name. One could understand this problem beyond personal ambition with Luhmann as one of the scarcity of time: a name like Gary Hall serves the purpose of providing readers with an advance orientation, granting credit. The name signifies that the author's works warrant attention, especially in light of his expertise in piracy. Undoubtedly, such acknowledgments of reputation involve an effect of exaggeration, yet they are not without factual basis.

under the category of essentials, for they should be possessed in the soul and not be reduced to mere trinkets or adornments.

These thoughts are rightly called utopian, because such a place of free sharing – of comprehensive sharing is caring – does not exist. And as such a non-place Plato or Socrates describes it then also: in the subjunctive, as possibility or demand. What if, he asks his interlocutor Glaucon, people would live like that? Wouldn't that be wonderful? In the words of pirate theorist Gary Hall: Doesn't this idea 'produce something of a dopamine rush in us?'[218] From the pirates' point of view, intellectual property is not the solution, but the problem. Based on this consideration, they fundamentally question property altogether. It is the reason why pirate theorists – with Hall: 'anti-bourgeois theorists' – are interested in piracy in the first place, despite the fact that 'even the left' finds it hard to question it these days: 'So-called piracy thus provides my collaborators and I with one starting point from which to develop an affirmative critique of private property and bourgeois subjectivity that is designed to help us be more consistent with the kind of radical politics many theorists espouse (but don't necessarily perform themselves) when writing about the commons'.[219]

The concept of the commons, which has gained new relevance not least in the context of pandemic control, is currently one of the favourite topics of pirate reflection. According to Sollfrank et al., piracy entails not only generating novel perspectives on the world – as a response to Hall's well-known manifesto from 2016, in which he urged theorists and philosophers to reinvent themselves amidst times of upheaval[220] – but also considering how to act from this standpoint, namely as someone who undertakes the responsibility of care.[221] By merging commons and art, and viewing aesthetics through the lens of 'a concept that has its origins in economics and political science',[222] the researchers try to do justice to this reflection. That this experiment would fail could be foreseen, as the function of art is not that of politics.[223] By the same token, one could demand

218 Hall, 'Postdigital Politics'.
219 Hall, 'Postdigital Politics'.
220 G. Hall, *Pirate Philosophy: For a Digital Posthumanities* (Cambridge, MA: MIT Press, 2016).
221 Sollfrank et al., *Aesthetics of the Commons*, 7.
222 Sollfrank et al., *Aesthetics of the Commons*, 7.
223 This does not mean that 'political art', for instance, is not possible, but only as art. The insistence on independent criteria might even, Luhmann suggests,

that politics once again be placed on the safe ground of ecclesiastical dogma – or, what might be more interesting, that ecclesiastical dogma be placed on the ground of piracy.

Nevertheless, the approach is one of the most interesting in recent pirate reflection for a number of reasons – and not only because it takes the casual motto of 'sharing is caring' seriously and makes it theoretically manageable. Pirate care understands piracy as 'manner in which communities all over the world sponta-neously self-organised to fill the gaps in care left by the state and market'.[224] Hall refers to Bollier, for whom such actions can be understood as commoning rather than 'volunteering', because they are more deeply committed and collective in character than individual 'do-gooding'.[225]

In this sense, pirate care could be understood as a piratical variant of social work. In order to be able to define it more precisely, a look at the function of social work is helpful. As already indicated: unlike in everyday language, which assumes that someone or something *has* a function (the cow has the function to give milk, piracy has the function to guarantee sharing contents), the concept of function used here assumes that an observer constructs a problem, in view of which 'world questions' are interpreted as solutions that can be compared with other interpretations of solutions. In this sense, the problem to which social work responds can be conceptualised as exclusion, and the solution it offers is the opening, re-opening (or simulation of these openings) of the opportunity for the chance of inclusion (although, strictly speaking, in the context of systems theory, inclusion is not used to refer to the inclusion or exclusion of people, but merely to refer to communications that specifically mark people's relevance to communication).

In this sense, pirates can indeed be seen as social workers – and just as in the case of the pirate, this designation is also only borrowed,

---

make for a stronger political impact. Conversely, politics seems to make use of art only as a staffage, as decoration, or as a momentary means of pageantry. 'But this is what one finds everywhere [...]. Each sphere sells the other to its own ends. But one should not let the abuse in other fields backfire on one's own criteria consciousness'. N. Luhmann, *Schriften zu Kunst und Literatur* (Frankfurt am Main: Suhrkamp, 2008), 90. Trans. M.H.

224 Hall, *Pirate Philosophy*; Sollfrank et al., *Aesthetics of the Commons.*
225 D. Bollier, 'Commoning as a Pandemic Survival Strategy', *News and Perspectives on the Commons* (26 March 2020), www.bollier.org/blog/commoning-pandemic-survival-strategy. See also M. Sitrin, *Pandemic Solidarity: Mutual Aid during the Covid-19 Crisis* (London: Pluto, 2020).

no more than a metaphor. Instead of the social worker, the pirate is called in the event of a disturbance. The disturbance here is: the unjust distribution of resources, the inappropriateness of the concept of copyright, the North–South divide, or, in the case of authoritarian states, censorship of certain works. Pirate care, just like the various forms of piracy, is thus not only about a form of resistance to sovereign power, but also about 'exposing the various forms of violence and inequality that prevail'.[226] It aims at what the economy formally excludes: the equal distribution of scarce goods for all. It is a social work that aims, as it were, to free the sick society as a whole from its shortcomings. It has proved highly effective in this role, against the opposition of power and rights holders, and has even partly ensured – and continues to ensure – 'de-dogmatisations' and the readjustment of these systems. Only it does not solve social problems in a profes- sional and science-based way, as social work does. But its work certainly amounts to something similar: piracy intervenes and reacts, by providing the alternatives that economics and law do not (initially) provide. Because certain normal paths are blocked, it provides other, extra-systemic ones, which make violations of law necessary. By thus keeping society moving and from stagnation, it ensures its continued existence, including the survival of the very systems it subverts (or 'attacks') – the economy and the law.

One could also understand the question of piracy as social work in a different, more lifeworldly way – as a question of a new 'habitus' of communication in piracy contexts. Here, piracy care could contribute to endow the habitus of social workers, which has long been subject to ridicule – a disgustingly approximate humanity, coupled with a canonical phrasing of mild kindness – with a sense of coolness and sophistication.

6 Conclusion

The figure of observer used in this text assumed a separation between piracy and the environment. This assumption has proven to be well-founded. Piracy appears as a both self-determined and externally determined entity. It is not a structure within the system of the economy or the system of law, but itself an observer. It takes place

226 D. Dragona, 'Commoning the Commons: Revisiting the Role of Art in Times of Crisis', in Sollfrank et al., *Aesthetics of the Commons*, 120.

in the environment of these systems, just as, conversely, the economy and law take place in the environment of piracy.

The unity of the piracy system results from its form, the preference for the unlicensed sharing of 'intellectual' or 'cultural' contents, which appears on the screen of the legal system as copyright infringement – that is, a 'no' to a legal demand for copyright confirmation. Like the protest movements, piracy is expressed in society against society.[227] It is not a pest that invades society from the outside, as it were (which is why it is important not to misunderstand the term parasite used in this and Danai Tselenti's text). Insofar as it reproduces specific communications, it always reproduces society – like every form of communication – and is to that extent, one could say, approved of. Piracy needs the other systems to reproduce itself, and the assumption is that the other systems (especially the economy) also need piracy. It is occasionally operationally coupled with the economy and the law. In the case of such a coupling, all three observers are used to synchronise their positions, and in this way the piracy operation of sharing becomes part of a system through the fact that this system refers to it. In the next moment, this coupling dissolves, the momentary knot loosens, and the systems' search for new events starts all over again.

Unlike counterfeiting and/or product piracy (industrial property infringement), which is aimed at financial gain, and its equivalent plagiarism (artistic and intellectual property infringement, which aims to profit from theft in the area of reputation or fame), piracy is about sharing content (usually without having to pay for it, or for extremely small amounts). Many economists and legal scholars usually do not distinguish between the form of piracy that seeks to share and the form which seeks financial gain or fame (counterfeiting and plagiarism). Both are observed to be economically damaging and even socio-economically harmful. From my point of view, it makes more sense to define the reality of piracy as the difference of sharing/ selling, and in this sense as a subcategory or special form of piracy that does not seek financial gain. In both cases, it seems justified to point to the productive moment of piracy, which is described in this text as its functionality.

As should have become clear, a large part of piracy's self-under-standing – as with other social movements – runs through moral

227 N. Luhmann, 'Protestbewegungen', in K.-U. Hellmann (ed.), *Protest: System-theorie und soziale Bewegungen* (Frankfurt am Main: Suhrkamp, 1996), 204.

communication. Morality, as a self-referential principle of self-assertion, allows 'existential gains'. However, in the case of the pirate theorists, first, it does not emerge in the almost religious form that is characteristic of other 'networks of outrage and hope' (Castells's designation of social movements); pirate theorists are, secondly, quite capable of making concrete proposals as to what could evolve in place of what already exists. This could have to do with the fact that they are always already active – or, rather, they are of service – precisely as pirates, i.e., they don't just say 'no', but act by literally taking the law in their own hands. From the concrete proposals of a reformer like Tim Wu to the activities of Gary Hall, ominously present in this text, who not only preaches open access, but also realises it.[228]

Unlike protest movements, pirates do not rely on alarmist communication. They are 'cooler', as it were, which, along with their symbols, makes them attractive – they steal, and they mark the theft as lawful, pointing at a sore point of the legal system: that it presumes to distinguish so irreconcilably between right and wrong. Their question could then, paradoxically, be: is the current difference between right and wrong right (lawful)? Why should I not copy? What could replace this *not*? They also possess a rudimentary instance of reflection, as demonstrated above, in which they engage with these questions, and as a result, they strive to comprehend the social structures against which they are directed.

Piracy points at the fact that the traditional copyright structures are rusty and need a general overhaul, and some go so far as questioning the concept of property altogether. As mentioned above, a complete abolition is not on the cards, either of property or of the present copyright. But the idea that the meritorious legal construct

---

228 After his book on open access published in 2008, Hall followed up with action: his Jisc-funded project LivBL presented a series of open access books on the topic of 'life' that attempted to provide a bridge between the humanities and the sciences, and the peer-reviewed journal *Culture Machine*, co-founded with Dave Boothroyd, also met open access requirements. After that, he established – together with Steve Green – the first open access archive for cultural and media studies research, CSeARCH and co-founded the publishing house Open Humanities Press, whose monograph project practices a remarkable collaboration with the University of Minnesota, the University of California, and Stanford University. Unsurprisingly, he did not compromise on his OA ideals in connection with this book project by signing all his publication rights away – not least because he is currently also working on 'opening up' the publisher of this very book for the future.

of intellectual property with regard to the digital transformation
of society needs an update is generally considered to be reasonable
(just as fundamental modifications of national constitutions are
considered advisable with regard to their historical nature, i.e., age).[229]
The only thing to bear in mind again here is that everything that
is possible in law must relate to the already established structures.
To repeat, legal decisions of the past, however questionable, remain
'law' and thus a connecting factor for further legal decisions. Not to
mention Burleson's concerns about the power of organised lobbies,
which stand in the way of appropriate solutions to problems – and
also massively irritate politics.[230] Or our habit of assuming selectors.
Even the Creative Commons regulation at least presupposes an
author (albeit a somewhat more generous one).

As I have shown, the law and the economy (but also politics, which
is not specifically dealt with in this text) have taken up piracy issues
to an astonishing extent, which in turn has had a knock-on effect on
piracy. An end to piracy is not yet in sight, not least because some of
the solutions (e.g., Spotify) have turned out not to be sufficient, but it
can hardly be denied that an astonishing amount of content is now
freely available. As the existence of piracy as a system depends on
the maintenance of difference, this success could cause the loss of
that difference. My speculation was whether the demands of piracy
theorists might be – or have become – deliberately unrealistic in
nature because their non-fulfilment ensures the continued existence
of piracy as a reproductive context.

A good example of this is Hall's linking up with the utopias
propagated by the so-called Internet gurus, especially Barlow's direct
reference to the American founding document.[231] The reference makes
sense when one thinks of the Magna Carta of liberalism, Locke's
justification for the separation of powers:[232] first, because it confirms it
(the governed must agree to what the government does, including, of
course, in matters of copyright); second, because it deftly wrests from
liberalism the justification for property that Locke had so wonderfully

229 Heidingsfelder, *Trump*, 326–7.
230 Burleson, 'Learning from Copyright's Failure', 1320.
231 Hall, *Pirate Philosophy*, 47. Barlow, 'Declaration of the Independence of
    Cyberspace'. See also Wagner, 'Information Wants To Be Free', 995, who
    starts his essay with a Jefferson quote ('Inventions then cannot, in nature,
    be a subject of property').
232 J. Locke, *Two Treatises of Government*, ed. P. Laslett (Cambridge: Cambridge
    University Press, 1988).

traced back to natural law and the necessity of production. That these words – human freedom, etc. – 'produce something of a dopamine rush in us', as Hall claims, may indeed be true if he wants to use this first-person pronoun to refer to himself and his fellow pirate companions. Positive emotional experiences ('reward effects') when hearing a word are, however, not a criterion for the attainability of these goals. Presumably the opposite is more likely to be the case: it is precisely the unattainability of the ideals of 'democracy, human freedom, sharing, caring, cooperation' that causes 'us' to continue to uphold them counter-factually – unconcerned about the defeats that these ideals have experienced again and again in the course of history.[233] And that could be what it is all about: as it is their non-fulfilment that ensures the continued existence of piracy. To use a line from a poem by Thomas Brasch: the pirates have to make sure they stay where they have never been – in utopia.

The fact that a pirate theorist of Hall's stature has – in addition to the central issues 'sharing, caring, cooperation' – fallen back on age-old thematic shopkeepers such as democracy and human freedom (in contrast to animal and/or plant freedom?), is in many ways more remarkable than it first appears. One can interpret this revival as an attempt to guarantee the continuity of piracy through unrealistic goals, as I have done above; but these unrealistic goals are of course also part of a left agenda which – despite the failures – still claims to want to realise them. The problem could be that this reference to the rhetoric of liberalism is a despecification, i.e., a softening of the piracy's theme of sharing. As piracy lives precisely on this one theme, while democracy and human freedom are commonplace topics, this could have damaging consequences. If piracy loses this theme – its unique selling point, in economic terms – the 'proprium' of piracy would be lost in the process. It will be absorbed by and vanish into society. Imagine, for example, if the pirate parties were to renounce their central issues – the reform of copyright and patent law, open access, and better data protection – in favour of a programme that promotes affordable housing, stable pensions, climate protection, creating jobs, supporting children, and strengthening families (all central points of the German SPD party, of which at least digitalisation

233 One could go so far as to deny Hall the right to the title of pirate. According to Michael D. High, this title can no longer be claimed if one focuses on 'ill-defined, idealised freedom' instead of emphasising the collective, economic transgression of piracy. High, 'Piratical Designations', 93.

represents the thematic focus of the Pirate Party). More positively, Hall's attempt could be seen as the production of indeterminacy: the use of a resource that allows the systemic reference of piracy to be complexly intertwined with that of politics.[234] But this is no more than mere speculation.

The pirates have not shaped the future, but the former present, and in this way contributed decisively to the present present. Moreover, they have long since realised the digital ethics that some political advisors are demanding.[235] Contrary to what they pretend to believe, the decision of 'what digital future do we want to live in as a society' is not ours to make. Society itself will answer this question for us. As tempting as it would be to declare the right to licence-free copying a human right – and there are numerous reasons to do so, which could be supported by economic arguments, and completely dispense with the foundational assumptions of Kant and Jefferson based on the concept of 'human dignity': declaring it does not lead to its social reality (as the example of the several Declarations of Independence clearly demonstrate, along with the one that declares an independent cyberspace). As Koselleck has shown, not even the legal act of equality is a political or economic act, and certainly not a

---

234 See E.M. Leifer, *Actors as Observers: A Theory of Skill and Social Relationships* (New York: Garland Publishing, 1991).

235 See, for instance, C. Piallat, *Der Wert der Digitalisierung*, which takes up central points of the pirate agenda for an apparently urgently needed digital value creation. The editor ties in with the commons discourse outlined above, he calls for digital infrastructure to be treated as a public collective good, and access to the Internet as a human right. 'Never before has the need for approaches to a value-led shaping of the digital world been so great'. Piallat, *Wert der Digitalisierung*, 52. The idea seems to be the stimulation of rational discussions (or discussions that take place within the framework of scientific rationality), which are then supposed to lead to a certain consensus on values that is finally translated into collectively binding decisions (Piallat is digital and network policy advisor for the Party Bündnis 90/Die Grünen). 'The digital future', he writes, cannot be 'sat out', i.e., endured. One could easily argue against this by pointing out that not taking action (*wei wu*) is always an option. What is noteworthy about Piallat's approach is not so much the concept of using the present as a testing ground for future events, or the commitment to the humanistic goal of enhancing society, but above all to attribute the pressure to take action to an entity called 'digitality' in order to absolve those who are responsible for taking action. He only carries out what is, as it were, timely: 'The individual deed reveals itself as an event that reaches through the agent'. Koselleck, *Begriffsgeschichten*, 160.

guarantee of equality for society as a whole.[236] On the contrary, these postulates can even block each other. Koselleck calls such a legal act a necessary 'but never sufficient condition'.[237] And who knows, maybe once recognised digital rights would be revoked again and linked to an ancestor test, or to a 'conformity test of constitutional fidelity' (whoever does not believe in the value of digital dignity as laid down in the Creative Commons Constitution forfeits these rights). I regard studies that cultivate the idea that everything can be done, provided only that the partner does not resist; in social terms, the illusion of perfect humanity, with the greatest scepticism (in Hall's figurative language: not in a mood excited by the effect of some neurotransmitter).

The first task for the theorist, before any calls for the improvement of society, is to recognise the operational differences of systems. As soon as scientific knowledge is used in politics (or other functional areas), it gives up important moments of its scientificity and becomes 'clouded', as it were.[238] In other words, it becomes politics – or economy or law – and thus in turn the object of theory. In politics, knowledge must be able to lead to results, it must be able to be translated into collectively binding decisions; in the economy it needs to be translated into payments; in law, translation into legal judgements is a necessary condition. Time pressure plays just as much a role here as the need to simplify complex contexts (whereby especially law is a system that is capable of massively slowing down its own processes). While I can point to the precarious status of the text at hand, this strategy is out of the question for political experts; they can hardly justify their own decisions by pointing to the uncertainty of all knowledge. Precisely that which protects scientific results as scientific against criticism would lead to the opposite here.[239] One can speak of two completely different levels of entitlement. Such texts are not science in the strict sense, but science that is called upon by politics to keep up with the rapid developments taking place on the Internet – in short, the 'digital pressure' that forces us to act comes from politics, which harbours fears with regard to the effect of Internet-mediated communication on so-called 'social cohesion', for example. (The solution that politics

236 Koselleck, *Begriffsgeschichten*, 197.
237 Koselleck, *Begriffsgeschichten*, 193.
238 Luhmann, *Die Wissenschaft der Gesellschaft*, 11.
239 Heidingsfelder, *Trump*, 319 ff.

has come up with for this uses the form of committees in which not only deliberations but also decisions are taken, which amounts to a multiplication of the decision-making burden – and a multiplication of the time required for votes on votes to be taken.[240] Not necessarily the best way to deal with time pressure. Kettemann and Paul name three committees alone that are currently dealing with issues of Internet reform within the United Nations: 'Within the UN General Assembly, the First Committee discusses Internet-related security issues. The Second Committee examines economic and social issues related to Internet regulation. The Third Committee discusses human rights aspects'.[241] Not to mention the special organisations: 'talking shops' such as the annual conference of the Internet Governance Forum (IGF), the various expert panels, work programs, or forums.)

A normative qualification of a digital human right would have to prove the validity of this right, which was also Habermas's concern (or more ironically with Luhmann: the validity of validity).[242] The attempt to fulfil this claim poses the greatest problems for digital ethicists. Of these, the idea of having all those affected by digitality vote on those forms of action is probably the most difficult to implement; not to mention the question of how it could be judicially reviewed.[243] Those who seek to replace Habermas's discourse ethics with a digital ethics inherit this legal fiction, along with the tactic of establishing validity through 'a kind of idealisation of the absent' (Luhmann). The fictional character becomes particularly clear in a brief sideways glance at the current attempts to realise global reform with regard to cyber norms within the framework of the UN, where the conflict between West and East does not contribute to the likelihood of agreement: resolutions supported by the United States, for instance, are perceived by some states as Western-dominated, and vice versa. The power blocs currently correspond to two different forums, here the Group of Governmental Experts (GGE), there the Open-Ended Working Group (OEWG) in the Context of International Security, on developments in the field of

---

240 N. Luhmann, 'Zwei Quellen der Bürokratisierung in Hochschulen', in A. Kieserling (ed.), *Universität als Milieu: Kleine Schriften* (Bielefeld: Haux, 1992), 75.

241 Kettemann and Paul, 'Ein Update', 1.

242 J. Habermas, *Faktizität und Geltung: Beiträge zur Diskurstheorie des Rechts und des demokratischen Rechtsstaats* (Frankfurt am Main: Suhrkamp, 1992).

243 Luhmann, *Das Recht der Gesellschaft*, 99.

information and telecommunications, which owes its existence to a Russian initiative. 'Ultimately, the two resolutions on the future of the UN debate on cyber norms contradict each other in substance and reveal and cement the continuing division'.[244] But I am equally sceptical about the potential of a systems theory of piracy vis-à-vis possible gains of order in politics, law, and economy – nor is it likely to have much impact on the practice of piracy itself. Apart from the incompatibility of these different functional levels, the idea of being able to recommend any kind of practice towards and away from piracy seems to make little sense, especially in the case of a universally applicable theory. No instructions for action or suggestions for optimising action are to be expected from systems theory, as if it were capable of better structuring and making more efficient the conversation with a prosecutor investigating pirates, a file sharer, an owner like Lars Ulrich. This does not of course mean that it cannot contribute anything to society. To paraphrase Keller: scientists can best make sense of piracy by being scientistic.[245] At least on this I unreservedly agree with Gary Hall: being a theorist means to explore ways of reimagining theory, for instance 'by challenging some of the taken-for-granted categories and frameworks concerning what critical theory is considered to be, especially the highly individualistic, liberal–humanist model that's performed by most theorists and philosophers today'.[246] In my view, the biggest problem with these theories is the humanistic overestimation of the possibilities of social control, which the present investigation explicitly distances itself from. Paradoxically, it is a direct result of functional differentiation, which precisely opposes it:

> The fact that society adjusts its structure to regulate communi-cations, and can only be a differentiated society in this way, has then also created, so to speak, pre-missive illusions, from which arguments are then made. These include, in temporal terms, the illusion that everything can be done, provided only that the partner does not resist; in factual terms, the illusion that there is

244 Kettemann and Paul, 'Ein Update', 3.
245 'Lawyers can make sense of this chaotic public dialogue by being lawyerly'. D. Keller, 'Toward a Clearer Conversation about Platform Liability', Knight First Amendment Institute's 'Emerging Threats' Essay Series (6 April 2018).
246 Hall, *Pirate Philosophy*, 3.

no lack, provided only that maldistributions are eliminated by society itself; in social terms, the illusion of perfect humanity.[247]

The basic idea can be summarised as the conviction that society can be controlled and that the aim must be to enable people to live a better, freer, fairer, more humane life. For some piracy theorists, piracy plays an essential role within this ideal. Even a Marxist like Castells has taken leave of these ideas:

> I have seen so much misled sacrifice, so many dead ends induced by ideology, and such horrors provoked by artificial paradises of dogmatic politics that I want to convey a salutary reaction against trying to frame political practice in accordance with social theory, or, for that matter, with ideology. [...] In the twentieth century, philosophers tried to change the world. In the twenty-first century, it is time for them to interpret it differently.[248]

Therefore, as Hall suggests, it must indeed be about transforming theories. Piracy can be a starting point here and be it to develop an affirmative critique of private property and bourgeois subjectivity, which would provide greater consistency with regard to the 'radical politics many theorists espouse [...] when writing about the commons' (Hall's central concern).[249] Theory, on the other hand, should refrain from attempts to transform society, i.e., to be politics itself. Not least because society as a whole cannot be addressed, it is only possible to address individual areas – namely, those which, thanks to certain organisations, have representational functions (politics, for example, in the form of parties or governments, or the economy in the form of companies and businesses). The suggestions for improvement addressed to them can, however, only be effective in the form of irritations.

The pirates have contributed to these irritations in no small way. But unlike the digital ethicists and political consultants they did not wait for the systems to translate them into their internal temporality. Instead of joining different committees and talking shops, they set their own temporality against it and put digital ethics into practice, while others are still negotiating what it might look like.

---

247 Luhmann, *Systemtheorie der Gesellschaft*.
248 Manuel Castells, *End of Millennium* (Chichester: Wiley-Blackwell, 1998), 359.
249 Hall, *Postdigital Politics*, 32.

***

What is a possible future of piracy? This much can be predicted: the next society will be as dramatically different from the book-printing society of modernity as it is from the writing society of antiquity.[250] It will leave behind the form of functional differentiation, operate in a more network-like way, and adapt to dealing with computers that communicate socially. I assume that it is already doing so – which is the reason for the conflicts we are currently facing, not only in the area of copyright. Piracy will continue to co-vary with this development. It has contributed to this – and still does. If this development is catastrophic – and there are many indications of this at present – piracy will also disappear. If not, there are good chances that it will remain and adjust its structures and processes to the state of this differentiation. This does not say much, so I will try to be more precise: my personal impression is that the system is currently exchanging its coupling favourites. It is further detaching itself from its parasitic, resistant, illegal past and tying itself even more than before to the economy, politics, and the law.

As a teacher, I would appreciate it if we could discuss the requirements of studying piracy – instead of chasing after the ever-next plagiarism and thus making Plato's dystopia come true. Shouldn't we put our energy and strength into something other than eyeing students with hostility? We could organise such a study around the inclusion/exclusion question, that is, around a very specific bundle of competencies for which it would have to be true that they are not available anywhere else in society, and thus create a unique selling point of the studied pirate. This pirate should be well versed in economic issues, for example, know about the paradox of scarcity (in short: that access – in the case of classical piracy a violent one – creates what it wants to eliminate), instead of naively delegitimising inequality and trusting the visible pirate hand.[251]

---

250 D. Baecker, *Studien zur nächsten Gesellschaft* (Frankfurt am Main: Suhrkamp, 2007). Whether this conversion requires a network-theoretical variant of systems theory, which has been overtaken by development, and which may even have to leave behind the basic distinction between system and environment, is an open debate. However, I think that systems theory can still claim validity, since the essential structures continue. See Luhmann, *Theory of Society*, 2.345 ff.

251 Luhmann, *Die Wirtschaft der Gesellschaft*, 179 ff.

Professionalisation would then also mean that the current moralising – piracy as collective 'do-gooding' (Bollier) – is already extirpated during studies. Systems theory could help with the cooling-out of such perspectives, especially of moral ones, which, as we have seen, parasitise the parasite – although not as much as it parasitises the field of social work – and, in practice, pumping away morality would clear the way for a professionalisation of which one result could be to define what one has to be able to do if one wants to do this job: if one wants to be a pirate. It would provide students of piracy with the knowledge of what 'real data piracy' (Goriunova) relies on, and inform them not only about 'the structures, tactics, and organizational forms of the Net',[252] but also of piracy itself (including its acting ontologies).

Instead of humanly finalising piracy, there would be a minimal ethics, which does not have to be constantly conjured up. I take it from Heinz von Foerster in slight modification: Always act in such a way that the alternative of the pirate increases.[253] And: Do not commit piracy to one or the other side of the alternatives. This is precisely the danger of conceptualising piracy as care. Pirates should instead be seen as people who take on social responsibility and therefore need a tough education. And students would have to be made second-order observers, that is, highly contingency-aware: piracy is only a possibility, not a necessity, and it cannot be referenced back and legitimised by a central authority (not even by an authority like Gary Hall, who admittedly does not make this claim either). That is why it is so important to provide one's own observation with an index that always already co-marks the view of one's own piratical view, thus setting it contingent in principle. Through pirate education, individuals would gain the competency to seamlessly transition between systems or remain loyal to them depending on the circumstances. This would eliminate functional ignorance, and improve perspective-taking abilities. As a result, the adept pirate would no longer prioritise their own system above all else. That which is necessarily so and not otherwise is realised as a social projection.

Piracy is nothing more, but also nothing less than a possibility. Its utilisation by society is undeniable, yet the interpretation of this

252 O. Goriunova, 'Uploading Our Libraries: The Subjects of Art and Knowledge Commons', in Sollfrank et al., *Aesthetics of the Commons*, 50.
253 Foerster, 'Ethics and Second Order Cybernetics', 295.

phenomenon remains subject to varying perspectives, not solely amongst pirates. This anthology provides information about it.

Select Bibliography

Adams, B., 'Martian Law: Is Mark Watney Really a Space Pirate?', *Overthinking It* (27 October 2015). www.overthinkingit.com/2015/10/27/martian-law-mark-watney-really-space-pirate/. Accessed 20 October 2022.

Albion, R.G., 'The "Communication Revolution"', *American Historical Review* 37, no. 4 (1932): 718–20.

—. 'The Communication Revolution, 1760–1933', *Transactions of the Newcomen Society* 14, no. 1 (1933): 13–25.

Amar, N., 'The Lives of Dakou in China: From Waste to Nostalgia', *Études chinoises* 38, no. 2 (2018): 35–60.

Anderson, B., *Imagined Communities: Reflections on the Origin and Spread of Nationalism*, rev. ed. (London: Verso, 2006).

Associated Press, 'Lars Ulrich to Sell Basquiat Painting', *Hollywood Reporter* (10 October 2008). www.hollywoodreporter.com/business/business-news/lars-ulrich-sell-basquiat-painting-120872/. Accessed 20 October 2022.

Baecker, D., *Studien zur nächsten Gesellschaft* (Frankfurt am Main: Suhrkamp, 2007).

Barlow, John Perry, 'A Declaration of the Independence of Cyberspace' (8 February 1996). www.eff.org/cyberspace-independence. Accessed 20 October 2022.

Baumgärtel, Tilman, 'Lob der Piraterie', *Zeitschrift für Medienwissenschaft*, vol. 13, *Überwachung und Kontrolle* 7, no. 2 (2015): 133–7.

BDB (Börsenverein des Deutschen Buchhandels), *Illegal aber egal? Ein Forschungsüberblick zum Unrechtsbewusstsein von Jugendlichen*, Börsenblatt (14 April 2010). www.boersenblatt.net/archiv/379078.html. Accessed 20 October 2022.

Becker, H.S., *Outsiders: Studies in the Sociology of Deviance* (Glencoe, IL: Free Press of Glencoe, 1963).

Bejan, A., 'Plagiarism Is Not a Victimless Crime', *ASEE Prism* 28, no. 7 (2019): 52.

Beltracchi, H., and W. Beltracchi, *Selbstporträt* (Reinbek bei Hamburg: Rowohlt, 2014). e-book.

Benjamin, W., 'Das Kunstwerk im Zeitalter seiner technischen Reproduzierbarkeit', in *Abhandlungen: Gesammelte Schriften*, vols 1–2, ed. R. Tiedemann and H. Schweppenhäuser (Frankfurt am Main: Suhrkamp, 1991), 1st version: 431–70, 3rd version: 471–508.

—. 'Über den Begriff der Geschichte', in *Abhandlungen: Gesammelte Schriften*, vols 1–2, ed. R. Tiedemann and H. Schweppenhäuser (Frankfurt am Main: Suhrkamp, 1991), 693–704.

Blumenberg, H., *Paradigmen zu einer Metaphorologie* (Bonn: Bouvier, 1960).

Bollier, D., 'Commoning as a Pandemic Survival Strategy', *News and Perspectives on the Commons* (26 March 2020). www.bollier.org/blog/commoning-pandemic-survival-strategy. Accessed 20 October 2022.

Burleson, K., 'Learning from Copyright's Failure to Build Its Future', *Indiana Law Journal* 89, no. 3 (2014): 1299–325.

Castells, Manuel, *End of Millennium* (Chichester: Wiley-Blackwell, 1998).

Chen, Qian, 'Plagiarism is Rampant in China, and Its Media Companies Are Raking in Billions', *CNBC* (23 January 2018). www.cnbc.com/2018/01/23/ip-plagiarism-is-rampant-in-china-and-media-companies-profit-from-it.html. Accessed 20 October 2022.

Correa, C.M., and Xuan Li, *Intellectual Property Enforcement: International Perspectives* (Cheltenham: Edward Elgar, 2009).

Dagenais, J., *The Ethics of Reading in Manuscript Culture: Glossing the* Libro de buen amor (Princeton, NJ: Princeton University Press, 1994).

de Kloet, Jeroen, 'Dakou Culture', in E.L. Davis (ed.), *Encyclopedia of Contemporary Chinese Culture* (London: Routledge, 2005), 183.

Deriso, N., 'Classic Rock Artists Who (Allegedly) Ripped Somebody Off', *Ultimate Classic Rock* (6 October 2017). https://ultimateclassicrock.com/classic-rock-rip-offs/. Accessed 20 October 2022.

Derrida, J., 'Die soufflierte Rede', *Die Schrift und die Differenz* (Frankfurt am Main: Suhrkamp, 1997).

Dery, M., "Culture Jamming: Hacking, Slashing, and Sniping in the Empire of Signs" [blog] (1993). www.markdery.com/books/culture-jamming-hacking-slashing-and-sniping-in-the-empire-of-signs-2/. Accessed 20 October 2022.

Farivar, M., 'US Intensifies Crackdown on China Intellectual Property Theft', *Voice of America* (15 May 2020). www.voanews.com/a/usa_us-intensifies-crackdown-china-intellectual-property-theft/6189373.html. Accessed 20 October 2022.

Fink, C., 'Enforcing Intellectual Property Rights: An Economic Perspective', in *The Global Debate on the Enforcement of Intellectual Property Rights and Developing Countries*, International Centre for Trade and Sustainable Development, Programme on Intellectual Property Rights and Sustainable Development, Geneva, 2009, 1–26. www.files.ethz.ch/isn/102256/2009-03_fink-correa-web.pdf. Accessed 20 October 2022.

Fink, C., K.E. Maskus, and Yi Qian, 'The Economic Effects of Counterfeiting and Piracy: A Review and Implications for Developing Countries', Policy Research Working Paper 7586, Washington, DC, World Bank Group (2016), 1–44. https://openknowledge.worldbank.org/handle/10986/23923. Accessed 20 October 2022.

Fiske, John, 'The Cultural Economy of Fandom', in L.L. Lewis (ed.), *The Adoring Audience: Fan Culture and Popular Media* (London: Routledge, 1992), 30–49.

Foerster, Heinz von, 'Ethics and Second Order Cybernetics', *Understanding Understanding: Essays on Cybernetics and Cognition* (New York: Springer, 2003), 287–304.

Foucault, Michel, 'What is an Author?', in S.B. Smith (ed.), *Modernity and its Discontents: Making and Unmaking the Bourgeois from Machiavelli to Bellow* (New Haven, CT: Yale University Press, 2018), 299–314.

Fuchs, P., *Die Metapher des Systems: Studien zu der allgemein leitenden Frage, wie sich der Tänzer vom Tanz unterscheiden lasse* (Weilerswist: Velbrück Wissenschaft, 2001).

—. *Das Weltbildhaus und die Siebensachen der Moderne: Sozialphilosophische Vorlesungen* (Konstanz: UVK Verlag, 2001), 30.

—. *Das System 'Terror': Versuch über eine kommunikative Eskalation der Moderne* (Bielefeld: Transcript, 2004).

—. 'Das WorldWideWeb – ohne Technik' (manuscript 2009). www.fen.ch/texte/gast_fuchs_www.htm. Accessed 20 October 2022.

—. *Das System Selbst. Eine Studie zur Frage: Wer liebt wen wenn jemand sagt: 'Ich liebe Dich!'?* (Weilerswist: Velbrück, 2010).

—. 'Die Verschränkung der Systeme' (manuscript 2022). www.fen.ch/texte/gast_fuchs_www.htm. Accessed 20 October 2022.

Fuchs, P., and M. Heidingsfelder, 'MUSIC NO MUSIC MUSIC: Zur Unhörbarkeit von Pop', *Soziale Systeme* 10, no. 2 (2004): 292–324.

Gilman, G., '"Game of Thrones" Tops "Breaking Bad" as 2013's Most-Pirated TV Show', *The Wrap* (26 December 2013). www.thewrap.com/game-thrones-beats-breaking-bad-2013s-pirated-tv-show/. Accessed 20 October 2022.

Goffman, E., *Interaction Ritual: Essays on Face-to-Face Behavior* (New York: Pantheon, 1967).

Goldblatt, D., 'Self-Plagiarism', *Journal of Aesthetics and Art Criticism* 43, no. 1 (1984): 71–7.

Goriunova, O., *Art Platforms and Cultural Production on the Internet* (London: Routledge, 2012).

—. 'Uploading Our Libraries: The Subjects of Art and Knowledge Commons', in Cornelia Sollfrank, Felix Stalder, and Shusha Niederberger (eds), *Aesthetics of the Commons* (Zurich: Diaphanes, 2021), 41–61.

Habermas, J., *Faktizität und Geltung: Beiträge zur Diskurstheorie des Rechts und des demokratischen Rechtsstaats* (Frankfurt am Main: Suhrkamp, 1992).

—. 'Keine Demokratie kann sich das leisten', *Süddeutsche Zeitung* (19 May 2010). www.sueddeutsche.de/kultur/juergen-habermas-keine-demokratie-kann-sich-das-leisten-1.892340. Accessed 20 October 2022.

Hall, Gary, *Pirate Philosophy: For a Digital Posthumanities* (Cambridge, MA: MIT Press, 2016).

—. 'Postdigital Politics: or, How to Be an Anti-Bourgeois Theorist' (2021). https://hcommons.org/deposits/item/hc:38325/. Accessed 13 March 2022.

Hall, Stuart, 'Encoding, Decoding', in S. During (ed.), *The Cultural Studies Reader* (London: Routledge, 1999), 507–17.

Heidingsfelder, M., *System Pop* (Berlin: Kadmos, 2012).

—. 'Retrology: Addicted to the Future', *Society & Culture in South Asia* 2, no. 2 (2016): 1–22.

—. 'Guest Editorial: Shifting Spheres', *Kybernetes* 40, no. 4 (2020): 861–907.

—. *Trump – beobachtet: Eine Struktursuche* (Berlin: Springer, 2020).

—. 'Untangling Pop: A Systems Theoretical Approach', *Systems Research and Behavioral Science* 39, no. 4 (2022): 786–806. https://doi.org/10.1002/sres.2804. Accessed 20 October 2022.

Hesse, U., 'St Pauli: The Club That Stands for All the Right Things ... except Winning', *Guardian* (2 September 2015). www.theguardian. com/football/blog/2015/sep/06/st-pauli-club-that-stands-for-all-the-right-things-except-winning. Accessed 20 October 2022.

High, M., 'Piratical Designations: Power and Possibility in Representations of Piracy', PhD thesis, Stony Brook University, 2014. https:// ir.stonybrook.edu/xmlui/bitstream/handle/11401/77209/High_grad. sunysb_0771E_12037.pdf. Accessed 20 October 2022.

Iseli, M. 'Wolfgang Beltracchi: Der Stachel im Kunstmarkt', *Handelszeitung* (6 August 2018). www.handelszeitung.ch/unternehmen/wolfgang-beltracchi-der-stachel-im-kunstmarkt. Accessed 20 October 2022.

Jenkins, Henry, *Textual Poachers: Television Fans and Participatory Culture*, 2nd ed. (London: Routledge, 2013 [1992]).

Jimenez, J., 'Russia Considers Legalizing Software Piracy to Combat Tech Bans', *PC Gamer* (10 March 2022). www.pcgamer.com/russia-considers-legalizing-software-piracy-to-combat-tech-bans/. Accessed 20 October 2022.

John, R.R., 'American Historians and the Concept of the Communications Revolution', in Lisa Bud-Frierman (ed.), *Information Acumen: The Understanding and Use of Knowledge in Modern Business* (London: Routledge, 1994), 98–110.

Johns, Adrian, *Piracy: The Intellectual Property Wars from Gutenberg to Gates* (Chicago: University of Chicago Press, 2010).

Johnson, M., K.B. Wagner, K.T. Yu, and L. Vulpiani, *China's iGeneration: Cinema and Moving Image Culture for the Twenty-First Century* (New York: Bloomsbury Academic, 2014).

Jullien, François, *Une seconde vie: essai* (Paris: Grasset, 2017). e-book.

Keane, Michael, and Elaine Jing Zhao, 'Renegades on the Frontier of Innovation: The Shanzhai Grassroots Communities of Shenzhen in China's Creative Economy', *Eurasian Geography and Economics* 53, no. 2 (2012): 216–30.

Kelber, W.H., *Imprints, Voiceprints, and Footprints of Memory: Collected Essays of Werner H. Kelber* (Atlanta, GA: Society of Biblical Literature, 2013).

Keller, D., 'Toward a Clearer Conversation about Platform Liability', Knight First Amendment Institute's 'Emerging Threats' Essay Series (6 April 2018). https://knightcolumbia.org/content/toward-clearer-conversation-about-platform-liability. Accessed 20 October 2022.

Kettemann, M.C., and S. Dreyer (eds), *Busted! The Truth about the 50 Most Common Internet Myths* (Hamburg: Verlag Hans-Bredow-Institut, 2019).

Kettemann, M.C., and A. Paulus, 'Ein Update für das Internet: Reform der globalen digitalen Zusammenarbeit', Global Governance Spotlight 4 (2020). www.econstor.eu/bitstream/10419/229428/1/1745911332.pdf. Accessed 20 October 2022.

Kix, M., 'Der Glaube an Kunst ist wie in die Kirche gehen', *Die Zeit* (8 March 2017). www.zeit.de/campus/2017/02/wolfgang-beltracchi-kunstfaelscher-haft-betrug-kunstmarkt/komplettansicht. Accessed 20 October 2022.

Koselleck, R., *Begriffsgeschichten: Studien zur Semantik und Pragmatik der sozialen Sprache* (Frankfurt am Main: Suhrkamp, 2010).

Lehmann, M., 'Enthemmter Dissens: Kommunikation in Netzwerken', in L. Koch and T. König (eds), *Zwischen Feindsetzung und Selbstviktimisierung: Gefühlspolitik und Ästhetik populistischer Kommunikation* (Frankfurt am Main: Campus, 2020), 203–28.

Leifer, E.M., *Actors as Observers: A Theory of Skill and Social Relationships* (New York: Garland Publishing, 1991).

Li, N., 'Rethinking the Chinese Internet: Social History, Cultural Forms, and Industrial Formation', *Television & New Media* 18, no. 5 (2017): 393–409.

Liang, Lawrence, 'Beyond Representation: The Figure of the Pirate', in Lars Eckstein and Anja Schwarz (eds), *Postcolonial Piracy: Media Distribution and Cultural Production in the Global South* (London: Bloomsbury, 2014), 69–70.

Litman, Patricia, *Digital Copyright* (Amherst, NY: Prometheus Books, 2006).

Locke, John, *Two Treatises of Government*, ed. P. Laslett (Cambridge: Cambridge University Press, 1988).

Lord, A., *The Singer of Tales* (Cambridge, MA: Harvard University Press, 1960).

Loughlan, P.L., '"You Wouldn't Steal a Car": Intellectual Property and the Language of Theft', Sydney Law School Research Paper 08/35 (2008), 1–10.

Luhmann, N., *Soziale Systeme: Grundriß einer allgemeinen Theorie* (Frankfurt am Main: Suhrkamp, 1984).

—. *Archimedes und wir*, ed. D. Baecker and G. Stanitzek (Berlin: Merve, 1987).

—. *Die Wirtschaft der Gesellschaft* (Frankfurt am Main: Suhrkamp, 1988).

—. *Die Wissenschaft der Gesellschaft* (Frankfurt am Main: Suhrkamp, 1990).

—. 'Der Ursprung des Eigentums und seine Legitimation – ein historischer Bericht', in W. Krawietz, A.A. Martino, and K.I. Winston (eds), *Technischer Imperativ und Legitimationskrise des Rechts* (Berlin: Duncker & Humblot, 1991), 43–57.

—. 'Status quo als Argument', in A. Kieserling (ed.), *Universität als Milieu: Kleine Schriften* (Bielefeld: Haux, 1992), 16–29.

—. 'Zwei Quellen der Bürokratisierung in Hochschulen', in A. Kieserling (ed.), *Universität als Milieu: Kleine Schriften* (Bielefeld: Haux, 1992), 74–9.

—. *Das Recht der Gesellschaft* (Frankfurt am Main: Suhrkamp, 1993).

—. 'Protestbewegungen', in Kai-Uwe Hellmann (ed.), *Protest: Systemtheorie und soziale Bewegungen* (Frankfurt am Main: Suhrkamp, 1996), 201–15.

—. 'Tautologie und Paradoxie in den Selbstbeschreibungen der modernen Gesellschaft', in Kai-Uwe Hellmann (ed.), *Protest: Systemtheorie und soziale Bewegungen* (Frankfurt am Main: Suhrkamp, 1996), 79–106.

—. *Die Gesellschaft der Gesellschaft* (Frankfurt am Main: Suhrkamp, 1997).

—. *Die Moral der Gesellschaft* (Frankfurt am Main: Suhrkamp, 2008).

—. *Ökologische Kommunikation: Kann die moderne Gesellschaft sich auf ökologische Gefährdungen einstellen?* (Wiesbaden: VS Verlag für Sozialwissenschaften, 2008).

—. *Schriften zu Kunst und Literatur* (Frankfurt am Main: Suhrkamp, 2008).

—. *Theory of Society*, vol. 1 (Stanford, CA: Stanford University Press, 2012).

—. *Theory of Society*, vol. 2 (Stanford, CA: Stanford University Press, 2013).

—. *Systemtheorie der Gesellschaft*, ed. J.F.K. Schmidt and A. Kieserling (Frankfurt am Main: Suhrkamp, 2018).

Macfarlane, A., *The Origins of English Individualism* (Oxford: Blackwell, 1978).

Maigret, Nicolas, and Maria Roszkowska (eds), *The Pirate Book* (Ljubljana: Aksioma, 2015). http://thepiratebook.net. Accessed 20 October 2022.

Malzer, M., 'Reflections on the Winter Olympics in Beijing' (manuscript 2022).

Manovich, L., 'What Comes after Remix', *Remix Theory* 10 (2007). http://manovich.net/content/04-projects/057-what-comes-after-remix/54_article_2007.pdf. Accessed 20 October 2022.

Maturana, H., and F. Varela, *Autopoiesis and Cognition: The Realization of the Living*, with a preface by Stafford Beer (Dordrecht: Reidel, 1972).

Mertha, A.C., *The Politics of Piracy: Intellectual Property in Contemporary China* (Ithaca, NY: Cornell University Press, 2005).

Negroponte, N., *Being Digital* (New York: Random House, 1996).

Niesyto, J., and K.D. Dapp (eds), 'Who Governs the Internet?', updated ed., Friedrich-Ebert-Stiftung Political Academy, Bonn, 2020.

Ong, W.J., 'Writing Is a Technology that Restructures Thought', *The Written Word: Literacy in Transition*, ed. Gerd Baumann (New York: Oxford University Press, 1986), 23–50.

Parsons, T., 'Durkheim's Contribution to the Theory of Integration of Social Systems', in K.H. Wolff (ed.), *Emile Durkheim 1858–1917* (Columbus: Ohio State University Press, 1960), 118–53.

Peukert, A., and A. Sonnenberg, 'Das Urheberrecht und der Wandel des wissenschaftlichen Kommunikationssystems', in P. Weingart and N. Taubert (eds), *Wissenschaftliches Publizieren. Zwischen Digitalisierung, Leistungsmessung, Ökonomisierung und medialer Beobachtung* (Berlin: de Gruyter, 2019), 211–41.

Piallat, C. (ed.), *Der Wert der Digitalisierung: Gemeinwohl in der digitalen Welt* (Bielefeld: Transcript, 2021).

Rammstedt, O., *Soziale Bewegung* (Frankfurt am Main: Suhrkamp, 1978).

Reed, R., 'Revisiting the Lessons of Metallica's Napster Lawsuit in the Era of Coronavirus', *Spin* (13 April 2020). www.spin.com/2020/04/revisiting-the-lessons-of-metallicas-napster-lawsuit-in-the-era-of-coronavirus/. Accessed 20 October 2022.

Renaud, Clément, 'An Archeology of Shanzhai Phones', in Clément Renaud, Florence Graezer Bideau, and Marc Laperrouza (eds), *Realtime: Making Digital China* (Lausanne: Presses polytechniques et universitaires romandes, 2020), 86–109.

Roth, S. and A. Schütz, 'Ten Systems: Toward a Canon of Function Systems', *Cybernetics and Systems Analysis* 22, no. 4 (2015): 11–31.

Schmidt, C.Y., *Allein unter 1,3 Milliarden: Eine chinesische Reise von Shanghai bis Kathmandu* (Dresden: Kahl, 2008).

Schneider, A., '"Es ist damals keinem leicht gefallen". Dr Florian Drücke, Leiter für Recht und Politik beim Bundesverband Musikindustrie im Interview', *Telemedicus* (5 October 2010). www.telemedicus.info/es-ist-damals-keinem-leicht-gefallen/. Accessed 20 October 2022.

Sitrin, M., *Pandemic Solidarity: Mutual Aid during the Covid-19 Crisis* (London: Pluto, 2020).

Smith, J.M., and E. Szathmáry, *The Origins of Life: From the Birth of Life to the Origin of Language* (Oxford: Oxford University Press, 1999).

Sollfrank, Cornelia, Felix Stalder, and Shusha Niederberger (eds), *Aesthetics of the Commons* (Zurich: Diaphanes, 2021).

Spencer-Brown, G., *Laws of Form* (New York: Julian Press, 1972).

Starr, P., *The Creation of the Media: Political Origins of Communications* (New York: Basic Books, 2004).

Steigrad, A., 'Sting Sells Music Catalog to Universal Music Group for $250 million', *New York Post* (10 February 2022). https://nypost.com/2022/02/10/sting-sells-music-catalog-to-universal-music-group-for-250m/. Accessed 20 October 2022.

Toma, A.V., 'Counterfeit, Piracy, Plagiarism: Comparison between These Crimes That Threaten National Security', *National Strategies Observer* 1 (2015). https://ideas.repec.org/a/iem/nosiem/v1y2015id2822000009354023.html. Accessed 20 October 2022.

Tse, E., K. Ma, and Y. Huang, Shan Zhai: *A Chinese Phenomenon* (Beijing: Booz & Company, 2009), 1. www.almendron.com/tribuna/wp-content/uploads/2014/10/shan-zhai-achinese-phenomenon.pdf. Accessed 20 October 2022.

Tyson, J., 'How the Old Napster Worked', *HowStuffWorks* (2016). https://computer.howstuffworks.com/napster.htm. Accessed 20 October 2022.

U.S. Government Accountability Office, 'Intellectual Property: Observations on Efforts to Quantify the Economic Effects of Counterfeit and Pirated Goods', Reports and Testimonies GAO-10-423 (12 April 2010). www.gao.gov/products/gao-10-423. Accessed 20 October 2022.

U.S. Supreme Court, *United States* v. *Furlong*, 18 U.S. 184 (1820). https://supreme.justia.com/cases/federal/us/18/184/. Accessed 20 October 2022.

Van der Sar, Ernesto, 'U.S. Government Recognizes Benefits of Piracy', *Torrentfreak* (13 April 2010). https://torrentfreak.com/es/u-s-government-recognizes-benefits-of-piracy-100413/. Accessed 20 October 2022.

Wagner, R.P., 'Information Wants To Be Free: Intellectual Property and the Mythologies of Control', *Columbia Law Review* 103, no. 4 (2003): 995–1034. www.law.upenn.edu/fac/pwagner/wagner.control.pdf. Accessed 20 October 2022.

Walsh, Nick Paton, 'Mom, I blew up the music industry', *Observer* (21 May 2000). www.theguardian.com/theobserver/2000/may/21/features.review27. Accessed 20 October 2022.

Wang, Shujen, *Framing Piracy: Globalization and Film Distribution in Greater China* (Lanham, MD: Rowman & Littlefield, 2003).

Ward, Edward, A *Journey to Hell: or, A Visit Paid to the Devil. A Poem* (London: British Library, 2010 [1700]). https://quod.lib.umich.edu/e/eebo/A67506.0001.001/1:6.3?rgn=div2;view=fulltext. Accessed 20 October 2022.

Warhol, A., and P. Hackett, *POPism: The Warhol Sixties* (Orlando, FL: Harvest, 1980).

Wittgenstein, L., *Philosophical Investigations*, German text, with an English translation by G.E.M. Anscombe, P.M.S. Hacker, and Joachim Schulte (Chichester: Wiley-Blackwell, 2009).

Wu, Timothy, 'Network Neutrality, Broadband Discrimination', *Journal on Telecom and High Tech Law* 2 (2003): 141–79. https://scholarship.law.columbia.edu/cgi/viewcontent.cgi?article=2282&context=faculty_scholarship. Accessed 20 October 2022.

Wyatt, R., 'Lines Drawn on Antipiracy Bills', *Tuscaloosa News* (13 December 2011). www.tuscaloosanews.com/story/news/2011/12/14/lines-drawn-on-antipiracy-bills/28397898007/. Accessed 20 October 2022.

Yan, J., *Génération dakou: écouter, recycler, expérimenter* (Paris: Van Dieren Éditeur, 2012).

Zach, S., *Labelgründung 2.0: Der Weg zum eigenen Label in Zeiten von Web 2.0* (MS 2008).

5 How to Be a Pirate: A Conversation

An Interview with Alexandra Elbakyan and Gary Hall
by Holger Briel

When Michael, Markus, and I first discussed the idea for publishing this book, it was very clear to us that we did not want to write yet another theoretical book on Internet piracy; practitioners from the field should also have a voice. After all, it is they who created this phenomenon in the first place and it is clearly grassroots-driven. In the following, two eminent actors in the field of Internet piracy will discuss their views on file sharing, piracy, and politics (of resistance).

The first practitioner to discuss her work is Alexandra Elbakyan, a young Kazakhstani computer programmer and creator of the website Sci-Hub, which provides free access to the majority of scientific journal articles. She has lectured on her idea of global open access all over the world and is famous throughout the digital world and beyond. She is also praised for her willingness to bear the brunt of legal action against her website. As a particular result of actions against her, at the moment she is unable to travel internationally and the interview with her was conducted in written form.

By way of an introduction to her thoughts, below is a text by Elbakyan which appeared in Russian in 2015 on the pages of VK. This is its first English translation.[1]

Sci-Hub: Open Access to Scientific Information

'This is theft' – something you can often hear from different people who learn about the existence of a project like Sci-Hub. Among these there are both outright opponents of the project (it would be more correct to say 'enemies', but let's not resort to military terminology) and ordinary people. But should one equate the scientific and educational

---

1   'Sci-Hub: Открытый доступ к научной информации' (26 September 2015), trans. Oksana Kryzhanivska, https://vk.com/wall-36928352_4635?lang=en. Translation authorised by author.

activities of the Sci-Hub project with theft? In this article, I will try to systematise all sorts of arguments on this topic.

First, let's look at the legal side of the issue. We immediately observe that 'theft' and 'computer piracy' are regulated by completely different laws – in all countries. For example, in our Criminal Code of the Russian Federation there are separate articles 158, 'Theft', and 146, 'Infringement of copyright and related rights'. If #пиратство is theft, then why come up with different laws for the same crime? So, piracy, or infringement of copyright, is not legally equivalent to theft.

Now let's consider not the legal but the semantic side of the issue. Piracy is essentially copying information. When information is copied, it grows larger. If you have a book and I make a copy of it, there will be two books. Copying is the production of new items. Not so with theft. If I steal a book from you, there is still only one book. Moreover, in this case, you will lose your book. With copying, the owner is not deprived of their owned object – on the contrary; with stealing, one is deprived. Through copying, new consumer goods are produced; in stealing, they are not. These are fundamentally important differences! A well-known saying, attributed to the Buddha, states: 'Thousands of candles can be lit from a single candle, and its life will not become shorter. Happiness does not become less when you share it'. We can add that information does not become less when it is copied. On the contrary, it gets bigger. Piracy is production! (and in the case of Sci-Hub it's a fairly complex and high-tech production).

One could counter-argue that theft means any violation of property rights. And since the information is intellectual, intangible property, its copying without the permission of the 'owner' can be equated to theft. I agree that 'property' in the modern sense is indeed a set of rights that can apply to both tangible and intangible objects. However, to equate piracy with 'theft' is nevertheless incorrect. After all, it is one thing to steal someone's wallet, take someone else's thing, and it is completely another 'illegally' to read a book. Is it right to describe all these actions with the same word? A person who does this is simply manipulating, trying to influence emotions rather than the mind. It is difficult to win support for the thesis 'copying information is bad', or 'spreading knowledge is bad'. However, everyone agrees with the thesis 'to steal is bad'. Therefore, arguments are sought to equate computer piracy to theft. It should be understood that this is a banal game of words and political rhetoric. By the way, historically, in the Russian, the word for 'thief' had a different meaning – a person so called was plotting a crime against state power; traitors were also called thieves.

There is also an argument that boils down to the fact that piracy is theft because the work of the author or publisher is not paid. A person invested time and effort, but someone took advantage of the fruits of his labours for nothing – that is, they stole. I note that this understanding of 'theft' is again not a classic. Is it possible in this case to consider an entrepreneur a thief who pays employees an unfairly low salary for their work and takes all the profits of the enterprise for himself? But this is constantly happening in a market society: the main income of the enterprise goes to the management, in comparison with which the person who really did the work receives little. Let's try to get to the bottom of the argument. Why should anyone's work be paid? 'Because it's fair', any sane person will immediately respond. Good, but also fair, if a person who does not have the money to subscribe to expensive scientific journals can read these journals for nothing. Instead, the rights holders act unfairly to obtain 'superprofits' – they set restrictively high prices for access to scientific and cultural heritage. In the case of Sci-Hub, the society that originally paid for the creation of scientific works from taxes does not have access to their results. The question arises: what if everything is actually the opposite – and it is the rights holders who stole science from society? As a whole, the argument about the 'need for paying the publisher for their work' comes down to the question of what is fair. Since it is impossible unequivocally to assert that piracy of scientific literature is unfair, then the argument is invalid.

To sum up, neither legally nor in its meaning, can the work of the Sci-Hub service be called 'theft' (#копирайт).

***

Interview with Alexandra Elbakyan

(The interview was conducted in March and April 2022 in written form.)

HB: As a concept, Internet file sharing has been around for about 25 years. What were the important factors that prompted the set-up of Z-Library and Sci-Hub?

AE: Well, Z-Library is not my project: it is a fork from Library Genesis, that was started around 2008 or so, earlier than Sci-Hub. The website became primarily a collection of books on science, but it did not have journals. Sci-Hub became the first website to provide free automatic access to research journals on a mass scale. After that, Library Genesis also added a section for journals on their website.

HB: With continued prosecution of piracy cases, do you see a possible end to piracy? How could that end be brought about?

AE: Piracy is a derogatory term that was invented by copyright holders to describe Internet freedom. When we stop calling Internet freedom 'piracy', piracy will end! On a practical note, there is more and more content on the Internet that does not require payment. Take for example YouTube, a gigantic collection of videos, all free to view. YouTube allows thousands of authors to live off the content they create, without any payment from viewers. Free content will prevail in future.

HB: Where would you locate the political dimension of Internet piracy? What larger social components does such piracy evidence?

AE: When we talk about book or journal piracy, it is essentially a fight for information freedom. Everyone has the right to information and knowledge and they must be freely distributed: that is one of the basic prerequisites for democracy, and one of the basic human rights. It would essentially be communist as well, though. Today we have that concept of 'intellectual property' that outlaws free distribution of, for example, academic books online, without permission of the owner: the publisher. We must move from the concept of 'intellectual property' to the concept of 'intellectual communism' when knowledge and information are free and belong to everyone.

HB: How do your own recent projects touch on piracy and how constitutive is it for your work?

AE: At the moment I'm working on Sci-Hub and on my PhD on the topic of Open Science. In the late 1980s, a movement emerged in science: the open access movement, that advocated that science journals must be free. The movement was supported by many prominent scientists and Nobel laureates and was quite successful; see, for example, 'Berlin Declaration on Open Access to Knowledge in the Sciences and Humanities'. My project Sci-Hub is so far the most radical, and I would say, the most successful, take on open access.

Sci-Hub made freely available more than 90 per cent of all academic journals; that is, more than 80 million published research articles.

HB: What kind of feedback have you been receiving from users? How does that make you feel?

AE: I received thousands of letters where people say that they were able to do their research projects thanks to Sci-Hub, that allowed them to access paid research literature for free, that they could not access because they do not have money. Many graduation theses were completed using Sci-Hub. Such feedback of course is a great motivation to continue! Sci-Hub is also used by medical professionals: many science journals are journals on medicine, so access that Sci-Hub provides helps saving human lives.

HB: What has been the personal cost/impact for you regarding your projects?

AE: Of course, I received lawsuits from big corporations such as Elsevier, Springer–Nature, Wiley, and others that hold copyright for their journals. Their corporations make huge profits from selling access to academic journals, and they do not pay authors. Sci-Hub is breaking this system by distributing this content for free, but is accused of copyright violation, or piracy. In 2016, a court in the United States fined Sci-Hub $US15 million in one case and $US4 million in another case. I did not pay anything, but Sci-Hub has a general reputation of an outlaw website. They also spread conspiracy theories that Sci-Hub is a project of Russian intelligence, and that I work for them. There was the danger of me having to go to prison. On the other hand, there are those who say that I deserve Nobel prize for Sci-Hub. That is another opportunity.

HB: If you had the choice, would you do it all over again? Why (not)?

AE: Of course! Because providing people with knowledge is a great idea to live for!

***

The second practitioner and theorist is Gary Hall, Professor of Media at Coventry University. I met him in 2019 at a Piracy Conference held in Suzhou, China. He had just recently finished two influential books, *Pirate Philosophy* (2016) and *The Inhumanist Manifesto* (2017) and had begun work on his most recent text, *A Stubborn Fury: How Writing Works in Elitist Britain* (2021). At the conference, he spoke to a rapt audience about the politics of creating and living a pirate mentality. And, indeed, this *Weltanschauung*, this world view, is at the heart of his undertakings, be they the writing of books, work on his theory journal *Culture Machine*, or the co-directing of the open access publishing house Open Humanities Press (OHP), which he co-founded. One of his most recent projects, and a very influential and necessary one at that, is his involvement in the community-led Open Publication Infrastructures for Monographs (COPIM) project, aiming at making more and more community-benefiting open access books available, thereby inverting the traditional academic practice of writing and publishing books with for-profit publishers and working towards a significant culture change within academia and the publishing world.

At the conference, Gary took participants to task, insisting on the close relation between theories discussed and their application in real life. I remember vividly that after my talk on the (justified) online appeal of piracy, he asked, and I paraphrase, 'What does this mean for the real world, for workers, for unions?' In other words, Gary rightfully insisted on thinking through and applying the kind of thinking that asserts the relationship between online and offline worlds, thereby displaying a comprehensive, organic understanding of how exploitation in one invariably leads to similar exploitation in the other.

In the best possible sense, Gary is an activist–academic, teaching students and writing about the benefits the online world can bring to the real one, but also making sure his audience understands that the material world and its inequalities provides subconscious routines to the online world. He sees it as his task to make these routines visible and to criticise them, in thought, action, and deed.

***

Interview with Gary Hall

(The interview was conducted in March 2022 in written form.)

HB: As a concept, Internet 'piracy' has been around for about 25 years. What were the important factors contributing to the rise of this concept?

GH: I'm aware that for a lot of people today, piracy might seem a slightly old-fashioned thing to be interested in, especially if history is measured in Internet years. At the beginning of the twenty-first century, pirating entertainment was something of a widespread desire, with Napster having 80 million users at the peak of its popularity in 2001. Now, more than 20 years after Napster's launch in October 1999, a lot of the energy and excitement around Internet piracy has been redirected. What has happened in the intervening years?

Back in 2007, my friends Pauline van Mourik Broekman and Simon Worthington published an issue of their pioneering journal *Mute* on Web 2.0. It contained a fascinating piece called 'Info-Enclosure 2.0', by Dmytri Kleiner and Brian Wyrick. 'Info-Enclosure 2.0' was about how Web 2.0, contrary to the hype that surrounded it at that time, did not in fact represent a democratising of the web by, for example, making it possible for just about anyone to create and publish content, be it with YouTube, MySpace, or Flickr, in a manner that 'previously would have required them to purchase desktop software and possess a greater technological skill set'.[2] Kleiner and Wyrick saw Web 2.0 rather as a 'second enclosure of the information commons': as capitalism's way of countering Internet piracy and the kind of peer-to-peer (P2P) file sharing that was the focus of your 20 Years of File Sharing: What is Next? Third Futures of Media Conference at Xi'an Jiaotong–Liverpool University, China, which was where we met in November 2019. Indeed, as I noted in *Digitize This Book!*, Kleiner and Wyrick went so far as to position blogs, wikis, and other forms of Web 2.0 as 'capitalism's preemptive attack against P2P systems'. As they wrote at the time:

> The mission of Web 2.0 is to destroy the P2P aspect of the internet. To make you, your computer, and your internet connection dependent on connecting to a centralised service that controls your ability to communicate. Web 2.0 is the ruin of free, peer-to-peer systems and the return of monolithic 'online services'.[3]

A decade and a half on, we can pick out two further (albeit related) aspects of capitalism's attack on P2P file-sharing systems and its

---

2   Dmytri Kleiner and Brian Wyrick, 'Info-Enclosure 2.0', *Mute* 2, no. 4 (January 2007), 12, www.metamute.org/editorial/articles/infoenclosure-2.0.

3   Kleiner and Wyrick, 'Info-Enclosure 2.0', 16, 18; Gary Hall, *Digitize This Book! The Politics of New Media, or Why We Need Open Access Now* (Minneapolis: University of Minnesota Press, 2008), 261–2n8.

rerouting of the energy and excitement around Internet piracy. The first was the development of Apple's iTunes in 2001. With its legal, pay-per-track download business model, iTunes built on the market created for sharing music online by the likes of Napster, Gnutella, Kazaa, and LimeWire. Having done its job in moving a lot of people away from piracy and P2P file sharing, a decision was then taken in 2019 for iTunes itself to be discontinued. (The introduction of macOS Catalina saw Apple replace iTunes with three apps: Apple Music, Podcasts, and Apple TV.)

The second aspect of capitalism's attack on P2P came with the launch in 2008 of Spotify, along with that of a number of other legal streaming services around the same time, including Netflix, Hulu, and iPlayer. As of the final quarter of 2021, Spotify – which was partly inspired by Napster – has logged 180 million paying users worldwide and has 406 million active users a month. Spotify, Netflix, and co. are notable for having easy-to-use interfaces (and very little unwanted porn and spam), which makes using them far more attractive to the average consumer than trying to get free content via a torrent.

Yet while a lot of the buzz surrounding Internet piracy has died down, file sharing is still happening. Dropbox and Bitcoin are both high-profile examples of what we might call non-pirate forms of file sharing, while there are numerous instances of actual 'pirate' file sharing too. They include YTS and The Pirate Bay, currently reported to be the two most popular sites.[4] Indeed, the American 'think tank' Institute for Policy Innovation has estimated that, regardless of Spotify and its rival Soundcloud, $12.5 billion worth of downloaded music has been pirated every year since 1999.[5] It is important to note that such pirate activity is not confined to the sharing of music, film, and television. Perhaps even more relevant to us as authors and academics is that of mass text digitisation projects. I'm thinking of pirate or shadow libraries such as Sci-Hub, LibGen, and Z-Library that offer unauthorised access to copyrighted material. These libraries are extremely popular and important because, for all the success of the open access movement, a lot of academic texts are still hard to get hold of in many places around the world.

4   Ernesto Van der Sar, 'Top 10 Most Popular Torrent Sites of 2022', *TorrentFreak* (3 January 2022), https://torrentfreak.com/top-torrent-sites/.
5   For more figures, see Damjan Jugovic Spajic, 'Piracy Is Back: Piracy Statistics for 2022', *DataProt* (4 March 2022), https://dataprot.net/statistics/piracy-statistics/.

So that's a brief history of the last 25 years of Internet piracy in the global North and West. (I'm conscious you are in China at the moment, which of course has a different relationship to Internet piracy.) What were the important factors contributing to the rise of this concept in the first place?

The simplest way for me to respond to this question is to say something about what, following McLuhan, I'll refer to as the Gutenberg galaxy of the printed codex book; and about how, for some, we are currently in the process of transitioning (albeit not in any straightforward linear or teleological manner) out of this galaxy into a post-Gutenberg world of densely layered information and data flows.[6] The latter has been made possible by factors such as the introduction of personal computers in 1981, the Internet in 1995, the cloud in 2006, smartphones in 2007, and 4G and 5G networks in 2009. Here, modern, liberal – 'Gutenbergian', if you will – concepts such as the distinction between public and private are becoming increasingly difficult to maintain. Evidence the reports released in the first part of 2019 that the five giant American tech companies, Alphabet, Amazon, Apple, Facebook, and Microsoft, had all been using human contractors to analyse a percentage of recordings from home voice assistants such as 'Alexa' (Amazon) and 'Siri' (Apple).

One response to such changes is that which is being put into action as we speak by Vladimir Putin as part of what's been called the first Great Information War. It takes the form of banning Facebook in Russia and restricting access to Twitter – as if information about the invasion of Ukraine can be controlled in the twenty-first century by means of twentieth-century-style centralised state censorship.

Another is that represented by the libertarian neoliberalism associated with Donald Trump and the post-Trump Republicans in the United States and Boris Johnson in the UK. From this point of view, our current period of transformation to a computational universe of high-volume waves of mediation is held as providing a few select individuals with a chance to generate new highly profitable business opportunities by disrupting much of the rules-based system by which liberal democracy and the state have traditionally kept a check on capitalism. (It's an approach that has its bible in James Dale Davidson and William Rees-Mogg's, *The Coming Economic Revolution: How to Survive and Prosper in It.*

---

6   Marshal McLuhan, *The Gutenberg Galaxy: The Making of Typographic Man* (Toronto: University of Toronto Press, 1962).

Rees-Mogg's son, Jacob, was Secretary of State for Business, Energy and Industrial Strategy in Johnson's government.)[7]

A third response to the emergence of the computational universe is that often adopted by governing bodies in Europe, including the European Union. This involves trying to force Alphabet, Amazon et al. back into a Gutenberg-shaped box precisely by introducing rules and regulations designed to maintain modern liberal democratic notions of privacy. An alternative is to accept that the latter is going to be extremely difficult if all we have to work with are the tools and concepts of yesteryear. Instead, this period of transition can be viewed more positively and productively. It can be seen as an opportunity to experiment with new social, economic, and legal possibilities for thinking–living that are very different from either the liberalism, neoliberalism, or centralised authoritarianism of the three approaches sketched above. It is an alternative response of this kind that I'm interested in exploring in my work.

Now, as a cultural phenomenon, Internet piracy is not unified and self-identical. It has many different elements and dimensions. Put crudely, some of them can be classified as liberal democratic. Shadow libraries, for example, can be perceived in certain aspects of their operation as trying to make up for the decline of the traditional public library. In other respects, Internet piracy can be positioned as being neoliberal. After all, is the P2P file sharing of music and films not a means for individual consumers to acquire capitalist commodities at little or no cost? Yet in some of its tendencies, at least, Internet piracy can be regarded as a response to our new post-Gutenberg condition and a means of exploring what comes next. Many of those involved may not understand it in these terms. In fact, it's likely most of them will not. Nevertheless, it is with trying out new modes of ownership and control, new attitudes toward intellectual rights, property rights and so on, that I would regard Napster and MegaUpload as having been engaged with in the past; and Monoskop and UbuWeb as being engaged with today. In the process, Internet piracy is helping us to invent the very laws and institutions by which its activities may be judged in the future.

7   James Dale Davidson and William Rees-Mogg, *The Sovereign Individual. The Coming Economic Revolution: How to Survive and Prosper in It* (London: Macmillan, 1997).

HB: With continued prosecution of piracy cases, do you see a possible end to piracy?

GH: It is possible that the performance of certain kinds of piracy may become more difficult. I gave the example above of how the widespread desire for Internet piracy of the early 2000s was rechannelled by the introduction of Web 2.0, iTunes, and Spotify.

Some forms of piracy may certainly decline and even die out as a result of no longer being appropriate. The 'Golden Age' of maritime piracy in the eighteenth century was created by a very specific historical, political, and social context. Relevant factors included the rise in the transatlantic shipping trade and the end of the War of the Spanish Succession, which led to many trained sailors being released from their nation's navies and left otherwise unemployed. Once this context changed, however, the 'Golden Age' of eighteenth-century piracy came to a close. It is perfectly possible that something similar could happen to the maritime piracy that is perpetrated by ex-fishermen in Somalia today – if the climate emergency results in a reduction in the use of container ships to transport goods and material over long distances as part of global supply chains, for example.

Internet piracy may likewise come to an end if *its* historical, political, and social context changes. However, I'm mindful that in the 'Pirates' chapter of his book on the future of creativity, *Free Culture*, Lawrence Lessig writes:

> If 'piracy' means using the creative property of others without their permission […] then the history of the content industry is a history of piracy. Every important sector of 'big media' today – film, records, radio, and cable TV – was born of a kind of piracy so defined.[8]

It is difficult to imagine an end to piracy when it is understood like this, for all the high-profile shutdowns of Napster and MegaUpload and repeated attempts by academic publishers to sue Alexandria Elbakyan and Sci-Hub. Nor should we necessarily wish for piracy to come to an end. As I say, piracy is an important means by which we can performatively invent the future.

8   Lawrence Lessig, *Free Culture: The Nature and Future of Creativity* (London: Penguin, 2004), 53.

HB: Where would you locate the political dimension of Internet piracy? What larger social components does such piracy evidence?

GH: Let me qualify that last point. When I say piracy is an important means by which we can performatively invent the future, I don't mean this so much in Lessig's content industry, 'big media' sense. I mean it more in the sense of viewing the shift to a post-Gutenberg galaxy as a chance to be the change we want to see, as it were, and in this way help invent an alternative future for ourselves and for society: a future that is neither neoliberal nor indeed liberal.

Actually, I'm not all that concerned whether piracy as it is conventionally understood comes to an end or not. I try to avoid the kind of moral approach that presumes to know what piracy *is* in advance: say, that it is using or stealing the property of others. This means I'm not overly invested in the idea of the pirate as deviant thief or subversive radical, which is the version often associated with the anti-copyright advocates of the pro-Internet piracy movement. (Nor, for that matter, am I invested in the image of the pirate as romantic outsider that is a feature of so much fiction and film, from Robert Louis Stevenson's *Treasure Island* to Disney's *Pirates of the Caribbean* franchise).

That I don't presume to know what piracy *is* in advance is also why I don't approach pirates and piracy as a direct object of study in my work. I've never written a straightforward political analysis of piracy, for instance. Not even in relation to the P2P file sharing of Gnutella and BitTorrent, or shadow libraries such as Aaaaarg. org and Public Library: Memory of the World. I'm more interested in trying to act as *something like* a pirate; and in explaining why, as intellectuals and academics, more of us might want to experiment with acting like this. We might want to do so for two reasons. First, because we too need to come to terms with the transformation from the analogue world of the codex book to the digital world of not just big data and Web 2.0, but now AI, the metaverse and Web3 as well. It seems to me that, in marked contrast to those operating in the spheres of music, film, television, and even politics, we have barely begun to do so as far as how we work, act, and think is concerned. When it comes to the manner in which we create and publish our work, we continue to operate for the most part as if we are still living in the Gutenberg galaxy of the codex book, along with its associated concepts of the possessive individual subject, the named biographical author, critical reflection, rational thought, and the public/private dichotomy.

The second reason we might want to do so as media theorists, in particular, is because theory helps us to be aware of our modes of being in the world, and to imagine them differently and so change them. Theory is thus one area of society in which we *can* invent new knowledges, new subjectivities, and new forms of social and political relations. An important part of this, for me, involves trying to enact alternative (non-liberal humanist) forms of subjectivity. In *The Posthuman*, Rosi Braidotti identifies a number of *conceptual personae* for dramatising alternative processes of becoming.[9] They include the feminist, the queer, and the cyborg. In my book, *Pirate Philosophy*, I add to these the figure of the pirate. I should stress, however, that I am using *pirate* in the classical sense of the term, where it refers to someone who *tries*, *tests*, *teases*, and *troubles* as well as attacks. (For the ancient Greeks, the word 'pirate' was connected to the root *peira*, 'to make an attempt, try, test'.)[10]

So, when I say I'm trying to act as something like a pirate philosopher, what I mean is that I'm making an attempt, trying, and testing alternatives to the modern, euro-Western, liberal humanist (Gutenberg galaxy) model of what it is to be a philosopher – or, indeed, academic – that is performed by most of us today, regardless of whether we are Marxists, feminists, new materialists, or posthumanists. It's a model that takes as its regulative norms: the named proprietorial author; the perfect object, published in uniform editions and distributed on a mass industrial basis; as well as self-expression, authenticity, and copyright.

In other words, I'm experimenting with the invention of alternative processes of becoming that are more consistent with the kind of politics that many of us espouse in our work, yet rarely manage to perform when it comes to how we live–work–think ourselves. Some of the non-oppositionally different norms of this model include intra-active collaboration (of both humans and non-humans); processuality; and creativity as modulation, *détournement*, 'piracy'. This is one of the political dimensions of piracy and of pirate philosophy, for me.

9   Rosi Braidotti, *The Posthuman* (London: Polity Press, 2013).
10   Gary Hall, *Pirate Philosophy: For a Digital Posthumanities* (Cambridge, MA: MIT Press, 2016).

HB: How do your own recent projects touch on piracy and how constitutive is it for your work?

GH: As you can see, a certain notion of piracy is very constitutive for my work, although perhaps not in a straightforward or obvious fashion. This is because, for all my references to pirate philosophy, here and elsewhere, and for all I've written a book of that title, I'm not actually concerned with coming up with a novel theory or original philosophy concerning piracy.

By way of further explanation, let me recall the argument John Gray develops with regard to the global public intellectual Slavoj Žižek. For Gray, Žižek is a creation of a capitalism that expands through the 'continuous production of novel commodities and experiences, each supposed to be different from any that has gone before'. And Gray sees this as being as true for contemporary theory and philosophy as for anything else. He thus concludes that Žižek's celebrity is due to the market logic of the very economy and media apparatus that Žižek himself criticises (and is unable to offer any alternatives to):

> In a stupendous feat of intellectual overproduction Žižek has created a fantasmatic critique of the present order, a critique that claims to repudiate practically everything that currently exists and in some sense actually does, but that at the same time reproduces the compulsive, purposeless dynamism that he perceives in the operations of capitalism.[11]

There's something conservative about such apparent creativity and overproduction when it comes to theory. And, for me, this is the case even when it takes the form of so-called 'low' or 'no-dads' theory. (McKenzie Wark defines low theory as referring to the 'organic conceptual apparatus a milieu composes for itself, at least partly outside of formal academic situations. [...] outside of the criteria of success of academia itself. [...] You could think of low theory as what organic intellectuals do. It's defined by who does it and why, rather than by any particular cognitive style'.)[12] If anything, I prefer Boaventura de Sousa Santos's idea. What we need is not

11   John Gray, 'The Violent Visions of Slavoj Žižek', *New York Review of Books* (12 July 2012), www.nybooks.com/articles/2012/07/12/violent-visions-slavoj-zizek/.

12   McKenzie Wark, in 'Alexander R. Galloway: An Interview with McKenzie Wark', *b20: the online community of the boundary 2 editorial collective* (7 April 2017), www.boundary2.org/2017/04/alexander-r-galloway-an-interview-with-mckenzie-wark/.

another theory – say, of political resistance and revolution – that we can position in a relation of contrast to all those others that have been provided over the course of the twentieth and early twenty-first centuries. What we need is 'rather to revolutionize theory'.[13]

When it comes to articulating what might be understood as *my* theory – but which really consists of collaborative performances of the theory of both myself and others – I don't always do so in terms of piracy or pirate philosophy, then. Instead, to make it more difficult to brand and celebrate as an original, self-identical, philosophical system, I continually shift between a number of different concepts and labels: new cultural studies, media gifts, radical open access, anti-bourgeois theory, masked media. I also repeat ideas and passages (including this one) across my written work so as to promote hetero-geneous, non-linear forms of engaging with it. Sometimes I make such sampling and remixing of material from myself and others explicit by means of the conventional system of citations, quotation marks, and endnotes. Sometimes I do not. (I am supposed to be something of a pirate philosopher, after all.)

HB: How do you see the future of piracy, especially in relation to the latest buzzwords of NFT and block chains?

GH: Just to explain for anyone reading this, NFTs (non-fungible tokens) use a cryptographic protocol of the kind that underpins cryptocurrencies such as bitcoin and Ethereum to track the ownership of a unique digital asset – say, the original digital file of Chris Torres's Nyan Cat gif or Twitter founder Jack Dorsey's first tweet – and guarantee its authenticity, thus enabling it to be monetised. First posted online in April 2011, an NFT of the original Nyan Cat was sold in February 2021 for £416,000.

I'm being asked about NFTs a lot at the moment. If NFTs have a marketing team behind them, then they're certainly doing a good job. That's meant to be a joke. But one reason why people may be asking about NFTs is because they are so new that no one is quite sure what to make of them. People are consequently – and quite understandably – looking for help and guidance. However, there is

---

13   Boaventura de Sousa Santos, *The End of the Cognitive Empire: The Coming of Age of Epistemologies of the South* (Durham, NC: Duke University Press, 2018), ix. For more, see Gary Hall, 'Pluriversal Socialism: The Very Idea', *Media Theory* 5, no.1 (2021), http://journalcontent.mediatheoryjournal.org/index.php/mt/article/view/126.

a great deal of new technology being developed at the moment. So why NFTs? What's so special about them? I suspect part of the reason NFTs – like blockchains, crypto, and Web3 – have become buzzwords is because there is the prospect of people making money out of them. Ideas that have fewer financial prospects are less likely to become such hot topics. How do I see the future of piracy in relation to NFTs? The correct answer to this question is that it's far too soon to know. However, that's perhaps a bit brief for our purposes here, so let me try to say a little more.

Earlier I described how, for Kleiner and Wyrick, Web 2.0 was a pre-emptive attack by capitalism against P2P systems. I mention it again because I wonder if we can't see NFTs in a comparable way? On the one hand, NFTs appear to have a certain democratic potential through their ability to subvert the art world by cutting out cultural intermediaries such as art dealers, galleries, and museums, and handing the selling of art over to its creators. Yet, if we update Kleiner and Wyrick's thinking for our contemporary context, can the development of NFTs not be seen as another business model, another 'Internet Investment Boom'? Yes, of course.[14] But also as one means by which the discourses of modernity and late capitalism are endeavouring to continue to privilege individualistic, original, and fixed modes of production and reception, and thus pre-emptively close off the possibility of artists and others inventing alternative ways of living–being – in this case perhaps by using blockchains, crypto, and Web3 somewhat piratically? You asked about a possible end to piracy. Certainly, my hope and expectation is that those social movements dedicated to radical open access, free and open-source software, peer production, the anti-privatised knowledge commons and their future equivalents will able to act as something like pirates in relation to NFTs.

14   Kleiner and Wyrick, 'Info-Enclosure 2.0', 13.

6 Sharing is Caring and Piracy is Theft

Ernesto Van der Sar

'Piracy is theft, clean and simple; it's smash and grab', Joe Biden, now US President, said a decade ago, effectively declaring war on pirate sites foreign and domestic. This quote was music to the ears of the entertainment industry. However, not everyone appreciated the warmongering. 'Sharing is caring', was a common response in pirate circles, where Biden's tough political stance failed to make much of an impact.

These polarised views are exemplary for the discussions around piracy and copyright. Today, more than a decade has passed since Biden's speech, but these opposing views are still ever present. In fact, they form a common thread in the news reporting at TorrentFreak. com, a piracy-oriented news site launched in 2005 that closely follows the file-sharing and piracy ecosystem. Over the years, it documented many high-profile copyright cases and ever-changing user, industry, and government behaviours. These writings are more or less second nature now. However, it's worth taking a step back to observe how it all started and what led us to where we are today.

1 The File-Sharing Revolution

The Internet opened the information gates to virtually any corner of the world. With relatively simple tools, people can share a message that previously took weeks to arrive. For me – a digital late bloomer – it all started in the late nineties. In my teenage years, my family didn't have an Internet connection at home. However, I vividly remember the first time I went onto the World Wide Web at a friend's house. It was a mesmerising experience.

The seemingly unlimited availability of knowledge, still relatively modest at the time, felt like a newly gained superpower. Hours flew by while frantically typing keywords into search engines and browsing through websites. Every new page that opened felt like a treasure trove, adding to a newly formed information addiction. Not much later I went to university. Looking back at the first few months, I spent more time at the library to scour through the Internet than actually studying. When you discover a superpower, it's hard to let go.

When before the turn of the millennium the MP3 and the first mainstream file-sharing services arrived, another dimension was added. As a music fan, I was used to spending hours in music stores browsing through and listening to the latest releases. Then, suddenly, a digital music library became accessible from home, turning music discovery sessions into night-long expeditions. The bricks-and-mortar music store was instantly outdated. It simply couldn't compete.

The fact that pirated music was available for free may have been an initial draw for many people, but to me it felt much bigger. And history shows that I wasn't the only one.

Initially, most music file sharing took place in dedicated applications such as Soulseek and Napster, but in the early 2000s BitTorrent added another element. This then novel file-sharing protocol spurred the development of dedicated sharing communities that were browsable on the web. This meant that they could also be indexed by search engines, which invited a whole new audience.

Public torrent indexers allowed people to openly share music, software, and video files. At the same time, hundreds of private sharing communities were formed, some of which were targeting very specific niches. These pirate sites became the ultimate media libraries for many people. In today's world, this may no longer seem that special, but before Spotify and Netflix started their streaming services, it was nothing short of a media revolution. Even today, many private torrent trackers have impressive collections that are far more complete than any commercial alternative.

Witnessing the rise of public torrent sites and private torrent trackers was fascinating to watch. In 2005, this fascination eventually led to the launch of TorrentFreak, a website dedicated to reporting news on file sharing. There wasn't much in-depth coverage on the file-sharing space at the time and the goal was to document the developments in this ecosystem, with a strong focus on news. This started as a solo journey, but after a year Andy Maxwell joined. Together, the two of us make up the entire writing team.

2 The (Dis)Information Battle

In the mid-2000s, various copyright industry groups were very vocal and their anti-piracy messaging was generally repeated in the media without question. TorrentFreak's goal was to present the other side as well and thus achieve – in our view – a greater balance in the discourse. This was accomplished in part by allowing the operators of major torrent sites, such as The Pirate Bay, to share their views. In addition, we also highlighted contrarian academic research and questioned results and conclusions from industry-supported studies.

In a way, these goals are partially rooted in the initial fascination I had for the Web. After consuming much online information and knowledge, the realisation came that one can also use it to create content and reach a global audience. The Internet had torn down the information barriers. Writing news and opinions was no longer exclusive to companies that had access to a printing machine or a television channel: everyone could become their own news publisher.

This self-publishing power may seem obvious today, but at the time it felt both empowering and liberating. TorrentFreak's advantage was that we launched at a time when relatively few Internet-native news sources were available, which made it relatively easy to build an audience. It is no coincidence that publications such as HuffPost, TechCrunch, Mashable, and Lifehacker all launched in the same year.

In the early years, TorrentFreak had a strong focus on giving a voice to the file-sharing community. This naturally meant that it offered a counterweight to the anti-piracy message pushed by rightsholder groups. We never endorsed piracy in any shape or form. However, we did try to fill information gaps and highlight the other side of often very polarised claims made by tendentious studies.

For example, while the music industry blamed piracy for its rapidly dropping revenues, we pointed out that, in all likelihood, the shift from physical sales to much less profitable downloads had a significant effect as well. At the same time, we highlighted academic studies which found that online piracy can have positive effects as well. It's not all black and white.

Similarly, when copyright groups started to portray pirate sites as one of the greatest malware threats on the Internet, we interviewed various anti-virus vendors to add some much-needed balance. All too often, news outlets simply repeat press releases without any critical thinking of their own. However, it's often not about what's reported in the press release but what's left out.

Another common theme is to point out erroneous DMCA takedown notices. We have covered dozens of these over the years, often focusing on extreme or bizarre examples. This included takedown notices that target bird humming or white noise. However, there are also more serious takedown problems – for example, when companies try to silence critics or competitors with DMCA notices.

The advantage of writing on an erstwhile niche topic is that we can cover subjects and topics in more depth. In recent years much of our reporting has been devoted to lawsuits and legal issues surrounding piracy and copyright. These consist of copyright troll lawsuits, site blocking efforts, as well as civil copyright infringement cases against pirates, operators, and third-party intermediaries such as ISPs.

This coverage also expanded to site owners who became the subject of criminal prosecutions. This includes The Pirate Bay founders and Megaupload's Kim Dotcom. Instead of simply covering these high profile cases based on prosecution press releases, we strove to add context by interviewing these defendants, allowing them to tell their story. The goal of our coverage has always been to add new information and that also remains the main driver today.

3 Changing Perspectives

Not everything remained the same, though. As the years passed, we increasingly realised that there are extreme positions on both ends. This was clearly visible in high-profile legislative issues such as the Stop Online Piracy Act (SOPA) battle in the United States and the EU Copyright Directive and its 'upload filters'. These public debates were skewed on and by both sides and made us more cautious in our reporting. After all, a counterweight should bring balance and not tip the scale in the other direction.

The polarised opinions and views can be quite a challenge from a news perspective. It's not the journalist's task to rebut one opinion with their own. This means that sometimes the balance should be found in contrasting two extreme positions, without adding any opinion. Highlighting all the relevant facts as context is the main goal. It is then up to the readers to weigh these accordingly.

We occasionally raise our voice with opinion pieces as well, but these are kept to a minimum today, since we're first and foremost a news site. The format of these articles is usually to question a report or claim that is unnuanced or clearly misleading. These claims may come from pro-copyright groups or media companies, as highlighted earlier, but we may also point out discrepancies in statements from big tech companies, pirate sites, or activist groups.

Another major change that TorrentFreak has witnessed over the past two decades is in the file-sharing ecosystem itself. In the early years, there were a lot of hobbyists running file-sharing sites and services. However, after people realised that money can be made from it, the profit opportunity invited a new breed of operators and developers. These people care very little about sharing: they're in it for the money.

This criminal element seems to be dominant today among operators of many sites and services. While there are still sites and small communities that are operated by idealists, these are now a minority. Many of the large streaming and download sites exist to make money. The same is true for most of the apps, sellers of dedicated piracy devices, and IPTV services.

Copyright holders are right to call out this angle and I'm the first to agree that sharing isn't always caring. However, locking up a dozen site operators or IPTV sellers is not the answer either. If there's money to be made, others will simply fill the gap and take over. This pattern has repeated itself numerous times of the past two decades.

People who occasionally consume pirated content are also not criminals. Many are actually avid consumers. Reports and research have repeatedly shown that people who download or share music or movies without permission also tend to spend a lot on legal content as well. Many pirates are loyal customers; cracking down on these people could prove to be counterproductive for the industry.

The above illustrates that piracy can be a crime. However, pirates can simply be caring fans, too. It's a matter of perspective.

4 The Piracy Compass

After observing the copyright battles and piracy ecosystem at TorrentFreak for nearly two decades, there are some personal conclusions that can be drawn. I don't claim to have a silver bullet or an ultimate answer, but sometimes a compass can be just as powerful.

When Joe Biden said that piracy is nothing more than theft, he was seen as Hollywood's hero. However, if the past decades have shown us anything, it's that threats and legislation won't stop piracy. At the same time, sharing isn't always caring either. There are criminals who exploit it to get rich at the expense of entertainment industry workers.

Real people are financially hurt in some cases. However, stronger enforcement isn't going to eliminate piracy. The easiest way to tackle the problem is by looking at what the motivations are that people have to go through unofficial channels for content and address these whenever and wherever possible. Making content easily available for a decent price often goes a long way already.

So, if we should compare piracy to anything, it's a compass. It tells us where legal availability of content is lacking. It's an instrument that will help the entertainment industries guide them on their way and give people what they want. If that point is reached, the compass is no longer needed.

7 Piracy in Nollywood: Dimensions, Contexts, Hazards, and Ways Forward

Nelson Obinna Omenugha

1 Introduction

For many, copyright protection is very key to the wellbeing of an intellectual property industry like the Nigerian film industry. Piracy is the negation of copyright protection; it is the destructive element which protagonists of copyright protection must deal with. Given the perennial challenge of piracy confronting Nollywood, discussions about the nature and impact of and solutions to piracy are critical for the industry's future and sustainability. This chapter, therefore, takes up this task. It examines the phenomenon of piracy in the Nigerian cinema industry, interrogating its dimensions and contexts, thus arriving at possible measures towards tackling it.

2 A Brief Overview of Nollywood

In the past three decades, the Nigerian film industry, popularly known as Nollywood, has emerged as an influential cultural industry within the country while also gaining impressive global visibility. The film industry in Nigeria dates to the 1960s when the first generation of filmmakers – such as Hubert Ogunde and Ola Balogun – started their productions. These pioneers were stage drama producers who in time started shooting on celluloid. Ogunde, who has been claimed to be the father of the Nigerian film industry, established the Ogunde Theatre in 1945, which was Nigeria's first professional drama production company.[1]

However, it was the 1992 blockbuster *Living in Bondage*, produced by businessman Kenneth Nnebue, that finally ushered in the modern cinema industry in Nigeria. Henceforth, the film industry

---

1   Similoluwa Daramola, 'Combating Piracy in the Nigerian Nollywood Movie Industry', *SSRN* (10 March 2021).

in the country never remained the same.[2] The remarkable success of Nollywood is evident from the fact that it has in a very short time emerged as one of the largest cinema industries in the world. On the average, it produces around one thousand films in a year, making it the second-most prolific film industry globally after India's Bollywood. Interestingly, figures from the Nigerian National Bureau of Statistics (NBS) show that in 2020 the industry released a total of 2,599 films, far more than the average annual production, during a year, curiously, that due to the COVID-19 pandemic saw many other social and economic activities in the country grounded.[3]

Apart from its enormous cultural influence as a form of entertainment and vehicle for sharing meaning, Nollywod has been noted for its huge economic impact. NBS data showed that the industry accounted for 1.49 per cent of the country's GDP.[4] And, of course, Nollywood is one of the nation's biggest employers of labour, accounting for over 300,000 jobs in 2021.[5]

Against this backdrop, Nollywood deservedly occupies a prominent position among subjects of public discourse in the cultural, economic, and even political spheres of Nigeria. In the same vein, issues touching on its wellbeing and survival, such as piracy, continue to be prominent in people's minds.

3 Piracy in Nollywood

The world over, piracy threatens the culture industry as it distorts the economic base of creativity and production. Nollywood has had its fair share of piracy. In fact, piracy has become a very disturbing and disruptive element in the Nigerian film industry, so much so that it has provoked concern about the very survivability of the industry.[6]

---

2 Daramola, 'Combating Piracy'; James Tsaaior, '"New" Nollywood Video Films and the Post/Nationality of Nigeria's Film Culture', *Research in African Literatures* 49, no. 1 (2018), 145–62.
3 National Bureau of Statistics, Nigeria, 'Nollywood Movies Production Data (Q2 2021)', Abuja, 2021.
4 (Amodu, 2020).
5 Bulus Bailey, 'Fast-Growing Nollywood Creates the Most Jobs in 5yrs', *Business Day* (10 January 2022).
6 Lanre Amodu, Chiamaka Isiguzoro, Oladokun Omojola, Babatunde Adeyeye, and Lanre Ajakaiye, 'Assessing Audience's Willingness to Curb Digital Piracy: A Gender Perspective', *Cogent Social Sciences* 6, no. 1 (2020), 1–14; Daramola, 'Combating Piracy'.

Following a survey on the trend and pattern of piracy in Nollywood, Ridwan et al. found the extent of the problem to be 'outrageous and alarming'.[7] This view reflects those of other scholars and stakeholders who have viewed piracy as the single most important factor threatening the progress and future of the industry.[8] Instructively, in 2009, the International Intellectual Property Alliance (IIPA) returned this damning verdict on the state of piracy in Nollywood:

> The video piracy situation in Nigeria has worsened, with remarkable high-quality counterfeit products, indicating a high level of criminality and sophistication not previously noted, particularly with respect to optical discs. Investment losses and levels of piracy, which have traditionally been very high, are getting higher, and are thus an indicator of serious danger for the video industry. Evidence of arrests and exhibits recovered during various anti-piracy raids conducted in Nigeria suggest that Chinese and Southeast Asian pirate gangs have infiltrated Nigeria and set up over a dozen optical-disc operations, some of which are reported to have mastering facilities, and that the growing piracy rate has destroyed the legitimate market in Nigeria for intellectual property media and digital products.[9]

Piracy is having a devastating effect on the ability of investors to recoup their expenses and then make a profit from film sales. The reduced profitability of investment in film because of piracy is also affecting the income of actors and other participants in the industry, so much so that many of them are threatened by poverty.[10] A popular filmmaker once had to sell his property to offset the bank loan he took out to produce his film, as piracy seriously prevented him from recouping his capital.[11] Hence, filmmakers are usually left in fear as to what will be the commercial fate of their next production, a situation

7   Adeyemi Ridwan, Ganiyu Akashoro, and Mukaila Ajaga, 'An Empirical Study of the Trend and Pattern of Video-Film Piracy in Nigeria', *European Scientific Journal* 9, no. 14 (2013), 81.

8   Daramola, 'Combating Piracy'; Ayoyemi Lawal-Arowolo, 'Copyright Exploitation: The "Nollywood" (Nigeria) Film Market', *SSRN* (8 February 2020); Edet Essien, 'Video Film Piracy in Nigeria: Interfacing to Integrate the Pirate', *LWATI: A Journal of Contemporary Research* 14, no. 1 (2016), 157–66; Ridwan et al., 'An Empirical Study'.

9   Ridwan et al., 'An Empirical Study', 67.

10   Amodu et al., 'Assessing Audience's Willingness'; Lawal-Arowolo, 'Copyright Exploitation'; Essien, 'Video Film Piracy in Nigeria'.

11   Daramola, 'Combating Piracy'.

that adversely affects investment in the industry.[12] Worse still, in the past, the series of efforts made to confront piracy have been largely ineffective.[13] This situation is empirically corroborated by Ajaga and Olugboji, whose findings show that producers' and marketers' attempts to eradicate piracy in Nollywood so far have failed.[14]

4 Forms of Piracy in Nollywood

Piracy in Nollywood occurs in several forms which are outlined below:

(1) Unauthorised rental of films. This is a form of piracy that emerged in Nollywood very early on in the life of the industry. In the 1990s and early 2000s, thousands of film rental shops started operating in the streets of Nigeria. These outlets rented out films recorded on VHS tapes and later CDs and DVDs. Most of these rental shops operated illegally, i.e., without having been registered by the Nigerian Copyright Commission (NCC). This meant that they did not pay the legally required royalties to the makers of the films they rented out. Nonetheless, such rental shops became the source through which millions of Nigerians consumed the large number of Nollywood films released on a weekly basis. This seriously undermined any successful return on investment on the part of filmmakers. In 2007, the World Intellectual Property Organization (WIPO) reported that over 40,000 film rental shops were operating in Nigeria while paying nothing to copyright owners. However, the more recent emergence of digital online platforms that enable Nigerians to download and watch films as well as share them via mobile phones and personal computers has undermined CD/DVD film rental as a profitable venture, and so substantially weakened that form of piracy.[15]

(2) Another form of piracy haunting Nollywood is the sale of pirated copies. These are unauthorised copies of legitimate films sold in various markets; the makers and sellers of illegal copies do not share sales proceeds with the filmmakers. Pirated Nollywood films can

---

12 Lawal-Arowolo, 'Copyright Exploitation'.
13 Daramola, 'Combating Piracy'; Lawal-Arowolo, 'Copyright Exploitation'.
14 Mikaila Ajaga and Femi Olugboji, 'Stakeholders' Perception of Piracy of Yoruba Nollywood Movies', *International Journal of Humanities & Social Studies* 2, no. 9 (2014), 6–13.
15 Chidi Izuzu, 'The Nollywood Video Club Days', *Pulse* (17 August 2017).

be found in all sorts of sales outlets. However, stakeholders have continued to point at the traders at the Alaba International Market, a popular electronics market in Lagos, as being the most notorious culprit regarding the creation and distribution of pirated copies.[16] The pattern of this form of film piracy is varied and dynamic. Apart from copies pirated locally and sold in the domestic market, some pirated copies are exported to be sold abroad, while there are also copies pirated abroad and clandestinely imported into Nigeria. According to a *New York Times* report, in November 2010, US officials confiscated more than 10,000 pirated Nollywood DVDs from nine shops in Brooklyn. Also, the pattern of piracy in Nollywood may come by way of a single film being recorded on a single CD/DVD or by way of recording of multiple films on one DVD, the latter being particularly attractive to buyers due to its relative cost.

Instructively, one significant factor working in favour of this form of piracy is that pirated copies usually end up much cheaper than original versions, thus giving market advantage to the pirates.[17] Worse still, the pirates have continued to improve their technology, so that differentiating a pirated copy from an original copy is becoming difficult if not impossible.[18]

(3) Online/digital piracy. This is the unauthorised online uploading and downloading of films as well as unauthorised sharing from user to user. As observed by Mauyakufa and Pradhan, while the introduction of online marketing of cultural products has greatly eased distribution and made it much more cost effective, it has significantly exacerbated piracy as unscrupulous individuals can more seamlessly distribute unauthorised digital copies of films.[19] Online/digital piracy in Nollywood occurs mainly via platforms like YouTube and piracy websites as well as via individual person-to-person file sharing (P2P).[20] Given the growing penetration of Internet access as well as access to digital platforms such as smartphones and

16 'Big Piracy Business in Alaba Market', *PM News* (11 March 2013), https://pmnewsnigeria.com/2013/03/11/big-piracy-business-in-alaba-market/.
17 Edet Essien, 'Video Film Piracy in Nigeria: Interfacing to Integrate the Pirate', *LWATI: A Journal of Contemporary Research* 14, no. 1 (2016), 157–66.
18 Ridwan et al., 'An Empirical Study'.
19 Fortunate Mauyakufa and Anup Pradhan, 'Cybercrime as a Detrimental Act to African Cinema: A Case Study of Nollywood', Proceedings of the International Conference on Industrial Engineering and Operations Management, Washington, DC, 27–29 September 2018.
20 Ridwan et al., 'An Empirical Study'.

personal computers, this form of piracy is becoming commonplace in Nigeria.[21] In fact, online/digital distribution of films is where the future lies, and the future of film piracy and the fight against it will be largely dependent on how both pirates and those who challenge them navigate through the dynamics of these technologies.

(4) Unauthorised broadcasting of films. This is another form of piracy thriving in Nollywood. In an ideal world, broadcast films are subject to the authorisation of the makers who are usually paid royalties for such dissemination. However, in Nigeria, unauthorised film broadcasting has become a thriving way for depriving filmmakers of the fruit of their labour. Of course, this does not go for all broadcasts; broadcasts of Nollywood films by popular satellite television stations such as African Magic are duly licensed, with fees being paid to the rightful owners.[22]

5 Causes of Film Piracy in Nollywood

What are the factors engendering piracy in Nollywood? This question remains germane, especially given how this situation has endured all these years and seemingly defies any solution. In the following, I will identify some of the causes of film piracy in Nigeria.

5.1 Economic Hardship in the Country

Economic realities in Nigeria are such that the income of an average Nigerian is quite low, making it difficult to afford a decent living. Recent data shows that over 4 out of every 10 Nigerians are living in poverty, with many more being continuously threatened by poverty. This situation is being aggravated by the severe weakening of the nation's currency (the naira) in recent months, which has grossly reduced individuals' purchasing power.[23]

This harsh economic reality has significant implication for protecting the copyright and economic interest of filmmakers. Poverty seriously limits the capacity of an average citizen to purchase legitimate CD/DVD or digital copies of Nigerian films, and therefore pirated physical copies and online copies are much cheaper alternatives.

21 Mauyakufa and Pradhan, 'Cybercrime'.
22 Daramola, 'Combating Piracy'.
23 World Bank, 'Poverty & Equity Brief: Nigeria' (October 2021). https://databank.worldbank.org/data/download/poverty/987B9C90-CB9F-4D93-AE8C-750588BF00QA/AM2021/Global_POVEQ_NGA.pdf

This has been pointed out as the major factor behind the thriving of illegal film renting and the sale of pirated CD/DVD copies. It has also continued to also encourage online/digital video piracy.

5.2 Ignorance of Copyright Law by the Public

A lot of people in the country are ignorant of copyright law. Scholars like Abdur-Raheem have found a very low awareness of copyright among Nigerians. Such ignorance tends to result in the violation of copyright law in general in the country, and this includes films. Even though awareness of law does not necessary guarantee compliance therewith, it is a critical first condition in the quest for achieving adequate obedience to the law amongst members of the public. As rightly observed by Arewa, 'members of the society must understand the protection of copyright before protection mechanism can become effective and piracy curbed'.[24]

A study by Onyejelem and Duru showed that the majority of Nigerian university undergraduates surveyed were ignorant of the legal implication of unauthorised online/digital distribution of music.[25] This is quite instructive in diagnosing causes of copyright infringements in the country.

5.3 Weak Law Enforcement

Copyright law enforcement in Nigeria has been adjudged to be too weak to reduce piracy effectively. As Andrews rightly observed, having a law alone is not enough; it must be backed by an effective implementation regime to be impactful.[26] This weakness in law enforcement is endemic in Nigeria and extends to several other areas apart from copyright.

Factors responsible include poorly trained, equipped, and motivated law enforcement agencies, an inefficient judicial system, and corruption.[27] Importantly, corruption has been identified as the number one enemy of law enforcement in Nigeria. Commenting on

---

24   Olufunmilayo Arewa, 'The Rise of Nollywood: Creators, Entrepreneurs, and Pirates', UC Irvine School of Law Research Paper, No. 2012-11.

25   Timothy Onyejelem and Henry Duru, 'Awareness and Attitude to Copyright Implications of Online Music Download among Undergraduate Students of Nnamdi Azikiwe University, Awka', *International Journal of Social Sciences and Humanities Reviews* 8, no. 2 (2018), 1–15.

26   Samuel Andrews, 'Reconceptualizing Nigerian Copyright Law to Protect Nollywood', PhD thesis, University of Suffolk, 2018.

27   (Kwaja, 2020).

the role of customs in preventing trans-border piracy in Nigeria, Umeh and Aniche write that 'corruption among customs officials seriously harm fight against importation of pirated materials'[28]

Dapo Adeniyi, a Nollywood filmmaker, was reported to have chosen to release his films in the United States instead of Nigeria, where he felt there existed a stronger law enforcement regime to check piracy (there are many audiences for Nollywood films in the United States, made up of expat-Nigerians and other Africans living there). Adeniyi stated, 'In the US, if you catch somebody infringing on your copyright you can call the police and they will assist you in bringing him to justice. Here in Nigeria, there is no police that you can call'.

Clearly, effective enforcement is critical to developing a strong and effective copyright regime in the Nigerian film industry. A survey by Amodu et al. indicates that even though people are aware of the copyright implications of unauthorised digital sharing of Nollywood films, they still do not consider stopping the behaviour.[29] This is probably because such persons are not envisaging any punitive consequences arising from their action. Studies in legal behaviour show that mere knowledge of the law in the absence of other motivating factors such as sanctions does not necessary translate to compliance thereto.

5.4 Weaknesses in the Existing Copyright Law

The existing copyright law in Nigeria is remarkably weak, especially regarding online/digital distribution of intellectual property which is the major form of piracy today. In fact, Ajaga and Olugboji are spot on when they argue that weak laws are a leading factor encouraging piracy in Nigerian film industry.[30]

Nothing validates the above point more than the fact that under the extant Copyright Act unauthorised sharing of digital works, save for commercial purposes, is not regarded as a criminal offence. Mauyakufa and Pradhan reason that this failure of the Nigerian law adequately to check Internet piracy has undermined productivity,

---

28 Samson Umeh and Charity Aniche, 'Contributions of the Nigerian Customs to the Fight against Piracy in Nigeria: Prospects and Challenges', *UNIZIK Law Journal* 16 (2020), 75.

29 Amodu et al., 'Assessing Audience's Willingness'.

30 Ajaga and Olugboji, 'Stakeholders' Perception of Piracy of Yoruba Nollywood Movies'.

which has kept Nollywood back from properly competing with Hollywood.[31] As filmmaker Dapo Adeniyi lamented, 'The problem is that there is no law that is strong enough to fight piracy in this country. So, how do you want to invest half a billion naira on a film and then watch it being frittered away by pirates?'[32] Andrews is therefore right when he observes that an amendment of the law is necessary in Nigeria to deal effectively with the digital/online dimension of piracy.[33]

6 Does Piracy Have Any Value for Nollywood?

While piracy is generally condemnable, both legally and morally, curiously there is an argument to the effect that it has its merits. In other words, some have argued that piracy plays a helpful role in advancing intellectual production. Drawing an analogy between the Marxist concept of primitive acquisition and piracy, Grassmuck has argued that piracy must have played an important role in the evolution of the modern capitalist commercial structure that propels the contemporary intellectual property industry.[34]

It has also been argued that piracy has played a positive role in making access to Nollywood films more widely available.[35] Elaborating on this view, Grassmuck contends that producers have responded to piracy by increasing their speed of mass production. In other words, pirates usually capitalise on circulation gaps to introduce pirated copies into the market, but Nollywood filmmakers, in a bid to beat them to it, have adopted the strategy of quickly flooding the market with authentic copies once they release any new production.[36] 'The viral spread of Nollywood films has thus far been a key element of Nollywood successes'.[37]

---

31   Mauyakufa and Pradhan, 'Cybercrime'.
32   Chux Ohai, 'Piracy Forces Filmmaker to Release Film Abroad', *Nigerian Voice* (20 May 2015), para. 5.
33   Andrews, 'Reconceptualizing Nigerian Copyright Law'.
34   Volker Grassmuck, 'On the Benefits of Piracy', in L. Eckstein and A. Schwarz (eds), *Postcolonial Piracy: Media Distribution and Cultural Production in the Global South* (London: Bloomsbury Academic, 2014), 79–98.
35   Emmanuel Akinwotu, 'Nollywood Moment: African Film Industries "Could Create 20m Jobs"', *Guardian* (20 October 2021); Grassmuck, 'On the Benefits of Piracy'.
36   Grassmuck, 'On the Benefits of Piracy'.
37   Grassmuck, 'On the Benefits of Piracy', 83.

Similarly, it has been contended that piracy has played a role in stimulating market competition in Nollywood, thus making films more affordable to consumers.[38] Stated differently, the rivalry represented by pirates has forced filmmakers to set lower prices for the products to enhance their competitiveness.

Be that as it may, while the above seemingly positive roles of piracy may appear desirable on the surface, piracy is ultimately harmful and portends dangers for the future of Nollywood. For instance, even though piracy may increase accessibility and affordability of films among the populace, the fact that filmmakers are not getting adequate returns on their investments or are not even recouping their production costs, becomes a greatly demotivating factor that may stall investment in the sector.[39] Stated differently, Nollywood, like every modern cinema industry founded on the profit principles of capitalism, would ultimately remain endangered as long as the capacity of the investors (who drive the industry) to recoup and make gains, continues to be undermined.

7 Conclusion and Recommendations

The discussion above reveals that Nollywood is burdened with piracy challenges which continue to threaten its sustainability. Consequently, this researcher concludes that addressing the problem of piracy is crucial to strengthening Nollywood and securing its future.

In so doing, it is of paramount importance that Nigerian copyright law be strengthened to meet the challenges of today's technological production dynamics. This is especially the case for online/digital distribution of intellectual property. The proposed amendment to the Nigerian Copyright Act contains provisions like those of the Digital Millennium Act of the United States, which seek to combat online piracy by instituting measures to hold websites and their hosting companies accountable in the event of copyright infringement. Like the US law, the bill seeks to reduce the freedom and protection which copyright infringers have enjoyed online. Section 44 criminalises hacking of any site for piracy purposes. It also prohibits the importing, selling, and distribution of any

---

38   Akinwotu, 'Nollywood Moment'; Grassmuck, 'On the Benefits of Piracy'.
39   Akinwotu, 'Nollywood Moment'; Karim Fahim, 'Pirated Films from Nigeria Are Seized in Brooklyn', *New York Times* (4 November 2010).

technology meant for piracy-related hacking. The bill empowers a copyright owner, whose work has been pirated on a website, to give notice to the appropriate Internet service provider (ISP) demanding that access or links to the pirated copy be taken down or disabled on its systems or networks (Section 47). The service provider is also required to remove such content or link within a prescribed period after carrying out necessary inquiry, as provided for in the bill (Section 48). Section 49 provides for suspension of accounts of an offender once a service provider is notified for a second time that the account has engaged in piracy. However, the above amendment bill has remained before the National Assembly since 2016 without passage.[40] Actions should be expedited as a matter of urgency to make the bill become law.

Similarly, there should be inter-agency collaboration to make enforcement of copyright law more effective. Such collaboration involving the Nigerian Copyright Commission (NCC), the police, customs, etc., is very critical to any successful fight against piracy in Nollywood.[41] Also important is adequate training of law enforcement agencies and technical equipment for more efficient detection of and dealing with piracy, especially in the context of today's technology-based piracy. Members of the public should also be sensitised as a way of making everyone aware of the issue to ensure more willing compliance with copyright law among the populace.

Select Bibliography

Abdur-Raheem, Adeyemi, 'The Legal, Economic, Social, Criminal, and Political Challenges of Video Piracy: The Nigerian Experience', PhD thesis, Universiti Utara Malaysia. https://etd.uum.edu.my/3350/2/Adeyemi_Ridwan_Abdur-Raheem.pdf. Accessed 7 March 2022.
Ajaga, Mikaila, and Femi Olugboji, 'Stakeholders' Perception of Piracy of Yoruba Nollywood Movies', *International Journal of Humanities & Social Studies* 2, no. 9 (2014): 6–13.
Akinwotu, Emmanuel, 'Nollywood Moment: African Film Industries "Could Create 20m Jobs"', *Guardian* (20 October 2021). www.theguardian.com/global-development/2021/oct/05/nollywood-booming-while-african-film-industries-could-create-20m-jobs-report. Accessed 7 March 2022.

40 Onyejelem and Duru, 'Awareness and Attitude to Copyright Implications of Online Music Download'.
41 Umeh and Aniche, 'Contributions of the Nigerian Customs to the Fight against Piracy'.

Amodu, Lanre, Chiamaka Isiguzoro, Oladokun Omojola, Babatunde Adeyeye, and Lanre Ajakaiye, 'Assessing Audience's Willingness to Curb Digital Piracy: A Gender Perspective', *Cogent Social Sciences* 6, no. 1 (2020): 1–14.

Andrews, Samuel, 'Reconceptualizing Nigerian Copyright Law to Protect Nollywood', PhD thesis, Suffolk University Boston, 2018.

Arewa, Olufunmilayo, 'The Rise of Nollywood: Creators, Entrepreneurs, and Pirates', UC Irvine School of Law Research Paper, No. 2012-11. https://papers.ssrn.com/sol3/papers.cfm?abstract_id=2011980. Accessed 4 March 2022.

Asogwa, Chika, Ibe Onoja, and Emmanuel Ojih, 'The Representation of Nigerian Indigenous Culture in Nollywood', *Journal of Scientific Research & Reports* 7, no. 2 (2013): 97–107.

Bailey, Bulus, 'Fast-Growing Nollywood Creates the Most Jobs in 5yrs', *Business Day* (10 January 2022). https://businessday.ng/big-read/article/fast-growing-nollywood-creates-the-most-jobs-in-5yrs/. Accessed 3 March 2022.

Carter, Michael, and Oluyemi Marenin, 'Law Enforcement and Political Change in Post-Civil War', *Nigerian Journal of Criminal Justice* 9, no. 2 (1981): 125–49.

Daramola, Similoluwa, 'Combating Piracy in the Nigerian Nollywood Movie Industry', *SSRN* (10 March 2021). https://ssrn.com/abstract=3770155. Accessed 3 March 2022.

Essien, Edet, 'Video Film Piracy in Nigeria: Interfacing to Integrate the Pirate', *LWATI: A Journal of Contemporary Research* 14, no. 1 (2016): 157–66.

Fahim, Karim, 'Pirated Films from Nigeria Are Seized in Brooklyn', *New York Times* (4 November 2010). www.nytimes.com/2010/11/05/nyregion/05nollywood.html. Accessed 9 March 2022.

Grassmuck, Volker, 'On the Benefits of Piracy', in L. Eckstein and A. Schwarz (eds), *Postcolonial Piracy: Media Distribution and Cultural Production in the Global South* (London: Bloomsbury Academic, 2014), 79–98.

Handzhiyska, Lawrence, and Clement Mackay, *Introduction to Media Law*. Vienna: Verein Freies Radio Wien, 2017. https://doksi.net/en/get.php?order=DisplayPreview&lid=24893. Accessed 20 October 2022.

Idachaba, Armstrong, 'Creating Wealth through Nigerian Video-Film' (March 2018). www.researchgate.net/publication/323936014_CREATING_WEALTH_THROUGH_NIGERIAN_VIDEO-FILM. Accessed 9 March 2022.

Ike, David, 'A Review of Copyright Governance in Nigeria', *NAU.JCPL* 8, no. 5 (2021): 57–72. https://journals.unizik.edu.ng/index.php/jcpl/article/download/799/713. Accessed 2 March 2022.

Izuzu, Chidi, 'The Nollywood Video Club Days', *Pulse* (17 August 2017). www.pulse.ng/entertainment/movies/throwbackthursday-the-nollywood-video-club-days/t404lm2. Accessed 2 March 2022.

Kwaja, Chris, *Policing, Police and the Feasibility of Their Reform in Nigeria* (Abuja: Friedrich-Ebert-Stiftung Nigeria Office, 2020).

Lawal-Arowolo, Ayoyemi, 'Copyright Exploitation: The "Nollywood" (Nigeria) Film Market', *SSRN* (8 February 2020). https://ssrn.com/abstract=2694906. Accessed 9 March 2022.

Mauyakufa, Fortunate, and Anup Pradhan, 'Cybercrime as a Detrimental Act to African Cinema: A Case Study of Nollywood', Proceedings of the International Conference on Industrial Engineering and Operations Management, Washington, DC, 27–29 September 2018. http://ieomsociety.org/dc2018/papers/201.pdf. Accessed 3 March 2022.

National Bureau of Statistics, Nigeria, 'Nollywood Movies Production Data (Q2 2021)', Abuja, 2021. https://nigerianstat.gov.ng/pdfuploads/Nollywood%20Movies%20Production%20Data%20%E2%80%93%20Q2%202021.pdf. Accessed 3 March 2022.

Nbete, AubaBari, and Somieari Ikiroma-Owiye, 'Film and Cultural Imperialism in Nigeria: A Critical Developmental Perspective', *The Crab: Journal of Theatre and Media Arts* 9, no. 4 (2014): 123–38.

Ohai, Chux, 'Piracy Forces Filmmaker to Release Film Abroad', *Nigerian Voice* (20 May 2015). www.thenigerianvoice.com/news/179860/piracy-forces-filmmaker-to-release-film-abroad.html. Accessed 5 March 2022.

Ojukwu, Ebele, Young Onyiuke, and Chinyere Esimone, 'Intellectual Property Rights Enforcement in Nigeria: A Prop for Music Industry', *US–China Education Review B* 5, no. 6 (2015): 373–81.

Oludayo, Tade, and Paul Okoro, 'Movie Piracy Networks at Alaba International Market, Lagos, Nigeria', *International Journal of Offender Therapy and Comparative Criminology* 62, no. 1 (2018): 214–26. https://doi.org/10.1177/0306624X17692208. Accessed 3 March 2022.

Omenugha, Nelson, 'The Utilization of Digital Platforms for Marketing in the Nigerian Entertainment and Media (E&M) Industry: Prospects and Challenges', *Case Studies in Business and Management* 5, no. 1 (2018): 61–79. www.macrothink.org/journal/index.php/csbm/article/view/13240/10464. Accessed 3 March 2022.

Onyejelem, Timothy, and Henry Duru, 'Awareness and Attitude to Copyright Implications of Online Music Download among Undergraduate Students of Nnamdi Azikiwe University, Awka', *International Journal of Social Sciences and Humanities Reviews* 8, no. 2 (2018): 1–15.

Onyeka, Rita, 'Awareness and Attitude of University Undergraduate Students in South East Nigeria to the Online Communication Laws', PhD thesis, n.d., Nnamdi Azikiwe University, Awka, Nigeria.

Ridwan, Adeyemi, Ganiyu Akashoro, and Mukaila Ajaga, 'An Empirical Study of the Trend and Pattern of Video-Film Piracy in Nigeria', *European Scientific Journal* 9, no. 14 (2013): 64–86.

Standeford, Dennis, 'Nigeria Prepares to Revamp its Copyright System for the Digital Age', Intellectual Property Watch (22 November 2015). https://web.archive.org/web/20210122033523/http://www.ip-watch.org/2015/11/22/nigeria-prepares-to-revamp-its-copyright-system-for-the-digital-age/. Accessed 15 October 2022.

Tsaaior, James, '"New" Nollywood Video Films and the Post/Nationality of Nigeria's Film Culture', *Research in African Literatures* 49, no. 1 (2018): 145–62. www.jstor.org/stable/10.2979/reseafrilite.49.1.09. Accessed 3 March 2022.

Umeh, Samson, and Charity Aniche, 'Contributions of the Nigerian Customs to the Fight against Piracy in Nigeria: Prospects and Challenges', *UNIZIK Law Journal* 16 (2020): 57–77.

World Bank (2021), 'Poverty & Equity Brief: Nigeria' (October 2021). https://databank.worldbank.org/data/download/poverty/987B9C90-CB9F-4D93-AE8C-750588BF00QA/AM2021/Global_POVEQ_NGA.pdf. Accessed 10 March 2022.

World Intellectual Property Organisation (WIPO), 'The Nollywood Phenomenon', *WIPO Magazine* (June 2007). www.wipo.int/wipo_magazine/en/2007/03/article_0004.html. Accessed 6 March 2022.

8 Poetic Prosumption and Disruptive Creativity: Social Media Uploaders and Influencers as the New Bandits, Pirates, and Guerrilla Winners

Zhen Troy Chen

This chapter focuses on fandom practices on Bilibili, a video-sharing social media site mediating anime, comics, games, and novels (ACGN), to investigate Chinese urban youth's poetic prosumption and co-creation, as both consumers and producers. Taking an ethnographic approach, this chapter problematises the Western conceptualisation of creativity by looking at the 'Shanzhai' (literally, 'mountain stronghold' in Chinese, meaning bandits, piracy, and imitation) and cultural adaptation as part of Chinese online entrepre-neurial vernacular cultures. Informed by de Certeau and Foucault, this chapter demonstrates how Chinese urban youth poetically and creatively poach and transcode media texts through parody, piracy, and their own agentic prosumption in the form of light novels, mash-up videos, and fanzines, among other genres. In doing so, fans construct a heterotopia, a place of otherness, where various tactics are employed by Chinese prosumers to challenge, counter, and negotiate control, social norms, and consumerism. Such poetic and tactical prosumption is also embedded in the process of shaping Chinese youth's negotiated identities and nurturing new socialites in the making. By doing so, this chapter aims to initiate a constructive conversation between Western and Eastern literature in a Chinese context and to understand the knowledge, attitude, and behavioural changes within networked communities on social media platforms. This is an up-to-date case that takes up the challenge to demonstrate the much-neglected agency of Chinese consumers and citizens of the new generation, given the fact that numerous, if not too much, research on communications in China has focused on top-down linear 'thought management' or seemingly irresistible 'market domination'.

Introduction

Fandom and (new) media-use research has proliferated in tandem with the ever-upgrading technologies of the past 20 years. Identified as manifesting 'the dialectic of value',[1] fandom studies has established its position in Western academia and universities, critically and successfully detaching itself from the 'fanatic' etymological association of the very term. The binary oppositional views on fandom and its varied effects have accelerated to a stage where on the one hand (media) fans are deemed perfect consumers in the developed Western societies where neoliberal market economy prevails. On the other hand, criticism over the 'active fan' thesis popularised by Fiske[2] and Jenkins,[3] persists where fans agency and subjectivity are destined to be captured by consumerism.

What is the case of fandom in China? Are Chinese fans showcasing their agency and subjectivity under the socialist market economy? If so, how are their agency and identities manifested through their everyday engagement with various media texts to achieve political and economic goals? To answer these questions, this chapter will dive deep into two cases in two respective geolocations across two generations in a transforming China. Using ethnographic approaches, including participant observation and in-depth interviews, the first case examines feminist gender reverse genre creation by Chinese urban youth based in the Jiangnan area (literally the South bank of the Yangtze River, including Shanghai, Hangzhou, and Ningbo), where tech giants are leading the booming platform economy; the second case explores aspirational and anxious female professionals and their self-cultivation processes based in Dalian, a coastal city in Dongbei, North-east China. This second case coincides with the transformation of Dongbei's industrialised and state-owned past to a globally connected, outsourcing-based, green future.[4] This chapter will next review the literature and contextualise the case in China

1   Matt Hills, *Fan Cultures* (London: Routledge, 2002), 9–10.
2   John Fiske, 'Audiencing: A Cultural Studies Approach to Watching Television', *Poetics* 2 (1992), 345–59.
3   Henry Jenkins, *Textual Poachers: Television Fans and Participatory Culture* (London: Routledge, 1992). See also Henry Jenkins, *Fans, Bloggers, and Gamers: Exploring Participatory Culture* (New York: New York University Press, 2006).
4   Zhen Troy Chen and La-Mei Chen, 'Chinese "Female Force" in an "American Factory": Women's Identity Formation in an English Reading Club', *Asian Journal of Women's Studies* 27, no. 2 (2021), 161–83.

before presenting the themes emerging from the two groups of informants.

Literature Review

The various fan groups under investigation in this chapter are emerging middle-class urbanities. Among the 128 million monthly active users,[5] Bilibili and ACGN fans are mostly Generation Z and millennials, while the female professionals working in call centres are establishing their careers and families in the expanding city centre of Dalian. Most of the informants are well educated, tech savvy, and culturally aware. However, their urbanity does not develop overnight. As the chapter will unpack, many informants come from economically challenged or even rural families. Dongbei used to be heavily reliant on a state-owned and planned economy, where the parents of the informants investigated worked 'within the system' (state-owned), while others work 'outside the system', as entrepreneurs and farmers. In particular, some informants come from less-well-off families and some of them are the first ever to attend college in their families and to aspire to be urban citizens. Obviously, for these informants, moving up the social ladder is largely through education and ongoing training, where social media offers opportunities for them.[6] Given the unique identity and demographics of the two groups, some literature on class identity is worth exploring in a Chinese context.

At the outset, scholars writing about Chinese (youth) culture 'naturally' took a conflict theoretical approach, beginning with censorship and ideological control,[7] where Gramscian theory contends that cultural hegemony reflects the interests of the dominant class, which is supported by the middle class. This support and conformity is deemed beneficial to middle-classes aspirations and interests as a kind of velvet prison.[8] However, cultural studies scholars, following Stuart Hall, who study Chinese youth culture, argue that such a focus

---

5   Karen Chiu, 'LoL, World of Warcraft and Kris Wu: Bilibili's New Year's Special Attracts Millions of Millennials', *Abacus* (*South China Morning Post*) (2 January 2020).

6   Chen and Chen, 'Chinese "Female Force"'.

7   Hai Ren, *Neoliberalism and Culture in China and Hong Kong: The Countdown of Time* (New York: Routledge, 2010).

8   Antonio Gramsci, *Selections from the Prison Notebooks of Antonio Gramsci* (New York: International Publishers, 1971).

on conflict 'unfortunately runs the danger of easy generalisations and oversights of peculiarities that are at odds with broad similarities' between China and the West.[9]

In a Chinese context, the idea of 'class struggle' was discouraged in mainstream discourses after the Cultural Revolution and opening-up and economic reform. 'Social stratum' has replaced class-sensitive notions.[10] From 2002 onwards, a discourse of a Chinese intermediate/ middle class was developed by the Chinese government to better tackle the issue of social inequality. The government-engineered discourse stays ambiguous on the concept of class where it is classified by both occupation and ideology.[11] Official government reports and policy documents suggests a 'leap forward' and overestimate the actual size of the middle class. However, for those who aspire to be part of the middle class, which is deemed to be the dominant force that maintains stability and economic growth, this discourse works well in orchestrating people's thoughts for such a common goal. Social stratum is further incorporated into Xi Jinping's 'China Dream', where Chinese people's aspirations are deeply connected with the furthering of the country and to which the middle class makes a significant contribution.

Under such a backdrop, much literature on media and communication from the West fails to study contemporary China within such reality and discourses, and is still, by and large, following a theoretical conflict tradition. This chapter instead brings the Marxian notion of hegemony and class conflicts into the contemporary context, where symbolic interactionism also plays a role.[12] This new approach is based on the premise that conflict theory or its radicalised activities are incorporated as part of interactions within a spectrum. Symbolic interactionists assume that people 'construct selves, social worlds and societies through interaction'.[13] That is, conflict, conformity, and resistance are negotiated in a developmental and 'becoming' process. *Agency* therefore plays a key role in defining and structuring this chapter, especially when fandom and

9   Jeroen de Kloet, *China with a Cut: Globalisation, Urban Youth and Popular Music* (Amsterdam: Amsterdam University Press, 2010), 182–4.
10   David Goodman, 'Locating China's Middle Classes: Social Intermediaries and the Party-State', *Journal of Contemporary China* 25 (2016), 1–13.
11   Goodman, 'Locating China's Middle Classes', 5.
12   Kathy Charmaz, Scott R. Harris, and Leslie Irvine, *The Social Self and Everyday Life* (Oxford: Wiley-Blackwell, 2019).
13   Charmaz et al., *The Social Self*, 6.

media use are increasingly being investigated and informed by the active fandom theorem.[14]

However, taking a sociological and cultural approach, this chapter also considers the 'agency-structure problem', where agent and structure work as a pair of contradictions or dialectics.[15] The agency, identities, and subjectivities of fans and users of the younger generation are in the making, co-shaped by new forms of technology and social contexts, which they in turn co-shape. Social media as a technology, social relationship catalyst, and space can be empowering. However, it is worth noting that these agents also operate, mobilise, and live in a given structure, a socio-cultural milieu. Therefore, the episteme of power needs some correction from the Chomskyan notion where power is an entity or object that can be projected upon a socio-cultural group made up by various agents. A Foucauldian notion of power, which is omnipresent, discursive, controlling, and, more importantly, *productive* is more suitable for such 'becoming' processes, since it envisages resistance and hope.[16]

In a recent study on Chinese urban youth's ACGN fandom,[17] I created a synthesis between the Foucauldian notion of power and de Certeau's strategy and tactics to argue that this fandom creates heterotopia, a place of otherness.[18] By doing so, Chinese urban youth and ACGN fans on Bilibili are agentic and tactical, utilising available resources and mobilising themselves, creating a discursive and symbolic power apparatus among their own communities. This is done through fandom organisation and creative media 'prosumption', a neologism signifying the blurring boundaries between producer and consumer, production and consumption.[19] Such practices and

---

14   See Fiske, 'Audiencing', and Jenkins, *Textual Poachers*. See also, Stuart Hall, Kuan-Hsing Chen, and David Morley, *Stuart Hall: Critical Dialogues in Cultural Studies* (London: Routledge, 1996).

15   John Hartley, Jason Potts, Terry Flew, Stuart Cunningham, Michael Keane, and John Banks, *Key Concepts in the Creative Industries* (London: Sage, 2012), 5–8.

16   Ian Buchanan, 'Assemblage Theory and its Discontents', *Deleuze Studies* 9 (2015), 382–92. See also Nicholas Gane, 'The Governmentalities of Neoliberalism: Panopticism, Post-Panopticism and Beyond', *Sociological Review* 60 (2012), 611–34.

17   Zhen Troy Chen, 'Poetic Prosumption of Animation, Comic, Game and Novel in a Post-Socialist China: A Case of a Popular Video-Sharing Social Media Bilibili as Heterotopia', *Journal of Consumer Culture* 21, no. 2 (2021), 257–77.

18   Michel Foucault, 'Of Other Spaces', *Diacritics* 16 (1986), 22–27.

19   Chen, 'Poetic Heterotopia'. See also George Ritzer and Nathan Jurgenson, 'Production, Consumption, Prosumption: The Nature of Capitalism in the Age of The Digital "Prosumer"', *Journal of Consumer Culture* 10, no. 1 (2010), 13–36.

tactics are worth exploring in such subcultural communities, where fandom publics in China are in the making, promising progressive everyday politics.[20] This tendency of subcultural politics has shifted the focus of cultural studies (subculture) from the political economy to everyday life, where resistance and negotiations are omnipresent, just as hegemonic power appears to be. 'Resisting without leaving' is therefore the ongoing endeavour of people who not only 'make do' with life, but also make their lives 'liveable' and 'poetic'.[21] Defined by de Certeau, 'poetic' means to create, to generate, and to invent.[22] This poetic productivity presents a starkly different conceptual framework from Lefebvre's controlling and pessimistic spaces projected in late capitalist and consumerist societies.[23]

Being poetic reflects the very resilience of 'technologies of the self', and creativity in an everyday sense. This is very much like the assessment of creativity in China, where Shanzhai is a much discussed phenomenon in a transforming society.[24] The term Shanzhai refers to the renegades' headquarters and the inhabitants therein – *including both activities and an alternative space* – hidden deep in the mountains and achieving guerrilla wins when their enemies are caught off-guard. There is an interesting equivalent of Western pirates over the sea, where the pirates are invisible and untraceable. On social media platforms, the uploaders and creators are also difficult to trace; however, they leave media and make impact without names. Discussed extensively in a book-length study, *Faked in China*, Chinese entrepreneurs, consumers, and fans initiate or engage in Shanzhai activities in domains as diverse as mobile phone manufacture, fake Apple stores, film and television fandom, as well as in Beijing's newly renovated Silk Street right before the 2008 Olympic Games.[25] In China, creativity is reconceptu-

20 Weiyi Zhang, *The Internet and New Social Formation in China: Fandom Publics in The Making* (London: Routledge, 2016).
21 Chen, 'Poetic Heterotopia'.
22 Ben Highmore, 'Michel de Certeau's Poetics of Everyday Life', in Ben Highmore (ed.), *Everyday Life and Cultural Theory: An Introduction* (London: Routledge, 2002), 145.
23 Henri Lefebvre, *The Production of Space*, trans. Donald Nicholson-Smith (Oxford: Blackwell, 1991).
24 Michael Keane and Elaine Jing Zhao, 'Renegades on the Frontier of Innovation: The Shanzhai Grassroots Communities of Shenzhen in China's Creative Economy', *Eurasian Geography and Economics* 53 (2012), 216–30.
25 Fan Yang, *Faked in China: Nation Branding, Counterfeit Culture, and Globalization* (Bloomington: Indiana University Press, 2016).

alised not as Western God-given and genius-like; rather, it is closely associated with imitation and adaptation, reworking, appropriating, and finding new meanings in new contexts.[26] In a similar vein, fandom becomes a rich site to investigate such creative prosumption activities, communities, platforms, and genres. These range from mash-up videos, commentaries, reviews, live streaming, ecommerce, vlogs, and MOOCs (Massive Open Online Courses). In the section below, I will lay out the methodology used and develop a historical account and cultural analysis of Bilibili, one of the most popular ACGN fandom communities and social media sites in China.

Contextualisation and Methodology

With the structure and theoretical framework laid out, namely, to investigate fans practices, in particular their tactical prosumption on Bilibili to see how a Foucauldian heterotopia is constructed and fans identities are negotiated, this chapter does not regard the active fandom premise as unproblematic. The proposed Foucauldian heterotopia works as a new episteme that sees the transformation of China at a particular historical juncture. Such an approach renders the 'becoming' and transforming possibilities of heterotopias to take different forms when analysing different socio-economic groups. It offers a more contextualised cultural analysis that also acknowledges the debates in fandom studies and changing realities in China. The 'dialectic of value'[27] between the dedicated fan communities and the perfect consumers, in addition to the divisions between academic fans and fans as academics, and the complicated views on their respective communities on various accounts, reflects moral, aesthetic, and even class divisions, even though there are also overlaps between these groups.

That said, 'fandom' here is working as an analogy, a new creature and agent that is the product of consumerist societies, including the post-socialist China (the post-reform China, from 1978 onwards). In this media rich, if not excessive, society, everyone can be a fan, enthusiastically following something, for pragmatist or instrumentalist reasons. Fandom also creates new forms of sociality and identities that connect people based on what they consume in isolated

26   Chen, 'Poetic Heterotopia'. See also Keane and Zhao, 'Renegades on the Frontier of Innovation'.
27   Matt Hills, *Fan Cultures*.

urban cities, where more and more young people are dating, learning, and ordering food, clothes, daily consumables, to name but a few, online. Even though offline consumption still takes place, the new consumerist fandom is becoming ever networked. *Networked fandom*, in this sense, also signifies community, space, genre, platform (to present and perform), and influence. Given fandoms' many faces and the many-faceted nature of Chinese reality,[28] the study of Chinese communication must be further contextualised given the fact that Western literature on Chinese communication has been dominantly focusing on censorship, surveillance, and oppression.

This chapter is based on the findings of two related ongoing projects: 'Becoming Identities: Consumption and Fandom on Social Media Platforms' and 'Poetic and Networked Identity Performance of Urban Young Prosumers'. These studies employ mixed qualitative methods, such as participant observation and in-depth interviews. Such methods are deemed appropriate to generate richer texture and to reveal the authenticities of informants' lived experiences.[29] They are widely used for cultural and social analyses.[30] These two projects span from cities in South China and North-east China along the developed and developing eastern seaboard, including, Dalian, Ningbo, Suzhou, Shanghai and Guangzhou, and Zhuhai. The fieldwork took place from 2015 to 2019, with ethical approvals from two universities. Pseudonyms are used to protect the anonymity of the informants.

Disruptive and Shanzhai Creativity

Bilibili originated from the poetic prosumption of fans and was built first as an imitation prototype of AcFun.com. AcFun was itself an adaptation of a Japanese video-sharing website, Niconico Donga ('Smiley Animations').[31] The reason why Bilibili is both poetic and creative is that it was based on a utopian vision to create a free sharing fandom community dedicated to Hatsune Miku, a female

28   Arif Dirlik and Xudong Zhang, *Postmodernism and China* (Durham, NC: Duke University Press, 2000).

29   Zhen Troy Chen, 'Data Collection, Analysis, and Small-Data Visualization: A Qualitative Interpretation of Novel Fandom Behaviors on Social Media Platforms', *SAGE Research Methods* (1 March 2022).

30   Anders Hansen and David Machin, *Media & Communication Research Methods* (London: Palgrave Macmillan, 2013).

31   Chen, 'Poetic Heterotopia'.

android and avatar for a Japan-based singing synthesiser, Vocaloid. Her name literally means 'the first voice coming from the future', which also celebrates a futurist and utopian vision that pushes the boundaries of human limits. With this synthesiser, the limits of the human voice are expanded and enhanced to achieve a very high pitch while still producing comfortable auditory sensations in the form of music.[32]

With the development of Internet technologies, the barriers to media production have diminished significantly. In most cities in China, RMB400–600 suffices as the annual subscription fee for a relatively fast broadband connection. With the proliferation of Shanzhai-ji (knockoff mobile phones imitating global brands)[33] and later affordable Xiaomi smart phones, even people in the countryside can surf the Internet at a relatively low cost. According to the product information from mi.com (as of December 2019), Xiaomi's RedMi smartphone series, targeted at the lower end of the market, costs RMB549, approximately $US78. Against such a backdrop, DIY musical works were developed, uploaded, and shared on AcFun, supported by the *danmaku* function with short comments bombarding the screen as barrage and overlaid texts on such videos. This is a gamification design inspired by the shoot'em up genre in early video games.[34]

However, the founder of Bilibili, Xu Yi, then a college student in Hangzhou, was not satisfied with the service provided by AcFun and created a new prototype with his friends in 2009. The new website was created and freely shared among dedicated fans who create, curate, and share videos revolving around music, animation, and other popular media, including digital games.[35] Such informal cultural agents make significant contributions to the establishment of the cultural circus of media production, distribution, consumption, and labour utilisation in China.[36] The open-source culture and its accompanying piracy activities fostered various amateur media and communities in China and later legitimatised themselves through

32 Chen, 'Poetic Heterotopia'.
33 See more in Yang, *Faked in China*, 67–74.
34 Zhen Troy Chen, 'Audiencing through Affects and Gamification Design: A Case of Bilibili and Danmaku Technology', in Cheung Ming (ed.), *The International Conference of Experience Design, Innovation and Entrepreneurship* (Gold Coast, Australia: Griffith University, 2019), 1–9.
35 Chen, 'Poetic Heterotopia'.
36 Elaine Jing Zhao, *Digital China's Informal Circuits: Platforms, Labour and Governance* (London: Routledge, 2019).

legally licensing copyrighted works from well-known studios. Therefore, Bilibili was incorporated into formal economics as part of the cultural and creative industries. This is in line with and orchestrated through the 'nation branding' campaigns from 2001 onwards, right after China joined in World Trade Organization.[37] In the past five years, Bilibili has collaborated with many enterprises and sate-owned entities, such as China Central Television (CCTV) and the Palace Museum, to produce signature media products ranging from animations and documentaries to video games and derivative works. Bilibili's 'Created in China' channel (*guochuang qu*) was well supported by fans with crowdfunding and donations, involving collaborators of other tech giants such as Tencent and NetEase. Over the past 20 years, Chinese informal markets and economies have undergone a 'copyrightisation' process to safeguard legal trading for cultural goods.[38] This orchestrated process is termed as 'the convergence of institutions' between the government and enterprises in China.[39]

Such transformation of previous piracy activities is not unique to China though. It is also evident in the developed economics of disruptive innovators in Silicon Valley, as documented by University of Southern California's Jonathan Taplin. In his book, *Move Fast and Break Things: How Facebook, Google and Amazon Cornered Culture and Undermined Democracy*, he uses the metaphor of a professional wrestling match to depict the business models of technological disruptors such as YouTube, where there are no rules for competition.[40] In an email exchange in 2005, YouTube founders regarded the posting of full-length movies on the site as an opportunity to get traffic and page views.

The '"play first, deal later" around hot content' strategy worked successfully for start-ups like YouTube and Bilibili since copyright was creatively and tactically bypassed based on either fair use or the

37 Yang, *Faked in China*.
38 Zhen Troy Chen, 'Flying with Two Wings or Coming of Age of Copyrightisation? A Historical and Socio-Legal Analysis of Copyright and Business Model Developments in the Chinese Music Industry', *Global Media and China* 6, no. 2 (2021), 191–206.
39 Jie Gu, 'From Divergence to Convergence: Institutionalization of Copyright and the Decline of Online Video Piracy in China', *International Communication Gazette* 80 (2018), 60–86.
40 Jonathan Taplin, *Move Fast and Break Things: How Facebook, Google and Amazon Cornered Culture and What It Means for All of Us* (London: Macmillan, 2017).

safe harbour provisions.[41] Fan-created reviews, commentaries, and fan art such as fanfiction, light novels, and cosplay are ambiguous legally in terms of copyright limitations. Under Chinese, English, and American copyright laws, fair use or fair dealing doctrines exempt such manipulation of primary works. These doctrines are based on the idea–expression dichotomy. That is, ideas per se are not subject to copyright protection, while only the expressions of certain ideas are protected.[42] In addition, in actual litigation processes, *originality tests* are not based on the amount of similarity but on a qualitative assessment.[43] Furthermore, for alleged copyright violations such as sharing full-length films online, the platform can seek for exemption under the safe harbour doctrine, where third parties are deemed not responsible for violations. This provision requires copyright holders to issue take-down notices to platforms and online intermediaries to make platforms *aware* of the issue. If no action is taken after receiving notice, the platform then bears liability. It is a whack-a-mole game which involves high transactional costs. Therefore, the lag between uploading and notification leaves a protection vacuum given the size of the audience and the frequency of such 'pirate' activities. Guerrilla wins thus can be achieved, where the new entrants to the market garner enough clout to force access to viral premium content, 'threaten a change in copyright policy', and 'use threat to get deal sign-up'.[44]

Bilibili also faced several 'Net Sword' campaigns initiated by the National Copyright Administration of the PRC, especially from 2015 to 2017. However, its traffic and network effect were not significantly affected due to the ongoing copyrightisation process. Many deals with established studios in Japan and China were achieved through capital investment and crowdfunding. Bilibili went for an IPO and became a publicly traded company in 2018. Perhaps more importantly, 70 per cent of its traffic was from consumption of user-generated content (UGC).[45] The IPO and copyrightisation have

41 Chen, 'Copyrightisation'.
42 Jerry Jie Hua, *Toward A More Balanced Approach: Rethinking and Readjusting Copyright Systems in the Digital Network Era* (London: Springer, 2014).
43 Howard B. Abrams, 'Originality and Creativity in Copyright Law', *Law and Contemporary Problems* 55 (1992), 3–44. See also John Cahir and Guido Westkamp, *International Copyright Law: International Conventions and Aspects of Private International Law* (London: University of London Press, 2005).
44 Taplin, *Move Fast and Break Things*, 151.
45 Chen, 'Poetic Heterotopia'.

generated mixed responses from the fandom community, given the fact that some fans regard this as a violation and betrayal of the site's initial vision, which was to make Bilibili a free sharing community. Others are concerned with the introduction of ad placements, which Bilibili promised not to engage with when it started. After the release of a public letter apologising for its strategic and commercial move, most fans accepted Bilibili's transformation from a grassroots, underground, and unofficial free sharing community to an official and professional company that provides better services.[46]

Bilibili's UGC is still largely free for all, including non-registered and non-subscribed users. The UGC uploaders and creators are aspirational media prosumers who aim to rely on subscription and sponsorship (patron) schemes developed by Bilibili. During my interviews, I found that many loyal fans do not hold a 'naive' view (using their own term) of Bilibili's commercialisation move even though they reject it emotionally. They appeared to be annoyed or betrayed by such a change; however, they also maintained that it was 'understandable', and many fans claimed to have seen through the disguise of the utopian discourse from the very beginning. 'It's bound to be going for monetisation', many informants pointed out. There is a cynicism revealed in these conversations. However, creativity and tactics are still evident on the site given Bilibili's initial grassroots inception. Relying on participant observation and analysis of policy documents and publicly available information released by the company, I have compiled a historical account of the development of Bilibili and Shanzhai creativity. The history of Bilibili clearly demonstrates how imitation and prototyping from prosumers, inspired by well-tested business models in the American and Japanese markets, can quickly achieve economy of scale.[47] In this way, guerrilla wins can be practised and achieved by both start-ups and fans through tactical prosumption.

Guerrilla Wins Through Tactical Prosumption

This section focuses on the fans and users on Bilibili and their everyday fandom practices following the development of the platform and then its strategic change. In addition, a female reading group from Dalian is used as a complementary case to demonstrate how learning in

---

46   Chen, 'Poetic Heterotopia'.
47   Keane and Zhao, 'Renegades on the Frontier of Innovation'.

a networked workplace leads to self-formation and self-cultivation within a changing techno and social environment.

Fandom as Heterotopian Space and Community

Similar to the 'active fan' premise, the study of youth culture tends to emphasise the rebellious and subversive potentials of various subcultures, such as Goths, Punks, and Skinheads.[48] Based on the paradigm of conflict theory, the binary oppositional pair of counter-culture and mainstream culture is established. However, such a collective practice-based approach tends to generalise subcultural groups.[49] As outlined in the literature review, I focus more on the spatiality and the actions that take place in such localities. I am particularly interested in Foucault's conceptualisation of heterotopia. It is neither the ideal utopian nor the hopeless and destructive dystopian. Instead, everything is different in heterotopia, in which a dialectical property of time and space can be achieved through creative manipulation of a liner timeline and sanctified spaces.[50] This is in line with Foucault's earlier account on power, discourse, and knowledge, where the neoliberal market economy is making everyone a perfect consumer[51] and an entrepreneur – the 'conduct of the conduct' that normalises people's behaviour.[52]

However, *danmaku* on Bilibili turn upside down many vocabularies rich with cultural references and shared only among an *exclusive* circle of vernacular cultures, which is a defining feature of hetero-topia.[53] This insider language, which transcodes and adapts from Japanese, Chinese, and emoji, is used in creative and provocative ways, and is rebellious in nature. For example, the 'sister complex', a cultural reference derived from the Freudian Oedipus complex, was widely used by the Otaku (geek) community on Bilibili. When

48 Susan Scott, *Negotiating Identity* (Cambridge: Polity Press, 2015).
49 Steve Bailey, *Media Audiences and Identity* (New York: Palgrave Macmillan, 2005).
50 Chen, 'Poetic Heterotopia'.
51 Matt Hills, *Fan Cultures*.
52 Zhen Troy Chen and Thomas William Whyke, 'Manufacturing and Commodifying "Chineseness": Micro-Celebrity Li Ziqi's Construction of an Idyllic Rural China and Her Media Representation on YouTube', in Xiaoling Zhang and Corey Shultz (eds), *China's International Communication and Relationship Building* (London: Routledge, 2022).
53 Foucault, 'Of Other Spaces'.

a show features a brother and a sister, 'the country owns you a sister!' will bombard the screen as barrage. Those with little insider knowledge of this community may find such comments out of context and even offensive, nasty, and immoral since they have an ambiguous undertone of incest. Mainstream media have furthered such an interpretation by reporting on *danmaku* with a moral panic framing.[54] However, the uploaders and disruptive creators think differently. They use such parodies as tactics meant for a comic and transgressive effect, resituated in everyday scenes at home in various media. In doing so, they even accuse commentators who make such criticism as obscene themselves, 'because they are simply thinking too much'. They speculate that the interpretation is more telling in terms of the 'unspeakable darkness' of the commentators' psyche rather than that of the creator fans. Informants who shared this insider knowledge with me also commented that there is a widely shared consensus on this meme (*geng*) as an implicit social critique of China's One Child Policy, since most informants belong to the very last single-child generation in China. Compared to the less networked media prosumption in the print and pre-Internet era,[55] such parodies and playful encounters make the meaning negotiation process visible and salient.

There are tens of thousands of such transcoding and creative examples in language use, which creates an emerging and ever accruing vernacular database. For the informants, mutations through *tucao* (vet out discontents) and parody are also created to bypass censorship. Similar but more vulgar versions of such mutations are cao-ni-ma ('grass mud horse') which plays on the similar sounding but differently toned and charactered 'Fuck Your Mother'. Another commonly used term, he-xie ('river crab'), is homophonic to harmony as in 'the construction of harmonious society', a national goal of the previous administration.[56] Such playful wordplay and parody not only take place in *danmaku* chat boxes, but also manifests in genres of fanfics or derivative works.

---

54 Zhen Troy Chen, 'Slice of Life in a Live and Wired Masquerade: Playful Prosumption as Identity Work and Performance in an Identity College Bilibili', *Global Media and China* 5, no. 3 (2020), 319–37.

55 Lisa Rofel, *Desiring China: Experiments in Neoliberalism, Sexuality, and Public Culture* (Durham, NC: Duke University Press, 2007).

56 Bingchun Meng, 'From Steamed Bun to Grass Mud Horse: E Gao as Alternative Political Discourse on the Chinese Internet', *Global Media and Communication* 7, no. 1 (2011), 33–51.

Fandom in Heterotopian Genres

On Bilibili, there are more than 20 channels featuring different genres of UGCs. Aspirational uploaders create fan arts such as, comic/animation review, cult tourism guide (pilgrimage or *seijijuenrei*), and cosplay. As a common trope in ACGN works, gender-reverse is widely used in fictions that involves time travel. Back in 2016, @超烦豆先森 @芦柑不是橘 (Mr Beans and Orange) from Z.Z. Studio – not a commercial entity but a format imitated and mocked from established film industries – created a derivative work of the mainland Chinese film, *The Founding of a Republic* (dir. Han Sanping and Huang Jianxin, PRC, 2006).[57] The film was a state-funded 'main melody' film aiming to celebrate the 60th anniversary of the founding of the People's Republic of China. After its debut on Bilibili, the derivative work received more than 559,000 pageviews within three days.[58] In the 7-minute parodic video, the creators changed all the leading characters into their opposite genders. The video was well received among the fan community and generated some coverage in Chinese media. Reviews from Zhihu.com celebrated it as yet another feminist and awakening message for Chinese women. WeChat blogger jzhshwd quoted a lengthy review from one follower, Diandian:

> I saw one *danmu* comment said, 'Why bother doing this (video), why not just make a mash-up video based on real historical heroines. I cannot diss (their point) that real heroines deserve presentation; however, I would feel less moe (burning or exciting) since they have never been carefully written or recorded – people don't know them'. Yes, our feelings and attention all come from patriarchy and the male gaze. What is being represented and created from this video is not only the underlining patriarchal structure or the male gaze (or its trans version based on the cisgender), but also something new. For example, in such an epic narrative, no matter what gender you are, you are beautiful and desirable. And the very beauty and desirability is transgressive, subverting the historical ethical and moral codes. In addition, compared with the conventional representation of 'masculinity', the switched 'heroes' have internalised both masculinity and femininity (please note that the whole video does not include any

---

57 For the remake mash-up video, see www.bilibili.com/video/av5002913/.
58 Shanshan Xiong and Liu Jingjing, 'Interpretation of the Female Subjectivity in Gender-Reverse Utopian Works', *Journal of News Research* 7 (2016), 171–2.

image of 'the iron lady'). I will watch this again with *danmu*, to feel this 'new' approach.

This is a case where Bilibili works as a heterotopia. Otherness is created through the gender-reserve; however, the patriarchal power relationship is still fixed. *Moe* (either 萌え or 燃え), in the review above literally means cute and budding, and in this case it also means burningly excited. The reviewer is excited about the fact that the female leaders imagined and actualised through the video played a more important role in founding the PRC, while the male counterparts' role gets reduced to a minimum level. The parody is still based on gender inequality reflected from the significant difference in the numbers of heroines and heroes. Tactics revealed from such a provocative work are resisting while not altering the strategy of the gendered social structure.

Another relevant practice is the 'shipping' of same-sex characters, known as slash in the West and as Yaoi in Japanese ACGN cultures. Even though the shipping or coupling include both Girl's Love or Boy's Love genres, Yaoi is said to be primarily about the pure love between two beautiful boys. Also known as Danbi (耽美), 'gazing the beautiful', the genre is either celebrated as female sexual liberation or criticised as queer baiting.[59] As a counterpart to male Otakus, Yaoi fans are normally identified as *fujoshi* (rotten girls) and the Yaoi genre is normally created *by* females, *for* females, with only with a small number of openly gay male writers and illustrators.[60] In China, there are a significant number of *fujoshi* writers, who are called *Oku-san/ Taitai* (a respectful term for married women in Japan/China) by fans as a register of respect for their 'productivity'.

Among my informants, most *fujoshi* engaged in reading, watching, curating, and sharing such derivative works. Scholars believe such queering of Chinese fandom makes a positive impact on Chinese gender politics.[61] Echoing the progressive role played by such works, a female informant from Dalian disclosed that she has sold two editions of her two fanfictions on Taobao, Alibaba's

59   Maud Lavin, Ling Yang, and Jing Jamie Zhao, *Boys' Love, Cosplay, and Androgynous Idols: Queer Fan Cultures in Mainland China, Hong Kong, and Taiwan* (Hong Kong: Hong Kong University Press, 2017).
60   Mark McLelland, Kazumi Nagaike, Katsuhiko Suganuma, and James Welker, *Boys Love Manga and Beyond: History, Culture, and Community in Japan* (Mississippi: University Press of Mississippi, 2015).
61   Lavin et al., *Queer Fan Cultures.*

e-commerce platform. Even though the number sold is not significant, it provides emotional incentive for her to make more fanfictions for her followers. Such fandom practice renders Bilibili a heterotopic space, displacing conventional gender roles and heteronormativity. However, such resistance does not transcend Chinese society's gendered power relationships in the sense that the relationship structure is still the same, switching only one agent within the gendered pair.

Fandom's Contradictory Influences

As Bilibili gets more and more popular among the younger generation, many entrepreneurial amateurs start to create media content for Bilibili for (non-)monetary incentives. These include the producers of MOOCs, especially language course producers. The female reading group I interviewed utilises these often free and abundant learning materials for their self-improvement. One female informant began her engagement with Bilibili when she was still a Year 3 student in high school while she was in Dalian. Owing to its proximity to Japan and its colonial history of occupation, Dalian has many Japanese companies and attracts many young people to learn Japanese at an early age. This informant was interested in Japanese ACGN culture and was among the early adaptors of Bilibili. Although she studied Japanese in college, a single, elective Japanese module 'was not enough' for her. She then started to learn by herself on Bilibili. She also acquired editing skills with a 'master-shifu', as she called the person. This experience was like an apprenticeship for her as she not only learnt how to 'get things done' but also how to engage with fans and followers. She runs her own Bilibili channel now, and even though the channel cannot support her as a full-time job, it generates extra pocket money for her and keeps her engaged in the new form of sociality:

> I was born in the countryside, and I never dreamed of learning two foreign languages. One from Bilibili. Our teachers always told us to learn from playing. The class I had was hardly playful for me. I had to figure it out myself. I still remember when I first came to the city, I did not even know how to take the Metro. I felt awkward. But Bilibili saved me. People there were nice, or I was just lucky enough to know my *shifu*. He taught me and encouraged me. Now my classmates seek advice from me to learn skills. It changes a lot of things for me (laugh).

Turning to the Internet for friendship is not new, however. Rather, what is striking in this case is that she landed a job offer in a Japanese call centre in Dalian after graduation and is involved in corporate marketing for her company now. Such a life-changing experience cannot be easily generalised. However, fandom worked for her by allowing her to learn more playfully while widening her access to resources for self-improvement, both professionally and socially. As one of China's many aspirational female professionals, moving up the social ladder can be difficult. Yet what enabled her were fandom's tactics and otherness, in turn fuelled by her own agency in such a heterotopia.

The 'capitalisation' of Bilibili is not limited to agentic individuals but has also expanded to established entities and organisations. What makes Bilibili obscure as a heterotopia is also evident in the last case I am going to present. Ranked as in the Top 5 among its video-sharing website rivals,[62] Bilibili's popularity also attracted the attention of the Central Committee of the Communist Young League (CCCYL), along with its provincial branches in Zhejiang, Guangdong, Shandong, and Anhui. Among Bilibili's more than one hundred million active users, CCCYL attracted 98,000 fans to its channel during its first month. As of December 2019, it has more than five million fans. Bilibili became a targeted platform by such organisations given that more than 74 per cent of its users are young people under 24 years of age, with an average age of 17 years old.[63]

'Post *danmu* like you are a youth league member next time' is one of the catch phrases used by CCCYL, covering issues such as the US–China Trade War, Hong Kong and the 'one country, two systems' policy, Taiwan politics, as well as military and foreign policies. This makes the channel (dubbed with a moe/cute term, *Tuantuan* by its followers) a heterotopia in the sense that it at once invites and excludes certain audiences and topics, as if it has an on/off switch.[64] Its novelty lies in the fact that a lot of the parodic videos are not conventional or official/professional news reports, but more like light-hearted and comic news commentaries.

---

62 'Top 10 Chinese Websites by Alexa Rank', www.webnots.com/top-10-chinese-websites-by-alexa-rank/.

63 Huai Xu, 'How Does the "Regular Army" Integrate into the Two Dimensions? Bilibili Will Give You the Answer', *Shangguan News* (2 November 2016), www.jfdaily.com/wx/detail.do?id=44373.

64 Foucault, 'Of Other Spaces'.

Such an approach is deemed to be more persuasive at orchestrating thoughts, as it creatively incorporates *logos* (by presenting
news), *pathos* (a welcoming tone and emotional appeal to younger
audience), and *ethos* (its official and authoritative status). Looking
from a Foucauldian perspective, such heterotopia works as an
in-between space mediating the 'technologies of the self' where
there is still space for subjects to negotiate their identities within
a perpetuating meaning–making apparatus. Such multiple and
diversified influences on prosuming agents also seems contradictory
since serious and authoritative news in China (mainly coming from
CCTV) has been originally parodied, if not radicalised, by Bilibili
users. However, such news, or rather its parodic forms and genres,
have been captured by CCTV and CCCYL alike to influence the
already stimulated younger generations. At the time of writing,
CCTV has launched their own channel on Bilibili as well, and its
news anchor, Guangquan Zhang, a figure with a parodic following
on the site, MC-ed the very successful Bilibili *New Year Gala*, which
streamed online and was broadcast on television at the same time.
Featuring well-received ACGN elements, such as World of Warcraft,
League of Legends, Bilibili also invited both traditional pop stars
and novel influencers – home-made Bilibili up-loaders – to appear
in the gala.[65] Co-organised with the state-run Xinhua News Agency,
the gala attracted 82 million fans and was said to have trampled
over all the other satellite television stations offering entertainment
extravaganzas on New Year's Eve.[66]

Conclusion

This chapter has presented multiple aspects of Bilibili prosumption
practices and fandom, with Chinese urban youth as informants
from the south and the north-east of the eastern seaboard of
China. Fandom was used as an analogy and an umbrella term
to mark identities, loosely shared and based upon various media
consumption and prosumption practices on the video-sharing
social media site. I argue that Bilibili is a heterotopia constructed
by multiple agents, ranging from the founder and the management

65 Gabriel Li, 'Bilibili to Hold Its First New Year's Eve Concert: "The Last
    Night of 2019"', *Pandaily* (19 December 2019), https://pandaily.com/bilibili-to-
    hold-its-first-new-years-eve-concert-the-last-night-of-2019/.
66 Chiu, 'LoL'.

team to its prosumers, including aspirational amateurs, govern-mental/state-run organisations, and business operators. The analyses of the cases span across the platform itself, the fandom space and community, its genres, as well as its multiple yet contradictory influences. The historical analysis of the platform showcased how Bilibili adopted Shanzhai and disruptive creativity and soon reached market scale, turning the site from a grassroots free sharing community to a commercialised and publicly traded company. This kind of transformation is not uncommon in the Chinese emerging economy over the past 40 years.[67] The chapter also demonstrated the complicated discursive strategy in which Shanzhai, as a form of national humiliation, can be turned into empowering, post-colonial, and developmental narratives for the South, attracting 'willing collaborators' from the West[68] who initially accused and still occasionally accuse China of 'intellectual property theft'. In addition, fandom communities across different geolocations and channels on Bilibili are constructing heterotopian spaces for themselves and achieving guerrilla wins through tactical prosumption. Such prosumption includes the novel use of playful language, irony and satire, parody and *tucao* in such formats as reviews and commentaries, *danmaku* comments, mash-up videos, fanfictions, and other fan arts. These practices are progressive and transgressive, dealing explicitly or implicitly with issues such as reproductive rights and gender equality (One Child Policy), sexuality, as well as domestic and foreign politics. In doing so, fans and prosumers write and narrate themselves into being. Within such a heterotopia, issues and identities which were deemed contro-versial and were little discussed are ever more visible. Even though it is still too early to judge how progressive or subversive such discourses are, ongoing negotiations are evident between Shanzhai and disruptive creativity from fandom communities and the efforts of orchestrating thoughts by the CCCYL and CCTV. Such negoti-ations will make discourses in emerging spaces on social media more exciting and diverse, which calls for future research on a transforming China.

67   Zhao, *Digital China's Informal Circuits*.
68   Michael Keane, Terry Flew, and Brian Yecies, *Willing Collaborators: Foreign Partners in Chinese Media* (London: Rowman & Littlefield, 2018).

Select Bibliography

Abrams, Howard B., 'Originality and Creativity in Copyright Law', *Law and Contemporary Problems* 55 (1992): 3–44.

Bailey, Steve, *Media Audiences and Identity: Self-Construction in the Fan Experience* (New York: Palgrave Macmillan, 2005).

Buchanan, Ian, 'Assemblage Theory and its Discontents', *Deleuze Studies* 9 (2015): 382–92.

Cahir, John, and Guido Westkamp, *International Copyright Law: International Conventions and Aspects of Private International Law* (London: University of London Press, 2005).

Charmaz, Kathy, Scott R. Harris, and Leslie Irvine, *The Social Self and Everyday Life* (Oxford: Wiley-Blackwell, 2019).

Chen, Zhen Troy, 'Audiencing through Affects and Gamification Design: A Case of Bilibili and Danmaku Technology', in Cheung Ming (ed.), *The International Conference of Experience Design, Innovation and Entrepreneurship* (Gold Coast, Australia: Griffith University, 2019), 1–9.

—. 'Slice of Life in a Live and Wired Masquerade: Playful Prosumption as Identity Work and Performance in an Identity College Bilibili', *Global Media and China* 5, no. 3 (2020): 319–37. https://doi.org/10.1177/2059436420952026. Accessed 20 October 2022.

—. 'Flying with Two Wings or Coming of Age of Copyrightisation? A Historical and Socio-Legal Analysis of Copyright and Business Model Developments in the Chinese Music Industry', *Global Media and China* 6, no. 2 (2021): 191–206. https://doi.org/10.1177/2059436421998466. Accessed 20 October 2022.

—. 'Poetic Prosumption of Animation, Comic, Game and Novel in a Post-Socialist China: A Case of a Popular Video-Sharing Social Media Bilibili as Heterotopia', *Journal of Consumer Culture* 21, no. 2 (2021): 257–77. https://doi.org/10.1177/1469540518787574. Accessed 20 October 2022.

—. 'Data Collection, Analysis, and Small-Data Visualization: A Qualitative Interpretation of Novel Fandom Behaviors on Social Media Platforms', *SAGE Research Methods* (1 March 2022). https://dx.doi.org/10.4135/9781529602098. Accessed 20 October 2022.

Chen, Zhen Troy, and La-Mei Chen, 'Chinese "Female Force" in an "American Factory": Women's Identity Formation in an English Reading Club', *Asian Journal of Women's Studies* 27, no. 2 (2021): 161–83. https://doi.org/10.1080/12259276.2021.1913850. Accessed 20 October 2022.

Chen, Zhen Troy, and Thomas W. Whyke, 'Manufacturing and Commodifying "Chineseness": Micro-Celebrity Li Ziqi's Construction of an Idyllic Rural China and Her Media Representation on YouTube', in Xiaoling Zhang and Corey Shultz (eds), *China's International Communication and Relationship Building* (London: Routledge, 2022).

Chiu, Karen, 'LoL, World of Warcraft and Kris Wu: Bilibili's New Year's Special Attracts Millions of Millennials', Abacus (South China Morning Post) (2 January 2020). www.scmp.com/abacus/news-bites/article/3044309/lol-world-warcraft-and-kris-wu-bilibilis-new-years-special. Accessed 20 October 2022.

de Kloet, Jeroen, *China with a Cut: Globalisation, Urban Youth and Popular Music* (Amsterdam: Amsterdam University Press, 2010).

Dirlik, Arif, and Xudong Zhang, *Postmodernism and China* (Durham, NC: Duke University Press, 2000).

Fiske, John, 'Audiencing: A Cultural Studies Approach to Watching Television', *Poetics* 2 (1992): 345–59.

Foucault, Michel, 'Of Other Spaces', *Diacritics* 16 (1986): 22–7.

Gane, Nicholas, 'The Governmentalities of Neoliberalism: Panopticism, Post-Panopticism and Beyond', *Sociological Review* 60 (2012): 611–34.

Goodman, David, 'Locating China's Middle Classes: Social Intermediaries and the Party-State', *Journal of Contemporary China* 25 (2016): 1–13.

Gramsci, Antonio, *Selections from the Prison Notebooks of Antonio Gramsci* (New York: International Publishers, 1971).

Gu, Jie, 'From Divergence to Convergence: Institutionalization of Copyright and the Decline of Online Video Piracy in China', *International Communication Gazette* 80 (2018): 60–86.

Hall, Stuart, Kuan-Hsing Chen, and David Morley, *Stuart Hall: Critical Dialogues in Cultural Studies* (London: Routledge, 1996).

Hansen, Anders, and David Machin, *Media & Communication Research Methods* (London: Palgrave Macmillan, 2013).

Hartley, John, Jason Potts, Terry Flew, Stuart Cunningham, Michael Keane, and John Banks, *Key Concepts in the Creative Industries* (London: Sage, 2012).

Highmore, Ben, 'Michel de Certeau's Poetics of Everyday Life', in Ben Highmore (ed.), *Everyday Life and Cultural Theory: An Introduction* (London: Routledge, 2002).

Hills, Matt, *Fan Cultures* (London: Routledge, 2002).

Hua, Jerry Jie, *Toward A More Balanced Approach: Rethinking and Readjusting Copyright Systems in the Digital Network Era* (London: Springer, 2014).

Jenkins, Henry, *Textual Poachers: Television Fans and Participatory Culture* (London: Routledge, 1992).

—. *Fans, Bloggers, and Gamers: Exploring Participatory Culture* (New York: New York University Press, 2006).

Keane, Michael, and Elaine Jing Zhao, 'Renegades on the Frontier of Innovation: The Shanzhai Grassroots Communities of Shenzhen in China's Creative Economy', *Eurasian Geography and Economics* 53, no. 2 (2012): 216–30.

Keane, Michael, Terry Flew, and Brian Yecies, *Willing Collaborators: Foreign Partners in Chinese Media* (London: Rowman & Littlefield, 2018).

Lavin, Maud, Ling Yang, and Jing Jamie Zhao, *Boys' Love, Cosplay, and Androgynous Idols: Queer Fan Cultures in Mainland China, Hong Kong, and Taiwan* (Hong Kong: Hong Kong University Press, 2017).

Lefebvre, Henri, *The Production of Space*, trans. Donald Nicholson-Smith (Oxford: Blackwell, 1991).

Li, Gabriel, 'Bilibili to Hold Its First New Year's Eve Concert: "The Last Night of 2019"', *Pandaily* (19 December 2019). https://pandaily.com/bilibili-to-hold-its-first-new-years-eve-concert-the-last-night-of-2019/. Accessed 20 October 2022.

McLelland, Mark, Kazumi Nagaike, Katsuhiko Suganuma, and James Welker, *Boys Love Manga and Beyond: History, Culture, and Community in Japan* (Mississippi: University Press of Mississippi, 2015).

Meng, Bingchun, 'From Steamed Bun to Grass Mud Horse: E Gao as Alternative Political Discourse on the Chinese Internet', *Global Media and Communication* 7, no. 1 (2011): 33–51. https://doi.org/10.1177/1742766510397938. Accessed 20 October 2022.

Ren, Hai, *Neoliberalism and Culture in China and Hong Kong: The Countdown of Time* (New York: Routledge, 2010).

Ritzer, George, and Nathan Jurgenson, 'Production, Consumption, Prosumption: The Nature of Capitalism in the Age of The Digital "Prosumer"', *Journal of Consumer Culture* 10, no. 1 (2010): 13–36.

Rofel, Lisa, *Desiring China: Experiments in Neoliberalism, Sexuality, and Public Culture* (Durham, NC: Duke University Press, 2007).

Scott, Susan, *Negotiating Identity: Symbolic Interactionism Approaches to Social Identity* (Cambridge: Polity Press, 2015).

Taplin, Jonathan, *Move Fast and Break Things: How Facebook, Google and Amazon Cornered Culture and What It Means for All of Us* (London: Macmillan, 2017).

Xiong, Shanshan, and Liu Jingjing, 'Interpretation of the Female Subjectivity in Gender-Reverse Utopian Works', *Journal of News Research* 7 (2016): 171–2.

Xu, Huai, 'How "Official Troops" Get Incorporated into the 2-D World? Bilibili is the Answer' [正规军'如何融入二次元? B站给你答案], *Shangguan News* (2017).

Yang, Fan, *Faked in China: Nation Branding, Counterfeit Culture, and Globalization* (Bloomington: Indiana University Press, 2016).

Zhang, Weiyu, *The Internet and New Social Formation in China: Fandom Publics in the Making* (London: Routledge, 2016).

Zhao, Elaine Jing, *Digital China's Informal Circuits: Platforms, Labour and Governance* (London: Routledge, 2019).

9 Growing Up a Pirate

Jiarui Tan, Yifan Li, and Holger Briel

Introduction by Holger Briel

As the previous chapters have already indicated, digital piracy has become a common enough practice in most parts of the world that it can be viewed as a new normal of online engagement. While this is a global movement, its local (or localised) practices differ immensely, depending on government intervention and market mechanisms. While Western media invariably designate China as the greatest 'evil empire' of piracy in the world, it is very rare indeed that Chinese netizens' stories are told, allowing for a look behind and beyond the various propaganda machines. This chapter seeks to remedy this situation. In the following, we will hear from two netizens from China who were willing to share their stories with us. These tell us much about the routines that separate, but also other day-to-day ones which draw us closer to each other, vis-à-vis and through techno-social developments.

As a way of introduction, and as an alternative foil, I would like briefly to reflect upon the history of my own life as a pirate. I suspect it is a rather pedestrian one, which happened a millionfold all over the Western world.

I had been a relative latecomer to computers; growing up, my best friends were fiddling with their Commodore 64s, something that did not interest me in the least. I did get a bit more interested when games such as *Leisure Suit Larry* (1987) started appearing and I gradually began to appreciate the more adult aspects of computing life. It would take until 1990, when I was presented with my first networked computer at work, that I began to realise the communicative opportunities the Internet had begun to offer just then. In the early 1990s, I was introduced to FTP servers, enabling me to access files at remote locations, most of them discovered via long hours of trial and error. Of course, file sharing was in its infancy then, mostly due to low bandwidth, low computing power, and limited content, but being able to connect to remote resources for work and leisure quickly began to pull me to its thrall. Back then, one 'surfed', haphazardly moving from website to website, just starting to appreciate the power that was hypertext.

In the late 1990s, I was living in England, Napster happened, and that changed everything. Having so far survived on my digital hunting prowess, having a single site from which music could be downloaded was a dream come true. I rapidly warmed to the medium, and also became involved in the fan ecology emerging around it, meeting new people from around the world. But what was the real magic of Napster and all the ensuing file-sharing websites was that they opened one's mind; especially with music or films, the horizon one had until then was typically the taste of one's social environment, largely based on availability. If rock 'n' roll had been a great unifier for a while (disregarding internecine battles of the bands and fans), in the 1980s much popular music would tribalise, with particular bubbles forming. Same for me, although perhaps due to my wanderings I had a fairly wide array of music I could get excited about already – punk, country, singer/songwriter, chanson, and rock – but that was it. Napster would infinitely broaden this horizon. Chill-out, (localised) world music, hip-hop, ambient – these were all musical genres I probably would not have found on my own and without the help of my new virtual friends. Plus, the opportunity to say, 'Mmm, what an interesting name ("Birdsongs of the Mesozoic"). Let's just download the file!'

Also, file-sharing sites do not just afford one the opportunity to discover new sounds and visons, they also help one better understand the past. I found many songs from German bands that I had never heard of before but which were popular when I was growing up, or even before then; creating playlists from the days my parent had been my age and listening to them together with them brought us closer and brought them many memories. For me, this led to a much more informed socio-cultural understanding of (my own cultural) history, especially when combined with instantaneous access to lyrics and band/singer information. Apart from becoming a much bigger fan, I also became aware of and started to analyse more the (political) environment within which these films and songs were created, disseminated, consumed. In other words, piracy made me a more cultured person (I hope).

Of course, all of this happened under the threat of impending doom; Napster barely lasted a year, and everybody tried to download as much as possible and as quickly as possible. But, already by then, my SysAdmin, a chap much more knowledgeable about computers than I, told me, 'There is no way they can shut down everything'. He proved to be right of course, and today, especially younger netizens are much more relaxed about content or websites disappearing, as their Internet's short history has shown its resilience, with content always reappearing somewhere else.

The stories to be told in the following not only give insights into how certain individuals grew up, but also tell the story of China's rapid rise in digitalisation. As the two contributors tell us, growing up in the China of the 1990s did not allow for much Internet engagement. Even gaming, already strongly established in the West and in Japan via console games, was still a novelty in China through lack of access to hardware and software (and, if indeed available, at horrendous prices).

The first story is Jiarui Tan's, a great lover of music, who twins her life story with the changing local availability of music. Growing up in small-town China, her musical tastes were shaped by what was available at the time – fairly little – and certainly reduced to local content. But then something magical happened. Here is her account.

For the Love of Music (Jiarui Tan's Story)

In this text, I will share my experiences and insights as a person who grew up and still lives in China, a country 'notorious' for its rampant piracy. Born in the mid-1990s, I can perhaps be classified as one of the youngest generations of digital immigrants in China. In the context of the rapid development of media and communication technologies in the last 30 years and the rise of China in the global marketplace, I, an ordinary urban-born young person of a certain age, have witnessed how our lives, our studies, and our thoughts have been influenced and changed by technological updates and the proliferation of piracy. My generation and I are part of China's unique piracy culture and the various subcultural landscapes that have emerged from the constant development of the Internet.

In Chinese, piracy literally means 'to steal a plate (盗版)', the word 'plate (版)' pointing out the original relationship between copyright and ancient printing technology. In a more profound sense, it relates to the relationship between information and its various carriers, and to technology and the dissemination of knowledge and culture. While copyright has always been seen in the West as a product of public policy to encourage and stimulate the creation of new works, since the new millennium, both in the West and in China, the spirit of sharing and the trend of DIY culture has expanded the boundaries of the concept of copyright, and at the same time has posed many challenges to the protection of individuals' intellectual property rights.

New media scholar Lev Manovich in 2007 defined the first decade of the twenty-first century as a decade dominated by the culture of remix.[1] When everything becomes digital, copying is replaced by pressing 'control + c' on the keyboard and the manipulability and fluidity of information has brought about the convergence of different fields, such as, music, art, design, software applications, user-created media, etc. Through 'copy, transformation, and combine', new cultural objects are created, new forms of culture are developed, and social evolution is made possible by the cooperation between and the collective intelligence of people.

Thinking about originality and piracy, data and knowledge, self-empowerment and copyright monopoly, I try to reflect on the following two questions through my personal stories. Is it right to copy? Who is protected by copyright? There may not be a standard answer to these questions, but I think they deserve and need to be discussed constantly in today's digital age.

1 The Beginning of Everything (1994)

When trying to string together my experiences growing up with Chinese piracy, I first attempted to find my coordinates in a linear history. One always wants to be special, to have oneself associated with big events that everyone knows about, as a way to get some kind of attention and explanation for one's insignificant life. The year 1994 was a rather special year, in my opinion. What follows is some of the information retrievable from any web browser.

In 1994, the World Wide Web, having been invented by Tim Berners-Lee a few years earlier, started to enter everyday use in the United States. Also in that year, Netscape, the first commercial web browser, was released. In the same year, China officially joined the Internet. The following year, 1995, is often regarded as the beginning of the Internet's commercialisation, the same year Echo Bay (later

1   Lev Manovich, 'What Comes after Remix', *Remix Theory* 10 (2007), http://manovich.net/content/04-projects/057-what-comes-after-remix/54_article_2007.pdf.

known as eBay) and amazon.com started to operate. In 1997, Netflix was founded, selling and renting out DVDs by mail. In the same year, NetEase, one of the largest game companies in the world, was founded in Guangzhou. One year later, in 1998, facing strong competition from Microsoft's IE browser, Netscape announced that its own browser would become open source. Google was established in 1998, bringing changes to the way people search for information on the Internet.

In China, Tencent was founded in Shenzhen. In 1998, Internet-based file sharing began to take root, and Napster opened the door for audio file sharing on the Internet in 1999. In the same year, Tencent's Internet-based instant messaging software QQ was released and began to occupy the social and entertainment lives of Chinese primary and secondary school students.

Returning to 1994, this was also the year I was born in a small town in the south-west of China. At that time, computers and cell phones were not yet popular. Most people were still living a simple and frugal life. Families around me started to have colour televisions, and watching television was the most attractive entertainment for children at the time. My first memories of watching films were not related to family outings, but to school activities. At that time, elementary schools would organise students to go to the only cinema in the local district. Although most of the films were on revolutionary or patriotic educational themes, the half-day would be the most anticipated and enjoyable one for all children.

In 1993, Chinese computer professor Jiang Wanmeng developed the first-ever VCD player, and from 1995 to 1997, Chinese VCD player usage grew exponentially. At that time, there were already various video stores on high street, selling video tapes and VCDs. After my parents had bought our first VCD player, I started to get in touch with foreign cartoons, my favourites being *Tom and Jerry* and Disney cartoons such as *The Little Mermaid*. But, as a child, I knew nothing about the United States and piracy. 'America' was a concept shaped by the media and adults then, and the word 'piracy' had not been heard of. It's worth noting that *Tom and Jerry* was broadcast on television as a phone-on-demand show and dubbed in the local dialect. The dubbed version is therefore more deeply rooted in my mind than the original version and until now many young people still remember the plot lines in dialect.

Having listed all of the above, I would like to explain that since the mid-1990s, the tech giants that surround our lives today came into the world, or, if already established, grew up with me. Like them, I have grown to feel the freedom and the embrace of openness and equality, and naturally became curious and eager to learn about urban life and the wider world outside. For the upcoming new millennium, technology could be the vision to change the world, driven by a utopian dream.

Back in 1984, Apple launched its groundbreaking Macintosh personal computer. Its successful advertising campaign, '1984', inspired by Orwell's dystopian novel, expressed Apple's values and goals: to put people, not governments or large corporations, in control of technology, to make computers accessible to ordinary people, and not to control their lives.

In 2002, the BitTorrent (BT) protocol was published, a P2P (peer-to-peer) communication protocol that promotes free sharing, collective cooperation, and faster download speeds. This decentralised technology allows everything to be shared as a torrent file and has revolutionised the way information is distributed.

In 2003, The Pirate Bay was created based on the anti-copyright mission of Piratbyrån, a Swedish anti-copyright organisation. It was a small website dedicated to storing, sorting, and searching BT seeds for free downloads of audio, video, apps, games, and other resources, run by three young men with anti-copyright ideals: Gottfrid, Fredrik, and Peter. All three personified the iconic labels young people follow: they were unruly, contemptuous of authority, advocated freedom and democracy, and also had the skills and bold ideas to change the world. They spent more than a decade countering attacks from governments and industries, using technology and the differences between countries' legal systems to keep their search engine running. On the Pirate Bay website, it is claimed that The Pirate Bay is 'the galaxy's most resilient BitTorrent site'.

When all that happened, I was still in elementary school. My parents had just bought our first computer, and the teacher was teaching us how to type in our computer class. I had no idea how everything that was happening in the world then would have such a profound impact on my future.

2 From the Dakou Generation to Fansub Groups

As a so-called 'small-town youngster', it wasn't until middle school that I officially started learning English. Languages, and here especially English, helped to open the door to more knowledge. Although I was lucky enough to receive a good education, my cultural enlightenment did not come from traditional school classes, but from pirated music, movies, and books. This free (cost-free and unbounded) journey has allowed me to know the world more deeply, to know myself, and to meet people who share my interests, which constitute the best memories of my adolescence.

According to official data on the government's confiscated pirated materials, from 1998 to 2005, the number of pirated audio/visual materials in China grew by a factor of nearly 100, and music and film piracy accounted for the largest share of the pirate market. This period was the 'golden age' of Chinese disc piracy,[2] as well as a time when personal computers and the Internet were gaining popularity in China. From offline to online, between the new and the old, I myself entered a golden age of knowledge-seeking.

Dakou CDs

When I was in secondary school, I became interested in foreign pop music. Listening to music became an effective way for me to learn English, and I tended to build up my English vocabulary through the lyrics of the songs I consumed. Before MP3s became commonplace, we usually listened to foreign songs on cassettes and CDs that came with English-learning newspapers and magazines, which usually contained one or two popular songs of the day. If one was 'Internet savvy' enough, one could find more information and music sources online by, for instance, searching for an artist by name. These were the days of student life before music streaming platforms and even before licensed CDs were introduced into the country.

Later on, I noticed a couple of stalls right in front of the school gate selling CDs by well-known and unknown musicians from abroad. The sellers were quiet and only spoke when approached by students. They didn't sell a lot of stuff, and what they sold was more like a personal collection. I found out later that they were selling *Dakou* discs. *Da* stands for strike or break, and *kou* stands for opening or cut. Dakou refers to the CDs and tapes that are dumped by the West as plastic rubbish, meant to be recycled, but instead are smuggled into China. There is a difference between a Dakou CD and a pirated CD: Dakou CDs are not pirated, but they are cut to prevent resale,

---

2   Jinying Li, 'From "D-Buffs" to the "D-Generation": Piracy, Cinema, and an Alternative Public Sphere in Urban China', *International Journal of Communication* 6 (2012), 542–63.

and often sold alongside pirated CDs. Dakou discs enabled Chinese musicians and audiences to listen to music that was not accessible before because of censorship or because they had been deemed too marginal to be distributed for a profit.

In his 'Popular Music and Youth in Urban China: The Dakou Generation' (2005), de Kloet explained in detail how since the second half of the 1990s Dakou CDs and tapes had contributed to the Chinese rock music scene. The Western music culture brought by Dakou nourished a generation of musicians who had grown up under the state-supported forces of marketisation and globalisation since China's reform and opening up in the 1980s. They express their complex experience and feelings through their music, which contains 'a cosmopolitan, national aspiration; a political, ironic critique and a nostalgic, idyllic longing'. Dakou is a uniquely Chinese cultural phenomenon, as well as a product of a particular era.

> Dakou cassette tape, dakou CD, dakou video, dakou MD, dakou vendors, dakou consumers, dakou musicians, dakou music critics, dakou magazines, dakou photo books; this is a dakou world, a new life where you don't even have to leave the country to realize your spiritual adventure. When Americans fiercely give themselves a cut, they also give the world a possibility of communism and unity.[3]

Pirated DVDs

Just as when we were watching *Tom and Jerry* on television as kids, we didn't realise until later that everything we watched or listened was pirated. A famous example for this fact is that China only acquired the copyright to Gabriel García Márquez's globally successful novel *One Hundred Years of Solitude* (1967) in 2010, although it had already been very successful in China in the 1980s and 1990s; it was, for instance, in 1984, that Chinese Nobel Prize winner Mo Yan first read the book and had been so enthralled by it that it significantly influenced his writing style.

In 2001, when DVDs started to become popular throughout the country, all kinds of pirated films were sold in video stores. This greatly enriched people's entertainment and, more importantly, allowed us to watch many of the best films and television shows

---

3   You Dali, www.guangzhou.elong.com/theme/themei48.html, cited in Jeroen de Kloet, 'Popular Music and Youth in Urban China: The Dakou Generation', *China Quarterly* 183 (2005), 617n27.

that had never been officially released in China. Among consumers of pirated DVDs, a unique group and a distinctive *D-buff* subculture began emerging. 'D' refers to both disc (disc) and 'piracy' (daoban), with 'D-buffs' (D-you, literally, D-friend) being a group of pirate consumers who treated disc searching as treasure hunting.[4]

Generally speaking, those films censored by the authorities and ignored by the legitimate film market received extra attention. Folk slang also emerged for pirated DVDs – 'Region 9' DVDs – a term derived from the international region codes for DVDs, meaning 'playable globally', a system developed by eight major US studios wherein DVD players sold in each region were only able to play DVDs from the same region. This protected the rights of distributors and resellers of AV products in each region. Depending on the region, the system also allowed each regional release to carry different textual matter, such as subtitle options, outtakes, director's cuts, extended versions, etc.

A 'Region 9' DVD is a 'cracked' version that does not belong to any one region and can be played on any DVD player. It even has better audio-visual effects, more special effects and subtitle options than the single-region licensed version. In the early years of the 21st century, China arguably possessed the most developed and complete film archives in the world. If you were patient enough, any film from any country could be found in the corner video shop – it was like a no-man's-land of images. Pirate disc vendors and buyers also formed a unique alliance and established an alternative underground distribution and circulation network for pirated films.

In 2005, a Chinese documentary called *Paigu* represented the d-buff movement from the perspective of a DVD vendor. Paigu is a young man who travels from the countryside to the big city to sell pirated DVDs for a living. The DVD vendors liked him; he may only have had a junior high school education and may never be able to understand the art films he sold, but he knew the names of the masters and their films by heart. His simple desire for information about the outside world, his curiosity about art, the great happiness of owning an art product, made his character touch our hearts. Like Dakou, the film and the phenomena it described, were products of its time. Nowadays, with the rise of video sharing and streaming platforms, buying DVDs has become obsolete. Video shops are fading fast from our life, becoming an ever-more marginal and nostalgic way of accessing films.

4   Li, 'From "D-Buffs" to the "D-Generation"'.

File Sharing

Starting in 2003, BitTorrents and BT forums swept through China. Among the first batch of video resource sites created, the most famous was BTChina.net. It was founded in 2003 by Huang Xiwei, and in 2009 reportedly had 40 million to 50 million active users and over 800,000 views per day.[5] In December 2009, an official announcement was made on its website that it had been shut down by the authorities for not holding a licence to disseminate audiovisual programs on the information network.

BTChina suffered a very similar fate to that of The Pirate Bay. In January 2008, Swedish prosecutors filed a criminal complaint against The Pirate Bay, charging the four administrators of the site with 'assisting others to infringe copyright'. In 2009, the three founders were each sentenced by a Swedish court to one year in prison and ordered to pay a hefty fine. True to its claim of resilience, The Pirate Bay nevertheless continues to be accessible even today. At the time, the significance of the trial went far beyond The Pirate Bay itself; the key question then was whether the tracker server in BT downloads represents an infringement of copyright since the tracker server establishes links between different downloaders but does not store content itself.

After BTChina had been shut down, Chinese legal scholars suggested that the determination of liability for copyright infringement of Internet movie and television works should be treated differently. According to Wang, a certain degree of tolerance should be extended to unauthorised downloading by netizens; websites seeking private profits should be strictly investigated for their infringement liability, but it is not appropriate to implement a 'one-size-fits-all' type of forced shutdowns, and the interests of netizens, websites, and copyright owners should be considered within the legal framework.[6] However, at the time of writing, there has not been any official response from the authorities.

VeryCD was established at the same time as BTChina. Its founder, Huang Yimeng, modified the source code of eMule, an open source P2P software developed on the eDonkey network, thereby creating a personal file-sharing website and software product. VeryCD has

5   X. Cong Wang, '"BTChina" kan wangluo zhuzuoquan baohu "shuangying" yuanze', [The Win–Win Principle of Online Copyright Protection from 'BTChina'], *Netinfo Security* 9 (2010), 26–8.
6   Wang, '"BTChina"'.

Web 2.0 properties, which attracted a large number of users to upload files onto the site, and at the time was one of the most visited file-sharing sites in mainland China. It even replaced its model eMule and became the 'official eDonkey' among Chinese netizens.

However, in 2011, the site was not able to escape the fate of consolidation; the music channel was closed and movies and television series were no longer available for download. In a 2010 news report, Wang had said:

> In this era of massive information, VeryCD is to be a Spartan website like Google, with a streamlined 'menu' online, without charging, without encouraging you to linger, without bothering you with ads, without selling products. The main theme of the design is to let you find information as soon as possible to connect, and as soon as possible to leave. Google is what we learned from, and this is how we share the Internet.[7]

Today, the founders of BTChina and VeryCD, two young people who have been deeply influenced by the spirit of sharing and the DIY culture of the Internet, have developed a product named TapTap. Their slogan is: 'Discover the world's best mobile games'. TapTap has since become a highly influential community for mobile games in China, 'the Steam of mobile gaming', gaining the favour of many talented independent game designers.

In 2012, Baidu launched its cloud storage service Baidu Cloud, later renamed Baidu netdisc, which allows users to easily upload their files to the network and view and share them across terminals anywhere, at any time. Through cloud storage, another form of P2P file sharing was opened up. Thus, for example, entering the search terms 'Love, Death & Robots 2 netdisc' into the Baidu search engine brings up over 2,830,000 results. If you click on the link, you might be lucky enough to get a valid download address directly. Nowadays, there are also engines that are designed to search for files within the netdisc, turning it into a cloud repository of pirated materials. However, this approach is no longer as secure as that of a personal website, as it is a closed space and the content that users upload and share is constantly censored and often deleted by Baidu without any notice.

---

7   See Li, 'From "D-Buffs" to the "D-Generation"'; Huang Yimeng, 'Shuzi Wutuobang', ['Keeper of the "Digital Utopia"', *Shanghai Informatization*] 9 (2010), 80–1.

With the rise of social media, pirated resources can also be accessed through Sina Weibo and WeChat groups. There are also bloggers on Weibo who collect all kinds of resources according to followers' demands and share them on Weibo and WeChat through netdisc links. The phenomenon of taking resources for personal gain has also emerged. For example, one of the most common types is to join WeChat groups to buy files. By scanning QR codes on file-sharing websites, one can join personal file-sharing groups. Moreover, pirates will also offer various levels of service, such as buying multiple films currently in theatres as a package and as a private order. File sharing has even become a kind of hook, attracting people to join and stay in a WeChat group with group leaders selling other products on their WeChat moments pages.

Fansub Groups

The first fansub groups in China appeared around 2000. In China, they mainly refer to amateur groups producing Chinese subtitles for overseas movies, television series, documentaries, animation, variety shows, public lectures, and other online videos and games, additionally providing free download services. In 2005, the FOX TV series *Prison Break* sparked such a frenzy in China that it brought fansub groups to the surface. The source of material to be fansubbed is mainly from P2P file-sharing sites and hacker communities who specialise in the removal of copy-protection schemes and in the distribution of copyrighted files. Compared to professional translators, members of fansub groups exhibit two significant differences: they do it voluntarily, and they rely on the Internet. They play multiple roles: they are viewers, listeners, consumers, Internet users, volunteer workers, publishers, distributors, advocates, and translators.

Source files that are directly ripped without Chinese subtitles are called 'raw meat', and those with Chinese subtitles are called 'cooked meat'. 'Raw meat' is suitable for those who have a basic knowledge of foreign languages, while most Internet users can only enjoy 'cooked meat' files. Since the translators themselves are fans of movies and television dramas, they often pay attention to the memes and interesting details that are passed around among fans and embed them into subtitles, giving fans an intimate feeling that the fansubbing team 'understands me'.

Yan Feng, a professor of Chinese at Fudan University, refers to the translation of massive amounts of film, television, and online learning materials by fansub groups as the 'fourth translation activity in history' that has had a huge impact on Chinese culture, following the translation of Buddhist scriptures in the Tang Dynasty, the translation of Western culture in modern China, and the systematic translation of modern Western humanities and social science works after the Cultural Revolution.

Thanks to the rapid development of information technology, numerous fansub groups have developed their own websites, social media accounts, and netdiscs, gradually expanding their reach while facing increasingly harsh censorship and crackdowns from the authorities. YYeTs used to be the largest and one of the hottest fansub group in China. In November 2014, five of YYeTs's servers were confiscated and the group announced the temporary closure of their website, with the following phrase on Weibo: 'invictus maneo', a Latin saying from the classic American television series *Person of Interest*, meaning, 'I am still unconquered'. The sentiment is constantly brought up under the pressure of the realities of the Chinese Internet world, resembling the stubbornness of the three young men who founded The Pirate Bay. I feel particularly fortunate to have grown up during a time when the spirit of sharing on the Internet has never been greater, thanks to the bravery and selflessness of strangers who have shown me the world and taught more people like me to use shared resources to educate themselves.

As I wrote earlier, I have been on a FREE journey. Free doesn't mean that we don't respect the authors and creators; on the contrary, a large number of works have found a wider audience in this alternative way, bringing unexpected benefits to both authors and audiences. Behind the piracy phenomenon, there is also a place where free labour is combined with a free gift economy. Websites, software, subgroups, and similar are typical examples of Internet users benefiting from the free gift economy, but also paying with their own free labour.

3 We Have Become Digital Refugees (2021)

On 3 February 2021, people had just celebrated the Chinese Lunar New Year. The police in Shanghai announced that they had solved a case of copyright infringement of film and television works. The YYeTs fansub group had been investigated, 14 suspects arrested, and the group officially shut down. In the minds of American television fans, YYeTs was a symbol, an icon that really brought American television into the lives of a generation of young people.

The shutdown caused a large number of 'American drama refugees' to express their sorrow and regret online.

For me, as a music fan, what was even more difficult to accept was that two days after YYeTs's demise, Xiami Music shut down its servers as well. Xiami Music was one of the first and most popular music websites in China during the PC era, launched in November 2008 and acquired by the Alibaba Group in 2013. Since 2015, after the National Copyright Administration issued the 'strictest copyright order in history', major online music platforms were investigated and forced to take down unauthorised songs. Various other music platforms in China are also still fighting a war for copyright. After a long melee, Xiami eventually lost out to copyright giants like QQ Music and NetEase Cloud Music and announced on 5 January 2021 that it would officially cease services on 5 February 2021.

As soon as the official news came out, users took to social media to share their grief over the demise of their beloved software and also to share their stories with Xiami. As a registered user for 11 years myself, with 44,173 plays and thousands of albums in my collection, I felt like I had suddenly become a homeless person. Users started to help each other out, with people writing code to help 'move' and 'rescue their possessions', downloading and transferring data and saving their digital memories. The night before the server shut down, there was also a party at Xiami, a virtual room where everyone could play their favourite songs. Nearly 4,000 people joined that party, playing songs one by one, leaving their contact details, and making an appointment to meet on another platform, saying goodbye to each other all the way to the moment when the server stopped working in the early hours of the morning.

Xiami playlists have always been considered to be of the highest quality in the industry. They are created by users themselves and reflect the aesthetics of their creators. To this day, it still doesn't rely on using algorithms to repeatedly suggest 'music that users might like'. Xiami staff still manually place songs in their lists that they feel should be heard. Xiami Music's utopia consist of the attempt to create 'the most comprehensive music library in China'. When new users inadvertently open this library, they are amazed by its completeness and beauty. This body of knowledge has helped many users enter the deeper world of music, including myself.

There is no other music streaming site in China that has the strength to nourish a generation of music lovers with such a free spirit, tolerance, artisanal perseverance and democratic atmosphere. [...] Xiami refuses to conform and insists on putting genres first. After years of refinement, this 'genre map' has now spread to 24 primary categories, including jazz, pop and rock, and all primary genres are followed by secondary genres, a level of dedication that is unparalleled by its peers. There are 32 categories of jazz, 59 categories of rock, 98 categories of electronic, 18 categories of blues, 17 categories of Chinese specialties, and 8 categories of experimental. Even pop has 46 branches. All primary and secondary categories have bilingual names, and the category pages consist of sections such as Style Radio, Hottest Songs, Hot Albums, Related Artists, etc. And the secondary genre pages have more genre introductions.[8]

The original name of Xiami is EMUMO, meaning 'earn music and money'. One of the main features of Xiami is its respect for music creators. It uses a P2P scheme, which means that songs are uploaded by Xiami staff and users themselves, while other users who want to download them have to pay in Xiami coins; Xiami then rewards the songwriters with a share of the coins. The founder, Wang Hao, says he wants to break the existing copyright system of the big record companies, with users uploading music first and the platform then negotiating with the musicians. In 2013, Xiami built a platform specially for musicians, which allows independent musicians and independent record labels to publish copyrighted music on the platform and set their own prices, as well as providing them with various operational support. But such an approach is undoubtedly too idealistic, and the obstacles Xiami faces are not only the record companies, the copyrights, but also a large group of young people nowadays who are beginning to readily accept the system and the algorithms and are no longer actively making a choice.

What we have experienced makes us understand that one of the intuitive evils of copyright protection is that it can lead to monopolies. Tencent Music has become the largest online music platform in China. In addition, it has aligned itself with the upstream copyright holders in the industry chain through cross-shareholdings in Spotify, a stake in Universal Music, and cross-shareholdings in Warner and Sony, putting pressure on other domestic competitors in terms of user traffic and copyright capacity. Although the domestic

8   Hu, *DigNow* vol. 1 (4 February 2021), https://mp.weixin.qq.com/s/fTVyW-fs_ lXd70jDO5BLaw (translated by the author).

music copyright battle is in the name of protecting copyright, it has actually resulted in a situation where multiple music companies are cut off from each other, each gaining profit, ultimately leading to the situation where users need to move to different platforms depending on what song they want to listen to. For many netizens, this has paved the way for them engaging in piracy, as pirate websites offer a more comprehensive choice of files.

4 Open or Closed?

The 'creative destruction' caused by the new technological revolution has changed the shape of cultural production and brought with it new ways of social interaction and a new ethos. With the participation of countless Internet users, the Internet is spontaneously mapping out and honing a new civilisation and the norms of information use under it. However, the old copyright system is still stubbornly blocking the advent of a new cyber civilisation. Looking back at the results of copyright actions, how many of them were welcomed by the general public? Arguably, neither the shutdown of fansub groups and file-sharing sites nor the positive advocacy of paid digital music was at all popular.

The notion that everything found on the Internet should be made available to share contrasted with the increasingly strict regime of copyright protection reveals two diametrically opposed extremes. One is that all resources should be free, which will inevitably lead to a lack of incentive for originality; the other is that all knowledge must be protected, which could eventually lead to an era where everything needs to be paid for, which would in turn only reinforce the survival of piracy. At a time when information stored in digital form makes it possible to reproduce and reconstruct works indefinitely, perhaps it is time to rethink what copyright is.

Over ten years ago, Google had become the centre of the Internet world, with its philosophy to distribute traffic so that people could find most comprehensively what they were searching for and therefore remain within the Google domain. For all of the big companies that have sprung up over the years since Google, the idea has been to try to keep users within their own service realm for as long as possible and to dissuade them from going elsewhere. After smartphones became popular, this trend towards concentration developed even faster. In addition to the concentration of traffic and time, investment and mergers and acquisitions at the capital level never stopped, with all these changes leading in the direction of greater concentration.

After this (still ongoing) centralisation of the Internet, user interests began constantly to be violated. In the past, content was scattered all over the Internet and it took time to find it, but it was not easy to remove it. Today, apart from removing publications 'in accordance with the law', a company can easily create numerous reasons to make content disappear from its platform. In the past, content was in the hands of the creators themselves, and companies could not easily take it away. To put it another way, access rights that used to be legal have now been devolved to companies.

What companies really control is data, data created by users and which does not belong to them. A clear example of this are the various digital products that people buy. Today, people can easily buy music, movies, games, and software online. But, unlike in the past, users now do not own these products even though they have paid money for them. What they have bought can suddenly disappear – for example if the copyright holder withdraws the copyright. And even if you had bought it, you might not be able to use it afterwards.

So, in the digital age, there will still be people committed to collecting old games cassettes and collecting CDs and records, because these are the things that actually belong to them. The digital versions purchased online can be seen as user data created at a cost that should have been private property, but in this day and age, corporations have taken this data out of the remit of the user's private property through various user agreements with which users have to comply. Companies tell you that you are only buying 'the right to use it', but they have the right to ban you from using it in the future, if they so desire.

For serious creators, this tactic also reduces great intellectual works to mere data controlled by algorithms. In his article 'Federico Fellini and the Lost Magic of Cinema' in the March 2021 issue of *Harper's Magazine,* director Martin Scorsese refers to the fact that the art of cinema is dying in the competition between the blockbuster studios and streaming media.[9] He acknowledges that streaming has helped his career, but still points out that the art of cinema is being cheaply conceptualised as 'content'. He stresses the importance of 'curating', as he puts it.

9   Martin Scorsese, 'Federico Fellini and the Lost Magic of Cinema', *Harper's Magazine* (March 2021).

Curating isn't undemocratic or 'elitist', a term that is now used so often that it's become meaningless. It's an act of generosity – you're sharing what you love and what has inspired you. (The best streaming platforms, such as the Criterion Channel and MUBI and traditional outlets such as TCM, are based on curating – they're actually curated.) Algorithms, by definition, are based on calculations that treat the viewer as a consumer and nothing else.

This reminds me of the philosophy that Xiami Music has always held, and I think it is the most important act to be cherished in the digital age, because it affirms the importance of people: no matter if it is authors, audiences, or distributors, their intelligence and value are decently respected. And that's really what democracy is all about.

In the face of pressure from censorship and monopolies, my own piracy journey also seems to have come to an end. It was because of this particular experience that I was able to grow up and re-examine what piracy meant to me, to my country, and to my time. If issues such as free versus paid, the amount of money paid, the purchaser's ownership and use of the product can be resolved and balanced in a future copyright protection system, piracy may eventually become a thing of the past. And I believe the root of all this may lie in putting people first.

***

The second story is Yifan Li's, who will talk about her love for video games and how this love was hard to fulfil when she was growing up.

Playing Video Games in China: A Personal Journey (Yifan Li's Story)

I am a hard-core video game player: PC and console games are my favourite. I barely play mobile games and casual games. That is mainly because of my video gaming experiences and in spite of the fact I am now working in a mobile game company where I officially have to like mobile games as products more than PC or console games.

Looking back on my video gaming experience in China, pirated video games occupy a large part. When I was in primary school (in around 2000), *Grand Theft Auto: Vice City Stories* was the first PC video game I played. In hindsight, it was too violent for a primary school student. *Sims* was also one of my favourite video games. I played these games via disc installations. At that time, I had no idea about pirated video games, I thought that since I had paid for these discs, that was it, and I did not feel sorry for the game production companies. At the time, I also didn't care about any game rating – whether the game was violent or pornographic. As there were not many games available to select and that supported Chinese, it was my regular practice to judge a game by the cover picture alone. I certainly miss those days when I used to pick and choose game discs in shady underground bookstores, as they were a formative and enjoyable part of my past.

With the development of the Internet, pirated video games became more easily accessible online. Websites such as 3DM offered free video games for players to download. By that time, I knew I was playing pirated video games; however, people around me were also playing pirated video games. It was very hard and costly for players to buy authentic games. Moreover, there were no stores in which to buy them. People like me who wanted to play new video games invariably had to go to websites to download them. The movers and translators on these websites were and remain heroic figures in the minds of myself and many other gamers. They made many great games available to us at a time when games were regarded to be as bad and addictive as heroin. When I found out that many of these websites had been forced to close down, with some of the figures behind them even punished, I remember I felt and continue to feel very sad.

When I was in middle school, I got a Sony PSP PlayStation. Although by then authentic game cartridges could be bought in some stores, I couldn't afford them; they were too expensive. In the early 2000s, the price of video games was higher than a normal family's monthly income. Choosing a pirated video games was considered a 'clever' move at that time, it was considered 'stupid' to pay so much money for a genuine copy.

After a busy high school, I went to university. By then, the Internet had become very sophisticated and the information and files I had access to was extensive. Steam (a very large digital distribution platform for PC gaming) became the first platform I came across and buying a game became more and more a matter of course and routine. During my time at university, pirated video games gradually disappeared. However, I knew they were still there; when I put a video game title into the Baidu search engine, I can still find a download link, even today. The same method I use to download a film, can also be used to download video games.

Nowadays in China, mobile games are more popular than PC or console games. Although people have more available income for mobile games, buying video games, especially 3A video games (costing up to RMB300) is still considered a financially worthwhile thing to do. When I see my 15-year-old cousin download for nothing the same video game that I just paid more than RMB300 to purchase, it seems clear to me that there are still many people playing pirated video games, not because they cannot find a way to buy them, but simply for economic and convenience reasons.

Cloud players are another species of video players today. Typically, these players do not buy or download a game, they just watch a host playing. Sometimes, watching a host playing is much more interesting than playing oneself, especially for horror video games. Some game companies, though, see such behaviour as piratical as well. However, in my opinion, few cloud gamers would not buy the game as well as watching others play it, simply because video games are produced to be played first of all, and then only to be watched; it is the interactive element that is the hook for video games, and their advantage over films.

Finally, how did pirated video games influence me? As I wrote above, in China in the 1990s it was very hard to buy and play authentic video games. My generation's parents were mostly born during the 1970s and so they were not familiar with video games. They often tried to dissuade us from playing them. Also, the government had and continues to have some very strong reservations about such games. But it is fair to say that without this 'bad' thing and without the years I invested in playing video games, mostly of the pirated kind, I would not have chosen video game topics for university essays and also would not have selected a video game company as my employer, a job I have come to dearly love.

Concluding Observations by Holger Briel

Jiarui's and Yifan's stories make a number of important points; for one, they show the raw emotional power and the beauty of minds opening up when introduced to artistic creations, new impressions, and the music from afar. They also tell of the hardships of gaining access to such content, something which is not only true for China, but for many countries of the global south. They describe the power of digital piracy to break down artificial walls and allow access to data otherwise unavailable due to legal or commercial top-down interventions.

These stories also talk of the positioning of individuals and generations within a techno-historical flow. Arguably, over the last 70 years or so, it was the Anglo-American cultural sphere that set standards for entertainment consumption; often it would take months, if not years, for US or British music and television shows to filter through to the rest of the world, if at all. With piracy, these carefully calibrated and revenue-maximising colonialist timeframes became inoperative; a reverse flow would even set in, with shows produced in India, Nigeria, Norway, or Germany now appearing on the US's netflixed screens, in part a result of the cultural power of piracy.

Furthermore, via piracy, it has become much harder to control the global flow of content, a situation with much political clout as well. Piracy had a large stake in the creation of proxy and mirror site and in the development of VPNs, all of which are nowadays used to tunnel underneath erstwhile seemingly unconquerable digital territorial barriers. It has also largely become impossible to divvy up the world into DVD regions and sell only to those who are deemed profitable or deserving.

The stories presented here do display a fair amount of nostalgia. This is perhaps unavoidable, as the Internet has become historic, accompanying people's changing lives and their growing older. While this is a typical situation, mirroring the development in music and film history ('Those were the Days: 100 Songs of the 1940s'), it should not allow us to become too complacent with the direction the Internet is taking. Just as with other maturing media, it is enormously powerful and therefore susceptible to abuse. There is political gain to be had from influencing the Internet, and while in many ways most users have much more access to information than ever before, this access has to be negotiated every day anew. Possible fracturing of the Internet would pose serious threats to its informational flow. Stories such as the ones presented here remind us what is gained from retaining access, and, indeed, what a wonderful thing it is to have, and thereby provide motivation to individuals and societies to fight for continued global access to information.

Select Bibliography

de Kloet, Jeroen, 'Popular Music and Youth in Urban China: The Dakou Generation', *China Quarterly* 183 (2005): 609–26.

Li, Jinying, 'From "D-Buffs" to the "D-Generation": Piracy, Cinema, and an Alternative Public Sphere in Urban China', *International Journal of Communication* 6 (2012): 542–63.

Manovich, Lev, 'What Comes after Remix', *Remix Theory* 10 (2007). http://manovich.net/content/04-projects/057-what-comes-after-remix/54_article_2007.pdf. Accessed 13 March 2022.

Scorsese, Martin, 'Federico Fellini and the Lost Magic of Cinema', *Harper's Magazine* (March 2021). https://harpers.org/archive/2021/03/il-maestro-federico-fellini-martin-scorsese/. Accessed 13 March 2022.

Wang, X. Cong '"BTChina" kan wangluo zhuzuoquan baohu "shuangying" yuanze', [The Win–Win Principle of Online Copyright Protection from 'BTChina'], *Netinfo Security* 9 (2010): 26–8.

10 Blockchains, Threats, and Parasites

Danai Tselenti

1 Introduction

During the last decade, the hype around blockchain technology has been constantly increasing. The overall popular discourse as well as a large share of the academic literature refers metaphorically to blockchain as a 'game changer' and portray it as a disruptive technology that can introduce a 'paradigm shift' in transaction modalities and reengineer interactions in a wide range of fields around the features of decentralisation, disintermediation, transparency, immutability, privacy, and security.[1] Blockchains represent distributed ledger systems, which rely upon cryptography in order to record and store transactions on a peer-to-peer basis. In this respect, they enable the operation of a 'trustless network' across which multiple participants can efficiently transact in an immutable and tamper-proof way without the intermediation of third parties such as governmental agencies, banks, etc., who act within the current digital economy as the necessary 'trusted authorities' for ensuring the validity of transactions.

The extant, rapidly evolving academic literature on blockchain technology emanates from a range of disciplines and approaches through often conflicting and polarising terms.

On the one hand, the advocates of blockchain technology focus on its disruptive potential to revolutionise interactions, foster privacy, and strengthen democracy.[2] The most enthusiastic advocates turn their attention to the unique cooperative properties of blockchain that make the technology ideal for sustaining non-hierarchical socialist

---

1 Melanie Swan, *Blockchain: Blueprint for a New Economy* (Sebastopol, CA: O'Reilly Media, 2015).
2 See Ahmed B. Ayed, 'A Conceptual Secure Blockchain-Based Electronic Voting System', *International Journal of Network Security & Its Applications* 9, no. 3 (2017), 1–9 and Maria Koletsi, 'Radical Technologies: Blockchain as an Organizational Movement', *Homo Virtualis* 2, no. 1 (2019), 25–33.

forms of governance.[3] On the other hand, a significant body of work takes a critical view on blockchain technology, emphasising its social and political dangers.[4] Blockchain critics generally invest blockchain technology with fears of a dystopian future closely aligned with neoliberal strategies that pose a threat to democracy and lead to greater control tendencies and other authoritarian outcomes.[5]

A third strand in this debate acknowledges that blockchains open up new avenues for interaction and decentralised transactions, yet also identifies a wide range of drawbacks, risks, and limitations, particularly regarding 'security issues' that they bring with them.[6] Within this stream of literature, 'security threats' are construed as grounded in individual or collective malicious intents.

Despite this engaging three-tier research approach, the existing literature that focuses on blockchain technology remains only tentatively connected to relevant new media studies scholarship. Particularly, there is a lack of studies that approach blockchain as an ecosystem and address the range of antagonistic relationships within it by promoting a different non-polarised understanding of the constellation of actors/actants that sustain it and the various ways they interrelate. In an attempt to alleviate the aforementioned discontinuities in the literature, this contribution will follow a new media studies perspective. Rather than argue for or against

3   See Steve Huckle and Martin White, 'Socialism and the Blockchain', *Future Internet* 8, no. 4 (2016), 49 and Brett Scott, *How Can Cryptocurrency and Blockchain Technology Play a Role in Building Social and Solidarity Finance?* (Geneva: United Nations Research Institute for Social Development, 2016).

4   See David Golumbia, 'Bitcoin as Politics: Distributed Right Wing-Extremism', in Geert Lovink, Nathaniel Tkacz, and Patricia de Vries (eds), *MoneyLab Reader: An Intervention in Digital Economy* (Amsterdam: Institute of Network Cultures, 2015), 118–31 and Marcella Atzori, 'Blockchain Technology and Decentralized Governance: Is the State Still Necessary?', *Journal of Governance and Regulation* 6, no. 1 (2017), 45–62.

5   Robert Herian, *Regulating Blockchain: Critical Perspectives in Law and Technology* (London: Routledge, 2019).

6   See Jennifer J. Xu, 'Are Blockchains Immune to All Malicious Attacks?', *Financial Innovation* 2, no. 25 (2016), 1–9; Oliver Boireau, 'Securing the Blockchain against Hackers', *Network Security* 1 (2018), 8–11; Marie Vasek, Joseph Bonneau, Ryan Castellucci, Cameron Keith, and Tyler Moore, 'The Bitcoin Drain: Examining the Use and Abuse of Bitcoin Brain Wallets', in Jens Grossklags and Bart Preneel (eds), *Financial Cryptography and Data Security* (Cham: Springer, 2017), 609–18; and Archana Prashanth Joshi, Meng Han, and Yan Wang, 'A Survey on Security and Privacy Issues of Blockchain Technology', *Mathematical Foundations of Computing* 1, no. 2 (2018), 121–47.

blockchain technology, this chapter studies the blockchain ecosystem in connection to piracy and particularly with regard to the ways it reconfigures and re-evaluates the concept of 'threat' in the general sense of the term. By focusing primarily on the Bitcoin and Ethereum ecosystems, the related objective is to challenge notions of security and disintermediation as illustrated within the extant blockchain literature by examining how processes of continuous interruptions, modifications, and respective optimisations become operationalised within the blockchain ecosystem.

In order to illustrate the theoretical arguments, this chapter draws primarily upon the work of Michel Serres and combines certain aspects of it with the insights of Katherine Hayles's theory of 'cognitive assemblages' and the 'regime of computation'.[7] By bringing disperse strands of literature on blockchain into conversation with the above-mentioned framework, this chapter introduces 'computational parasitism', a novel concept that highlights the numerous parasitic relations that are simultaneously ongoing in, around, and across the blockchain ecosystem and can thus capture the complex and constantly evolving blockchain ecology.

The chapter is organised as follows: section 2 sets out the theoretical framework by introducing Serres's notion of parasitism; section 3 traces blockchain's ideological underpinnings and briefly outlines the basic ways that blockchain technology and specifically Bitcoin function; and section 4 fleshes out the core argument of the essay, presenting four discrete chains of blockchain parasitism structured around three different types of parasitic relations (disorderly, intermediating, and centralising relations). In particular, section 4 utilises specific examples of the successive developments that have taken place within the blockchain ecosystem and introduces 'computational parasitism' as a novel theoretical concept that grasps the interrelations sustaining the blockchain ecosystem. The concluding section reviews the central argument and reflects on the inherently contradictory relation of blockchain to piracy, disintermediation, and the notion of threat in general. It also emphasises the need for future work to focus more carefully on the specific interdependencies and processes of one-way resource-transfers within the blockchain ecosystem.

---

7   Katherine Hayles, 'Literary Texts as Cognitive Assemblages: The Case of Electronic Literature', *Electronic Book Review* (5 August 2018), https://doi.org/10.7273/8p9a-7854.

2 Serres's Parasites as a Framework

Serres recasts the Western conceptualisation of relationality as binary by introducing the concept of the parasite as the fundamental 'third term' in order for communication to take place. Serres combines science studies and humanities in an innovative way, drawing from a mixture of heterogeneous sources ranging from information theory, biology, literature, and even mythology. He advances a general theory of parasitism that concerns human and non-human relations by merging three notions of the parasite: the informational, in the form of noise in a communication channel; the biological, in the form of an organism that feeds off its host; and the social, in the form of an abusive guest who benefits at the expense of a host. According to Serres, parasites need to be understood as types of relations and not as ontological entities or fixed identities. In his most influential work, *The Parasite* (1982), Serres draws on La Fontaine's famous fable about the city rat and the country rat in order to illustrate how different forms of parasitism interrelate and entangle with each other.[8] In the tale, a city rat invites his cousin, a country rat, to eat the left-overs from an extravagant meal held at a tax collector's house. As they eat, a noise is heard which interrupts the rats' meal and forces the country rat to return to his home out of fear for his life. The parable illustrates the asymmetrical transfer of recourses and the ways that one parasite gives access to the next: the tax collector who provides the left-overs is a parasite to the extent that he is not the producer of the food served. In a parallel manner, the city rat parasitises the tax collector by drawing on his resources as an 'uninvited guest' and is in turn parasitised by the country rat who is hosted at a meal where he unequally exchanges his company for food. Both rats are parasitised consequently by the noise that interrupts their parasitic activities.

In this sense, Serres depicts parasitism as a one-way relationship organised around taking without giving, or more generally around unequal exchange, and conceptualises parasitical relations as the necessary condition for the operation of any system. By positioning itself at the intersections of relationships, the parasite intermediates between the inside and the outside boundaries of a system. As Serres famously argues, 'A third exists before the second. A third exists

8   Michel Serres, *The Parasite*, trans. Lawrence R. Schehr (Baltimore, MD: Johns Hopkins University Press, 1982).

before the other. [...] I have to go through the middle before reaching the end. There is always a mediate, a middle, an intermediary'.[9]

3 An Overview of the Blockchain Technology

The idea of a decentralised peer-to-peer network can be traced back to the libertarian visions of the crypto-anarchist and cypherpunk movements of the early 1990s. Stating their core principles in the 'Crypto Anarchist Manifesto'[10] and the 'Cypherpunk Manifesto'[11] respectively, they envisage the elimination of governmental control over currency and promote individualism, privacy, and anonymous transactions secured by cryptography as the fundamental prerequisites of political and social change. As May particularly emphasised, the technology for this prospective 'social and economic revolution' would evolve in the years to come and threaten the state, which would try to slow or halt its spread.[12] In this sense, blockchain's underlying technology is inscribed within one of the most significant aspects of digital piracy, namely the challenge to state power.[13] Blockchain emerges thus as 'the uninvited guest': a parasitic, pirate technology posing a substantial threat to the power of the state.

Blockchain has been popularised as the undergirding technology of the Bitcoin cryptocurrency. Designed as a response to the 2008 financial crisis, Bitcoin emerged as an interruption to the established order of transactions. Introduced in a white paper written by an unidentified individual or group named Satoshi Nakamoto,[14] and in line with libertarian ideology, one of Nakamoto's primary objectives was to emancipate financial transactions from government control and central banks. To quote him, 'What is needed is an electronic payment system based on cryptographic proof instead of trust,

---

9 Serres, *The Parasite*, 63.
10 Timothy C. May, 'The Crypto Anarchist Manifesto' [Electronic mailing list message, 1992], www.activism.net/cypherpunk/crypto-anarchy.html.
11 Eric Hughes, 'A Cypherpunk's Manifesto' (9 March 1993), www.activism.net/cypherpunk/manifesto.html.
12 May, 'The Crypto Anarchist Manifesto'.
13 Jessica L. Beyer and Fenwick McKelvey, 'You Are Not Welcome Among Us: Pirates and the State', *International Journal of Communication* 9 (2015), 890–908.
14 Satoshi Nakamoto, 'Bitcoin: A Peer-to Peer Electronic Cash System' (2008), https://web.archive.org/web/20110303162115/https://bitcoin.org/bitcoin.pdf.

allowing any two willing parties to transact directly with each other without the need for a trusted third party'.[15]

In Bitcoin, transactions are encrypted via digital signatures, which involve two inextricably connected keys: a private and a public key. Every transaction is signed by the private key of the sender and is sent to the public key of the receiver. Each transaction is broadcast to the whole network, and in order to be added to the blockchain it necessitates collective validation through a mechanism of consensus established on what is known as 'proof-of-work'. More specifically, the nodes in the network are asked to solve a complex cryptographic puzzle. The nodes performing the proof of work are called 'miners' and the process of adding new blocks to the chain 'mining'. Miners are incentivised to provide their computational resources in order to validate blocks by a reward in bitcoins.[16]

As soon as a solution to the cryptographic puzzle is generated by one node, it is broadcast to all the other nodes in the network. The level of difficulty is adjusted in such a way that on average it takes ten minutes for a node in the network to come to the right solution, while mathematically the possibility of multiple miners providing proofs-of-work for the same block simultaneously is highly unlikely. Once a transaction is validated by the majority of miners it is timestamped and grouped into a 'block', which is then linked in a chronologically linear fashion with other blocks and is stored across the network. This means that each block is identified by a hash value on its header, which is essentially a digital fingerprint. Hash values are stored in each block in such a way that they are affected by the values of the previous blocks. This inter-dependence of hash values results in the synchronisation of the distributed ledger in real time, something that ensures the integrity of the entire blockchain, as any alteration of data will immediately become apparent to the whole network. In cases where multiple chains – based on valid hash values – compete for network legitimisation, the rule of the 'longest chain' prevails, which is to say, the chain which exhibits the most proof-of-work becomes accepted.

Modifying or adding a block to the chain would necessitate a 'mathematical race' in order to outpace the honest nodes of the network and generate subsequent valid blocks and thus the expenditure

15 Nakamoto, 'Bitcoin'.
16 Andreas M. Antonopoulos, *Mastering Bitcoin: Unlocking Digital Crypto Currencies* (Sebastopol, CA: O'Reilly Media, 2014).

of excessive computational power. As Nakamoto points out, '[t]he system is secure as long as honest nodes collectively control more CPU (Central Processing Unit) power than any cooperating group of attacker nodes'.[17]

It is precisely upon this technical rupture that serves as 'ground zero', that a first instance of parasitical interference is introduced into the blockchain scene. Construed through a Serresean framework, the parasite introduces a 'third', which modifies the order of existing relations by working beside or next to it and threatening the integrity of the primary system.

4 The Chains of Blockchain Parasitism

Chain of Parasitism #1
Although blockchain is premised on immutability, under specific circumstances, previous blocks can be modified. In this respect, the so-called '51% attack' is possible if a single node controls more than 51 per cent of the mining resources. In this case the dominant node can 'insert fraudulent transactions, double-spend funds, or even steal assets from others'.[18] The 51% attack is classified among the most important security 'threats' of the blockchain ecosystem in a significant share of the literature.[19]

Parasite #1.1
As computational power plays a pivotal role within the blockchain ecology, an issue in respect to accessibility to adequate computational resources arises. In this sense, 'as bitcoin gained monetary value, it fuelled a hardware-driven, energy intensive arms race […] as people sought to gain an advantage within the network'.[20] While a modern CPU can calculate a SHA-256 algorithm, the number of hashes computed is rather low in comparison to other technologies, such as the GPUs (Graphics Processing Units), which are able to perform calculations at significantly higher speeds. In this respect, in the last few years, a new market for Application-Specific-Integrated-Circuit

17   Nakamoto, 'Bitcoin'.
18   Xu, 'Are Blockchains Immune?'
19   Dmitry Efanov and Pavel Roschin, 'The All-Pervasiveness of the Blockchain Technology', *Procedia Computer Science* 123 (2018), 116–21.
20   Matthew A. Zook and Joe Blankenship, 'New Spaces of Disruption? The Failure of Bitcoin and the Rhetorical Power of Algorithmic Governance', *Geoforum* 96 (November 2018), 252.

(ASIC) devices has emerged, namely optimised, high-performance machines especially customised for bitcoin mining.

Parasite #1.2

This proliferation of specialised devices has been followed by the emergence of a series of mining pools where miners combine their computational resources in order to increase hash rates and computing power, and to share the rewards. This development has resulted in the centralisation of resources, so that the biggest mining pools currently hold over 50 per cent of the hash power and are concentrated in China.[21] Following Gehl and McKelvey,[22] we can approach large mining farms as 'top parasites' who have pushed the mining difficulty to such a high degree that it is practically impossible for small-scale miners to get block rewards, highlighting in this way that the blockchain protocol can be centrally controlled by a few powerful players.

Parasite #1.3

Consequently, the power consumption for the operation of bitcoin mining is constantly increasing. The escalating demands on computing power are correlated to high costs of electricity, leading miners in search of cheaper energy in order to consume massive amounts of electricity. Subsequently, such enormous power consumption is linked to environmental risks through the generation of excessive heat. According to some recent estimations, bitcoin's energy consumption is equivalent to the energy consumed by the country of Singapore and by the power used by more than 4.3 million houses in the United States.[23] In this sense, gigantic mining pools are eating environmental material resources, in the same way that parasites eat their host's resources, contributing thereby to the earth's warming.[24] Bitcoin's material dependence on power infrastructures, inherently tied to high computational demands, appropriate climate conditions, and cheaper access to electricity supply, results in an immensely uneven material geography based on a set of interdependent parasitic relations, all

21   Jordan Tuwiner, 'Bitcoin Mining Pools', *Buy Bitcoin Worldwide* (11 February 2022).
22   Robert Gehl and Fenwick McKelvey, 'Bugging Out: Darknets as Parasites of Large-Scale Media Objects', *Media, Culture & Society* 41, no. 2 (2018), 219–35.
23   Zook and Blankenship, 'New Spaces of Disruption?', 252.
24   Finn Brunton, 'Heat Exchanges', in Geert Lovink, Nathaniel Tkacz, and Patricia de Vries (eds), *MoneyLab Reader: An Intervention in Digital Economy* (Amsterdam: Institute for Network Cultures, 2015), 158–72.

of which revolve around feeding off the host environment while providing little in return.[25]

Chain of Parasitism #2

Bitcoin was followed by the emergence of a range of rival altcoins. Specifically, within a decade since its advent, over 2,300 digital cryptocurrencies have been launched (e.g., Litecoin, Cardano, Dash, Tether, etc.), not all of which are minable.[26] It is interesting to note, that although bitcoin was premised on the exclusion of transactional intermediation, 'an articulate ecosystem of Bitcoin intermediaries [...] gradually introduced the digital currency into the international networks of commerce and finance'.[27] Since its inception, we have witnessed a proliferation of exchange platforms and a series of third-party companies which provide a range of services and applications for the Bitcoin infrastructure (like wallet providers, payment processors, etc.).[28] This development formed a host system upon which a series of parasitic activities operate. In this respect, several exchange platforms have been hacked throughout the history of bitcoin, through the exploitation of internal software 'weaknesses'. The narrative of bitcoin security was severely challenged when in 2014 the largest bitcoin exchange platform based in Tokyo was hacked and bitcoins worth more than 450 million dollars were stolen. Throughout the years, a series of other bitcoin hacking attacks have occurred.[29]

---

25 Nick Lally, Kelly Kay, and Jim Thatcher, 'Computational Parasites and Hydropower: A Political Ecology of Bitcoin Mining on the Columbia River', *Environment and Planning E: Nature and Space* 5, no. 2 (2019), 1–2.

26 Eunice Mensah, 'Chasing the Wind? A Case for Competitive Popularity as an Approach to Regulating Cryptocurrencies', *SSRN* (5 March 2020), https://ssrn.com/abstract=3529921.

27 Francesca Musiani, Alexandre Mallard, and Cecile Meadel, 'Governing What Wasn't Meant to be Governed: A Controversy-Based Approach to the Study of Bitcoin Governance', in Malcolm Campbell-Verduyn (ed.) *Bitcoin and Beyond: Cryptocurrencies, Blockchains, and Global Governance* (London: Routledge, 2017), 138.

28 See Alan Cohn, Travis West, and Chelsea Parker, 'Smart after All: Blockchain, Smart Contracts, Parametric Insurance, and Smart Energy Grids', *Georgetown Law Technology Review* 1, no. 2 (2017), 284 and Jack Parkin, *Money Code Space: Hidden Power in Bitcoin, Blockchain and Decentralization* (Oxford: Oxford University Press, 2020).

29 Primavera De Filippi and Benjamin Loveluck, 'The Invisible Politics of Bitcoin: Governance Crisis of a Decentralized Infrastructure', *Internet Policy Review* 5, no. 4 (2016), 17.

Parasite #2.1

Another set of parasitic activities concerns the storage of the private key of transactors. Although a series of digital wallets by different companies have been developed (software wallets or multi-signature wallets), they remain vulnerable to various types of hacking which use malware that searches for private keys. Even the most recently advanced solution of hardware wallets is threatened through 'fault injections' that corrupt the processed data.[30]

Parasite #2.2

It is worth noting that the use of bitcoin is also linked to money laundering and illegal activities within black market economies. The most famous example is the darknet platform Silk Road, which was using bitcoin for trading illegal drugs, weapons, and other illicit products.[31] In an explicit connection to piracy, Silk Road's site founder used the pseudonym, Dread Pirate Roberts (DPR), promoting the cryptomarket as an anarcho-capitalist resistance to state power and taxation.[32]

Chain of Parasitism #3

Ethereum Blockchain

The next blockchain platform examined here is Ethereum, which emerged as an upgraded version of the cryptocurrency blockchain-based system. It was first introduced in Vitalik Buterin's white paper, 'A Next Generation Smart Contract and Decentralized Application Platform'.[33] Ethereum introduces additional functions to the blockchain technology as it supports a Turing-complete programming language, 'allowing for small snippets of code to be deployed directly on the blockchain and to be executed in a decentralised manner by every node in the network'.[34] These are the so-called 'smart contracts'. Smart contracts are designed as an optimised solution to traditional forms of contracts in an effort to

30 Boireau, 'Securing the Blockchain against Hackers', 9.
31 De Filippi and Loveluck, 'The Invisible Politics of Bitcoin', 8.
32 Rita Zajácz, 'Silk Road: The Market Beyond the Reach of the State', *Information Society* 33, no. 1 (2017), 23–34.
33 Vitalik Buterin, 'A Next Generation Smart Contract and Decentralized Application Platform', Ethereum White Paper (2014).
34 Primavera De Filippi and Samer Hassan, 'Blockchain Technology as a Regulatory Technology', *First Monday* 21, no. 12 (2016).

promote cost-efficient contractual processes without the intervention of third parties and aimed at enhancing transactional security and reducing contractual breaches. Ethereum-hosted smart contracts extend beyond financial applications (supply chain, insurance, property rights, real estate, voting, Internet of Things, etc.) and can be depicted as 'self-regulating autopoietic agencies',[35] which encode contractual relations into an 'if-then' computer logic.

The idea of smart contracts builds upon the concept of 'freedom of contract', or the ability for two parties to decide the terms and the nature of a transaction among themselves 'without intervention of an outside party' and thus 'aligns with libertarian ideology'.[36] Ethereum also supports its own cryptocurrency, Ether, which is mainly used for rewarding application authentication and development.[37] Ether mining is more sophisticated than in the case of Bitcoin, in that it does not rely exclusively on computational power but on memory-intensive tasks as well.

Ethereum was conceived as the underlying infrastructure for Decentralised Autonomous Organizations (DAOs), namely 'long-term smart contracts that contain the assets and encode the by-laws of an entire organization'.[38] A DAO may be understood as analogous to a legal organisation, with legal documents (by-laws) that define the rules of interaction among members.

Parasite #3.1

In September 2016, a DAO was set up using the Ethereum software. Shortly thereafter, it was attacked and more than 60 millions worth of Ether were stolen. The attacker exploited a loophole in the code of a smart contract.

The 'Dao Attack' resulted in splitting the blockchain coding community into two opposing groups: a 'pro-fork' group in favour of intervening in the code for restoring order and an 'anti-fork'

35 Luciana Parisi, 'Critical Computation: Digital Automata and General Artificial Thinking', *Theory Culture & Society* 36, no. 2 (2019), 6.
36 Kristin B. Cornelius, 'Smart Contracts as Evidence: Trust, Records, and the Future of Decentralized Transactions', in Jeremy Hunsinger, Lisbeth Klastrup, and Mathew M. Allen (eds), *Second International Handbook of Internet Research* (Dordrecht: Springer, 2018), 6.
37 Suyash Gupda and Mohammad Sadoghi, 'Blockchain Transaction Processing', in S. Sakr and A. Zomaya (eds), *Encyclopedia of Big Data Technologies* (Cham: Springer, 2018), 8.
38 Buterin, Ethereum White Paper, 1.

group, opposing every act of intervention as compromising the fundamental principles of blockchain's decentralised governance.[39]

In the end, the 'pro-fork' group prevailed and Ethereum's core developers introduced a 'hard fork', rolling back the blockchain to a previous – unaffected by the hack – state. On the contrary, the 'anti-fork' group refused to update the software and maintained the original blockchain, which resulted in the creation of a new but less popular cryptocurrency known as Ethereum Classic.

The 'Dao Attack' highlights the governance structure of blockchain as grounded in a specialised technocratic elite, which acts as the central gatekeeper of security. At the same time, the hard fork that occurred constitutes an illustrative example of computational parasitic relations. A fork could be approached as a particular kind of parasite, which introduces noise in terms of what Serres conceptualised as the joker, the wild card, the white domino, which takes all values. Serres writes: 'The noise is a joker. It has at least two values, like the third man: a value of destruction and a value of construction. It must be included and excluded'.[40]

That said, the aim to chase out the parasitic actors brings about new developments in the blockchain economy. Since the 'Dao Attack', a series of companies have been emerging that promise to enhance smart contract security by delivering bug-free contracts through the use of artificial intelligence.[41]

Chain of Parasitism #4

Moving to the last chain of parasitic relations, we can witness a proliferation of corporations (Microsoft, Intel, IBM), banks (Goldman Sachs), and even governmental and regulatory agencies (like the Delaware Blockchain Initiative created by the state of Delaware) that are adopting blockchains for private or permissioned use. In this respect, financial and governmental institutions (the primary 'excluded thirds') return to the blockchain ecosystem.

Serres identified two primary responses to parasitic interference: incorporation or expulsion. As Steven D. Brown explains regarding the parasitical dynamics between hosts and parasites: 'either they

39   Moritz Huetten, 'The Soft Spot of Hard Code: Blockchain Technology, Network Governance and Pitfalls of Technological Utopianism', *Global Networks* 19, no. 3 (2019), 329–48.
40   Serres, *The Parasite*, 67.
41   See, for instance, *AnChain.Ai*, www.anchain.ai/.

incorporate the parasite into their midst – and thereby accept the new form of communication the parasite inaugurates – or they act together to expel the parasite and transform their own social practices in the course of doing so [...] [H]ere then is the origin of human relations: the struggle to incorporate or expel the parasite'.[42]

The appropriation of blockchains by corporations has resulted in the enclosure of the distributed peer-to-peer network and the creation of private or 'permissioned' blockchains. Private blockchains 'are instantiations of' the basic features of the blockchain technology 'in a fully private space, such as a private server or a cloud-based environment', while permissioned blockchains 'are administered by a single entity', 'can be configured to restrict access only to approved users',[43] and can alternate commands if necessary.[44]

To put it in Serres's terms, 'privatization begins with the emission of a phenomenon that expands. Then a whole country is tied up by appropriating all the transmitters'.[45] Closely related to this parasitic logic of expansion and centralisation is Facebook's Libra crypto-currency project. Initiated in June 2019, it was designed to operate as a permissioned and centralised network under the third-party governance of the 28 member-firms of the Libra Association. Following Tischer, 'Third-party involvement may thus be understood as an attempt to parasite the Libra ecosystem by gaining technical power to divert income flows to themselves as occupants of the last position in the parasitic chain'.[46]

Moreover, as blockchain has been identified as the technology that can support the general digitalisation of society towards the Internet of Things (IoT), many corporations (like IBM, Samsung) have begun to invest large amounts of money in order to build their own IoT versions. As Serres argues, the parasite's 'immediate activity is to seek to appropriate for itself what is temporarily in common [...] The phenomenon of expansion is its proper business and its

42 Steven D. Brown, 'Science, Translation and the Logic of the Parasite', *Theory, Culture & Society* 19, no. 3 (2002), 17.
43 Cohn et al., 'Smart After All', 279.
44 Gopala K. Behara and Tirumala Khandrika, 'Blockchain as a Disruptive Technology: Architecture, Business Scenarios, and Future Trends', in Moses Strydom and Sheryl Buckley (eds), *AI and Bid Data's Potential for Disruptive Innovation* (Hershey, PA: IGI Global, 2010), 130–73.
45 Serres, *The Parasite*, 143.
46 Daniel Tischer, 'Cutting the Network? Facebook's Libra Currency as a Problem of Organization', *Finance and Society* 6, no. 1 (2020), 30.

appropriation'.[47] In this sense, the spectre of centralisation casts a giant shadow over the blockchain ecology.

Quantum Computing: A Parasite from the Future

Last but not least, the advent of quantum computing increases the chances of cracking cryptographic keys by speeding exponentially processes of algorithmic computations, a development that disrupts the fundamental basis upon which blockchain technology relies and creates security vulnerabilities.[48] Advancements in quantum computing and cryptography, thus, introduce a parasitic stage of imbalance and disorder within the blockchain ecosystem, forcing it to differentiate and adapt.

Computational Parasitism

As we study each new round of blockchain's technological advancements, optimisations, and expansions that get inscribed on top and across the previous ones, it becomes evident how relevant Serres's theoretical articulations are for conceptualising the antagonistic parasitic relations and power asymmetries within the blockchain ecosystem. Acting not as single actors but at the intersections of multiple parasitic interconnections between algorithms, human practices, and computational and material resources, blockchain ecosystems can be exemplified as 'cognitive assemblages'. Following Hayles,

> Cognitive assemblages are distinct (technologies) because their transformative potentials are enabled, extended, and supported by flows of information, and consequently cognitions between human and technical participants. Hybrid by nature, they raise questions about how agency is distributed among cognizers, how and in what ways actors contribute to systemic dynamics, and consequently how responsibilities – technical, social, legal, ethical – should be apportioned. They invite ethical inquiries that recognise the importance of technical mediations, adopting systemic and relational perspectives rather than an emphasis (I should say overemphasis) on individual responsibility.[49]

47   Serres, *The Parasite*, 143–4.
48   Brian S. Haney, 'Blockchain: Post-Quantum Security & Legal Economics', *North Carolina Banking Institute* 24, no. 1 (2020).
49   Katherine Hayles, *Unthought: The Power of the Cognitive Unconscious* (Chicago: University of Chicago Press, 2017), 119.

Within the context of what Hayles calls 'the regime of computation',[50] 'blockchain cognitive assemblages' are characterised by an evolving proliferation of human and non-human actors, which can be understood to be sustained and structured by 'computational parasitic' relations. Particularly, it can be argued that 'computational parasitism' is configured by what Serres calls 'parasitic cascades', processes in which each actor in the parasitic cascade takes something from the prior actor and reappropriates something from the prior flow without offering an equal share. As Serres puts it, 'the parasite parasites the parasites'.[51] This means that at the same time multiple parasitic relations coexist in which the positions of host and parasite are interchangeable. The particular understanding of 'threat' that comes to matter under the lens of computational parasitism manifests the different ways that piracy is inherently inscribed within the very structure of the blockchain ecosystem. In this sense, the range of blockchain 'pirate activities' provoke on the one hand new forms of complexity and consequently engineer systemic transformation, while on the other hand they mobilise the emergence of other chains of intermediaries and become themselves successively parasitised.

As shown throughout this chapter, computational parasitism is enacted on the basis of three major relation types: one type of parasitic relations represents all the 'disorderly elements' within the blockchain ecosystem. They mostly concern security threats associated with acts of hacking and forms of illicit behaviour that introduce 'a chaotic element within a system based on security and order'.[52] A second type of parasitic relations represents all the intermediating actors that entail the creation of new service providers and markets open to competition. As Marcella Atzori argues, 'Although originally designed as disintermediation tools, the ecosystems of fully distributed blockchains are characterized by a great amount of third parties and profitable offering intermediation services, with strong asymmetries of information and power between developers and users'.[53] A third type of parasitic relations encompasses all

---

50 Katherine Hayles, *My Mother Was a Computer: Digital Subjects and Literary Texts* (Chicago: University of Chicago Press, 2005).

51 Serres, *The Parasite*, 55.

52 Jussi Parikka, 'Viral Noise and the (Dis)Order of the Digital Culture: Introduction', *M/C Journal* 7, no. 6 (2005).

53 Atzori, 'Blockchain Technology', 31.

centralising actors that divert the blockchain's decentralised character through processes of imitation, adaptation, and incorporation. All of the above-mentioned parasitic types of relationships play out by posing a threat to the integrity of a previous system, resulting in a constant readjustment of system boundaries.

5 Conclusion

What has happened since blockchain's first inception? As shown, blockchain emerged as a pirate technology threatening the power of the state and central banks. However, at the time of writing this chapter, blockchain technology is being proposed as a solution to digital piracy.[54] The main conclusion that can be drawn is that blockchain is connected to the concept of piracy and consequently the general notion of threat in a contradictory way that follows the paradoxical logic of the 'excluded third, included': on the one hand it is designed as a revolutionary technology which holds promise of optimising transactional processes by reducing intermediation, security threats, and costs, while on the other hand it gives rise to an evolving 'intermediation and centralisation race' as well as a complex set of security issues, grounded in mutually dependent and threatening relationships. In this respect, although blockchain's theoretical promise is premised upon a vision of noise-free exchange, subject to no mediation, the blockchain ecosystem can be depicted as 'a complex topology' of intermediations, 'interruptions and interceptions',[55] based on a 'computational parasitic logic'. Approaching the blockchain technology through the analytic prism of the parasite delineates an asymmetric structure of relations that recur across various sites and scales of the blockchain ecosystem. As seen, the ways that parasitic relations manifest within the blockchain economy are numerous. We are currently witnessing a race by a variety of heterogenous actors – entangled in human-computational assemblages – to outpace each other across the parasitic chain.

Blockchain is being proposed as a disruptive technology that can transform a vast variety of fields, which range from the domain

---

54   Yasiru Jayasinghe, Kavinga Y. Abeywardena, Tharika Munasinghe, Sumala Mannage, Thisuri Warnasooriya, and Gihan Edirisinghe, 'VANGUARD: A Blockchain-Based Solution to Digital Piracy', *Global Journal of Computer Science and Technology* 20, no. 4 (2020), 19–28.
55   Brown, 'In Praise of the Parasite', 97.

of supply chain management,[56] energy systems,[57] digital voting,[58] education,[59] healthcare,[60] gaming,[61] and even human thinking.[62] It is even presently being proposed as the most cutting-edge technology able to provide a trusted infrastructure to support a shared virtual world, also known as metaverse.[63] These developments designate blockchain as a key technology that will play a central role in the next digital revolution of Web 3.0 and thus call for a close examination of its parasitical ubiquity. By following the parasitic chains, we can better grasp the relations of power and the dynamics within the contemporary blockchain ecology.

This contribution hopes to open the door for future studies that might reveal more complex understandings and further deepen the analysis of blockchain's systematisation of parasitic relations. Two directions of future research can be outlined that could build on the notion of 'computational parasitism' and offer more nuanced theorising that fully captures the power dynamics underpinning blockchain's parasitic relations. One direction could focus on

56   Sara Saberi, Mahtab Kouhizadeh, Joseph Sarkis, and Lejia Shen, 'Blockchain Technology and its Relationships to Sustainable Supply Chain Management', *International Journal of Production Research* 57, no. 7 (2018), 2117–35.

57   Zhaoyang Dong, Fengji Luo, and Gaoqi Liang, 'Blockchain: A Secure, Decentralized, Trusted Cyber Infrastructure Solution for Future Energy Systems', *Journal of Modern Power Systems and Clean Energy* 6, no. 5 (2018), 958–67.

58   Roberto Casado-Vara and Juan M. Corchado, 'Blockchain for Democratic Voting: How Blockchain Could Cast off Voter Fraud', *Oriental Journal of Computer Science and Technology* 11, no. 1 (2018).

59   Alex Grech and Anthony F. Camilleri, *Blockchain in Education* (Luxembourg: Publications Office of the European Union, 2017).

60   Marko Hoolbl, Marko Kompara, Aida Kamissalic, and Lili N. Zlatolas, 'A Systematic Review of the Use of Blockchain in Healthcare', *Symmetry* 10, no. 10 (2018).

61   Alesja Serada, Tanja Sihvonen, and J. Tuomas Harviainen, 'CryptoKitties and the New Ludic Economy: How Blockchain Introduces Value, Ownership, and Scarcity in Digital Gaming', *Games and Culture: A Journal of Interactive Media* 16, no. 4 (2020), 457–80.

62   Melanie Swan, 'Blockchain Thinking: The Brain as a Decentralized Autonomous Organization', *IEEE Technology and Society Magazine* (17 December 2015).

63   Hyun-joo Jeon, Ho-chang Youn, Sang-mi Ko, and Tae-heon Kim, 'Blockchain and AI Meet in the Metaverse', in Tiago M. Fernández-Caramés and Paula Fraga-Lamas (eds), *Advances in the Convergence of Blockchain and Artificial Intelligence* (London: IntechOpen, 2021).

identifying the specific strategies and tools used for the creation of parasitic interferences. At the same time, based on the concept of one-sided exchange, one other future research direction could centre on identifying the specific ways that actors position themselves within parasitic cascades and benefit from the unequal exchange of resources. As Serres specifically emphasises, 'He who is well-placed has the right to eat the others'.[64] In this respect, the position of power, the 'lion's share', depends on the position a parasite occupies within a parasitic cascade. The one who comes last has the power to parasitise all the others and benefit from the flow of all resources. Who shall be the last?

Select Bibliography

Antonopoulos, Andreas M., *Mastering Bitcoin: Unlocking Digital Crypto Currencies* (Sebastopol, CA: O'Reilly Media, 2014).

Atzori, Marcella, 'Blockchain Technology and Decentralized Governance: Is the State Still Necessary?', *Journal of Governance and Regulation* 6, no. 1 (2017): 45–62.

Ayed, Ahmed B., 'A Conceptual Secure Blockchain-Based Electronic Voting System', *International Journal of Network Security & Its Applications* 9, no. 3 (2017): 1–9.

Behara, Gopala K., and Tirumala Khandrika, 'Blockchain as a Disruptive Technology: Architecture, Business Scenarios, and Future Trends', in Moses Strydom and Sheryl Buckley (eds), *AI and Big Data's Potential for Disruptive Innovation* (Hershey, PA: IGI Global, 2010), 130–73.

Beyer, Jessica L., and Fenwick McKelvey, 'You Are Not Welcome Among Us: Pirates and the State', *International Journal of Communication* 9 (2015): 890–908.

Boireau, Oliver, 'Securing the Blockchain against Hackers', *Network Security* 1 (2018): 8–11.

Brown, Steven D., 'Science, Translation and the Logic of the Parasite', *Theory, Culture & Society* 19, no. 3 (2002): 1–27.

—. 'In Praise of the Parasite: The Dark Organizational Theory of Michel Serres', *Porto Alegre* 16, no. 1 (2013): 83–100.

Brunton, Finn, 'Heat Exchanges', in Geert Lovink, Nathaniel Tkacz, and Patricia de Vries (eds), *MoneyLab Reader: An Intervention in Digital Economy* (Amsterdam: Institute for Network Cultures, 2015), 158–72.

Buterin, Vitalik, 'A Next Generation Smart Contract and Decentralized Application Platform', Ethereum White Paper (2014). https://ethereum.org/en/whitepaper/. Accessed 20 October 2022.

64 Serres, *The Parasite*, 26.

Casado-Vara, Roberto, and Juan M. Corchado, 'Blockchain for Democratic Voting: How Blockchain Could Cast Off Voter Fraud', *Oriental Journal of Computer Science and Technology* 11, no. 1 (2018). DOI : http://dx.doi.org/10.13005/ojcst11.01.01. Accessed 20 October 2022.

Cohn, Alan, Travis West, and Chelsea Parker, 'Smart After All: Blockchain, Smart Contracts, Parametric Insurance, and Smart Energy Grids', *Georgetown Law Technology Review* 1, no. 2 (2017): 273–304.

Cornelius, Kristin B., 'Smart Contracts as Evidence: Trust, Records, and the Future of Decentralized Transactions', in Jeremy Hunsinger, Lisbeth Klastrup, and Mathew M. Allen (eds), *Second International Handbook of Internet Research* (Dordrecht: Springer, 2018), 1–20.

De Filippi, Primavera, and Benjamin Loveluck, 'The Invisible Politics of Bitcoin: Governance Crisis of a Decentralized Infrastructure', *Internet Policy Review* 5, no. 4 (2016).

De Filippi, Primavera, and Samer Hassan, 'Blockchain Technology as a Regulatory Technology', *First Monday* 21, no. 12 (2016).

Dong, Zhaoyang, Fengji Luo, and Gaoqi Liang, 'Blockchain: A Secure, Decentralized, Trusted Cyber Infrastructure Solution for Future Energy Systems', *Journal of Modern Power Systems and Clean Energy* 6, no. 5 (2018): 958–67.

Efanov, Dmitry, and Pavel Roschin, 'The All-Pervasiveness of the Blockchain Technology', *Procedia Computer Science* 123 (2018): 116–21.

Gehl, Robert, and Fenwick McKelvey, 'Bugging Out: Darknets as Parasites of Large-Scale Media Objects', *Media, Culture & Society* 41, no. 2 (2018): 219–35.

Golumbia, David, 'Bitcoin as Politics: Distributed Right Wing-Extremism', in Geert Lovink, Nathaniel Tkacz, and Patricia de Vries (eds), *MoneyLab Reader: An Intervention in Digital Economy* (Amsterdam: Institute of Network Cultures, 2015), 118–31.

Grech, Alex, and Anthony F. Camilleri, *Blockchain in Education* (Luxembourg: Publications Office of the European Union, 2017). https://publications.jrc.ec.europa.eu/repository/handle/JRC108255. Accessed 20 October 2022.

Gupda, Suyash, and Mohammad Sadoghi, 'Blockchain Transaction Processing', in S. Sakr and A. Zomaya (eds), *Encyclopedia of Big Data Technologies* (Cham: Springer, 2018).

Haney, Brian S., 'Blockchain: Post-Quantum Security & Legal Economics', *North Carolina Banking Institute* 24, no. 1 (2020). https://scholarship.law.unc.edu/ncbi/vol24/iss1/8. Accessed 20 October 2022.

Hayles, Katherine, *My Mother Was a Computer: Digital Subjects and Literary Texts* (Chicago: University of Chicago Press, 2005).

—. *Unthought: The Power of the Cognitive Unconscious* (Chicago: University of Chicago Press, 2017).

Herian, Robert, *Regulating Blockchain: Critical Perspectives in Law and Technology* (London: Routledge, 2019).

Hoolbl, Marko, Marko Kompara, Aida Kamissalicm, and Lili N. Zlatolas, 'A Systematic Review of the Use of Blockchain in Healthcare', *Symmetry* 10, no. 10 (2018): 470.

Huckle, Steve, and Martin White, 'Socialism and the Blockchain', *Future Internet* 8, no. 4 (2016): 1–15.

Huetten, Moritz, 'The Soft Spot of Hard Code: Blockchain Technology, Network Governance and Pitfalls of Technological Utopianism', *Global Networks* 19, no. 3 (2019): 329–48.

Hughes, Eric, 'A Cypherpunk's Manifesto' (9 March 1993). www.activism.net/cypherpunk/manifesto.html. Accessed 20 October 2022.

Jayasinghe, Yasiru, Kavinga Y. Abeywardena, Tharika Munasinghe, Sumala Mannage, Thisuri Warnasooriya, and Gihan Edirisinghe, 'VANGUARD: A Blockchain-Based Solution to Digital Piracy', *Global Journal of Computer Science and Technology* 20, no. 4 (2020): 19–28. https://computerresearch.org/index.php/computer/article/view/2008. Accessed 20 October 2022.

Jeon, Hyun-joo, Ho-chang Youn, Sang-mi Ko and Tae-heon Kim, 'Blockchain and AI Meet in the Metaverse', in Tiago M. Fernández-Caramés and Paula Fraga-Lamas (eds), *Advances in the Convergence of Blockchain and Artificial Intelligence* (London: IntechOpen, 2022).

Joshi, Archana Prashanth, Meng Han, and Yan Wang, 'A Survey on Security and Privacy Issues of Blockchain Technology', *Mathematical Foundations of Computing* 1, no. 2 (2018): 121–47.

Koletsi, Maria, 'Radical Technologies: Blockchain as an Organizational Movement', *Homo Virtualis* 2, no. 1 (2019): 25–33.

Lally, Nick, Kelly Kay, and Jim Thatcher, 'Computational Parasites and Hydropower: A Political Ecology of Bitcoin Mining on the Columbia River', *Environment and Planning E: Nature and Space* 5, no. 2 (2019). DOI: 10.1177/2514848619867608. Accessed 20 October 2022.

May, Timothy C., 'The Crypto Anarchist Manifesto' [Electronic mailing list message, 1992]. www.activism.net/cypherpunk/crypto-anarchy.html. Accessed 20 October 2022.

Mensah, Eunice, 'Chasing the Wind? A Case for Competitive Popularity as an Approach to Regulating Cryptocurrencies', *SSRN* (5 March 2020). https://ssrn.com/abstract=3529921. Accessed 20 October 2022.

Musiani, Francesca, Alexandre Mallard, and Cecile Meadel, 'Governing What Wasn't Meant to be Governed: A Controversy-Based Approach to the Study of Bitcoin Governance', in Malcolm Campbell-Verduyn (ed.), *Bitcoin and Beyond: Cryptocurrencies, Blockchains, and Global Governance* (London: Routledge, 2017).

Nakamoto, Satoshi, 'Bitcoin: A Peer-to Peer Electronic Cash System' (2008). https://web.archive.org/web/20110303162115/https://bitcoin.org/bitcoin.pdf. Accessed 20 October 2022.

Parikka, Jussi, 'Viral Noise and the (Dis)Order of the Digital Culture: Introduction', *M/C Journal* 7, no. 6 (2005). https://doi.org/10.5204/mcj.2472. Accessed 20 October 2022.

Parisi, Luciana, 'Critical Computation: Digital Automata and General Artificial Thinking', *Theory Culture & Society* 36, no. 2 (2019): 1–33.

Parkin, Jack, *Money Code Space: Hidden Power in Bitcoin, Blockchain and Decentralization* (Oxford: Oxford University Press, 2020).

Saberi, Sara, Mahtab Kouhizadeh, Joseph Sarkis, and Lejia Shen, 'Blockchain Technology and its Relationships to Sustainable Supply Chain Management', *International Journal of Production Research* 57, no. 7 (2018): 2117–35.

Scott, Brett, *How Can Cryptocurrency and Blockchain Technology Play a Role in Building Social and Solidarity Finance?* (Geneva: United Nations Research Institute for Social Development, 2016).

Serada, Alesja, Tanja Sihvonen, and J. Tuomas Harviainen, '*CryptoKitties* and the New Ludic Economy: How Blockchain Introduces Value, Ownership, and Scarcity in Digital Gaming', *Games and Culture: A Journal of Interactive Media* 16, no. 4 (2020): 457–80.

Serres, Michel, *The Parasite*, trans. Lawrence R. Schehr (Baltimore, MD: Johns Hopkins University Press, 1982).

Swan, Melanie, *Blockchain: Blueprint for a New Economy* (Sebastopol, CA: O'Reilly Media, 2015).

—. 'Blockchain Thinking: The Brain as a Decentralized Autonomous Organization', *IEEE Technology and Society Magazine* (17 December 2015). https://ieeexplore.ieee.org/stamp/stamp.jsp?arnumber=7360255. Accessed 20 October 2022.

Tischer, Daniel, 'Cutting the Network? Facebook's Libra Currency as a Problem of Organization', *Finance and Society* 6, no. 1 (2020): 19–33.

Tuwiner, Jordan, 'Bitcoin Mining Pools', *Buy Bitcoin Worldwide* (11 February 2022). www.buybitcoinworldwide.com/mining/pools/. Accessed 20 October 2022.

Vasek, Marie, Joseph Bonneau, Ryan Castellucci, Cameron Keith, and Tyler Moore, 'The Bitcoin Drain: Examining the Use and Abuse of Bitcoin Brain Wallets', in Jens Gros99klags and Bart Preneel (eds), *Financial Cryptography and Data Security* (Cham: Springer, 2017): 609–18.

Xu, Jennifer J., 'Are Blockchains Immune to All Malicious Attacks?', *Financial Innovation* 2, no. 25 (2016): 1–9.

Zajácz, Rita, 'Silk Road: The Market Beyond the Reach of the State', *Information Society* 33, no. 1 (2017): 23–34.

Zook, Matthew A., and Joe Blankenship, 'New Spaces of Disruption? The Failures of Bitcoin and the Rhetorical Power of Algorithmic Governance', *Geoforum* 96 (November 2018): 248–55. https://doi.org/10.1016/j.geoforum.2018.08.023. Accessed 20 October 2022.

Notes on Contributors

Holger Briel is currently Dean of the School of Culture and Creativity at the joint Hong Kong Baptist–Beijing Normal University in Zhuhai, China. He holds a PhD in comparative cultural theory from the University of Massachusetts, Amherst, and his research interests lie in media and cultural studies, philosophy, and digital social sciences. He is also a correspondent for several international newspapers. For many years, he has been the Editor-in-Chief of the IAFOR *Journal of Cultural Studies* and on numerous journal boards. In 2021, he was the recipient of a National South Korean Senior Fellowship in Cultural Studies. In recognition of his expertise in global education, he has also been elected to many national education supervisory bodies and holds a membership in the EU Council for Higher Education. He is currently working on a book on changing visual regimes in the twenty-first century.

Zhen Troy Chen, PhD, FHEA, is Senior Lecturer in Media, City University of London and an Adjunct Research Fellow of MXII Innovation Institute, Nanjing University of Information Science and Technology. His research interests are in digital media and advertising, cultural and creative industries, cultural and media policy (copyright), journalism, and experience design. He has authored a research monograph entitled *China's Music Industry Unplugged: Business Models, Copyright and Social Entrepreneurship in the Online Platform Economy* (2021). His research papers have appeared in *Journal of Consumer Culture, International Journal of Cultural Policy, Ethics and Information Technology, Social Semiotics, Asian Journal of Women's Studies, SAGE Research Methods*, and *Global Media and China*. He has also contributed book chapters to several edited collections.

Alexandra Elbakyan received her BSc in computing and data security in 2009 from the Technical University Almaty. After a practicum at the Georgia Institute of Technology she returned to Kazakhstan where in 2011 she founded Sci-Hub, the premier website indexing and offering free access to more than 80 million scientific articles. She has been called the 'Pirate Queen' due to her engagement in file sharing, and has polarised opinions about herself, with some comparing her to Edward Snowdon, and supporting her for a Nobel Prize, and others seeing her as one of the main offenders against copyright laws. At the moment, she is finishing her PhD on the Open Access movement.

Gary Hall is a critical theorist and media philosopher working (and making) at the intersections of digital culture, politics, art, and technology. He is Professor of Media at Coventry University, where he directs the Centre for Postdigital Cultures, which brings together a plurality of media theorists, practitioners, activists, and artists. He is the author of a number of books, including *A Stubborn Fury: How Writing Works in Elitist Britain* (2021), *The Inhumanist Manifesto* (2017), *Pirate Philosophy* (2016), and *The Uberfication of the University* (2016). In addition, he is co-author of *Open Education: A Study in Disruption* (2014) and co-editor of *New Cultural Studies: Adventures in Theory* (2006). He is currently completing a new monograph, entitled *Masked Media: Why Liberalism Must Be Defeated – And How to Do It*. He also has a history of creating norm-critical collaborative research contexts. In 1999, he co-founded the contemporary theory journal *Culture Machine*. In 2006, he co-founded the open access publishing house Open Humanities Press (OHP), which he still co-directs. He also co-edited OHP's Liquid Books series and the Jisc-funded Living Books About Life series. OHP is a founder member of both the Radical Open Access Collective and ScholarLed, with Hall being one of those behind the Community-led Open Publication Infrastructures for Monographs (COPIM) project.

Markus Heidingsfelder, PhD, is Associate Professor of Media Studies, Division of Humanities & Social Sciences, United International College Zhuhai. His work has appeared in *Soziale Systeme, Zeitschrift für Semiotik, Kybernetes, Systems Research & Behavioral Science, Cybernetics & Human Knowing*, among others. His most recent books are *Trump – beobachtet* (2020), *Corona – Weltgesellschaft im Ausnahmezustand* (editor, with M. Lehmann, 2020), *George Spencer-Brown's 'Design with the NOR': With Related Essays* (editor, with S. Roth, L. Clausen, and K.B. Laursen, 2020).

Michael D. High is Assistant Professor of Media Studies in the Department of Media and Communication at Xi'an Jiaotong–Liverpool University, China. His research interests are media piracy, Hollywood cinema, American popular culture, and digital fandom. His research papers have appeared in the *International Journal of Communication* and

Jump Cut: A Review of Contemporary Media. He has also contributed book chapters to several edited collections.

Yifan Li was born in Wuxi, Jiangsu, and graduated from Xi'an Jiaotong–Liverpool University, China, taking both her Bachelor and Master's degrees in communication studies. She is an avid console and PC video game player who thinks she is particularly good at playing *Elden Ring*. She works as marketing specialist in the department of overseas marketing and games publishing in a games company.

Nelson Obinna Omenugha is a lecturer in the Department of Mass Communication at Nnamdi Azikiwe University, Awka, Nigeria. He undertook his studies both in Nigeria and abroad, gaining degrees in mass communication, strategic marketing, and media management and technology. He graduated top of his class in his undergraduate studies, a BSc in mass communication from Nnamdi Azikiwe University, Awka, winning the 2011/12 Vice Chancellor Best Student Merit Award of the department. Nelson holds an MA in strategic marketing communications and an MSc in international marketing communication strategy from the University of Greenwich and France Business School (ESCEM), Poitiers respectively. He was awarded a Global Youth Leaders Certificate by Coady International Institute, Antigonish, Canada. Most recently, he obtained his doctorate degree from the media and communications program of Xi'an Jiaotong–Liverpool University, China. His research interests span the scope of media studies and management, strategic marketing, disruptive technologies, digital economy, youth entrepreneurship, and leadership.

Jiarui Tan was born and raised in Beibei, Chongqing. She received her MSc in media and communication from Xi'an Jiaotong–Liverpool University, China. She is a lover of plants, music, and the Internet, currently working as a content creator and community manager for an Ethereum-based virtual city.

Danai Tselenti obtained her BA and Master's degrees from the Faculty of Political Science and Public Administration of the University of Athens. Since December 2015, she holds a PhD from the Department of Early Childhood Education of the University of Athens. Her current research focuses on new media and particularly contemporary online reading communities (Bookstagram, Instapoetry, online book reviewing platforms), wherein she uses a broad range of qualitative methods in order to get a deeper understanding of the cognitive and affective dimensions underlying user-generated content and online audience responses. Currently, she is a postdoctoral researcher at the University of Porto working within the context of the project 'The Myth of Innocence: A Mixed Methods Approach toward the Understanding of Female Sexual Behavior', a collaborator of the Research Group in Human Sexuality at the Faculty of Psychology and Educational Sciences of Porto University, and a research member at the National Technical University of Athens. Her research interests lie in the areas of new media studies, reader response research, and cognitive and affective processes in reading, feminism, and educational theory.

Ernesto Van der Sar received his PhD in behavioural and social sciences at Groningen University. He is a journalist for and founder and editor-in-chief of TorrentFreak (TF), the prime website covering all things related to piracy and copyright. Van der Sar also conducts research on piracy-related trends and occasionally appears as a commentator and expert in articles on piracy in the *New York Times*, *Washington Post*, for the BBC, and elsewhere.

Index

Printed and bound by CPI Group (UK) Ltd, Croydon, CR0 4YY

27/10/2024

14580405-0001